I

FARM
HOLIDAY GUIDE
GREAT BRITAIN & IRELAND
1993

RAC
Publishing

Published by RAC Publishing, RAC House,
Bartlett Street, South Croydon CR2 6XW.

ISBN 0 86211–206–0

Compiled and edited by Felicity Clarke/Kim Worts
Picture credits
Cover illustration Highgate Farm, Cumbria
pp.5–12 Alastair Bruce

Cartography ESR Ltd, West Byfleet

Advertising Agents
Kingslea Press Limited, 137 Newhall Street,
Birmingham B3 1SF. ℗ 021-236 8112

Typeset by Tradespools Ltd, Frome, Somerset.
Printed in Spain by Grafo S.A. Bilbao

CONTENTS

CONTENTS

Introduction

Farmers and Visitors at Nurstead Court Farm

There is something special about staying on a farm. A friendly welcome, comfortable accommodation and good, fresh food are all there to attract the visitor. But above all, it is the indefinable lure of the land that holidaymakers find hard to resist. Whichever one of Britain's beautiful areas you choose to visit, and there are more than a thousand farmhouses listed in this guide to help you decide, the sights and smells of the countryside and the reassuring daily routine of the farm will prove a unique and fulfilling experience.

Those who stay at Nurstead Court Farm, near the village of Meopham in Kent, will certainly enjoy these pleasures. They will also discover many unexpected delights. This working dairy farm, on the rim of the North Downs, has the oldest Guernsey herd on mainland Britain. As well as feeling part of farming history, guests at Nurstead Court find themselves living in a traditional English manor house dating back to the 14th century.

Set in beautiful rolling pastures, the farm is the hub of a small, close knit parish. Remarkably, it has been in the hands of the same family for more than 400 years. The owners are Michael and Suzanne Edmeades-Stearns. An ancestor of Suzanne, Henry Edmeades, bought the estate in 1767 but the family had lived there as tenants for at least 200 years before. By marrying a local heiress Henry hoisted the family into the squirearchy and the Edmeades tradition continues today.

While proud of their heritage, Nurstead Court is mentioned in the Domesday Book, the present owners run a modern organic farm which is a perfect example of the growing trend in diversification or agri-tourism. Five years ago they looked for new ways of making a living to supplement the traditional ones of raising cattle, producing milk and growing crops. They decided to open their home to guests. By looking beyond the old farming methods, Michael and Suzanne hope to secure the future of the family home. Alongside the normal routine of the farm a typical day at Nurstead Court can include many different activities. Guests arrive all year round and are often part of these varied and colourful events.

Besides the dairy herd, around which everything else revolves, Michael and

Suzanne keep a dozen Jacobs sheep, five ponies and a donkey. A peacock and some guinea fowl adorn the lawn and garden while Spike, a handsome cockatiel, keeps a beady eye on proceedings from his cage by the library window. Two friendly terriers, Nellie and Sweep, complete the menagerie.

The working day at Nurstead Court starts at 7am. After breakfast with her

Michael and Suzanne Edmeades-Stearns, pictured outside the farmhouse.

children, Annabelle 22, Guy 19, and Pippa 11, all live at home, Suzanne prepares breakfast for the guests who eat betweem 8am and 9am in the panelled library where the oldest book dates back to 1575. "They can choose between traditional English fare, cereal, bacon, eggs and toast or a Continental style breakfast," says Suzanne, "and we tend to be fairly flexible about eating times."

The guests are still eating, but Michael is in the fields rounding up the herd of 65 pedigree cows for milking. The milking parlour can accommodate six cows at a time and the job, which takes about an hour and a half to complete, is repeated at 6pm. The morning and evening milking sessions are highlights of the farm day. In winter there is less to see as the cows merely walk through from their winter home in the big byre by the milking parlour, but in summer the great parade of 60-70 large beasts coming in from the fields, tramping up the well-worn path, is an impressive sight. Few visitors are awake enough to enjoy the scene at the morning milking. However, in summer at the evening session the herd often comes in to quite an audience of guests with their families.

Although milking by hand is rare these days, it still has to be done when a cow has an infection. The idea of milking a cow in the old-fashioned way holds a great appeal, but guests at Nurstead Court can only watch, not participate. "It is really not possible to let visitors do this," explains Michael. "An infected cow needs the tender handling of an expert, and a healthy cow needs to be milked quickly and efficiently. If amateurs start they might be injured by the cow if the animal moves the wrong way." Michael is understandably protective of his animals, not only

Michael Edmeades-Stearns cajoles the cattle back from the fields for the evening milking session.

does he have a great rapport with these gentle beasts, but the Guernsey herd is, at today's prices, very expensive. It has always been so. "The original six heifers came over from Sark around 1870. Suzanne's great grandfather married the daughter of the Seignieur of Sark and the cows were part of the dowry."

After the cattle have returned to pasture, they stay out day and night during the summer, Michael moves on to other tasks like cleaning the milking equipment and feeding the calves. There is no particular calving season, so there are always between 60 and 70 young stock to look after. If the demands of the herd allow Michael and Guy spend the rest of the morning catching up on other essential jobs, most particularly that of making silage for the cows winter feed. At midday, however, it is back to the dairy for the arrival of the tanker to collect the milk. Twice a week Michael separates the cream from the milk. Guests on the farm are offered fresh milk daily and it is sold on the farm at weekends.

Following a lunch break, Michael might be found making or mending fences in a far flung corner of the farm, or coppicing to add to the store of winter fuel for the

Pippa, the youngest member of the family, brushes down her pony, Hoppy, and Mum looks on.

house. At the end of the evening's milking, the dairy cleaning starts all over again. It is usually 8pm before Michael finishes work.

The running of the house and the walled kitchen garden, a lovely Victorian legacy, occupies most of Suzanne's day. With a full time gardener to look after it, the newly restored half acre garden is the latest business venture. Fruit and vegetables along with young plants and cuttings are sold on the farm. In keeping with modern trends, all are organically-grown. "We have recently gone fully organic following a three year period of conversion," says Suzanne, "and no chemical fertilisers are used anywhere on the farm."

A strong sense of history is what most guests feel when they arrive at Nurstead Court. The oldest part of the house, a Grade 1 listed building with 20 rooms, dates back to 1320. It is a gem of medieval architecture. The unusually grandiose aisled hall survived until 1825, and half of it still stands, enclosed in walls of dressed flint and supported by carved oak pillars. There is Georgian furniture and even a couple of four poster beds.

Dinner is not provided and so in the evenings most guests make use of the various pubs and restaurants in Meopham (pronounced Mepp'm). Michael and Suzanne claim there is no such person as the typical guest, their visitors are drawn from all walks of life. Because of the farm's proximity to tourist attractions like Canterbury, Leeds Castle and the Dickens Centre at Rochester, some use it as a base for sightseeing in the area. Motor racing fans and competitors often stay at Nurstead to attend sports car and saloon car events at Brands Hatch only four miles away. Racing drivers keep their competition cars on trailers at the farm. Others come simply for the tranquillity of the countryside. Walking along the Wealden Way and the many footpaths which criss cross the farm is a favourite occupation for many. The farm covers 220 acres. This includes 50 acres of woodlands which are rich in wildlife, particularly birds, and many a guest turns amateur ornithologist during a stay at Nurstead. Badgers are in evidence too and there is a good

One of the original medieval windows on the north wall of Nurstead Court's famous aisled hall.

chance of sighting foxes in the woods which, although interesting for the guests, is also why Michael decided against keeping poultry.

Obviously for children the big attraction is the animals. All are friendly and enjoy being petted and fed occasional tit bits. Those who remember the children's TV adventure serial "The Country Boy" will recognise the farm as one of the locations used in filming. An advance crew of BBC designers stayed here as B&B guests for six weeks.

In March and April the lambs are born. If any need bottle feeding visiting children are always eager to help. With so few sheep on the farm, summer tasks like dipping and shearing are done by outside labour and completed very quickly. The fleeces are sold to local people and the wool used in cottage industries. The dairy is the true business of the farm, the sheep really arrived by accident. "They were brought here for a fete once, part of pets corner, and never taken away by their owner," explains Suzanne.

There are no riding facilities for guests at Nurstead. Pippa, the pony enthusiast of the family, hopes to organise this when she is older. Visitors wishing to bring their dogs to the farm should ask first, but generally pets are welcomed all year round. "Obviously it depends on the dog," says Michael, "but if owners can keep them under control and common sense is applied, then we have no objection."

The main summer sports here are tennis and croquet which guests play on the east lawn. Guests of many nationalities find their way to the farm, like the Russian museum curator who stayed here to pick up tips on how best to market a newly privatised palace in St Petersburg, and the young Czechoslovakian couple eager to see England following their country's revolution, who made Nurstead their first port of call after driving all the way from Prague in a battered old Skoda.

Day visitors to the farm include many local people involved in community activities. Suzanne is particulary fond of the flower arranging courses, run by Meopham Flower Studio, which take place in the drawing room between spring and late summer. Sometimes guests staying on the

Pippa prepares to take her pony,
Hoppy for a gallop.

10

farm join a course. "During these courses the house is a mass of fresh flowers," says Suzanne.

Occasionally, English Heritage bring groups from historical societies to view the house and the medieval hall, ending their tours with cream teas in the library. An annual art exhibition is staged in the house during July and a local art group regularly uses the garden and grounds for sketching and painting. Indeed guests have been known to set up their easels too. As the manor house of the parish, tied to nearby St Mildred's Church, Nurstead Court is in great demand for wedding receptions. The house and grounds are hired out several times a year for this purpose. It is not unusual to see a marquee on the lawn and as many as 200 people gathered there for the celebrations. Sometimes the honeymoon couple choose to spend their first night of married life at Nurstead Court, frequently accompanied by some of the wedding guests.

With the arrival of autumn, life on the farm remains as varied as ever. Michael harvests his single crop of oats for use as winter feed. By the end of October the empty fields are ploughed and almost immediately are sown with oats and clover leys for the following year. Meanwhile the guests are often to be found tramping through the surrounding woodland enjoying the autumn colours.

With the onset of frosts the farm routine changes dramatically. The cows are brought in from the fields and kept under cover, returning to pasture the following spring. Winter feeding of the herd means more work for Michael and mucking out the byre becomes an added daily chore. Meanwhile the breeding process

continues apace and Guernsey bulls are regularly brought to the farm to sire calves. All heifer calves born on the farm are kept in the herd but the bull calves are sold at market.

Although Michael and Suzanne each have their particular areas of responsibility on the farm, they are happy to help each other out. Suzanne is quite at home herding the cattle and Michael willingly makes up beds for the guests. For the visitor, it is wonderful to come to the farm at any time of year. There is no better place to escape from the stresses of urban life and to breathe in that precious commodity – fresh air. After the rigours of sightseeing, it is a joy to be transported back to the gentler world of Nurstead Court.

And what of Suzanne and Michael's opinion of their guests? When they began this new venture they were both understandably wary of taking strangers into their home. But now their enthusiasm is obvious. What they enjoy most is the constant variety of guests, they come from towns, from cities, from overseas or just from over the county border. Without the B&B enterprise, they would never have had the chance to meet so many different people, and long may it continue for it has been "five fascinating years".

Alastair Bruce

HOW TO USE THIS BOOK

Symbols

	English	French	German
©	Telephone number	Numero de telephone	Telefonnummer
♒	Bath	Bain	Privatbad
🛁	Bathroom	Salle de bain	Badezimmer
∬	Shower	Douche	Dusche
♿	Disabled facilities	Amenagements pour handicapés	Einrichtungen fur Behinderte
⚘	Children Welcome	Enfants bienvenus	Kindern wilkommen
⌇	Dogs by arrangement	Accès aux chiens	Mitführen von Hunden
⚹	No smoking	Défense de fumer	Nicht rauchen
⌑	Light refreshments	Boissons/sandwich	Imbisstube
✗	Restaurant	Restaurant	Restaurant
B&B	Price of bed and breakfast	Prix d'une chambre et petit dejeuner	Preis fur Einzelzimmer und Fruhstuck
EM	Price of evening meal	Prix du diner	Abendessenpreise

Further Information

© When telephoning Ireland from the UK remember to prefix the listed number with the country code (010353) plus the relevant county code.

♿ this denotes farms which, in the owners' opinion, meet the needs of disabled guests. Disabled visitors are recommended to contact the establishment direct to check whether their particular requirements can be met.

⚘(5) minimum age is given in brackets where a restriction exists.

⌇ dogs are welcome for most of the year, but always check with the proprietor before arriving with your pet. Farming schedules could mean your dog will be a danger or nuisance.

✘ where this symbol does not appear, smoking may nevertheless be restricted to certain areas.

B&B Two prices denotes a minimum and maximum price per person, unless otherwise stated, and is based on low and high season, single and sharing, and the quality of the accommodation. If only one price is given, this is a minimum. The prices quoted here are forecasts made by the owners of what they expect to charge in 1993. As they have to be set so far in advance there may well be changes. It is advisable to confirm prices with the owner before finalising a booking.

Maps – The map references on each town entry refer to the map page and square in the section at the end of the book. Farms are often in isolated positions some distance from the nearest town or village. Map references and directions in the text are for general guidance, always request detailed instructions from the farms when booking.

THE COUNTRY CODE

Enjoy the countryside and respect its life and work

Guard against all risk of fire

Fasten all gates

Keep your dogs under close control

Keep to public paths across farmland

Use gates and styles to cross hedges, fences and walls

Leave livestock, crops and machinery alone

Take your litter home

Help to keep all water clean

Protect wildlife, plants and trees

Take special care on country roads

Make no unnecessary noise

ENGLAND

AVON

CHEW MAGNA
Map 2 A3

Valley Farm, Sandy Lane, Stanton Drew, Nr Bristol
✆ (0275) 332723   Mrs D.E. Keel

Valley Farm lies in a quiet and ancient village just 7 miles from Bristol (M32/A37/B3130 Chew Magna road then left by Toll House to Stanton Drew). The new farmhouse offers every comfort, tea/coffee facilities in rooms. Quiet position available for caravans away from the farmhouse. The farm has a beef herd and its location is ideal for trout fishing, birdwatching, and delightful country walks. There are Druid Stones in the village. Chew Valley Lakes 4 miles, Bath 10 miles, Wells and Cheddar 12 miles.

Open Mar-Nov.
2 double bedrooms inc. 1 ens. ⋔/WC, 1🛏, 2WCs.
🐕(3) ⅍ ETB 🏅 🏅Highly Commended
Prices:B&B £18–21, weekly £120–140. 🐕 rates.

Woodbarn Farm, Denny Lane, Chew Magna, Bristol BS18 8S2
✆ (0275) 332599   Mrs Judi Hasell

Woodbarn Farm stands on the outskirts of the village of Chew Magna, on the B3130 off the A37 south of Bristol. This working beef and arable farm is only 5 minutes from the peace and beauty of Chew Valley Lake. An ideal location for trout-fishing, birdwatching or as a base for touring the region. Cot and highchair provided. Bath 15 miles. Wells 12 miles. Bristol 8 miles. Cheddar 12 miles.

Open Mar-Nov.
2 bedrooms (1 double; 1 family ens. ⋔/WC),1🛏, 2WCs.
🐕 ⅍ ETB Listed
Prices: B&B £15–20. 🐕 rates.

PENSFORD
Map 2 A3

Leigh Farm, Pensford, Bristol BS18 4BA
✆ (0761) 490281   C. & J. Smart

In an attractive stone-built farmhouse quietly situated half a mile off the A37 south from Bristol, the Smarts offer a holiday for all the family on their corn and sheep farm with coarse fishing. A pony and donkey are kept for children. Cot and highchair provided. Stanton Drew stone circles 2 miles. Pensford Viaduct 1 mile.

Open Mar-Nov.
3 bedrooms (1 twin; 1 double; 1 family), 1🛏, 1WC. 🐕
Prices: B&B £17. 🐕 rates.

TEMPLE CLOUD
Map 2 A3

Temple Bridge Farm, Temple Cloud, Bristol BS18 5AA
✆ (0761) 452377   Mrs Dinah Wyatt

Just south of the village of Temple Cloud, off the A37 Bristol-Wells road, stands this 17th-century, white-painted farmhouse complete with old beams, log fires and central heating for your extra comfort. Temple Bridge is an arable farm offering an attractive rural base for exploring the cities of Bath, Bristol and Wells (10 miles). Cheddar and Longleat 20 miles.

Open Mar-Oct.
2 family bedrooms, 1🛏, 1WC.
🐕(2)ETB 🏅Commended
Prices: B&B £14–16. 🐕 rates.

KEY TO SYMBOLS

Bath	🛁
Shower	⋔
Bathroom	🛏
Disabled Guest Facilities	♿
No Smoking	⅍
Children Welcome	🐕
Dogs by Arrangement	🐕

WESTON-SUPER-MARE   Map 2 A3

Purn House Farm, Bleadon, Weston-Super-Mare BS24 0QE
℃ (0934) 812324   Mrs T.G. Moore

Within this creeper-clad 17th-century farmhouse you will find every comfort. The family-run 500-acre working dairy and arable farm is conveniently placed for touring at Bleadon, off the A370 Taunton road 3 miles from Weston-Super-Mare. Cheddar Gorge 10 miles. Wells and Glastonbury 20 miles.

Open Mar-Nov
6 bedrooms (1 twin; 1 double ens. ⋔/WC; 4 family inc. 2 ens. ⇨/WC), 1➡, 1WC.
⬩ ⸙ ETB ⚘ ⚘Approved
Prices: B&B £16–20, weekly £90–110. EM £7, B&B plus EM weekly £134–154. ⬩ rates.

WICK   Map 2 A2

Pool Farm, Wick, Bristol BS15 5RL
℃ (0272) 372284   Mrs P. Wilmott

Pool Farm is a listed 350-year-old building of Cotswold stone on the A420, Bristol-Chippenham road, to the east of the village. A stay on this 70-acre dairy farm offers the opportunity to tour the Cotswolds, visit Longleat and Bath or cross the Severn Bridge into South Wales. Children's games and cot provided. Bath 6 miles. Bristol 9 miles.

Open all year
2 bedrooms (1 twin; 1 family), 1➡, 1WC. ⬩
Prices: B&B £13–16. ⬩ rates.

Self-Catering

PENSFORD   Map 2 A3

Leigh Farm, Pensford, Bristol BS18 4BA
℃ (0761) 490281   C. & J. Smart

For full farm description, see p. 15. Built of natural stone and standing near the trout lake behind the main farmhouse, the outbuildings have been converted into 8 self-contained units to sleep 2, 4 and up to 8 persons respectively.

Open all year
Prices: £88 (2 person, low season) £330 (up to 8 person, high season).

BEDFORDSHIRE

HIGHAM FERRARS   Map 2 B1
Rifle Range Farm, Yielden, Bedford MK44 1AW
✆ (0933) 53151   Mrs A. Paynter

This quiet modern farmhouse stands on the edge of a small village, 3 miles south of A45 Kimbolton-Higham Ferrars road. The mixed farm is surrounded by many country walks with the understated charm of the Rivers Nene and Ouse only a few miles away. The Three Shires Way passes through the farm. Packed lunches on request. Wellingborough 8 miles. Bedford 14 miles.

Open all year
2 bedrooms (1 double; 1 single), 1🛏, 1WC.
🖧 🏃 ETB Listed Commended
Prices: B&B £14–15, weekly £70–95. EM £7–10. B&B plus EM weekly £125. 🖧 rates.

PULLOXHILL   Map 3 A2
Pond Farm, 7 High Street, Pulloxhill MK45 5HA
✆ (0525) 712316   Judy Tookey

Pond Farm is situated opposite the village green in Pulloxhill: 3 miles from the A6 and 5 miles from M1, Jct12. We are within easy reach of Woburn Abbey and Safari Park, Whipsnade Zoo and the Shuttleworth Collection of Historic Aircraft at Old Warden. Luton Airport 11 miles. Pond Farm, built in the 17th century, is mainly arable, although we have horses grazing on the meadowland and a resident Great Dane. No guest lounge but TV in all bedrooms.

Open all year
3 bedrooms (1 twin; 1 double; 1 family), 1🛏, 1WC.
🖧 ETB Listed
Prices: B&B £13.50-16.50. 🖧 rates.

ROXTON   Map 3 A2
Church Farm, High Street, Roxton, Bedford MK44 3EB
✆ (0234) 870234   Mrs Janet Must

This historic farmhouse is set in a secluded village on a family owned arable farm. Many guests return seeking the relaxed surroundings and pleasant atmosphere we offer. Situated just off the A1 between Sandy and St Neots, the area is excellent for golf, fishing, walking and cycling. RSPB 6 miles. Shuttleworth Collection 8 miles. Bedford 7 miles. Cambridge 19 miles. Cot and highchair available.

Open all year
2 bedrooms (1 twin; 1 family), 1🛏, 1WC.
🖧 ⚡ 🏃 ETB Listed
Prices:B&B £14–19. 🖧 rates.

SANDY   Map 3 A2
Highfield Farm, Tempsford Road, Sandy
✆ (0767) 682332   Mrs Margaret Codd

Highfield Farm extends a warm welcome and a friendly atmosphere to guests. This attractive arable farm is set back off the A1 (southbound carriageway, after A428 roundabout) giving peaceful seclusion yet within easy reach of London and Cambridge. Ground-floor bedrooms available. Cot and children's games provided. RSPB Sandy 1 mile. Shuttleworth Collection 5 miles. Cambridge 22 miles. London 50 miles.

Open all year
6 bedrooms(3 twin inc. 2 ens. 🛁/WC; 2 double inc. 1 ens. 🛁/WC; 1 family ens. ▽/WC), 1🛏, 1WC.
🐴 ⊁ ETB 👑 👑 Highly Commended
Prices: B&B £14–25. 🐴 rates.

STAGSDEN   Map 3 A2

Firs Farm, Stagsden West End, Bedford MK43 8TB
✆ (02302) 2344   John & Pam Hutcheon

Firs Farm has an old timber-framed farmhouse set in a large garden with outdoor swimming pool, standing in the middle of a 500-acre family-run arable farm. Breakfast is taken in the old bakehouse, and guests have separate sitting room and TV. Tea/coffee facilities. Firs Farm is 6 miles from Bedford, A428/A422 toward Milton Keynes then turning signposted West End. Stagsden Bird Gardens 1 mile, Cranfield College and Airfield 5 miles.

Open all year
2 bedrooms (1 twin; 1 double), 1🛏, 1WC.
🐴 ⊁ ETB 👑
Prices: B&B £15 weekly £98. 🐴 rates.

Self-Catering

TURVEY   Map 3 A2

Elderswell Farm, Turvey MK43 8BD
✆ (023064) 281

This detached Georgian-style farmhouse, surrounded by parkland and a stable conversion, is on an arable and sheep farm a short distance from the pretty stone-built village of Turvey (off A428 from Bedford). There is a Saxon-based church and a choice of river and country walks. A detached 200-year-old stonebuilt cottage and farmhouse in the village are also available. Accommodation is in 4 units with 1–4 bedrooms, sleeping 2–6. Ground floor bedrooms available. TV, telephone and linen provided. Bedford 7 miles.

Open all year
🐴 ⊁
Prices: Daily £20-35, weekly £120–280.

BERKSHIRE

BRADFIELD

Map 2 B2

Boot Farm, Southend Road, Bradfield, Nr Reading RG7 6EJ
✆ (0734) 744298

Boot Farm is a comfortable Georgian house with an attractive garden, beyond which lies the working dairy farm and a busy livery yard. Packed lunches and afternoon teas on request. Situated in Southend village, west of Reading 3 miles off the A4, Boot Farm is ideally placed for visiting Newbury Races, Henley Regatta, Pangbourne, the Thames Valley and the rolling Berkshire Downs.

Open all year
4 bedrooms (1 twin; 1 double ens. ⋔/WC; 2 single), 2➡, 2WCs.
⚱(12) ⊁ ETB ♛ ♛Commended
Prices: B&B £16.50–20.

CHADDLEWORTH

Map 2 B2

Manor Farm, Chaddleworth, Newbury RG16 0EG
✆ (04882) 215   Mrs Margaret Cooper

Mrs Cooper provides a warm and friendly atmosphere on this mixed farm set on the rolling Berkshire Downs, under a mile east of the A338 with easy access to the M4, J14. The Georgian farmhouse offers beautiful views and walks. Good eating places locally. Ridgeway 3 miles. Lambourn racing establishments 6 miles. Newbury racecourse 10 miles. Newbury and District Agricultural Show 8 miles.

Open all year
2 bedrooms (1 twin; 1 double), 2➡, 1WC.
⚱(6) ⊁ ETB ♛Commended
Prices: B&B £17.50–20. ⚱ rates.

MAIDENHEAD

Map 3 B2

Moor Farm, Holyport, Nr Maidenhead SL6 2HY
✆ (0628) 33761   Mrs G. Reynolds

Guests have exclusive use of one wing of this 700-year-old listed farmhouse, within 5 mins walk of village green of the conservation village of Holyport. The farmhouse is timber-framed, heavily beamed, and furnished with antiques. Pleasant local village pubs serve good food. Moor Farm has a flock of pedigree Suffolk sheep and stabling for local and guests' horses. Riding tuition available. Easy access to M4 Jct 8/9 and just off the A330 (take A308 from Maidenhead).

Open all year
2 twin bedrooms inc. 1 priv. ⋔/WC, 1 priv. ☞/WC.
⚱⊁ ETB ♛ ♛Commended
Prices: B&B £18–20 per person.

NEWBURY

Map 2 B2

Manor Farm, Brimpton, Nr Reading RG7 4SQ
✆ (0734) 713166

Manor Farm lies just outside Brimpton village, one mile south of the A4 midway between Reading and Newbury. This 500-acre dairy and arable farm boasts a comfortable Georgian house and garden. Earlier parts of the building include a Norman chapel that once belonged to the Knights Hospitallers. Good pub food available locally. Highchair and cot provided.

Open all year
2 bedrooms (1 twin; 1 family), 1➡, 2WCs.
⚱ ETB Listed
Prices: B&B £16–20, weekly £96–120.

Mousefield Farm, Long Lane, Shaw, Newbury RG16 9LG

✆ (0635) 40333/524331   Mrs R. Houghton

Mousefield Farm is located a mile along the B4009 from the A4 Newbury Robin Hood roundabout. Staying in this beautiful 300-year-old farmhouse you can follow nature trails through the 25-acre woodland, or just relax in the large garden after sampling some excellent home cooking. Packed lunches and afternoon teas are available on request. The farm supports a 150 Friesian dairy herd, beef cattle and wheat, barley and maize. Cot, playroom and children's games provided. Small listed caravan site (5 vans). Newbury race course 1 mile. Donnington Castle 2 miles. Windsor Castle 15 miles.

Open all year
5 bedrooms (1 twin; 1 double; 1 family; 2 single), 3🛁, 3WCs.
🐕 🎠
Prices: B&B £15–18, weekly £100–120. EM £6. B&B plus EM weekly £142–160. 🐕 rates. 🎠 £1 per night.

Woodlands Park Farm, Ashford Hill, Newbury RG15 8AY

✆ (0635) 268258/(0734) 814821

As its name suggests, 60 acres of woodland form part of this 240-acre grass dairy farm. The attractive countryside surrounding the Georgian farmhouse has many rights of way and areas of commonland for walking and riding. Home cooking includes packed lunches on request. Ashford Hill is 6 miles southeast of Newbury, on the B3051 west off the A340. Kennet & Avon Canal 4 miles. Highclere Castle 4 miles. Watership Down 6 miles. Whitchurch Silk Mill 10 miles. Easy access M4 Jcts 12 & 13, M3 Jct 6.

Open all year
4 bedrooms (1 twin; 2 family; 1 single), 1🛁, 2WCs.
🐕 🎠ETB 👑 👑Commended
Prices: B&B £18–19. EM £3.50–5. 🐕 rates.

READING   Map 3 B2

Parsons Farm, Stratfield Saye, RG7 2DX
✆ (0734) 333607   Mrs A.E. Floyd

For Parsons Farm turn to Strathfield Saye off the A33 Reading-Basingstoke road at the Wellington Arms Hotel, the farm lies beyond the village. The house was at one time part of the Duke of Wellington's estate. It is no longer a working farm, although sheep, ducks and geese are kept on a small acreage. Accommodation is offered in a self-contained two-storey annexe amid well-restored barns and farm buildings surrounding a garden courtyard with a large swimming pool. Silchester Roman town 3 miles.

Open all year
1 double bedroom ens.🚿/WC.
🐕 🎠
Prices: B&B £17.50–25.

STOKE ROW   Map 2 B2

Neals Farm, Wyfold, Reading, RG4 9JB
✆ (0491) 680258   Lady Silsoe

Our spacious Georgian farmhouse is secluded and quiet, set high in the Chilterns and flanked by beechwoods with a wonderful view. This is a 100-acre working farm with horses, beef and sheep. We offer our guests an informal, relaxed atmosphere with comfortable beds, good food and a heated swimming pool. Packed lunches on request. Cot and children's games provided. To reach Neals Farm from the A423 Henley-Oxford road, take the B481 south from Nettlebed, fork right to Stoke Row. In Stoke Row turn left towards Peppard, after less than a mile turn right into Neals Lane. Henley 6 miles. Stonor Park 6 miles.

Closed Xmas
4 bedrooms (2 twin; 1 double; 1 single), 1🛁,2WCs.
🐕 ✖️ 🎠ETB 👑
Prices: B&B £16.

KEY TO SYMBOLS	
Bath	🛁
Shower	🚿
Bathroom	🛁
Disabled Guest Facilities	♿
No Smoking	✖️
Children Welcome	🐕
Dogs by Arrangement	🎠

Self-Catering

MAIDENHEAD   Map 3 B2

Courtyard Cottages, Moor Farm,
Holyport, Nr Maidenhead SL6 2HY
✆ (0628) 33761   Mrs G Reynolds

For full farm description, see p. 19. Accommodation is offered in attractively converted barns and Georgian stable block. Three cottages have 2 bedrooms, sleeping 4. A one-bedroom cottage, sleeping 2, has been specifically designed for the use of disabled guests.

Open all year
& ⌇ ETB♪♪♪♪Highly Commended
Prices: weekly £210–240 1-bedroom, £310–340 2-bedroom.

READING   Map 3 B2

Parsons Farm, Stratfield Saye, Nr
Reading RG7 2DX
✆ (0734) 333607   Mrs A.E. Floyd

Accommodation is offered in a self-contained 2-storey annexe to the farmhouse sleeping 2–3. For full farm description, see p. 20.

Open all year ⛨
Prices: daily £15–20, weekly £180.

YOUR ROUTE TO SUCCESSFUL MOTORING

*L*et the RAC prepare you an individually tailored route to your holiday destination. We'll take the strain out of your journey by supplying a route designed to your requirements, avoiding major road works and so ensuring a smooth start to your holiday.

1. European Route and Travel Pack

- Choose from: the fastest, most scenic, most suitable for towing or to avoid motorways or toll roads.
- Junction by junction route directions from your port of arrival to your destination *(coverage includes France, Benelux, Germany, Spain, Portugal, Austria and Switzerland. Elsewhere marked mapping is provided).*
- Total and intermediate distances in miles/km.
- Through-route town plans for major centres.
- Route planning maps for every country visited.
- Information booklets for each country.

  Member £16.50   Non Member £18.50

2. European Route and Town Plans only   Member £11.00   Non Member £13.00

3. UK and European Route and Travel Pack

European Route and Travel Pack plus the best route from your home town to your port of departure, UK town and port plans and UK road map.

Member £18.50   Non Member £ 20.50

4. UK and Irish Route

Tell us the type of route you want - motorway, picturesque, towing, etc - and receive the best junction by junction driving instructions, information on motorway facilities, road numbers, town plans, UK roadworks report and route planning map of the UK and Ireland.

UK Route: Member £5.00   Non Member £10.00
Irish Route: Member £5.00   Non Member £10.00

To obtain your route:

☎ 0345 333222 - charged at local rate. Please have your credit card details available. Allow 14 days for route preparation and return by post.

Express Route Service - Next day delivery guaranteed for a £3.00 supplement.

RAC Telephone Traffic and Travel Information Lines

Before you set out be prepared:

☎ 0891 500242   The latest traffic conditions for London and the UK motorways.
☎ 0891 500241   Traffic and roadworks in Europe.
☎ 0891 500243   European Touring Information - documentation and motoring regulations - make sure you comply.

RAC Weatherline   For UK weather information:

☎ 0891 500249   The national 1-5 day weather forecast *(updated daily)* or 30 day weather outlook.

Calls cost 36p per minute cheap rate and 48p per minute all other times.

BUCKINGHAMSHIRE

AYLESBURY Map 2 B2

Poletrees Farm, Brill-Ludgershall Road,
Aylesbury HP18 9TZ
✆ (0844) 238276 Anita Cooper

This 140-acre farm lies just north of Brill, off the A41, Bicester-Aylesbury road. The 500-year-old, oak-beamed farmhouse in peaceful surrounds is ideally placed for plenty of delightful country walks. Waterperry Gardens 4 miles. Waddesdon Manor 5 miles. Quainton Steam Railways 5 miles.

Open all year
3 bedrooms (1 twin; 2 doubles) 1🛏, 1WC.
⌇ETB Listed
Prices: B&B £16–20. EM £12.

HANSLOPE Map 2 B2

Spinney Lodge Farm, Forest Road,
Hanslope, Milton Keynes
✆ (0908) 510267

Enjoy good home cooking at this attractive Victorian farmhouse set in pleasant open countryside. Packed lunches on request. The farm is mainly arable with sheep and beef, situated midway between Milton Keynes (7 miles) and Northampton just west of the M1. Silverstone 8 miles. Woburn Abbey 9 miles.

Open all year
3 bedrooms (1 twin ens.🛁/WC; 2 double), 1🛏,
1🛁, 1WC.
⌂(12) ⌇ETB ♨
Prices: B&B £16–18.EM £6–8. ⌂ rates.

LONG CRENDON Map 2 B2

Foxhill Farmhouse, Kingsey, Aylesbury
HP17 8LZ
✆ (0844) 291650 Mr & Mrs N.M.D. Hooper

On the A4129 from Thame in the hamlet of Kingsey stands Foxhill, a spacious oak-beamed farmhouse listed as being of architectural interest. It has a large attractive garden with views to the Chiltern Hills and there is a heated swimming pool available in summer. It is not a working farm. Waddesdon Manor 7 miles. Hughenden Manor 14 miles.

Open Feb-Nov.
3 bedrooms (2 twin inc. 1 ens. 🛁; 1 double ens.
🛁), 1🛏,1WC.
⌂(5) ⌇ ETB Listed
Prices: B&B £17–19, weekly £119–133.

Manor Farm, Shabbington, Aylesbury
HP18 9HJ
✆ (0844) 201103

Manor farmhouse is an architect-designed bungalow in a secluded rural location between Oxfordshire and Buckinghamshire. The county border is at the gate. The farm covers 188 acres and has sheep and cattle. Locally there is fishing in the Thames, and riverside walks and tours. Windsor Castle, Blenheim, Oxford all within easy reach. The farm is 2 miles from Thame off the A418 Oxford road.

Open all year
4 bedrooms (2 double; 2 single), 2🛏, 2WCs.
⌇ ETB Listed
Prices: B&B £17.50.

WINSLOW   Map 2 B2

Foxhole Farm, Little Horwood Road,
Winslow, Buckingham MK18 3JW
© (0296) 714550   Mrs W.M.A. Bates

Foxhole Farm stands between the A421 and the A413 south of Milton Keynes. The well appointed, fine modern farmhouse is set in 70 acres of pasture and woodland. Close to Buckingham and the market town of Winslow its location places several NT properties within easy reach.

Open all year
3 bedrooms (1 twin; 1 double; 1 single), 1🛏,
2WCs.
ETB registered
Prices: B&B per night £17 single, £32 double.

See STOP PRESS
for more farms

CAMBRIDGESHIRE

ELY
Map 3 A1

Hill House Farm, 9 Main Street, Coveney, Ely CB6 2DJ
☎ (0353) 778369

Hill House Farm is an arable working farm in a quiet fenland village 3 miles west of Ely, and 3 miles from the A10 Kings Lynn-Cambridge road. Enjoy high quality accommodation and food in this fine Victorian farmhouse with open views of the surrounding countryside. Cot and highchair provided. Welney Wildfowl Trust 9 miles. Newmarket 12 miles. Cambridge 17 miles.

Closed Xmas
4 bedrooms (1 twin ens. ᵮ/WC; 1 double ens. ᵮ/WC; 1 family suite of 2 rooms inc. ens. ᵮ/WC).
⚑ ⚞ ETB ♛ ♛ ♛Commended
Prices: B&B from £16. EM £14. ⚑ rates.

Spinney Abbey, Wicken, Ely CB7 5XQ
☎ (0353) 720971   Mrs V. Fuller

Just off the A1123 south of Ely, Spinney Abbey is a grade 2 listed building of historical interest, rebuilt from the former priory in 1775. It stands in a large garden adjacent to our mixed dairy and arable farm which borders Wicken Fen, NT Nature Reserve. Easy access to Cambridge and Newmarket.

Open all year
3 bedrooms (1 twin private ᵮ/WC; 1 double ens. ᵮ/WC; 1 family ens. ᵮ/WC).
⚑(5) ETB ♛ ♛.
Prices: B&B £16.

HUNTINGDON
Map 3 A1

Molesworth Lodge Farm, Molesworth, Huntingdon PE18 0PJ
☎ (08014) 309   Mrs R. Page

Molesworth Lodge Farm is situated a mile from the A14 (A604) Huntingdon-Kettering road. Mrs Page has created a warm, comfortable and friendly atmosphere for guests at this non-working farm. The farmhouse is quiet and peaceful standing in 300 acres of grassland. Cot, highchair and children's games provided. Trout fishing and sailing at Grafham Water 10 miles. Hamerton Wildlife Centre 6 miles.

Open all year
2 bedrooms (1 twin; 1 family), 1 ⇥, 1WC.
⚑ ETB Listed
Prices: B&B £12–15. ⚑ rates.

LANDBEACH
Map 3 A1

The Willows, 102 High Street, Landbeach, Cambridge CB4 4DT
☎ (0223) 860332   Mrs D.J. Wyatt

This 100-acre arable farm is in the village of Landbeach, 3 miles north of Cambridge, off the A10. Mrs Wyatt offers a friendly welcome to visitors to her Georgian farmhouse. Cot, highchair and children's games are provided. Ely 10 miles.

Open all year
3 bedrooms (1 double; 1 family; 1 single), 1 ⇥, 3WCs.
⚑ ⚞ ⼎
Prices: B&B £13–15. ⚑ rates.

Manor Farm, Landbeach, Cambridge CB4 4EA

✆ (0223) 860165   Vicki Hatley

Located in the village of Landbeach, 3 miles north of Cambridge, off the A10, Manor Farm is a

620-acre mixed beef, sheep and arable farm. The grade 2 listed Georgian house stands in an enclosed walled garden. Separate guest lounge and dining room. All rooms individually decorated. Anglesey Abbey and Wicken Fen close by. Ely 10 miles. Newmarket 13 miles.

Closed Xmas
3 bedrooms (1 twin; 1 double; 1 family ens. ▥/WC), 1🛁, 1WC.
⚘ ETB ♛ ♛Commended
Prices: B&B £15–20. ⚘ rates.

CHESHIRE

BALTERLEY
Map 4 B3

Green Farm, Deans Lane, Balterley Green,
Nr Crewe CW2 5QJ
✆ (0270) 820214

Green Farm is less than 2 miles from the A531, south of Crewe, M6 Jct16. In our lovely old farmhouse on a working dairy farm we offer you a warm welcome. Relax in our large garden – our aim is to make your stay happy and comfortable. This is a good base for exploring Cheshire and The Potteries. Cot and highchair provided. Bridgemere Gardens 8 miles. Stapeley Water Gardens 8 miles. Nantwich 8 miles. The Potteries 10 miles.

Open all year
3 bedrooms (1 twin; 1 family; 1 single), 2🛏,
2WCs.
&. 🐕 ⊁ ETB Listed
Prices: B&B £12.50–13.50, weekly £84.🐾 rates.

BETLEY
Map 4 B3

Adderley Green Farm, Betley, Nr Crewe
✆ (0270) 820203   Mrs Sheila Berrisford

Situated a mile from the A531, easy access M6 Jct16, this large attractive farmhouse on a 250-acre dairy farm offers luxury accommodation in Laura Ashley style decor. Packed lunches supplied on request. Fishing and horse riding available. The Potteries 6 miles. Stapeley Water Gardens 10 miles. Alton Towers 15 miles.

Open all year
4 bedrooms (1 twin; 2 double ens. 🛁/WC; 1 single ens. 🛁/WC),
🐾 ⊁ ETB ♛ ♛
Prices: B&B £14–20. ⊁ £1 per night.

CONGLETON
Map 5 A2

Cuttleford Farm, Astbury, Congleton
✆ (0260) 272499   Mrs M.C. Downs

This 150-acre mixed farm is located on the A34, 4 miles south of Congleton, opposite the NT property of Little Moreton Hall. Mrs Downs offers the hospitality of a 16th-century farmhouse, equipped with a hard tennis court and extensive gardens. Cot and highchair provided. Alton Towers 25 miles. The Potteries 10 miles.

Open all year
3 bedrooms (1 twin; 2 double inc. 1 ens. 🛁/WC),
1🛁/WC, 1WC.
🐾 ⊁ ETB Listed
Prices: B&B £12–20. 🐾 rates.

MACCLESFIELD
Map 5 A2

Hardingland Farm, Macclesfield Forest,
Macclesfield
✆ (0625) 425759   Mrs A.S.Read

This early Georgian farmhouse stands in a picturesque location in the Peak District just 4 miles east of Macclesfield in Macclesfield Forest. Here you can enjoy good home cooking and every comfort in a house tastefully furnished with antiques to suit the period. The surrounding smallholding has sheep and beef cattle. Macclesfield Silk Museum and Heritage Centre 4 miles. Gawsworth and Capesthorne Halls 10 miles.

Open Mar-Nov.
3 bedrooms (1 twin ens.☜/WC; 2 double inc. 1 ens. ☜/WC), 1🛁, 2WCs.
𝒴 ETB Listed Highly Commended
Prices: B&B £16–19, weekly £112–133. EM £10.50. B&B plus EM weekly £175–198.

MIDDLEWICH   Map 4 B2
Forge Mill Farm, Warmingham, Middlewich CW10 0HQ
✆ (027077) 204   Mrs Susan Moss

Forge Mill Farm is a mixed farm off the A533, easy access M6 Jcts 17 & 18. This spacious Victorian farmhouse is set in peaceful countryside close to the Middlewich canals and Cheshire Circle walks. Highchair provided. Northwich Salt Museum 6 miles. Oulton Park Racing 6 miles.

Open all year
2 bedrooms (1 twin; 1 double), 1🛁, 1WC.
𝒶 ETB ♛ ♛
Prices: B&B £15–16.𝒶 rates.

NANTWICH   Map 4 B3
Lea Farm, Wrinehill Road, Wybunbury, Nantwich CW5 7NS
✆ (0270) 841429   J. Callwood

Lea Farm lies off the A500 towards Nantwich from M6 Jct 16. The charming farmhouse is set in landscaped gardens where peacocks roam on a 150-acre dairy farm. As well as good home cooking Lea Farm also offers a pool/snooker table and fishing in a well-stocked pool and stream. Packed lunches and afternoon teas on request. Stapeley Water Gardens 2 miles. Bridgemere Garden World 2 miles. Dagfields Craft Centre 1 mile.

Closed Xmas
3 bedrooms (1 twin; 1 double; 1 family ens. 🛁/WC), 1🛁, 1WC.
𝒶 🛏 ETB ♛ ♛
Prices: B&B £13–16, weekly £86–100. EM £7–8. Weekly B&B plus EM £130–150. 𝒶 rates.
🛏 £1 per night.

Stoke Grange Farm, Chester Road, Nantwich
✆ (0270) 625525   Mrs Georgina West

Stoke Grange Farm, 1991–92 Cheshire Tourism Development Award Winner, is on the A51, just over 2 miles northwest of Nantwich. The attractive farmhouse dates from 1838, on a working farm with chickens, geese and ponies. Relax on the verandah with splendid views and watch the canal boats pass by the farmhouse. Packed lunches on request. Cot, highchair, playroom and children's games provided. Self-catering also available. Nantwich 2 miles. Dorfold Hall 2 miles. Churches Mansion 3 miles. Cholmondeley Castle and Gardens 5 miles. Stapeley Water Gardens 5 miles.

Open all year
3 bedrooms (2 twin ens. 🛁/WC; 1 double), 1🛁, 1WC.
𝒶 ETB ♛ ♛
Prices: B&B £15-20. 𝒶 rates.

Self-Catering
CONGLETON   Map 5 A2
Pedley House Farm, Pedley Lane, Congleton CW12 3QD
✆ (0260) 273650   Dorothy Gilman

The beamed farmhouse stands on a beef and sheep farm a short walk from the village of Pye Ash. Modernised to a high standard, the large and comfortable house sleeps 10, with a ground floor sitting room also usable as a bedroom suitable for disabled guests. The farm is situated on the edge of the Peak District, off the A523 south of Macclesfield (M6 Jct 17/18, then A54), the drive is opposite the Boars Leigh Restaurant at Bosley. Little Moreton Hall 5 miles.

Open all year
𝒶 ETB⌁⌁⌁⌁Commended
Prices: weekly £200–375.

Planning a day out?
See RURAL ATTRACTIONS

CORNWALL

BODMIN
Map 1 A3

Mennabroom, Warleggan, Bodmin PL30 4HE
✆ (020882) 272

Reputedly the oldest house on Bodmin Moor, the medieval Cornish farmhouse of Mennabroom is full of character with oak beams and granite fireplaces and stands on a working farm with a beef suckler herd. Here you can enjoy good home cooking, sensational moorland walks and explore the famous local attractions. For Mennabroom, take the A30 Bodmin-Launceston road eastwards, then turn south by Colliford Lake to Warleggan. St Neot 3 miles, Jamaica Inn 4 miles, Lanhydrock (NT) 8 miles, Tintagel 30 mins drive.

Open Apr-Sept.
3 double bedrooms inc. 1 ens. ☜/WC), 1🛁,
1WC.
♨(10)
Prices: B&B £13–16, weekly £86–107. EM £7,
B&B plus EM weekly £135–155.

Moss Farm Riding, Blisland, Bodmin PL30 4LF
✆ (0208) 850628   Mr & Mrs P. Dibb

This large Cornish granite farmhouse is dramatically situated on open moorland, off the A30 six miles north of Bodmin. The surrounding farm has horses, cats and dogs. Riding for experienced adults available. Only half an hour's drive from both north and south Cornish coasts, the farm is an ideal base for touring. Jamaica Inn 6 miles. Dozemary Pool 6 miles. Tintagel 13 miles.

Open all year
3 bedrooms (2 double inc. 1 ens. ⋔/WC; 1 family ens. ⋔), 2🛁, 3WCs. ☘
Prices ex. VAT: B&B £13, weekly £90. EM £7.
Weekly B&B plus EM £140.

Treffry Farm, Lanhydrock, Bodmin PL30 5AF
✆ (0208) 74405   Mrs Pat Smith

This delightful 18th-century listed slate-hung Georgian farmhouse stands on a 200-acre dairy farm adjoining NT property of Lanhydrock, off the B3268 Bodmin-Lostwithiel road. Enjoy plentiful and delicious home cooking, packed lunches on request. Licensed. Restormel Castle 2 miles. Bodmin Moor 5 miles.

Open Easter-Oct.
3 bedrooms (2 twins ens. ⋔/WC; 1 double ens. ⋔), 1🛁, 2WCs.
♨(6) ETB ♚ ♚Commended
Prices:B&B £18, weekly £120. EM £9. Weekly B&B plus EM £180. ♨ rates.

BUDE
Map 1 B2

Hallagather, Crackington Haven, Bude
EX23 OLA
✆ (08403) 276   Mrs Pat Anthony
✆ From August 1993 (08403) 230276

Part of the Heritage Coast, and set in an Area of Outstanding Beauty, Hallagather farmhouse is a grade 2 listed building, parts of which date from the 14th century. It has oak beams, granite fireplaces with open fires, slate flagstones, and offers guests a superb base for exploring the local beaches, and surrounding National Trust countryside. The farm covers 184 acres with Charollais and Limousin cattle and a breeding flock of sheep. Tintagel and Boscastle a few mins drive. The farm lies north off the B3263, (A39 south from Bude).

Open Apr-Oct.
3 bedrooms (1 double ens.⋔/⇔/WC;1 family ens.⋔/⇔/WC;1 single ens. ⋔/WC).
⚬⚬ ⋔ ETB ⚘ ⚘Commended
Prices: B&B £11.50–15.50, weekly £77–100.⚬⚬ rates.

Lower Northcott Farm, Poughill, Bude
EX23 7EL
✆ (0288) 352350   Mrs Sally-Ann Trewin

Poughill is immediately north of Bude. Our Georgian farmhouse stands in secluded grounds with outstanding views of the heritage coastline. There is a children's safe play area and you are welcome to wander around, meet the animals and see the working of our farm. Home cooking, packed lunches on request. Highchairs, cots and games room provided. Milky Way 15 miles.

Open all year
5 bedrooms (1 twin ens. ⋔/WC; 1 double ens. ⇔/WC; 2 family ens.⋔/WC; 1 single), 1⇔/WC.
⚬⚬ ETB ⚘ ⚘Approved
Prices: B&B £14, weekly £98. EM £6–9. Weekly B&B plus EM £135. ⚬⚬ rates.

CAMBORNE
Map 1 A3

Cargenwen Farm, Blackrock, Praze-an-Beeble, Camborne TR14 9PD
✆ (0209) 831442   Mrs C.R. Peerless

Cargenwen Farm is a comfortable, fully modernised and quiet base for exploring southwest Cornwall. Set on a southwest facing hillside the house has extensive country views from all bedrooms. Good traditional homemade meals are provided using fresh home and local produce. Vegetarian and special diets catered for. Excellent country walks from the farm with regular sightings of foxes, badgers and birds of prey. Golf courses, pony trekking, Cornish beam engines nearby, and a wide selection of beaches. Cargenwen Farm is 3 miles from Camborne, take B3303 for Praze-an-Beeble.

Closed Xmas and New Year
4 bedrooms (1 twin; 2 double inc. 1 ens. ⋔/WC; 1 family), 2⇔, 2WCs.
⚬⚬ ⅍
Prices: B&B £13–16, EM £8.⚬⚬ rates.

HAYLE
Map 1 A3

Rosehill Farm, Leedstown, Hayle TR27 6DH
✆ (0736) 850315   Mrs J. Christophers

This traditional Cornish farmhouse in a central rural location is an ideal base for touring the coasts. Mrs Christophers provides good cooking and a homely atmosphere. Afternoon teas on request. The small farm has cattle and family pets and grows vegetable crops: courgettes, potatoes and cauliflowers. For Rosehill, take B3302 from Hayle to Leedstown, then B3280 towards Praze-an-Beeble. Hayle 6 miles. Penzance 9 miles. Gweek Seal Sanctuary 10 miles.

Open Jan-Nov.
2 bedrooms (1 twin; 1 double), 1⇔, 1WC.
⚬⚬ ⋔
Prices: B&B £10–12, weekly £70–84. EM £7, B&B plus EM weekly £119–133. ⚬⚬ rates,⋔ £5 per week.

HELSTON
Map 1 A3
Little Pengwedna Farm, Helston TR13 0BA
✆ (0736) 850649

This traditional Cornish granite farmhouse is located on a working farm with pedigree Charollais show cattle, 4 miles outside Helston on the B3302 St Ives road. The house is beautifully furnished to provide a comfortable and relaxing holiday. Tea/coffee facilities in all rooms. Many golden beaches and secluded fishing coves within easy reach.

Open all year
3 bedrooms (1 twin; 2 double inc. 1 ens. ℍ/WC), 1🛏, 2WCs.
⌂ ⊁ ETB ⚌ Commended
Prices: B&B £12.50, weekly £84. ⌂ rates.

Polgarth Farm, Crowntown, Helston TR13 0AA
✆ (0326) 572115   Mrs Maureen Dale

This farm is mainly market-gardening. Babysitting by arrangement. Pets welcome. Central for both coasts, Polgarth Farm is on the B3303, Helston-Camborne road. Helston 3 miles.

Open Jan-Nov.
3 bedrooms (2 double; 1 family), 1🛏, 3WCs.
⌂ ⊁ ETB ⚌ ⚌Approved
Prices:B&B £13–14, weekly £84. ⌂ rates.

Tregaddra Farm, Cury, Helston
✆ (0326) 240235

Tregaddra is an early 18th-century farmhouse set in half an acre of well-kept gardens, providing high class accommodation. Ideally situated in the Lizard peninsula with views of the sea, coast and countryside for 15 mile radius. Good farmhouse cooking with own produce used, packed lunches available. Heated swimming pool and games room. Lounge has inglenook fireplace, log fires in cooler season. The farm is mainly arable, potatoes, cabbage and corn, and a beef cattle herd. The farm lies off the Lizard road (A3083) 5 miles from Helston. Mullion Golf Club 3 miles. Seal Sanctuary 5 miles. Poldark Mine 8 miles.

Open all year
5 bedrooms (2 double ens. ℍ/WC; 2 family ens. ℍ/WC; 1 single), 1🛏. ⌂
Prices: B&B £17–20, weekly £119–140. EM £6, B&B plus EM weekly £160–175. ⌂ rates.

LAUNCESTON
Map 1 B3
Hurdon Farm, Launceston PL15 9LS
✆ (0566) 772955   Mrs Margaret Smith

This elegant 18th-century stone farmhouse is a listed building, superbly situated in picturesque surroundings. The accommodation is comfortable and spacious with log fire in the lounge. In the dining room, at separate family tables, a typical dinner starts with spinach roulade, major mushrooms, followed by roast beef or fresh salmon en croute. Desserts such as steamed chocolate pudding, apple dappy or strawberry Pavlova, are followed by cheese and coffee. The traditional mixed working farm of 400 acres lies south of Launceston (1 mile from A30 bypass), ideal for visiting both north and south Cornish coasts or inland to wild Bodmin Moor or Dartmoor.

Open May-Oct.
6 bedrooms (1 twin ens.▭/WC; 2 double inc. 1 ens.▭/WC; 2 family ens.▭/WC; 1 single), 1 🛏, 1WC.
♿ ⌂
Prices: B&B £13.50–16.50, weekly £80.50–98. EM £8. Weekly B&B plus EM £128.50–146.⌂ rates.

Middle Tremollett Farm, Coads Green, Launceston PL15 7NA
✆ (0566) 82416

The stone-built farmhouse, centrally heated but with log fires in winter, stands on a working mixed farm with corn, beef cows, calves and 100 sheep. Lambing time Feb-Mar. Afternoon teas available on request. The farm lies 8 miles southwest of

Launceston (A30/B3257 to village of Coads Green). Cheesewring on Bodmin Moor 5 miles. Kitt Hill 7 miles.

Closed Xmas
2 bedrooms (1 double; 1 family) 1🗋, 1🛏, 2WCs.
🐾 ⅍ ETB 🏅
Prices: B&B £12–16, weekly £80–100. 🐾 rates.

Trethorne Leisure Farm, Kennards House, Launceston PL15 8QE
ℂ (0566) 86324   Dorothy Davey

Just off the A30 west of Launceston on the junction with the A395 stands Trethorne Leisure Farm. A 140-acre working dairy farm where you can milk a cow, ride a pony or watch ducks hatch. Staying in the farmhouse you can enjoy delicious home-cooked food in a relaxed atmosphere. Packed lunches available. Golf driving range and 9 hole pay and play golf course 36 par on the farm and a licensed restaurant separate to the farmhouse.

Closed Xmas
6 bedrooms (1 twin ens. 🗋; 2 double ens. 🗋/WC; 3 family ens.🗋/WC), 1🛏, 2WCs.
🐾 ⋔
Prices: B&B £14–15, weekly £98. EM £8. Weekly B&B plus EM £154. 🐾 rates.

LISKEARD   Map 1 B3
Tregondale Farm, Menheniot, Liskeard PL14 3RG
ℂ (0579) 342407   S. Rowe

Follow the signs off the A390, east of Liskeard, to find this characteristic farmhouse on a 180-acre mixed farm where animals are naturally reared in the peace of the countryside amidst wildlife, flowers and woodland walks, a pony for riding. The farmhouse is beautifully set with rural views surrounded by a walled garden including a tennis court, swing, and seesaw. Home grown produce is used to prepare tastefully presented four course evening meals. Children's facilities and babysitting available. Looe and Polperro 6 miles. NT properties and Bodmin Moor 5 miles. St Mellion Golf and Country Club 5 miles.

Open all year
3 bedrooms (1 twin; 1 double with 🗋/🖵/WC; 1 family with 🖵/WC), 1WC.
🐾ETB 🏅 🏅 Highly Commended
Prices: B&B £15–17.50, weekly reductions. EM £8.50. 🐾 rates.

Tresulgan Farm, Nr Menheniot Station, Liskeard PL14 3PU
ℂ (05034) 268   Mrs E.R. Elford

Tresulgan is a 140-acre dairy farm situated on the A38 4 miles east of Liskeard. The 17th-century farmhouse is very comfortable and provides good home cooking. Every care is taken to make your stay a memorable one. Beaches 4–6 miles. Popular fishing villages of Looe and Polperro 6–10 miles. A choice of NT properties and children's amusements within 15 miles.

Closed Xmas
3 bedrooms (1 twin ens. 🗋/WC; 1 double ens. 🗋/WC; 1 family ens. 🗋/WC).
🐾 ⋔ ETB 🏅 🏅Highly Commended
Prices: B&B £15–16, weekly £105–112. EM £6–7. B&B plus EM weekly £147–154. 🐾 rates.

Trewint Farm, Menheniot, Liskeard PL14 3RE
ℂ (0579) 347155/62237   M.E. Rowe

Trewint working farm is situated less than 2 miles off the A38 in peaceful rural surroundings, 4 miles from the old market town of Liskeard. The 200-acre working farm has attractive valley walks, pedigree South Devon cattle, sheep, pigs, a pony for children and a play area. Sample true country fare using home produced vegetables and naturally fed meat. Packed lunches and afternoon teas on request. Cot, highchair, babysitting provided. The family suite consists of 2 adjoining rooms. Dobwalls Railway and Theme Park 4 miles. Monkey Sanctuary 5 miles. Morwellham Copper Mine and village 10 miles. Looe, Polperro, Whitsand Bay 6 miles. Ideal base for golfing holiday.

Open all year **RAC**
2 bedrooms (1 double ens. ⋒/WC;1 family ens. ⋒/WC).
Prices: B&B £12–16, weekly £84–112. EM £6.50–8. Weekly B&B plus EM £126–168. rates.

LOOE   Map 1 B3

Bucklawren Farm, St Martins, Looe PL13 1NZ
✆ (05034) 738   Mrs Jean Henley

Bucklawren is a 500-acre dairy and arable farm off the B3253, 2 miles east of the picturesque fishing village of Looe. In this large and spacious farmhouse, set in glorious countryside with beautiful sea views, you can enjoy farmhouse cooking from local produce in a friendly and relaxed atmosphere. Packed lunches and afternoon teas on request. Cot and highchair provided.

Open Mar-Nov.
5 bedrooms (2 twin inc. 1 ens. ⋒/WC; 1 double ens. ⋒/WC; 2 family ⋒/WC), 1🚼, 1WC.
ETB 🏅 🏅Commended
Prices: B&B £14–17, weekly £94–108. EM £8. Weekly B&B plus EM £147–160. rates.

Coombe Farm, Widegates, Nr Looe PL13 1QN
✆ (05034) 223   Alexander & Sally Low

On the B3253 between Hessenford and Looe stands this lovely country house furnished with antiques. Although no longer attached to a working farm the house is set in 10 acres of lawns, meadows, and ponds with superb views down a wooded valley to the sea. Enjoy the luxury of log fires, delicious home cooking and candlelit dining. The bedrooms are fully equipped with TV, tea/coffee facilities, telephone, etc. A heated

swimming pool, croquet lawn, and a stone barn for snooker and table tennis. Nearby are golf, fishing, tennis, horse riding as well as glorious walks and beaches. Packed lunches on request. Licensed. Monkey Sanctuary 3 miles. Whitsand Bay 5 miles.

Open Mar-Oct. **RAC**
10 bedrooms (3 twin; 3 double; 4 family) all rooms ens. ⋒/WC.
♿ (5) 🚼 🐕 ETB 🏅 🏅 Highly Commended
Prices: B&B £16.50–22.50. EM £10. rates.

Trenake Manor Farm, Pelynt, Looe PL13 2LT
✆ (0503) 220216

Trenake is 5 miles from Looe, off the B3359 after Pelynt village. The 14th-century farmhouse, centrally heated, stands on a 285-acre working dairy farm. Ideally situated for exploring this picturesque part of the Cornish coast. Cot provided. Polperro 3 miles. Liskeard cattle markets (Mondays and Thursdays) 12 miles. Monkey Sanctuary 8 miles. Bodmin Farm Park 12 miles.

Open April-Oct.
3 bedrooms (2 double; 1 family), 1 🚼, 1WC.
ETB 🏅 🏅Commended
Prices:B&B £12-14. rates.

MEVAGISSEY   Map 1 A3

Treberrick Farm, Tregony, Truro TR2 5SP
✆ (087253) 247   Mrs M.E. Retallack

6 miles south of the A390 St Austell-Truro road lies Treberrick, a 250-acre family run farm. Here you can relax in comfort in a spacious farmhouse and enjoy traditional country cooking. Guests are welcome to watch the cows and sheep being milked. Situated on the edge of the Roseland Peninsula, the unspoilt beaches of Portholland and Caerhays are only 2 miles distant. Mevagissey 6 miles.

Open Mar-Oct.
3 bedrooms (1 twin; 2 double), 1🚼, 1WC.
Prices: B&B £13–14. EM £7–8.

MORWENSTOWE   Map 1 B2
Darzle Farm, Woodford, Morwenstowe, Nr Bude EX23 9HY
✆ (028883) 222

Just 15 minutes north of Bude, Darzle Farm offers the chance to stay on a fully modernised dairy farm and enjoy good farm cooking with home grown produce, including our own clotted cream and butter. Children welcome to feed the chickens, collect eggs, etc. Packed lunches on request. Cots, highchairs, slides, swings, table tennis, Wendy house and playroom provided. Beaches, woodland walks and coastal footpath 2 miles. Kilarny Springs 3 miles. Pixieland 6 miles. Tamar Lakes 6 miles. Gnome Reserve 10 miles.

Open all year
3 bedrooms (1 double ens.⌂/WC;2 family inc. 1 ens. ⌂/WC, 1 ens. ⌂), 1 suite inc. 1 double, 1 twin, ens. ⌂/WC. 3 ➥, 1WC.
⚱ ⊁ ETB ♛ ♛
Prices: B&B £14–16, weekly £90–97. EM £6–8. Weekly B&B plus EM £135–140. ⚱ rates.

Dene Farm, Morwenstowe, Bude
✆ (028883) 330   Mrs Irene Heard

The stone-built farmhouse surrounded by gardens stands in a pleasant wooded valley and offers good home cooking and a relaxing stay. This small mixed farm is at Morwenstowe, west off the A39 Bude-Clovelly road. Bude 9 miles. Clovelly 10 miles. Tintagel 22 miles.

Open all year
3 bedrooms (2 double inc. 1 ens.⌂/WC; 1 family), 1➥, 2WCs.
⚱ETB Recommended
Prices: B&B £13–16, weekly £96–103. EM £6.50–8. B&B plus EM weekly £141.50–159. ⚱ rates.

MULLION   Map 1 A3
Polhormon Farm, Polhormon Lane, Mullion, Helston TR12 7JE
✆ (0326) 240304   Mrs Alice Harry

Situated off the A3083 Helston-Lizard road, past Poldhu Cove, Polhormon is a working dairy farm with magnificent coastal and country views. A choice of seven sandy beaches within 5 miles of the farm. The Victorian farmhouse offers old-fashioned comfort and a relaxed atmosphere. Cot, highchair, babysitting available. Lizard Head 5 miles. Helford River (Frenchman's Creek) 10 miles. St Michael's Mount 16 miles.

Open Easter to mid-Oct.
3 bedrooms (1 double; 2 family), 1➥, 2WCs.
⚱ ⊁ ETB ♛
Prices: B&B £14–15, single from £18, weekly £98–105.

NEWQUAY   Map 1 A3
Manuels Farm, Newquay
✆ (0637) 873577   Mrs Jean Wilson

This small working family farm lies in a sheltered peaceful valley, signposted from the A392, 3 miles from Newquay. Staying in a 17th-century listed farmhouse you can enjoy the comforts of log fires and traditional cooking using local produce. Fresh bread baked daily. Packed lunches on request. Cot, highchair and babysitting available. Trerice (NT) 1 mile.

Open all year
4 bedrooms (2 double; 2 family), 2➥, 2WCs.
⚱ ⊁ ⊁ ETB ♛ ♛Commended
Prices: B&B £14–17. EM £9.50. Weekly B&B plus EM £150–180. ⚱ rates.

PADSTOW   Map 1 A3
Trevornick Farm, St Issey, Wadebridge PL27 7QH
✆ (0841) 540574   Wg Cdr & Mrs P.J. Patterson

This lovely old Cornish slate farmhouse with converted farm buildings is surrounded by well tended gardens overlooking Little Petterich Creek. The 11-acre general farm with cattle, sheep and crops, offers guests every comfort, amidst rural peace by the Estuary. Take the A39/A389 from Wadebridge (5 miles) to St Issey, and thereafter follow farm signs. Padstow 1 mile. A choice of beaches within 5 miles.

Open all year
3 bedrooms (1 twin; 2 double), 2➥, 2WCs.
⚱ ⊁ ETB Highly Commended
Prices: B&B £15–17.50, weekly £105–122.50.

See STOP PRESS
for more farms

PENZANCE
Map 1 A3
Menwidden Farm, Ludgvan, Penzance
✆ (0736) 740415   Mrs A.R. Blewett

Menwidden Farm lies off the A30, 4 miles north of Penzance (turn off at Crowlas). Mrs Blewett provides good farm cooking in a friendly atmosphere at this small working dairy farm. Cot and highchair provided. St Michael's Mount 3 miles. St Ives 5 miles. Land's End 14 miles.

Open Feb-Nov.
6 bedrooms (1 twin; 3 double; 2 family), 2🛏, 2WCs.
🐾 ETB Listed
Prices: B&B £12, weekly £80. EM £5. Weekly B&B plus EM £110. rates.

POLBATHIC
Map 1 B3
Hendra Farm, Polbathic, Torpoint PL11 3DT
✆ (05035) 225

Hendra is a slate-fronted farmhouse with a large garden and spacious comfortable rooms. The relaxed family atmosphere will make you feel at home at all times. On this mixed working farm there are cows, sheep, ducks and chickens. Cot, highchair and toys available. South of the A38 Saltash-Liskeard road, Hendra is just 2 miles from Downderry beach. Looe 6 miles. Mount Edgecombe 8 miles. Plymouth 12 miles.

Open April-Oct.
3 bedrooms (1 twin; 1 double; 1 family ens. /WC), 1🛏,1WC.

Prices: B&B £12-15, weekly £80-100. rates.

PORT ISAAC
Map 1 A3
Trewetha Farm, Port Isaac PL29 3RU
✆ (0208) 880256

Leave the A39 before Camelford on the B3314/B3267 to reach Trewetha, a mile from the old fishing village of Port Isaac. The 18th-century farmhouse is set in 20 acres of grazing land with panoramic sea and countryside views. The farm keeps sheep, pigs, chickens and miniature Shet-

land ponies. Highchair provided. Fishing trips from Port Isaac, surfing at Polzeath (7 miles) and golf at Rock (7 miles).

Open all year
2 bedrooms (1 double; 1 family), 1🛏, 2WCs.
ETB
Prices: B&B £13.50, weekly £87.50. rates.

ST AUSTELL
Map 1 A3
Poltarrow Farm, St Mewan, St Austell
✆ (0726) 67111

Just west of St Austell off the A390, this beautiful and comfortable farmhouse is set in Du Maurier country, close to beaches and a quaint harbour. Traditional Cornish fare makes Poltarrow Farm an ideal choice for the discerning visitor. Licensed. Various NT properties to visit locally. Coastal footpaths 3 miles.

Open all year
3 bedrooms (1 twin ens. /WC; 1 double ens. /WC;1 family ens. /WC).
ETB Commended
Prices: B&B £16. EM £8. rates.

St JUST
Map 1 A3
Manor Farm, Botallack, St Just, Penzance TR19 7QE
✆ (0736) 788525

Just north of St Just lies Manor Farm. Built in 1665 the farmhouse may seem familiar as it has starred in two BBC TV series, 'Poldark' and 'Penmarric'. The manor is on a working dairy and mixed farm, ideally placed for exploring the westernmost points of Cornwall. Cape Cornwall 2 miles. Land's End 4 miles. Minack Open Theatre 6 miles. St Michael's Mount 8 miles.

Open all year
3 bedrooms (1 twin ens. /WC; 2 double inc. 1 ens. /WC), 1🛏, 2WCs.
ETB Commended
Prices:B&B £14-19. rates.

ST JUST-IN-ROSELAND — Map 1 A3

Commerrans Farm, St Just-in-Roseland, Nr Truro TR2 5JJ
✆ (0872) 580270   Mrs Wendy Symons

A warm welcome and good home cooking await you at Commerrans on the beautiful Roseland peninsula, off the B3289 north of St Just-in-Roseland. The small working farm, mainly sheep and bulb growing, lies peacefully by the River Fal. Cot, highchair and children's games provided. Trelissick Gardens 2 miles. Coastal paths 2 miles. St Mawes Castle 4 miles. Veryan Round-houses 5 miles.

Open April-Nov.
3 bedrooms (1 twin; 2 double), 1🛉, 1WC.
🕮(1) 🛉
Prices: B&B £12-15. EM £7. 🕮 rates.

SALTASH — Map 1 B3

Burcombe Farm, St Dominick, Saltash PL12 6SH
✆ (0579) 50217   Peter & Violet Batten

Burcombe Farm extends to 160 acres, mainly arable, corn, potatoes and beef cattle, with a history that dates back to 1722. The farmhouse is large with wonderful views across the River Tamar to Plymouth. Less than 5 miles from Callington, turn off the A388 Saltash road for St Dominick. St Mellion Golf and Country Club with its two 18 hole courses 3 miles. Plymouth 12 miles.

Open Apr-Oct.
3 bedrooms (2 twin inc. 1 ens. 🛁/🖘/WC; 1 double ens. 🛁/🖘/WC), 1🛉, 1WC.
ETB ⚜ ⚜Approved
Prices: B&B £17.50-20, weekly £110-120.

TRURO — Map 1 A3

Arallas, Ladock, Truro TR2 4NP
✆ (0872) 510379   Mrs B. Holt

Turn south off the A30 Bodmin-Redruth road at Summercourt to reach Arallas, an elegant farmhouse formerly used as a gentleman's sporting retreat. It is in a truly peaceful rural area with good walks through 400 acres of woodland and superb views. Cot provided. North and South coasts are both within easy reach.

Open Feb-Nov.
3 bedrooms (1 twin ens. 🛁/WC; 2 double inc. 1 ens. 🖘/WC, 1 ens. 🛁/WC).
🕮 ETB ⚜ ⚜ ⚜ Commended
Prices: B&B £14-21, weekly £91-123. EM £8-11. 🕮 rates.

Great Hewas Farm, Grampound Rd, Truro TR2 4EP
✆ (0726) 882218   Mrs D. Dymond

Great Hewas is a 140-acre working farm situated in the centre of Cornwall, ideal for touring and safe sandy beaches. Set in peaceful countryside, 3 miles north of the A390 St Austell-Truro road, it is an excellent place for just relaxing and enjoying good home cooking. The farmhouse is tastefully furnished and all main bedrooms have extensive views.

Open Easter-Sep.
3 bedrooms (2 double inc. 1 ens. 🛁/WC; 1 family/twin), 1🛉, 2WCs.
🕮 ETB Registered
Prices: B&B £12.50, weekly £84. EM £5. Weekly B&B plus EM £112.

Nanteague Farm Guest House, Marazanvose, Nr Truro
✆ (0872) 540351

On the A30 north of Truro, 2 miles from Zelah, Nanteague can give you a real country holiday with everything on your doorstep. We can arrange clay pigeon shooting, gliding, flying, diving, sailing and horse riding. Set in 130 acres of beef farmland, there is an outdoor heated pool, 9 hole golf course, a lake with canoes and riverboat, inland beach and a large children's play area. Cot and highchair also provided. The farm is just 10 minutes' drive from Truro, Newquay, Perranporth and all surrounding beaches. Licensed.

Open Easter-Oct.
5 bedrooms (1 twin ens. 🛁/WC; 1 double ens. 🛁/WC; 3 family 🛁/WC), 1🛉, 1WC.
🕮 ETB ⚜ ⚜ ⚜Highly Commended
Prices: B&B £14-16.50, weekly £98-115.50. EM £8.50. 🕮 rates.

Pengelly Farm, St Erme, Truro TR4 9BG
✆ (0872) 510245

Pengelly Farm is a working dairy farm set in its own 230 acres. The views from the farm are breathtaking. The house has been totally renovated and restored to its original state with polished beams and open fireplaces. Cot, highchair, and children's games provided. Off the A3076 a mile south of the A30, its central location makes it ideal for touring the whole of Cornwall. North coast 6 miles. South coast 10 miles. Lappa Valley Railway 4 miles. Newquay 6 miles.

Open April-Oct.
4 bedrooms (1 double; 2 family inc. 1 ens. 🛁, 1 ens. 🚽/WC; 1 single), 1🛏, 1WC. ⚘
Prices: B&B £12–17, weekly £80–110. ⚘ rates.

Penhale Farm, Grampound Road, Truro
TR2 4ER
✆ (0726) 882324   Mrs Sue Lutey

Penhale Farm is a working farm of 240 acres in the centre of the county, south off the A30 Bodmin-Redruth at Indian Queens. The farm's enterprises are cereal, beef cattle and sheep. The spacious farmhouse looks out over a large pleasant garden. The house is decorated to a high standard. Cot, highchair and children's games provided. Motor Car Museum 1 mile. A choice of NT properties in the locality. Truro 10 miles. Coast 20 mins drive.

Open April-Oct.
3 bedrooms (1 twin; 2 double;), 1🛏, 2WCs. ⚘
Prices: B&B £12.50. EM £6.50. ⚘ rates.

Polsue Manor Farm, Tresillian, Truro
✆ (087252) 234   Mrs Geraldine Holliday

The farmhouse on this 190-acre working farm is set in glorious countryside overlooking the tidal Tresillian River in one of the prettiest parts of Cornwall on the edge of the Roseland Peninsula. Many delightful country walks locally. Home cooking. Cot and highchair available. Centrally situated, on the A39 2 miles east of Truro, Polsue Manor is ideally placed for exploring both coastlines.

Open most of the year
5 bedrooms (1 twin; 2 double; 2 family),1🛏, 1🛁, 2WCs.
⚘ ⛏ ETB 👑
Prices: B&B £14–16. EM £7. ⚘ rates.

> Planning a day out?
> See RURAL ATTRACTIONS

Self-Catering

BODMIN   Map 1 A3

Moss Farm Riding, Blisland, Bodmin
PL30 4LF
✆ (0208) 850628   Mr & Mrs P. Dibb

For farm description, see p. 29. An attractively converted barn provides self-catering accommodation for 4–6.

Open all year
Prices: weekly £70–250.

FALMOUTH   Map 1 A3

Boskensoe, Mawnan Smith, Falmouth
TR11 5JP
✆ (0326) 250257   Mrs G Matthews

Boskensoe Farm has an attractive granite farmhouse and two bungalows standing on a mixed working family farm. Part of the farmhouse is available for self-catering from April to October. The bungalows are open all year. Each unit sleeps 8. The farm lies 5 miles from Falmouth. Helford River and NT Gardens under 2 miles.

Open all year ⛏
Prices: weekly £125–350.

LISKEARD   Map 1 B3

Tregondale Farm, Menheniot, Liskeard
PL14 3RG
✆ (0579) 342407   S. Rowe

For farm description see p. 32. Accommodation is available in a traditional country cottage, sleeps 4, full of character with beams and original oven.

Open all year
ETB Highly Commended
Prices: weekly £150–325.

CORNWALL

PADSTOW
Map 1 A3

Trevornick Farm, St Issey, Wadebridge
PL27 7QH
✆ (0841) 540574   Wg Cdr & Mrs P.J. Patterson

For full description see p. 34. Accommodation is offered in 5 cottages, sleeping 2–5. One double cottage is Accessible Category One for Disabled. Cots available.

Open all year
♿ ✈ ✂ ETB ♪♪♪♪Highly Commended
Prices: weekly £120–550.

PORT ISAAC
Map 1 A3

Trewetha Farm, Port Isaac PL29 3RU
✆ (0208) 880256

For farm description see p. 35. Accommodation is available in a barn which has been converted into 2 fully equipped units, each sleeping 4.

Open all year
Prices: weekly £165–365.

38

CUMBRIA

ALSTON
Map 7 A3

Middle Bayles Farm, Alston, CA9 3BS
℡ (0434) 381383   Mrs Pat Dent

The number of visitors who return is proof of the warm farmhouse hospitality and good home cooking we offer. You are welcome to wander around our 300-acre hill farm, located a mile from Alston off the A686. It is an ideal area for walking and exploring the beauty of the North Pennines. The 17th-century farmhouse is tastefully furnished with superb views overlooking the South Tyne Valley. Packed lunches on request. Cot, highchair and children's games provided. Kilhope Weel 7 miles. Lakes, Hadrian's Wall, Durham all within 30 miles.

Closed Xmas and April
2 bedrooms (1 double ens. ☞/WC; 1 family private ☞/WC), 1WC.
ঞ ⅍ ETB ♕ ♕Commended
Prices: B&B £14–17, weekly £98. EM £8. Weekly B&B plus EM £146.(No EM Tues) ঞ rates.

Stonehall, Slaggyford, Carlisle CA6 7PB
℡ (0434) 381349

A warm welcome and good farmhouse cooking await you at this 1500-acre hill farm of mainly beef cattle and sheep. The peaceful surroundings of the Pennine Way are a delight for walkers, packed lunches provided on request. Cot and highchair available. Stonehall is reached by the A689 from Alston, the farm is a mile north of

Slaggyford at Knarsdale. Haltwhistle 8 miles. Hadrian's Wall 10 miles. Lake District 23 miles.

Open Apr-Oct.
3 bedrooms (1 twin; 1 single; 1 family), 2➡, 2WCs.
ঞ ⋔ ETB Registered
Prices: B&B £14–15, weekly £92. EM £7, B&B plus EM weekly £140. ঞ rates.

AMBLESIDE
Map 4 B1

Tock How Farm, High Wray, Ambleside
℡ (05394) 36481   Patricia Benson

A working dairy beef and sheep farm once owned by Beatrix Potter, it now belongs to the National Trust. There are wonderful views from all the spacious, well equipped bedrooms. In the farmyard there are peacocks, chickens and ducks. Separate lounge and dining room for guests. Homemade jams a speciality. Cot available. The farm is south of Ambleside off the B5286 Hawkshead road.

Open all year
3 bedrooms (2 double; 1 family), 1➡, 2WCs.
ঞ ⅍ ⋔
Prices: B&B £12–15. ঞ rates,⋔ £2 per night.

BEWCASTLE
Map 7 A3

Bank End Farm, Bewcastle, Roadhead, Carlisle CA6 6NU
℡ (06978) 644   Dorothy Downer

Peace and relaxation await you on this small sheep farm close to the Scottish border (east of the A7 at Longtown, off the B6318). Private sitting room with TV and tea-making, friendly atmosphere and excellent home cooking. Packed lunches on request. River Black Lyne 100yds. Riding and pony trekking 1 mile. Fishing (sea trout and salmon) 6 miles.

Open Apr-Nov.
1 twin bedroom ens. ⋔☞/WC).
✂ETB ♨ ♨ ♨Commended
Prices: B&B £17.50–21, weekly from £122. EM £11. Weekly B&B plus EM from £190.

BRAMPTON   Map 7 A3
Cracrop, Kirkcambeck, Brampton, Carlisle CA8 2BW
✆ (06978) 245   Mrs Marjorie Stobart

Prizewinners in conservation and wildlife, Cracrop has 425 acres of arable, permanent pasture and woodland located off the B6318, 7 miles north of the A69 Carlisle-Haltwhistle road. Deer, pheasant, rabbit and duck are continually seen. The farm's main enterprises are milk, beef and sheep. Farm trails are marked for guests to see the variety of farm life at first hand. The large farmhouse dates from 1847. Delicious home cooking. Packed lunches on request. Games room, snooker, spa bath and sauna.

Closed Xmas
3 bedrooms (1 twin ens. ⋔/WC; 1 double ens. ⋔/WC; 1 family ens. ⋔/WC), 3➡, 2WCs.
⚲ (12) ✂ETB ♨ ♨ ♨Highly Commended
Prices: B&B £18–21, weekly £120. EM £12.

High Nook Farm, Low Row, Brampton CA8 2LU
✆ (06977) 46273   Mrs Annabel Forster

High Nook Farm offers a warm friendly welcome and good home cooking in the rural peace of Irthing Valley. Off the A69 east of Brampton, this stock rearing farm covers 100 acres. Built in 1857, the farmhouse has good sized rooms. Packed lunches on request. Cot and highchair available. Naworth Castle 2 miles. Hadrian's Wall 3 miles. Lanercost Priory 3 miles.

Open April-Oct.
2 bedrooms (1 double; 1 family), 1➡, 1WC.
⚲ ⫟ ETB Listed
Prices: B&B from £10, weekly £65. EM £6. Weekly B&B plus EM £105. ⚲ rates.

CALDBECK   Map 7 A3
Friar Hall, Caldbeck, Wigton CA7 8DS
✆ (06998) 633   Mrs Dorothy Coulthard

Friar Hall is a working farm with dairy and sheep in the small village of Caldbeck, northwest of Penrith (B5305/5299). You can enjoy the comforts of an attractively modernised farmhouse, oak beams retained in most rooms. The superb view from the farmhouse takes in the church, river and Caldbeck Fells. Well placed for touring the Lake District, Hadrian's Wall and the Scottish Borders. Cot and highchair provided.

Open Mar-Oct.
3 bedrooms (1 twin; 1 double; 1 family), 2➡, 2WCs.
⚲ ⫟ ETB Listed
Prices: B&B £14.50–15.50. ⚲ rates.

CARLISLE   Map 7 A3
Bessiestown Farm, Catlowdy, Penton, Carlisle
✆ (0228) 577219   J & M Sisson

Bessiestown is a small beef and sheep rearing farm overlooking the Scottish Borders. It lies northeast of Carlisle off the B6318 (leave A7 at Longtown). The farmhouse has been delightfully decorated to create the relaxed atmosphere you would expect in a comfortable family home. Indoor heated swimming pool for guests' use.

Scottish Borders 2 miles. Hadrian's Wall 10 miles. Lake District 30 miles.

Open all year
5 bedrooms (2 twin inc. 1 ens. ⌂/WC, 1 ens.♨/WC; 2 double ens. ⌂/WC; 1 family ens.♨/WC), 1WC.
⚶ ETB ♨ ♨ ♨Highly Commended
Prices: B&B from £19, EM £9. ⚶ rates.

Craigburn Farm, Catlowdy, Penton, Carlisle CA6 5QP
✆ (0228) 577214　　　　Mrs Jane Lawson

Northwest of Carlisle (east of the A7), on the edge of Kershope Forest, this 18th-century farmhouse is set in 250 acres of family run farmland. Delicious home cooking (licensed), including traditional Sunday lunch, comfortable surroundings and a friendly atmosphere provide the winning combination for a relaxing and peaceful holiday. Packed lunches on request. Cot, highchair, playroom and games provided. Well placed for exploring the Lakes, Hadrian's Wall, Gretna Green and south Scotland.

Open all year
6 bedrooms (2 twin ens. ⌂/WC; 2 double ens. ♨/WC; 2 family inc. 1 ens. ⌂/WC, 1 ens. ♨/WC).
& ⚶ ↟ ETB ♨ ♨ ♨Commended
Prices: B&B £17–18, weekly £107–113.40. EM £8–10. Weekly B&B plus EM £157.50–176.40. ⚶ rates.

Meadow View, New Pallyards Farm, Hethersgill, Longtown, Carlisle
✆ (0228) 577308　　　　J. Elwen

Meadow View stands on New Pallyards Farm, a 65-acre working farm supporting ponies, sheep and beef cattle. Its location, northeast of Carlisle and 6 miles east of Longtown (A7), is 9 miles from M6. Kielder Water, the largest man-made lake in Europe, Hadrian's Wall, woodland walks and fishing are nearby. Packed lunches on request. Ground floor access bedroom. Cot, highchair and children's games provided.

Open all year
6 bedrooms (2 twin inc. 1 ens. ⌂/WC, 1 ens. ♨/WC; 2 double inc. 1 ens. ⌂/WC, 1 ens. ♨/WC; 2 family inc. 1 ens. ⌂/WC, 1 ens. ♨/WC), 1↟, 1WC.
& ⚶ ↟ ETB ♨ ♨ ♨ Commended
Prices: B&B £16–18, weekly £100–120. EM £9.50. Weekly B&B plus EM £150-175. ⚶ rates. ↟ rates.

New Pallyards Country Farmhouse, Hethersgill, Longtown, Carlisle
✆ (0228) 577308　　　　Mrs G.A. Elwen

The award winning main farmhouse at New Pallyards Farm also offers every hospitality to guests. For details of farm location and amenities, see previous entry. Ground floor access bedroom. Packed lunches on request.

Open all year
7 bedrooms (3 double ens. ♨/WC; 2 family inc. 1 ens. ⌂/WC, 1 ens. ♨/WC; 2 twins inc. 1 ens. ⌂/WC, 1 priv. ♨/WC).
& ⚶ ↟ ETB ♨ ♨ ♨Commended
Prices: B&B £19, EM £9.50. Weekly B&B plus EM £150–175. ⚶ rates.↟ rates.

Streethead Farm, Ivegill, Carlisle CA4 0NG
✆ (06974) 73327　　　　Mrs J. Wilson

Streethead Farm offers the opportunity to stay in a very old listed building, situated in unspoilt countryside midway between Penrith and Carlisle, west off M6, Jct 41. It makes an ideal base for exploring the Lake District. Packed lunches on request. Hutton Hall 4 miles. The Lakes 13 miles.

Open Mar-Oct.
2 bedrooms (1 double; 1 family), 1↟.
⚶(7) ETB Listed
Prices: B&B £13–14. EM £8. ⚶ rates.

COCKERMOUTH　　　　　　　　Map 7 A3

Brook Farm, Loweswater, Cockermouth CA13 0RP
✆ (0900) 85606　　　　Mrs Ann Hayton

This 250-acre stock rearing hill farm stands in a lovely area of the Lake District, on a quiet back road between Loweswater and Lorton, south of Cockermouth. Mrs Hayton serves good home cooking at the comfortable farmhouse. Packed lunches on request. Cot provided. This is a centre for beautiful scenery and good walking. Loweswater and Crummock Lakes 2 miles. Cockermouth 5 miles.

Open May-Oct.
2 bedrooms (1 double; 1 twin), 1➡, 1WC.
⚗ ✂ ♜ ETB ⚜Commended
Prices: B&B £14.50–15.50, weekly £98–105.
EM £6. Weekly B&B plus EM £140–147. ⚗
rates.

High Stanger Farm, Cockermouth CA13 9TS

✆ (0900) 823875   Mrs A.P. Hewitson

A warm welcome awaits you at this 17th-century farmhouse with attractive low ceilings, oak beams and open fires. Packed lunches on request. Cot, highchair and babysitting available. High Stanger is a working Cumbrian sheep farm set in the beautiful Lorton Vale, south of Cockermouth on the B5292. Wordsworth's birthplace 2 miles. Crummock Water 3 miles. Bassenthwaite Lake 4 miles. Buttermere 7 miles.

Open all year
2 family bedrooms, 2➡, 2WCs.
⚗ ♜ETB Listed
Prices: B&B £13.50–14. ⚗ rates.

Stanger Farm, Cockermouth CA13 9TS

✆ (0900) 824222   Mrs Carolyn Heslop

We are a small family lakeland dairy farm, situated on the River Cocker in the glorious Vale of Lorton. Relax in comfort by an open log fire in our farmhouse. Friendliness and hospitality are our bywords. Packed lunches on request. Evening meals by arrangement. Stanger Farm is conveniently placed for Buttermere, Keswick and the Western Lakes. Fishing on site, pony trekking close by, footpaths and bridleways around the farm.

Open Easter-Oct.
2 bedrooms (1 twin; 1 double), 1➡, 2WCs.
⚗ ETB ⚜ ⚜
Prices: B&B £13.50.

GREAT LANGDALE   Map 4 B1

Bayesbrown Farm Great Langdale, Ambleside LA22 9JZ

✆ (09667) 300   Mrs J. Rowand

Bayesbrown Farm is set at the beginning of the Great Langdale valley, northwest of Ambleside off the B5343. It has 825 acres with beef cows and Herdwick sheep. Our own hens supply the eggs for breakfast. Enjoy the comfort of an open log fire after a home cooked meal. Packed lunches on request. Cot and children's games provided. Beatrix Potter's House 6 miles. Grasmere 7 miles. Tarn Hows 9 miles. Windermere Steamers 9 miles.

Open all year
4 bedrooms (1 twin; 1 double; 1 family; 1 single), 1➡, 2WCs.
⚗ ♜
Prices: B&B £13, weekly £84. EM £7. Weekly B&B plus EM £133. ⚗ rates.♜ £1 per night.

Stool End Farm, Great Langdale, Ambleside

✆ (09667) 615   Mrs J. Rowand

Enjoy a break on this 17th-century working farm owned by the NT, with comfortable dining/sitting room and woodburner. Stool End farms beef cows, sheep, goats, Shire horses and sheep dogs. Situated amid the beauties of Langdale Valley, northwest of Ambleside off the B5345, it is ideal for walking the Langdales, fishing, boating and visiting the attractions of the Lake District. Sawrey Farm (Beatrix Potter's) and Dove Cottage 8 miles. Coniston 7 miles. Eskdale railway 10 miles.

Closed 25–26 Dec.
2 bedrooms (1 double; 1 family), 1➡, 1WC.
⚗
Prices: B&B from £14, weekly £85. EM £7. ⚗ rates.

KENDAL   Map 4 B1

Cragg Farm, New Hutton, Nr Kendal

✆ (0539) 721760   Mrs Olive M. Knowles

Cragg Farm is a 260-acre dairy and sheep farm, situated in beautiful countryside, convenient for both the Lake District and the Yorkshire Dales, and easily accessible being only 3 miles from M6, Jct37. The 17th-century farmhouse offers excellent modern facilities yet has retained its old world character. Guests will find traditional Cumbrian hospitality. Cot provided. Kendal 4 miles. Levens Hall 7 miles. Windermere 12 miles. Yorkshire Dales 10 miles.

Open Mar-Oct.
2 bedrooms (1 double; 1 family), 1➡, 1WC.
⚗ ♜
Prices: B&B £13.50–14.50. ⚗ rates.

Garnett House Farm, Burneside, Kendal LA9 5SF

✆ (0539) 724542   Mrs S. Beaty

A rare opportunity to stay in a 15th-century listed farmhouse with 4ft thick walls, oak panelling and doors. You can enjoy modern comforts and good home cooking in period surrounds. The large dairy and sheep farm is sited off the A591, Kendal-Windermere road. Kendal 2 miles.

Windermere 6 miles. Levens Hall 5 miles. Sizergh Castle 5 miles.

Open all year **RAC**
3 bedrooms (1 twin; 1 double; 1 family ens. 🛏/WC), 2🛁, 2WCs.
⚷ ETB 👑 👑
Prices from: B&B £13, weekly £88. EM £6.50. ⚷ rates.

Low Hundhowe Farm, Burneside, Kendal LA8 9AB
✆ (0539) 722060

Low Hundhowe is a 235 acre family run mixed farm set in the beautiful Kent Valley. The 350-year-old farmhouse faces south to the River Kent. Nestling in the hillside below Potter Fell it is a peaceful retreat yet only minutes from the A591 and M6. Situated midway between Kendal and Windermere it is well placed for exploring the Lake District. Packed lunches available. Good walking area.

Open Jan-Nov.
3 bedrooms (1 twin; 2 double), 1🛁, 2WCs.
⚷(2) ETB 👑 👑
Prices: B&B from £13, weekly £90. EM from £6. Weekly B&B plus EM £126. ⚷ rates.

Murthwaite Farm, Longsleddale, Kendal LA8 9BA
✆ (053983) 634   Mrs Nancy Waine
✆ from 7 April 1993 (0539) 823634

This 17th-century stonebuilt farmhouse has an idyllic setting in the picturesque Longsleddale Valley, off the A6 north of Kendal. Murthwaite is a traditional Lakeland working farm where you can enjoy modern comfort and delicious home cooked meals. Windermere 8 miles. Kendal Castle 6 miles. Haweswater 8 miles. Sizergh Castle 10 miles.

Open Mar-Nov.
3 bedrooms (1 twin; 2 double), 2🛁, 2WCs.
✂ ETB Listed
Prices: B&B £13–13.50. EM £6.50.

Patton Hall Farm, Meal Bank, Kendal LA8 9DT
✆ (0539) 721590   Mrs Margaret Hodgson

Patton Hall is a cosy well-equipped 17th-century farmhouse, just 3 miles north of Kendal, off the A6. Relax in comfortable surroundings, well placed for exploring the Lakes and enjoying the rugged scenery.

Closed Xmas and New Year
3 bedrooms (1 twin; 2 double), 1🛁, 1WC.
⚷(2) 🐾 ETB 👑 👑
Prices: B&B £12–16, weekly £84–105. ⚷ rates. 🐾 £0.50 per night.

KESWICK-ON-DERWENTWATER
Map 7 A3

Lonscale Farm, Threlkeld, Keswick CA12 4TB
✆ (07687) 79603   Helen Scrimgeour

This large Victorian farmhouse is the ideal place to get away from the crowds. Attractively situated between Lonscale and Latrigg Fells in the heart of the Lake District, it is east of Keswick off the A66. The Cumbrian Way for walkers runs just 400 yds above the house. Working Sheep Dog Demo every Thursday evening.

Open Easter-Oct.
3 bedrooms (1 double; 1 family; 1 single), 1🛁,

1WC.
🏠 ETB Member
Prices: B&B £11–12.50, weekly £77–87.50.

Low Grove Farm, Millbeck, Keswick CA12 4PS
✆ (07687) 72103   Mrs M.E. Thompson

Under 2 miles north of Keswick, off the A591 Carlisle road, this mixed grazing farm enjoys an enviable setting with panoramic views at the foot of Skiddaw. The farmhouse, built in 1764, is a listed building. At Low Grove you will find a comfortable and homely atmosphere. Packed lunches on request. Derwentwater 2 miles. Bassenthwaite Lake 5 miles.

Open Apr-Nov.
3 bedrooms (2 double; 1 twin),1🛏,1WC. 🏠
Prices: B&B £11–12.

Stybeck Farm, Thirlmere, Keswick CA12 4TN
✆ (07687) 73232   Mrs Jean Hodgson

Stybeck is a traditional working farm situated just off the A591 Keswick-Grasmere road. It lies at the foot of the Helvellyn range of mountains, in the picturesque Thirlmere Valley. Good farm cooking. Packed lunches on request. Fishing on Lake Thirlmere 1 mile. Ponytrekking and golf 6 miles. Castlerigg Stone Circle 4 miles.

Open all year
3 bedrooms (2 double inc. 1 ens. 🛁/WC; 1 family), 2🛁, 1🛏, 2WCs.
🏠 🍴 ETB Listed
Prices: B&B £14–16. EM £10. 🏠 rates.

KIRKBY LONSDALE   Map 4 B1

Barnfield Farm, Tunstall, Nr Kirkby Lonsdale
✆ (046834) 284   Mrs J.M. Stephenson
✆ from early 1993 (05242) 74284

The farmhouse was built in 1702 and has been in the same family for four generations. We have 200 acres and are a working farm. Barnfield is under 4 miles from Kirkby Lonsdale (M6, Jct34,

then A683), with its famous Devil's Bridge. Cot available.

Open all year
2 bedrooms (1 double; 1 family), 1🛏, 2WCs.
🏠 🍴
Prices: B&B £12–14. 🏠 rates.

KIRKBY STEPHEN   Map 7 A3
Augill House Farm, Brough, Kirkby Stephen CA17 4DX
✆ (07683) 41305   Jeanette Atkinson

Augill House, built in 1825, is a small hill farm in the Upper Eden Valley, off the A66 east of Penrith. In the farmhouse you can enjoy truly luxurious five-course dinners, which in summer are served in our lovely conservatory overlooking the garden. All bedrooms have TV and tea/coffee facilities. We are ideally situated for visiting the Lakes, Yorkshire Dales and Teesdale as well as walking on the Northern Pennines.

Closed Xmas and New Year
3 bedrooms (1 twin ens. 🛁/WC; 2 doubles inc. 1 ens. 🛁/WC, 1 with priv. 🛏), 1🛏, 1🛁, 2WCs.
🍴 ETB 👑 👑Commended
Prices: B&B £14–16. EM £8.50.

PENRITH   Map 4 B1
Highgate Farm, Penrith CA11 0SE
✆ (07684) 83339

Highgate Farm has a good stone built farmhouse dated 1730, attractively decorated with old beams and brasses. Two of the bedrooms have king size old brass beds. The farm is on the A66 Penrith-Keswick road, 4 miles from M6, Jct 40.

Swimming 2 miles. Hill walking and horse riding 3 miles.

Open mid Feb-mid Nov.
4 bedrooms (1 twin; 1 double; 1 family; 1 single), 1🛏, 1🛁, 2WCs.
ETB 👑 👑
Prices: B&B £15.

Park House Farm, Dalemain, Penrith CA11 0HB
✆ (07684) 86212   Mary Milburn

Situated in our own private valley off the A592 Penrith-Ullswater road (3 miles M6 Jct40). Entrance via Dalemain House, ignoring no cars sign. Park House is a 270-acre sheep farm with stunning views of our Lakeland hills. Enjoy Cumbrian hospitality from a welcome cuppa with home-baking to a generous breakfast. Good evening meals served locally. Packed lunches on request. Cot available. Dalemain House Country Museum and Gardens are close by. Ullswater Lake 3 miles. Penrith Steam Museum 4 miles. Many lovely walks.

Open Apr-Oct.
2 bedrooms (1 double; 1 family), 2🛏, 2WCs.
👑ETB 👑
Prices: B&B £13–15, weekly £84-91. Short breaks offer.👑 rates.

Tymparon Hall, Newbiggin, Stainton, Penrith
✆ (07684) 83236   Mrs Margaret Taylor

Staying on this 150-acre sheep farm you can enjoy the comforts of a typical Cumbrian home, with a large garden and comfortable spacious rooms.We offer good home cooking and packed lunches on request. Cot available. Ullswater and Penrith 4 miles. Golf, swimming, ponytrekking within easy reach.

Open April-Oct.
3 bedrooms (1 twin; 1 double; 1 family ens. 🛁/WC), 2🛏, 1WC.
👑 🐎 ETB Listed Approved
Prices: B&B £15–17, weekly £100–115. EM £8.50. Weekly B&B plus EM £160–174. 👑 rates.

TROUTBECK   Map 7 A3

Gill Head Farm, Troutbeck, Penrith CA11 0ST
✆ (07687) 79652   Mrs J. Wilson

Gill Head is a working farm with cattle, sheep and ponies, under a mile off the A66 on the A5091. The 17th-century farmhouse with oak beams and log fire offers comfort and relaxation. Fishing, boating, riding, golf and climbing all nearby.

Open all year
3 double bedrooms inc. 1 ens. 🛁/WC, 2 ens. 🍽/WC. 👑 🐎
Prices:B&B £16, B&B plus EM £20. 👑 rates.

Self-Catering

KENDAL   Map 4 B1

High Swinklebank Farm, Longsleddale, Nr Kendal LA8 9BD
✆ (053983) 682   Mrs O. Simpson
✆ From early 1993 (0539) 823682

High Swinklebank Farm is a hill sheep farm in a lovely valley setting, off the A6 north of Penrith. The cottage is a self-catering annex to the farmhouse, completely self-contained and recently fitted out. Cot, games and garden available for children. The farm offers immediate access to the beautiful fell-walking countryside that surrounds us. Kendal 9 miles.

Open all year
2 bedrooms (1 double; 1 bunk), living room,

kitchen, 1🛁, 1WC.
🎠 🍖 ETB 𝒥𝒥𝒥Commended
Prices: weekly £100–160. Weekends available
low season.

PENRITH   Map 7 A3
Skirwith Hall, Skirwith, Penrith CA10 4DX
✆ (0768) 88241   Mrs L.I. Wilson

The large dairy and mixed farm of Skirwith Hall
stands off the A686 on the outskirts of Skirwith village. Well placed for exploring the Lakes and the
Yorkshire Dales. Accommodation is in two attractive cottages of Georgian sandstone situated
on the farm. The cottages sleep 8 and 4. Both are
equipped with all the comforts of home, and have
open fires. Cot and highchair available. Acorn
Bank Gardens 2 miles. Long Meg Stone Circle
and Lacy's Caves 3 miles. Wetherights Pottery
Museum 8 miles.

Open all year
🎠 🍖 ETB𝒥𝒥𝒥𝒥 & 𝒥𝒥𝒥 Commended
Prices: weekly £92–290.

TROUTBECK   Map 7 A3
Gill Head Farm, Troutbeck, Penrith CA11
0ST
✆ (07687) 79652   Mrs J. Wilson

For full farm description, see p. 45. Accommodation sleeping 2/4 is available in a separate
apartment on the farm. Fishing, boating, riding,
golf and climbing all nearby.

Open all year
♿ 🎠 🍖
Prices: £160 minimum.

See STOP PRESS
for more farms

DERBYSHIRE

AMBERGATE
Map 5 A3

Lawn Farm, Whitewells Lane, off Holly Lane, Ambergate DE56 2DN
✆ (0773) 852352   Mrs Carol Oulton

This comfortably furnished and fully appointed farmhouse stands on a 150-acre working beef and sheep farm on a quiet country lane (off A6 Belper-Matlock road). Every attention given to guest's enjoyment, cot and highchair provided. Its location makes it ideal for visiting many of the county's attractions. National Tramway Museum 5 miles. Matlock Bath 10 miles. Chatsworth House 20 miles. Ashbourne and Dovedale 20 miles. Alton Towers 35 miles.

Open all year
2 bedrooms (1 double ens. ☞/WC; 1 family), 1🛁.
⚲ 🛉 ETB Listed
Prices: B&B £12–18, weekly £75–110. ⚲ rates.

ASHBOURNE
Map 5 A3

Beechenhill Farm, Ilam, Dovedale, Ashbourne DE6 2BD
✆ (033527) 274   Mrs Sue Prince

Take the A515 north from Ashbourne and turn left after 1 mile for Beechenhill Farm. We live in the best place in the world and we delight in sharing our home with guests! Our warm listed farmhouse nestles on the south-facing hill beside Dovedale. We have 92 acres, a dairy herd and sheep. Our breakfasts are fresh, healthy and traditional, using the best of local produce. Our rooms have wonderful views. Cot, highchair, garden swings available. Within walking distance are glorious Dovedale Gorge, Ilam Country Park and beautiful Manifold Valley. Local picturesque villages and jolly good local pubs (2–3 miles).

Closed Xmas
2 double bedrooms, 1🛁, 1WC.
⚲ ⌇ ETB ♛ ♛Highly Commended
Prices: B&B £16–18.50. ⚲ rates.

Coldwall Farm, Okeover, Nr Ashbourne DE6 2BS
✆ (033529) 249   Mrs M.A. Griffin

Guests are welcome to watch the activities on this working farm with milking cows, calves, sheep, lambs, and Shire Horses. The comfortable stone-built house is 200 years old, and is well placed for exploring the Peak District. There are lovely walks through the woods and by the river on the farm. Coldwall Farm is 4 miles from Ashbourne, A52 towards Leek then via Okeover Park. Dovedale 1 mile. Alton Towers 5 miles.

Open Easter-Oct.
2 bedrooms (1 double; 1 family), 1🛁, 1WC. ⚲
Prices: B&B £12.50–14, EM £6.50–7.50.⚲ rates.

Dairy House Farm, Alkmonton, Longford, Ashbourne DE6 3DG
✆ (0335) 330359

Relax in this spacious old oakbeamed farmhouse comfortably furnished with two lounges and guests' dining room. Enjoy good home cooking,

Residential License and packed lunches on request. The house stands on a stockrearing farm and is surrounded by a pleasant walled garden. The farm is in a peaceful rural location 8 miles from Ashbourne. Take the A515 south to Cubley, then turn to Alkmonton. Dovedale 8 miles. Manifold Valley 10 miles. Chatsworth and Calke Abbey 40 mins.

Open all year
7 bedrooms (1 twin ens. ☜/WC; 3 double inc. 2 ens. ⋔/WC; 1 family ens. ⋔/WC; 2 single), 1�, 2WCs.
♿(5) ⅍ ETB ♛ ♛ ♛Commended
Prices: B&B £16–22, weekly £105–147. EM £10–15, B&B plus EM weekly £175–217.

Little Park Farm, Mappleton, Ashbourne DE6 2BR
✆ (033529) 341   Mrs Joan Harrison

Enjoy the peace and quiet of this 123-acre dairy farm situated in the Dove Valley, 3 miles from Ashbourne. Take A52 for Leek, at Mayfield turn right for Okeover, then left to Blore. Farm lane opposite Okeover Hall. The 300-year-old listed farmhouse has oak beams and tasteful furnishings. Guests have own TV lounge and dining room. Dovedale, Ilam, Tissington Trail and bike hire 2 miles. Alton Towers 6 miles.

Open Mar-Oct.
3 bedrooms (1 twin; 2 double), 1➍, 1WC.
ETB ♛Commended
Prices: B&B £13–14, EM £7.50.

Throwley Hall Farm, Ilam, Ashbourne DE6 2BB
✆ (0538) 308202   Mrs M.A. Richardson
✆ (0538) 308243

After being greeted with afternoon tea on your arrival, your enjoyment of your stay at Throwley Hall Farm is assured. This Georgian farmhouse is on a large working beef and sheep farm 5 miles northwest of Ashbourne (off the A523). Packed lunches on request. Cot and highchair available. Dovedale 2 miles. Manifold Valley, with cycle hire, 3 miles. Alton Towers 6 miles.

Open all year
3 bedrooms (1 twin; 1 double ens. ⋔/WC; 1 family), 1➍, 2WCs.
♿ ⋔ ETB ♛ ♛Commended
Prices: B&B £14–18, weekly £84.

Planning a day out?
See RURAL ATTRACTIONS

BAKEWELL   Map 5 A2
Bubnell Cliff Farm, Baslow, Bakewell DE4 1RH
✆ (0246) 582454   Mrs S. Mills

Bubnell Cliff Farm lies 5 miles northeast of Bakewell (A621/619). This mixed family farm covers 300 acres amidst some of the most breathtaking scenery in Derbyshire. Good farmhouse cooking. Ideal spot for walkers. Chatsworth House 1 mile. Haddon Hall 6 miles.

Open all year
2 bedrooms (1 double; 1 family), 1➍, 1WC.
♿ ⅍
Prices: B&B £12–13. ♿ rates.

Highfield Farm, Ashford-in-the-Water, Bakewell
✆ (0629) 812482   Mrs Brocklehurst

Comfort and beauty combine to charm in this limestone farmhouse furnished to a very high standard in the lovely village of Ashford-in-the-Water, off the A6 Bakewell-Buxton road. Highfield's 500 acres encompass beef, sheep and corn. There are wonderful views from every window, especially the large sunlounge. Well dressing end of May. Haddon Hall 4 miles. Chatsworth House 4 miles. Monsal Dale 1 mile.

Open May-Oct.
2 bedrooms (1 twin; 1 double), 1➍, 1WC.
ETB Listed
Prices: B&B £14–16.

BELPER   Map 5 A3
Dannah Farm Country Guest House, Shottle, Belper DE5 2DR
✆ (0773)550273/550630

Relax and be pampered in this lovely Georgian farmhouse standing amidst beautiful countryside on a mixed working farm. Luxurious accommodation includes a 4-poster suite and ground floor bedrooms. Winners of the 1992 National Award for Farmhouse Catering and shortlisted for the Alternative Farmer of The Year. Licensed (restaurant and residential). Dannah Farm lies 3 miles from Belper, A517 then turn right to Shottle after Hanging Gate Inn. Kedleston Hall 15 mins drive. Chatsworth House and Alton Towers 30 mins.

Closed 25–26 Dec.
7 bedrooms (2 twin inc. 1 ens. ☞/🛁/WC, 1 ens. 🛁/WC; 4 double inc. 3 ens. 🛁/WC; 1 ens. ☞/🛁/WC; 1 family ens. ☞/🛁/WC), 2WCs. ⚘ ETB ☙ ☙ ☙Highly Commended
Prices: B&B £24.50–35, weekly £165–215. EM £7.95–16.50, B&B plus EM weekly £220–330. ⚘ rates.

BUXTON   Map 5 A2

Blackwell Hall, Blackwell in the Peak, Taddington, Nr Buxton
✆ (0629) 85271   Mrs Christine Gregory

Your comfort is our main concern at Blackwell Hall, a 300-acre dairy farm with an early 18th-century farmhouse set in a mature 2-acre garden. On the edge of Cheedale and Millers Dale, we offer private accommodation, with an oak beamed lounge. In the dining room traditional farmhouse breakfasts await you. The farm is situated off the A6 midway between Bakewell and Buxton. Monsal Dale 4 miles. Dovedale and Chatsworth 6 miles.

Open all year
3 bedrooms (1 twin ens. 🛁/WC; 1 family ens. 🛁/WC; 1 double ens. ☞/🛁/WC). ⚘ ✠ETB ☙
Prices: B&B £14–18.

Fernydale Farm, Earl Sterndale, Buxton
✆ (0298) 83236   Joan Nadin

Fernydale Farm comprises 200 acres set amid the beautiful and rugged Peak District National Park. From the comfortable farmhouse you can enjoy the splendid views whilst relaxing in a warm and friendly atmosphere. This working dairy and sheep farm, situated off the A515 Ashbourne-Buxton road on the B5053, is an excellent base for exploring the region. Buxton, Bakewell and Ashbourne are all within easy reach.

Closed Xmas
2 double bedrooms ens. 🛁/WC. ETB ☙ ☙
Prices:B&B from £17.50.

Mosley House Farm, Maynestone Road, Chinley SK12 6AH
✆ (0663) 750240   Mrs B Goddard

Enjoy a stay in the Peak District on our 150-acre mixed dairy farm with beautiful views surrounding our 17th-century farmhouse. Accommodation is spacious, tea/coffee facilities, TV and own sitting room. Large garden and patio. 10 mins walk from village. Chinley is off the A624 Glossop-Buxton road. Cracken Edge is on the farm, Chinley Churn and old quarries on the boundary. Castleton 30 mins drive.

Open Apr-Oct.
1 family bedroom ens.☞/WC), 1🛁, 1WC. ⚘
Prices: B&B £12–15, weekly £120.⚘ rates.

Shallow Grange, Chelmorton, Nr Buxton
✆ (0298) 23578
✆ Fax (0298) 78242

Shallow Grange is a delightful 18th-century farmhouse, fully modernised without detracting from its character. This working dairy farm is in the heart of the Peak District, on the A5270 just off the A515 Ashbourne-Buxton road. At the farmhouse you can enjoy excellent homecooked meals in comfortable surrounds. Licensed. Packed lunch on request. Within 20 minutes drive are Buxton, Bakewell, Dovedale, Millers Dale, Haddon hall, Goyt Valley and Chatsworth House.

Open all year
3 bedrooms (1 twin ens. ☞/WC;1 double ens. ☞/WC;1 family ens. ☞/WC). ⚘(5)
Prices: B&B £17.50. EM £12.

Wolfscote Grange Farm, Hartington, Nr Buxton SK17 0AX
✆ (0298) 84342   Jane Gibbs

Away from it all is the perfect way to describe Wolfscote Grange. Set high above Wolfscote Dale, overlooking Berrisford Dale with Dovedale less than 2 miles downstream, this old 15th-century farmhouse has great character. All rooms are traditionally furnished. Guests are encouraged to explore our beef and sheep farm and the hill and dale walks leading from our door. The farm is situated just over a mile outside Hartington (A515 Buxton-Ashbourne road, then B5054). Ashbourne, Bakewell, Buxton 10 miles.

Open Mar-Nov.
3 bedrooms (1 twin; 1 double; 1 family), 1🛏,
1WC.
♨ETB Approved
Prices: B&B £14–15, weekly £88–95. ♨ rates.

CHESTERFIELD   Map 5 A2

Old School Farm, Uppertown, Ashover, Chesterfield S45 0JF
✆ (0246) 590813   Dawn Wootton

A warm welcome awaits you at this large comfortable modern farmhouse/bungalow. Old School Farm offers a friendly atmosphere and good home cooking. Cot and highchair provided. It is a mixed working farm and covers 25 acres in the small hamlet of Uppertown, on the B5057 off the A632 Chesterfield-Matlock road. Hardwick Hall, Haddon Hall and Chatsworth House all within 9 miles.

Open Mar-Oct
4 bedrooms (1 double; 2 family; 1 single), 1🛏,
1WC.
♨
Prices: B&B £14, EM £6.♨ rates.

Oakwood Farm, New Mills Road, Chisworth SK14 6SB
✆ (0457) 854627   Mr & Mrs M. Wilde

A small working farm offering you a warm and friendly welcome in our comfortable home. With extensive views all around, this is a perfect place for peace and relaxation. Situated on the edge of the Peak District, just off the A626 Glossop-Marple road, this is an excellent base for touring. Buxton, Bakewell, Castleton's Caves, Chatsworth House, and Haddon Hall are all within easy reach.

Closed Xmas and New Year
1 family bedroom inc. priv.☜/WC.
♨ ⅄
Prices: B&B £15–17.♨ rates.

CHISWORTH   Map 5 A2

Shire Cottage, Ernocroft Farm, Benches Lane, Chisworth, Hyde SK14 6RY
✆ (0457) 866536   M. Sidebottom

This home from home bungalow on a hill farm overlooks Etherow Country Park. In this quiet and secluded location you can enjoy the magnificent views over an early breakfast. Ground floor bedroom and ramp to door. Cot, highchair and games supplied. Ernocroft Farm is off the A626 Marple-Glossop road, on the edge of the Peak District. Local attractions include Lyme Park 5 Miles, Forge Bank Water Wheel 2 miles, Bramhall Hall 4 miles, Quarry Bank Mill 6 miles, Granada Studio Tour 14 miles.

Open all year
4 bedrooms (1 twin ens.🛁/WC; 1 twin and double ens. 🛁/WC; 1 single), 1🛏, 3WCs.
♨ 🐾
Prices: B&B £16–18. ♨ rates.

DOVERIDGE   Map 5 A3

The Beeches Farmhouse, Waldley, Doveridge DE6 5LR
✆ (0889) 590288

Winners of 1992 top national award for farm based catering. Enjoy dining on fresh food and homemade desserts in our oak-beamed licensed restaurant, after exploring the beautiful Derbyshire countryside or the thrills of Alton Towers. Excellent family rooms retain the character of our 18th-century farmhouse. Children love feeding the animals on our working dairy farm. Ground floor bedrooms, cot, highchair and playroom available. Packed lunches available. The Beeches lies 5 miles from Uttoxeter, A50 to Doveridge then turn onto Marston Lane opposite the Cavendish pub for 2 miles. Riding stables, lessons and treks, locally.

Closed Xmas
12 bedrooms (3 twin inc 1 ens. ⋔/🚻/WC; 2 double inc. 1 ens. ⋔/WC; 7 family inc. 1 ens. ⋔/WC; 5 ens. ⋔/🚻/WC), 2🛁, 3WCs.
⚭ ETB 👑 👑 👑 Highly Commended
Prices: B&B £15–35, weekly £105–245. EM from £9.50, B&B plus EM weekly £171–315. ⚭ rates.

MATLOCK
Map 5 A2

Farley Farm, Farley, Matlock DE4 5LR
✆ (0629) 582533

Farley Farm is in the picturesque countryside just north of Matlock, off the A6. A warm welcome awaits you in the stonebuilt farmhouse of the working dairy and arable farm. Delicious farmhouse cooking and packed lunches on request make this a good choice for exploring the magnificent scenery on your doorstep. Cot, highchair, swings available. Arbor Low, Dovedale and the Manifold Valley, Crich, Chatsworth House, Haddon Hall, American Adventure Park – all are within easy reach.

Open all year
3 bedrooms (1 twin; 1 double; 1 family), 2🛁,2WCs.
⚭ ⊁ ETB 👑 👑
Prices: B&B £14, EM £5. ⚭ rates.

Packhorse Farm, Tansley, Matlock
✆ (0629) 582781

Packhorse Farm stands on the edge of the Peak District, a couple of miles east of Matlock on the A615. It is a working farm with 40 acres. The modernised farmhouse is quietly situated in extensive grounds. Its location makes it ideal as a touring base. Good walking country. Packed lunches on request. Gulliver's Kingdom 4 miles, Tramway Museum 5 miles, Haddon Hall and Chatsworth House, 6 miles, Castleton 18 miles, Alton Towers 22 miles.

Closed Xmas and New Year **RAC**
4 bedrooms (1 twin; 1 double; 2 family), 1🛁, 2WCs.
⚭(3) ETB 👑 👑
Prices: B&B £14. ⚭ rates.

MICKLEOVER
Map 5 A3

Bonehill Farm, Etwall Road, Mickleover, Derby DE3 5DN
✆ (0332) 513553   Mrs Catherine Dicken

This 120-acre mixed farm with Georgian farmhouse is set in peaceful rural surroundings, yet offers all the convenience of being only 3 miles west of Derby, on the A516 between Mickleover and Etwall. Cot and highchair provided. Within 10 miles there is a choice of historic houses to visit; Calke Abbey, Kedleston Hall, Sudbury Hall. Peak District 20 miles. Alton Towers 25 miles.

Open all year
3 bedrooms (1 twin; 1 double; 1 family), 1🛁, 2WCs.
⚭ ⊁ ETB Listed
Prices: B&B £15. ⚭ rates.

Self-Catering

ASHBOURNE
Map 5 A3

Beechenhill Farm, Ilam, Dovedale, Ashbourne DE6 2BD
✆ (033527) 274   Mrs Sue Prince
For full farm description see p. 47. Accommodation is available in two self-catering cottages: the larger is purpose designed to meet the needs of disabled guests and sleeps 6. The smaller cottage sleeps 2.

Open all year
♿ ⊁ETB ♦♦♦♦Highly Commended
Prices: small cottage £110–190, large cottage £170–350.

See STOP PRESS
for more farms

Dairy House Farm, Alkmonton, Longford, Ashbourne DE6 3DG
✆ (0335) 330359

For full farm description see p. 47. Accommodation is offered in two attractively converted Victorian farm buildings, the Pig Sty sleeps 4, and the Loose Boxes sleeps 2 (plus baby). Both are equipped to the highest standard.

Open all year
ETB♪♪♪♪Highly Commended
Prices: weekly Pig Sty £140–275, Loose Boxes £120–225.

BELPER Map 5 A3
Chevin House Farm, Chevin Road, Belper
✆ (0773) 823144 J. Jordan

Accommodation is offered in a 2-bedroomed country cottage, sleeps 6, on an elevated sight overlooking the Derwent Valley and Derbyshire Hills. The main farmhouse and cottage stand in 100 acres of grass and woodland. The farm is mainly dairy with lots of interesting poultry roaming free around the farmyard and fields. The cottage is comfortable and tastefully furnished in traditional style. The farm lies a mile from Belper, take the A6 to Milford and turn opposite Strutt Arms. Kedleston Hall 4 miles. Ripley Railways 5 miles.

Open all year
ETB♪♪♪♪Commended
Prices: weekly £80-200.

Planning a day out?
See RURAL ATTRACTIONS

BUXTON Map 5 A2
Old House Farm, Newhaven, Hartington, Buxton SK17 0DY
✆ (0629) 636268 Sue Flower

Staying in this attractively renovated self-contained cottage adjacent to the farmhouse gives you the opportunity to watch the work on a 500-acre dairy and stock farm, milking up to 150 cows and lambing 500 sheep. Definitely a home base you will enjoy returning to each day. The cottage sleeps 6, and has been equipped to the highest and most modern standards. Hartington is in the centre of the local dales and the Manifold Valley. Scenic walks abound. Cycle hire locally.

Open all year
🐾 🦅 ETB♪♪♪♪Commended
Prices: £150–250.

Wolfscote Grange 'Cruck' Barn, Wolfscote Grange Farm, Hartington, Nr Buxton SK17 0AX
✆ (0298) 84342 Jane Gibbs

For full farm description, see p. 49. The old 15th-century cruck barn has great character and is fully equipped for your comfort, with 1 double gallery bedroom and 1 twin.

Open all year
Prices: £150–230.

CHISWORTH Map 5 A2
Shire Cottage, Ernocroft Farm, Benches Lane, Chisworth, Hyde SK14 6RY
✆ (0457) 866536

For full farm description, see p. 50. A separate self-catering unit has been formed by a modern 2-bedroomed bungalow adjoining the farmhouse. Sleeps 6.

Prices: weekly £150–250.

DEVON

ASHBURTON
Map 1 B3

Lower Southway Farm, Widecombe-in-the-Moor, Ashburton
✆ (03642) 277   Mrs Dawn Nosworthy

Lower Southway Farm stands within the Dartmoor National Park with superb views across the country from the farmhouse, which lies 5 miles north of the A38. On this mixed farm Mrs Nosworthy provides excellent food in a friendly atmosphere. Ground floor access bedroom and cot provided. Packed lunches on request. Ideal for walking and riding.

Open all year
3 bedrooms (1 twin; 1 double; 1 family), 2 🛏,
2WCs.
🐾 ETB Listed
Prices: B&B from £12.50, weekly £77. Weekly B&B plus EM £140. 🐾 rates.

Middle Stoke Farm, Holne, Nr Ashburton TQ13 7SS
✆ (03643) 444   Pamela Neal

Middle Stoke is a stud farm and guests are welcome to meet the thoroughbreds, mares, foals, youngstock and racehorses. Also a pony and some sheep. You can enjoy a good English breakfast and packed lunches supplied on request. Cot available. The farm is managed with conservation in mind, natural hedges harbour a wide variety of wildflowers, birds and wildlife. Situated on Dartmoor, west of the A38 Plymouth-Exeter road from Ashburton, the farm has magnificent views across Dartmoor with all its delightful walks and beauty spots. Buckfast Abbey, Butterfly Farm, Steam Railway 4 miles. Torbay beaches 15 miles.

Closed Xmas
6 bedrooms including twins, doubles, singles and family sizes, 1🛏, 2WCs.
🐾 🐴
Prices: B&B £14.50–16.50, weekly £101.50–108.50. 🐾 rates,🐴 £1.50 per night.

Mill Leat Farm, Holne, Ashburton, Newton Abbot TQ13 7RZ
✆ (03643) 283   Mrs Dawn Cleave

Mill Leat is a 120-acre farm on the edge of beautiful Dartmoor, farming sheep and cattle. Situated 3 miles from Buckfast Abbey off the A38, the 18th-century farmhouse nestles in a quiet and peaceful valley. Amid such delightful surrounds you can enjoy plenty of good farmhouse cooking. Packed lunches on request. Dartmoor 2 miles, Hembury Woods (NT) 1 mile, Buckfastleigh Steam Railway, Butterfly Farm and Otter Sanctuary 3 miles.

Closed Xmas
2 family bedrooms, 1🛏.
🐾 ⚹
Prices: B&B £12–13, weekly £78. EM £7.50. Weekly B&B plus EM £130. 🐾 rates.

New Cott Farm, Poundsgate, Newton Abbot
✆ (03643) 421   Margaret Phipps

A friendly welcome, beautiful views and pleasing accommodation at New Cott Farm, north off the A38 Ashburton-Buckfastleigh road. This is a working farm with fishing in our own trout ponds and a nature trail, lovely walks and birdwatching. Enjoy our excellent food with lots of clotted cream, free range eggs and fresh vegetables. Packed lunches on request. Ground floor bedrooms. Relax in the solitude of Dartmoor. Guided walks. Pony trekking. Many NT properties within easy reach.

Open all year
3 bedrooms (1 twin ens. 🛁/WC; 1 double ens. 🚿/WC; 1 family ens. 🛁/WC).
♿ 🐾(3) ETB 👑 👑Commended
Prices: B&B £15–17. EM £9–9.50. Weekly B&B plus EM £145–150.

Wellpritton Farm, Holne, Ashburton TQ13 7RX
✆ (03643) 273   Sue Townsend

We warmly welcome you to Wellpritton, our beautiful farmhouse on the edge of Dartmoor near Buckfast Abbey off the A38. We keep goats, donkeys, rabbits, chickens and sometimes sheep and cattle. We serve farm-produced food and have a games room and swimming pool for you to relax in. Riding, fishing sailing and golf locally. Exeter, Plymouth and Torbay 30 minutes' drive.

Closed Xmas   RAC
4 bedrooms (2 twin inc. 1 ens. ☺/WC; 2 double ens. ⏷/WC), 1🛌, 2WCs.
👪 ETB 👑 👑Highly Commended
Prices: B&B £17, weekly £105. EM £8. Weekly B&B plus EM £140.

BAMPTON   Map 1 B2

Newhouse Farm, Oakford, Tiverton EX16 9JE
✆ (03985) 347   Mrs Anne Boldry

We welcome you to our 17th-century Devon Longhouse, featuring heavy oak beams and inglenook fireplace. The house has been tastefully modernised to provide every comfort. We offer quality country cooking using home and local produce wherever possible. Our beef and sheep farm is set in its own wooded valley off the B3227 (A396 north from Tiverton). Exmoor

National Park starts 5 miles away. North and South Devon coasts, Exeter, Taunton, Barnstable 25 miles.

Closed Xmas
3 bedrooms (1 twin ens. ☺/WC;2 double inc. 1 ens. ☺/WC), 1🛌, 1WC.
👪(10) ETB 👑 👑
Prices: B&B £15.50–17, weekly £100–110. EM £9.50. Weekly B&B plus EM £155–165.

BARNSTAPLE   Map 1 B2

Higher Clifton Farm, East Down, Barnstaple EX31 4LX
✆ (0271) 850372   Mrs Elizabeth Smyth

East Down is a small village off the A39 north of Barnstaple. This comfortable 17th-century farmhouse is on a family-run farm with lots of animals. Guests enjoy good farmhouse cooking using mostly home produce, and relax in a lounge/dining room with TV and tea/coffee facilities. The house stands in a secluded spot at the end of its own drive with lovely views of the surrounding countryside. An ideal area for walkers, with plenty of wildlife, flowers and birds. Riding school 3 miles. Arlington Court (NT) 2 miles. Exmoor 4 miles. Woolacombe and Ilfracombe 8 miles.

Open May-Sept.
3 bedrooms (1 twin; 1 double; 1 family), 1🛌, 2WCs.
👪 ⚹ ETB 👑Approved
Prices: B&B £14–16, weekly £90. EM £8. Weekly B&B plus EM £120–125.

Home Park Farm, Lower Blakewell, Muddiford, Barnstaple EX31 4ET
✆ (0271) 42955   Mrs Mari Lethaby

Home Park is a sheep and beef farm of 70 acres situated in the midst of the beautiful Devonshire countryside north of Barnstaple (off the B3230). Every attention is paid to your comfort, most especially with good home cooking. A country and garden lovers paradise. TV and tea trays in rooms. Packed lunches and afternoon teas on request. Cot, highchair, play area with slide, swings and Wendy house available for children. A choice of beaches 10 miles. Lynton, Lynmouth,

Ilfracombe, Exmoor and Dartmoor all within easy reach.

Open Mar-Nov.
2 family bedrooms ens. shower/WC. [child symbol]
Prices: B&B £15–17.50, weekly £90–110. EM £6. Weekly B&B plus EM £135. [child symbol] rates.

Huxtable Farm, West Buckland, Barnstaple EX32 0SR
✆ (0598) 760254 Jackie Payne

Huxtable Farm and Barn are carefully restored listed buildings. The medieval longhouse, dated 1520, has oak beams, screen panelling and open fireplaces with bread ovens. Enjoy superb 4-course candlelit dinners with homemade wine and food using farm and local produce. The 80-acre farm supports mainly sheep. Children welcome to feed the animals: lambs, goats and Shetland pony. Cot, highchair, sauna, quarter-size snooker and table tennis available. Packed lunches on request. Standing 5 miles east of Barnstaple, close to North Devon beaches, NT properties, golf, woodland and moors.

Closed Xmas and New Year
6 bedrooms (1 twin ens. bath; 2 double ens. bath/WC; 2 family ens. bath/WC; 1 single ens. shower), 6 bath, 6WCs.
[child symbol] [no smoking symbol] ETB ♛♛♛ Commended
Prices: B&B £18–21, EM £11. Weekly B&B plus EM £196.70–245. [child symbol] rates.

Rowden Barton, Roundswell, Barnstaple EX31 3NP
✆ (0271) 44365 Mrs V. Dallyn

The modern farmhouse at Rowden Barton is set on a peaceful 90-acre beef, sheep and arable farm. Here you will find comfortable accommodation and traditional home cooking in a warm and friendly atmosphere. The sun lounge has extensive views across Dartmoor. The farm lies on the B3232 2 miles south of Barnstaple.

Open all year
2 bedrooms (1 twin; 1 double), 2 bath, 2WCs.
[child symbol](12) [no smoking symbol] ETB Listed
Prices: B&B £14, weekly £98.

Stone Farm, Brayford, Barnstaple EX32 7PJ
✆ (0271) 830473

Stone Farm is quietly situated in peaceful countryside 6 miles east of Barnstaple (A361/B3226). It is a 180-acre working sheep farm, and has 7 acres of woodland with a circular walk. This charming 17th-century beamed farmhouse, with inglenooks and a games room with a league-size pool table, offers spacious and comfortable accommodation. Cot, highchair, swing, slide available. Packed lunches on request. Barnstaple and Exmoor 6 miles. North Devon coast 12 miles. A variety of NT properties within easy reach.

Open May-Nov.
3 bedrooms (1 twin; 1 double; 1 family ens. bath/WC), 1 bath, 2WCs.
[wheelchair symbol] [child symbol]
Prices: B&B £14–15, weekly £90. EM £8. Weekly B&B plus EM £135. [child symbol] rates.

Waytown Farm, Shirwell, Barnstaple EX31 4JN
✆ (0271) 850396 Mrs H. Kingdon

Waytown Farm is a mixed beef and sheep farm of 240 acres 3 miles northeast of Barnstaple on the A39. The spacious 17th-century farmhouse offers every comfort, and good farmhouse food using own produce when available. Children may help milk Jersey cow, feed calves and collect eggs. Cot, highchair and games provided. Riding and fishing 2 miles. Arlington Court (NT) 3 miles. Croyde, Woolacombe, Putsborough beaches 8 miles.

Open Easter-Nov.
3 bedrooms (1 twin; 2 double ens. shower/WC), 1 bath, 2WCs.
[child symbol] ETB ♛♛ Commended
Prices: B&B £15–18, weekly £100. EM £7. Weekly B&B plus EM £130–145.

BIDEFORD Map 1 B2

Church Farm, Horwood, Nr Bideford EX39 4PB
✆ (0271) 858254 Mrs Kathy Clements

A warm and friendly welcome awaits you at this new and comfortable farmhouse set on a small working farm, mainly sheep with a few cows and calves. Church Farm lies east of Bideford off the B3232, and is ideally placed for enjoying all the area has to offer along the North Devon coast. Riding in Horwood village. Sailing at Instow 3 miles. Golf at Westward Ho! and Saunton 7 and 12 miles. Dartington Glass Factory 7 miles.

Open all year
4 bedrooms (1 twin ens. ▥/WC; 2 double inc. 1 ens. ▱/WC, 1 ens. ▥/WC; 1 single), 1🛏.
🐾(1🐕) ⛵
Prices: B&B £12. EM £8.

BUCKFASTLEIGH   Map 1 B3
Well Park Farm Bungalow, Dean Prior, Buckfastleigh
✆ (0364) 43775

Set on the edge of Dartmoor National Park, 3 mins from the A38 Buckfastleigh-Plymouth road. Sample delicious farmhouse food, afternoon teas with homemade Devon scones. Tea/coffee making facilities, large TV lounge, wood-burning stoves in colder months. Cot, highchair, play area with swings and slide. Many excellent local eating places. Ideal base for touring beaches. Buckfast Abbey, Steam Railway and Butterfly Farm 2 miles.

Open Mar-Oct.
2 bedrooms (1 double; 1 family), 1🛏.
🐾 ⛵ ETB Listed Commended
Prices: B&B £13.50–15, weekly £90–100. EM £6.50–7. B&B plus EM weekly £130.

CHAGFORD   Map 1 B3
Frenchbeer Farm, Chagford TQ13 8EX
✆ (0647) 432427   Christine Malseed

This thatched 16th-century longhouse is situated in beautiful unspoilt countryside, west of Exeter (A30/A382), 2 miles west from the moorland village of Chagford in Dartmoor National Park. Enjoy the friendly and informal atmosphere on our working sheep and beef farm. Frenchbeer Farm makes an ideal base for walking, riding, birdwatching, fishing, touring or simply to relax and unwind. Good local eating places. NT properties 3 miles.

Open Jan-Nov.
3 bedrooms (1 twin; 2 double), 1🛏, 2WCs.
⛵ 🛏 ETB ⚜
Prices: B&B £14–17, weekly £98.

Teigncombe Farm, Chagford TQ13 8ET
✆ (0647) 433410   Mrs H. Stanbury

Stay in a secluded hill farm on the edge of the moor and enjoy good Devon hospitality while you explore the area. Packed lunches provided on request. The farmhouse is a traditional granite Dartmoor longhouse. Teigncombe Farm lies 3 miles from Chagford on the road to Kestor Rock.

Open Apr-Oct.
2 bedrooms (1 twin; 1 double), 1🛏, 1WC.
🐾(8) 🛏 ETB Listed
Prices: B&B £12. 🐾 rates.

CLOVELLY   Map 1 B2
Burscott Farm, Clovelly, Nr Bideford
✆ (0237) 431252

Our working dairy farm overlooks Bideford Bay and the beautiful village of Clovelly. The farmhouse is surrounded by gardens with lovely views on all sides. Good home cooking and packed lunches on request. The coastal footpath runs by the edge of the farm. Burscott Farm is on the road into Clovelly off the A39. Milky Way Dairy 1 mile. Local potteries 3 miles.

Open Mar-Nov.
3 bedrooms (1 twin; 1 family; 1 double), 1🛏, 1WC. 🐾
Prices: B&B £11.50–15, weekly £80.50–105. EM £5–7. Weekly B&B plus EM £115.50–130. 🐾 rates.

Stroxworthy Farm, Woolsery, Nr Clovelly, Bideford
✆ (0237) 431333

Stroxworthy Farm lies in peaceful countryside just 4 miles from Clovelly (turn off the A39 at Buck's Cross west of Bideford). Staying on our dairy farm, you are perfectly placed for relaxing on this attractive part of the coast or for touring. Rosemoor Gardens 10 miles. Dartington Crystal 13 miles. Tapeley Park 10 miles.

Open Mar-Oct.
4 bedrooms (2 twin inc. 1 ens. ▥/WC, 1 ens. ▱/WC; 2 double ens. ▱/WC).
🐾(4) 🛏
Prices: B&B from £15, weekly £105.

COLYTON
Map 2 A3

Smallicombe Farm, Northleigh, Colyton EX13 6BU
✆ (0404) 83310 Mrs Margot Todd
✆ From spring 1993 (0404) 831310

This small working farm stands in an area of outstanding natural beauty. Children are encouraged to make friends with the farm animals, including Jersey cows, calves, pigs, sheep and goats. You can enjoy good farmhouse cooking and every comfort. Packed lunches on request. Ground floor accommodation available, the twin room is equipped to meet the needs of the elderly or partially disabled. Cot, highchair, laundry, games room and babysitting service available. Situated south of the A35 Axminster-Honiton road, convenient for the coast, and ideal for touring the region. Golf, riding, swimming pool 4 miles. Honiton and Colyton 4 miles. Coast 6 miles. Brochure on request.

Open all year.
3 bedrooms (1 double ens. 🚿/🛁/WC; 1 twin ens. 🛁/WC;1 family ens. 🚿/🛁/WC).
♿ ⌂ ETB ♛♛
Prices: B&B £15–17, weekly £95–115. EM £8. Weekly B&B plus EM £145–165. ⌂ rates.

COMBE MARTIN
Map 1 B2

Brinscott Farm, Combe Martin EX34 0PA
✆ (0271) 883609 Mrs Jean Chugg

Situated on the A3123 in a beautiful part of the Devonshire countryside, our working farm supports sheep and cattle. The farmhouse is a comfortable bungalow where you can enjoy good home cooking. It is ideal for the older guest looking for a relaxed holiday. Combe Martin 3 miles. Arlington Court 3 miles. Exmoor 6 miles. Lynton and Lynmouth 12 miles.

Open all year
2 bedrooms (1 twin; 1 double), 1🛁, 1WC.
Prices: B&B £8.50–12.50. EM £6.

CREDITON
Map 1 B3

Brindiwell Farm, Cheriton Fitzpaine, Nr Crediton EX17 4HR
✆ (0363) 866357

Brindiwell is a sheep farm covering 120 acres, situated north of Exeter (off the A396/A3072). The delightful Devon longhouse is a listed building with oak beamed ceiling and panelling, surrounded by a large garden with outstanding views over the rolling countryside. You can enjoy good home cooking. Afternoon teas on request. Noted beauty spot on River Exe, 3 miles, with working water mill.

Open all year
3 bedrooms (1 double; 1 family; 1 single), 1🛁, 1WC.
⌂ ETB Listed
Prices:B&B £12–15, weekly £85. EM £7. Weekly B&B plus EM £100–110. ⌂ rates.

Hayne Farm, Cheriton Fitzpaine, Crediton EX17 4HR
✆ (0363) 866392

Guests are welcomed to our 17th-century working beef and sheep farm which lies north of Exeter (off the A396/A3072). Relax in our oak-beamed dining room before a log fire in winter, or enjoy our garden and sun lounge in summer. We serve good farm fare and packed lunches on request. Cot and highchair provided. From our central situation the South and North coasts, Exmoor and Dartmoor are all within easy reach. Fursdon House 2 miles. Bickleigh Castle 3 miles. Killerton House 8 miles. Tiverton 8 miles. Exeter 9 miles.

Open Mar-Dec.
3 bedrooms (1 twin; 1 double; 1 family), 1🛁.
⌂ ETB Listed
Prices: B&B £8–12, EM £5–6. ⌂ rates.

CROYDE
Map1 B2

Combas Farm, Croyde, Braunton EX33 1PH
✆ (0271) 890398 Mrs G.M. Adams

Stay in a traditional 17th-century Devon longhouse with inglenook fireplaces set in a secluded valley, off the B3231 out of Braunton, within walking distance of the beaches and coastal path. Combas is a mixed farm covering 140 acres. From the farmhouse and its lovely garden you can enjoy unspoilt views of the North Devon countryside. In a wonderfully relaxed atmosphere you can sample a varied menu using our own farm produce. Packed lunches on request. Ground floor bedroom, cot, highchair and play area available. Braunton Burrows 3 miles. Golf course 3 miles. Arlington Court (NT) 8 miles.

Open Apr-Nov.
6 bedrooms (1 twin; 2 double; 2 family; 1 single), 1 ➡, 1 ♒, 3WCs.
♨ ETB Listed Commended
Prices: B&B £14.50–17, weekly £91–107. EM £6.50. Weekly B&B plus EM £132–151. ♨ rates.

EXETER   Map 1 B3

Lochinvar, Shepherds Park Farm, Woodbury, Nr Exeter EX5 1LA
✆ (0395) 32185   Mrs J.H. Glanvill

Lochinvar is part of a dairy farm in tranquil rural surroundings, with panoramic views over the countryside. Shepherds Park Farm is south of Exeter (A376), and its location offers a wide choice of activities. Packed lunches on request. Cot and highchair available. Riding stables within walking distance. Fishing 1 mile. Golf 3 miles. Farm Museum 3 miles. Adventure Farm Park 4 miles.

Open all year
3 bedrooms (1 twin; 1 double ens. ♒/WC; 1 family ens ♒/WC), 1➡, 1WC.
♨ ⛏ ETB ♔
Prices: B&B £14–18, weekly £98–120. ♨ rates.

Marianne Pool, Clyst St George, Exeter EX3 0NZ
✆ (0392) 874939   J. Bragg

A warm welcome awaits you at this thatched Devon longhouse standing on a mixed farm down a quiet country lane south of Exeter (A376). Easy access M5, Jct30. Historic city of Exeter 4 miles. Beaches, Exmouth 6 miles. Budleigh Salterton 8 miles. Dartmoor 15 miles.

Open Easter-mid Oct.
2 bedrooms (1 twin; 1 family), 1➡, 1WC.
♨ ETB Listed
Prices: B&B £13.50–15, weekly £90. ♨ rates.

Mill Farm, Kenton, Exeter EX6 8JR
✆ (0392) 832471   Delia Lambert

In this large redbrick farmhouse you will find every comfort. Cot, highchair, and large children's play area provided. The farm, mainly beef, is in a lovely rural setting off the A379 Exeter-Dawlish road. There is much to explore in the area: Powderham Castle 1 mile, Exeter Canal 2 miles, Exeter, Haldon Forest and Dawlish Warren 4 miles.

Open Mar-Oct
5 bedrooms (1 twin; 2 double; 2 family), 1➡, 2WCs.

♨ ETB Listed Commended
Prices: B&B £13, weekly £85–91. ♨ rates.

Pierces Farm, Upton Pyne, Exeter EX5 5JA
✆ (0392) 841252   Mrs Yvonne Taverner

On this 300-acre working farm a warm welcome awaits you in the 16th-century farmhouse. Your comfort is our priority. Cot and highchair provided, and a garden for you to relax in. The farm is situated off the A377, 3 miles north of historical Exeter. University Campus 2 miles.

Open Easter-Sept.
2 bedrooms (1 twin; 1 family ens. ♒/WC), 1➡, 1WC. ♨
Prices: B&B £14–19, weekly £95–115. ♨ rates.

Whitemoor Farm, Doddiscombsleigh, Nr Exeter EX6 7PU
✆ (0647) 52423   Mrs Barbara Lacey

The listed 16th-century farmhouse at Whitemoor is thatched, with oak beams, doors and staircase, and log fires in winter. The house is set in the seclusion of a mature garden and surrounded by 280 acres of arable and wooded farmland. Here you can enjoy traditional farmhouse cooking with homemade preserves and farm produce. Packed lunch on request. Cot provided. Whitemoor lies just 7 miles southwest of Exeter and is an ideal base for exploring the area. Extensive forest walks 1 mile. Birdwatching 2 miles. Haldon Racecourse 3 miles. Sea 10 miles. Dartmoor 12 miles.

Open all year
4 bedrooms (1 twin; 1 double ens. ♒⛺/WC; 2 single),1➡, 2WCs.
♨ ⛝ ⛏ ETB ♔
Prices: B&B £14–15, weekly £91–98. EM £7–7.50. Weekly B&B plus EM £136.50–147. ♨ rates,⛏ £2 per night.

HARTLAND   Map 1 B2

Elmscott Farm, Hartland EX39 6ES
✆ (0237) 441276   Mrs Thirza Goaman

Located off the A39, Bideford-Bude road, Elmscott is a mixed dairy and arable farm, consisting of 200 British Friesians. The house is built of natural stone and lies by one of the most attractive parts of the coast. Mrs Goaman provides good home cooking. Games room, pool, table tennis and garden available for guests. The coastal footpath is on the farm. Golf, indoor swimming pool and tennis courts 6 miles.

Open Easter-Oct.
3 bedrooms (1 twin; 1 double ens. ☞/WC; 1 family), 1➡.
⌂ (10) ⚹
Prices: B&B £13, weekly £91. EM £7. Weekly B&B plus 6EM £133. ⌂ rates.

Summerwell Farm, Hartland, Bideford
✆ (0237) 441304   Mrs Roberta Macer

This 180-acre dairy farm lies in the parish of Hartland, just 5 miles from the sea. The comfortable farmhouse is attractively furnished with chintz, antiques and open fires. Cot provided. Summerwell is situated off the A39, 14 miles south of Bideford, in an Area of Outstanding Natural Beauty and is easily accessible to many beaches and the magical Devon countryside. Big Sheep and Milky Way within 10 miles. Stunning cliffs at Hartland 5 miles. Clovelly 6 miles.

Open April-Oct.
2 bedrooms (1 twin; 1 double), 1➡, 1WC.
⌂
Prices:B&B £11–12, weekly £75–80. EM £8.50.
⌂ rates.

West Titchberry Farm, Hartland, Bideford
EX39 6AU
✆ (0237) 441287   Mrs Yvonne Heard

West Titchberry is a mixed farm of 150 acres, set on the coast at Hartland Point (A39 Bideford-Bude road, then B3248). Guests are warmly welcomed into our comfortable family farmhouse which is dated 1746. Farm produced meat and fresh vegetables feature strongly on the dinner menu. Packed lunches on request. Cot, highchair, games room available. Shipload Bay in walking distance. Hartland Lighthouse 1 mile. Hartland Abbey 2 miles. Clovelly 6 miles. Bude and Bideford 16 miles.

Closed Xmas
3 bedrooms (1 twin; 1 double; 1 family), 1➡, 2WCs.
⌂
Prices: B&B £12, weekly £80. EM £6.50. Weekly B&B plus EM £106–110. ⌂ rates.

HAYTOR   Map 1 B3
Narracombe Farm, Ilsington, Newton Abbot TQ13 9RD
✆ (0364) 661243   Mrs Sue Wills

Come and relax and enjoy the hospitality that is always assured at Narracombe. This lovely home, mostly dating back to the 16th century, is surrounded by beautiful countryside and spectacular views. Cot, highchair and games provided. The farm is 4 miles north of Ashburton. Haytor Rocks and Dartmoor Granite Tramway under 2 miles. Devon Guild of Craftsmen 2 miles. Becky Falls 4 miles. Medieval Hut Circles 5 miles.

Closed Xmas and New Year
2 bedrooms (1 twin; 1 double), 1➡, 1WC.
⌂ ⚹ ETB Listed and Commended
Prices: B&B £14.⌂ rates.

HOLSWORTHY   Map 1 B2
The Barton, Pancrasweek, Holsworthy EX22 7JT
✆ (028881) 315

This large 16th-century farmhouse stands in a peaceful position on a 200-acre dairy farm. Good farmhouse fare served using homegrown produce. There is a TV lounge, dining room and games room. The large garden includes a childrens' play area. The Barton is off the A3072 Holsworthy-Bude road. Holsworthy 3 miles. Bude 5 miles. Cornish coast 6 miles.

Open May-Sept.
5 bedrooms (2 twin; 2 double; 1 family), 2➡, 2WCs.
⌂ ⋔ ETB ♕
Prices: B&B £12–13, weekly £84–91. EM £6.50–7.50, B&B plus EM weekly £129.50–143.50. ⌂ rates.

Elm Park, Bridgerule, Holsworthy
✆ (028881) 231   Mrs S. Lucas

Elm Park is a working farm of 205 acres with dairy, beef, sheep and turkeys, located west of Holsworthy (A3072/B3254). Children are welcomed with pony rides, tractor and trailer rides. Our modern farmhouse, with large lawns and games room, is near surfing beaches and ideal for touring Devon and Cornwall. Plenty of home cooked food is served and everyone is made most welcome. Cot and highchair. Surfing 6 miles. Holsworthy Cattle Market 4 miles. Tamar Lakes 6 miles. Clovelly 15 miles.

Open Mar-Oct.
4 bedrooms (1 twin; 3 family inc. 2 ens. ☞/WC), 1➡, 1WC.
⌂ ETB ♕ ♕

Prices: B&B £12–14, weekly £80–90. EM £6. Weekly £115–125. ⌂ rates.

IVYBRIDGE — Map 1 B3

Venn Farm, Ugborough, Ivybridge
✆ (0364) 73240

Venn Farm's attractive farmhouse is set in large gardens in a peaceful location just 2 miles from the A38 east of Plymouth. Children are welcome to help around our mixed farm. Plenty of good farmhouse cooking, carve your own roast is a popular feature with guests. Snooker table. This is a good choice for touring South Devon. Wrangaton golf course 2 miles. South Dartmoor 2 miles.

Open Mar-Oct.
4 bedrooms (2 twin inc. 1 ens. 🚿/WC; 2 family ens. 🚿/WC), 1🛁, 2WCs.
⌂ ETB ♛♛ Commended.
Prices: B&B £16, EM £9. Weekly B&B plus EM £160. ⌂ rates.

KINGSBRIDGE — Map 1 B3

Burton Farm, Galmpton, Kingsbridge TQ7 3EY
✆ (0548) 561210 — Anne E. Rossiter

Burton Farm is situated in the South Huish Valley, a mile from the old fishing village of Hope Cove and 3 miles from Salcombe. The farm has a dairy herd and two pedigree flocks of sheep, guests are welcome to look around. We are always happy to answer your questions. We provide traditional farmhouse cooking with our own produce where possible. Packed lunches and children's teas on request. Cot and highchair available. The area is ideal for walking and there is a wide choice of sandy coves and beaches.

Open all year
7 bedrooms (1 twin ens. 🛁/WC; 3 double inc. 1 ens. 🚿/WC; 2 family ens. 🛁/WC; 1 single), 2🛁, 2WCs.
⌂ ETB ♛♛
Prices: B&B £16–18.50, EM £8.25. ⌂ rates.

Court Barton, Aveton Gifford, Kingsbridge TQ7 4LE
✆ (0548) 550312 — John & Jill Balkwill

Court Barton is a fine 16th-century Grade 2 listed manor farmhouse nestled in the beautiful South Hams beside the church 100 yds from the village, off the A379 northwest of Kingsbridge. The farm dates from Domesday times and is now a mixed farm of 40 acres. Cot, high chair, playroom and afternoon teas provided. Lots of sandy beaches within 5 miles. Dartmoor, Plymouth, Totnes, Dartmouth all within 20 miles.

Closed Xmas
7 bedrooms (2 twin inc. 1 ens. 🚿/WC, 1 ens. 🛁/WC; 2 double ens. 🚿/WC; 2 family inc. 1 ens. 🛁/WC, 1 ens. 🚿; 1 single ens. 🚿/WC), 1🛁, 1WC.
⌂ ETB ♛♛Commended
Prices: B&B £16–22. ⌂ rates.

Helliers Farm, Ashford, Aveton Gifford, Kingsbridge TQ7 4ND
✆ (0548) 550689 — Mrs C.M. Lancaster

Helliers Farm lies off the A379 northwest of Kingsbridge. You will enjoy the friendly atmosphere in this recently modernised farmhouse. Cot, highchair and children's games provided. It is well placed for the beaches of Bantham, Bigbury-on-Sea, Thurlestone and Salcombe. Golf courses, riding school and coastal path nearby.

Open all year
4 bedrooms (1 twin; 1 double; 1 family/double with priv.🛁; 1 single), 2🛁, 2WCs.
⌂ ⊁ ETB ♛♛
Prices: B&B from £15.

Shute Farm, South Milton, Kingsbridge
✆ (0548) 560680 — Marion Luscombe

Shute Farm is a working mixed farm of 140 acres, situated in a quiet position a mile and a half from Thurlestone Sands. Take the Salcombe road out of Kingsbridge and turn off for South Milton after 2 miles. The 16th-century farmhouse has plenty of character with an open fireplace and all the downstairs rooms are beamed. Tea/coffee facilities in all rooms, cot and highchair provided. Golf 2 miles. Sharpitor NT Gardens 3 miles. Dartmoor 15 miles.

Open Mar-Nov.
3 bedrooms (1 double; 1 family; 1 single), 2🛁, 2WCs.
⌂ ETB Listed
Prices: B&B £12–14, weekly £84–98. ⌂ rates.

South Allington House, Chivelstone, Kingsbridge TQ7 2NB
© (054851) 272 Edward & Barbara Baker

South Allington House is a working farm set in beautiful grounds in a quiet hamlet, surrounded by farms between Start Point and Prawle Point (off A379 Kingsbridge-Dartmouth road). At the farm we have a croquet lawn, bowls and coarse fishing for guests' amusement. Packed lunches and afternoon teas on request. Cot and highchair provided. Kingsbridge 7 miles. Salcombe 4 miles (ferry). Dartmouth (historic naval town and river trips) 10 miles.

Open Easter-Nov.
11 bedrooms (3 twin inc 1 ens. ⇔/🛁/WC; 4 double inc. 1 ens. ⇔/🛁/WC, 2 ens. 🛁/WC; 2 family inc. 1 ens.⇔/🛁/WC; 2 single), 3🛌, 3WCs.
🏵️ ⚌ ETB ⚌ ⚌Commended
Prices: B&B £33–46 per 2 in room; weekly £200–298 per 2 in room. 🏵️ rates.

MORETONHAMPSTEAD Map 1 B3
Budleigh Farm, Moretonhampstead TQ13 8SB
© (0647) 40835 Mrs J. Harvey

This old thatched farmhouse has a pretty level garden with swimming pool for guests use. Budleigh Farm is a sheep farm with a small suckler herd, just outside Moretonhampstead on the A382 Newton Abbot road. The local area has good country walks to offer, the pretty villages of Luscombe and North Bovey are 2 miles away. Dartmoor 3 miles.

Open Feb-Dec.
3 bedrooms (1 twin; 1 double; 1 single), 1🛌, 1🛁,

2WCs.
🏵️ ETB ⚌Commended
Prices: B&B £11.50–17.50, weekly £72.50–110.25. 🏵️ rates.

Little Wooston Farm, Moretonhampstead TQ13 8QA
© (0647) 40551 Mrs J.S. Cuming

Enjoy the good home cooking and friendly atmosphere on this 250-acre dairy, beef and sheep farm. The stone farmhouse offers comfortable accommodation, and the area is a delight for walkers. Packed lunches available on request. The farm lies 2 miles outside Moretonhampstead. Attractive villages, Manor House and golf course 3 miles.

Open Apr-Sept.
3 bedrooms (1 double; 1 family; 1 single), 1🛌, 1WC.
🏵️ 🐓 ETB Listed
Prices: B&B £11–12, weekly £77–84. EM £6–7, B&B plus EM weekly £119–126. 🏵️ rates.

OKEHAMPTON Map 1 B3
Higher Cadham Farm, Jacobstowe, Okehampton EX20 3RB
© (083785) 647 Mrs Jenny King

Enjoy the period surroundings of our 16th-century longhouse with beams and log fires. Our family farm, dating back over 3 generations, covers 139 acres, with sheep, beef cattle and a few poultry. It lies just 5 miles north of Okehampton. We provide traditional home cooking and a warm welcome. Packed lunches on request. Kitchenette for parents, playroom games and toys. Licensed. The farm is on the Tarka Trail and has several interesting walks. Dartmoor and several NT properties, swimming, golf and horse riding 5 miles.

Open Mar-Nov.
4 bedrooms (1 twin; 1 double; 1 family; 1 single), 1🛌, 2WCs.
🏵️(3) ETB ⚌ ⚌Commended
Prices: B&B £12, weekly £80. EM £7. Weekly B&B plus EM £115. 🏵️ rates.

The Knole Farm, Bridestowe, Nr Okehampton
© (083786) 241 Mrs Mavis Bickle

The farmhouse dates back to the Victorian era and is approached by an short drive through an avenue of beech trees. It is set in just under an acre of grounds and surrounded by farmland. The farm is family run, comprising beef and sheep over 100 acres. This tranquil setting is within easy reach of the main A30 (west of Okehampton). Home cooking and packed lunches on request. Ideal for walkers, Dartmoor 2 miles. Lydford Gorge 3 miles. A variety of NT properties locally, also Morwellham Quay, beaches and sports facilities.

Open Easter-Nov.
5 bedrooms (1 twin; 2 double; 1 family; 1 single), 1🛏, 1WC.
🏠 🟊 ETB 👑 👑Commended
Prices: B&B £13–14, weekly £91–98. EM £7–8. Weekly B&B plus EM £130. 🏠 rates,🟊 rates.

Middlecott Farm, Broadwoodkelly, Winkleigh EX19 8D2
✆ (0837) 83381   Mrs June Western

This mixed family run farm is the ideal base for a relaxed country holiday. Winkleigh is 8 miles north of Okehampton (A386/A3072/B3219). Mrs Western provides good farmhouse cooking, and there is much to see and explore in the local area. Dartmoor, fishery and cider factory nearby. Tarka Country 6 miles.

Open Feb-Nov.
3 bedrooms (1 twin; 1 double; 1 family), 1🛏, 2WCs.
🏠 🟊 ETB 👑 👑
Prices: B&B £14–16, EM £8–10. 🏠 rates.

OTTERY-ST-MARY   Map 1 B3

Home Farm, Escot, Ottery-St-Mary
✆ (0404) 850241

At Home Farm you can enjoy the modern comfort and period beauty of the 16th-century farmhouse, situated in attractive parkland on a 300-acre mixed working farm. Plenty of local pubs and restaurants and pretty rural walks. Located

off the A30 east of Exeter, it is within easy reach of the coast and the moors. The historic town of Ottery-St-Mary 3 miles. Sidmouth 6 miles. Exeter 10 miles.

Open Easter-Oct.
3 bedrooms (1 double; 1 family; 1 single), 1🛏, 1🛁, 2WCs.
🏠 🥢 ETB 👑
Prices: B&B £14–15.50, weekly £94.50. 🏠 rates.

SIDMOUTH   Map 1 B3
Higher Coombe Farm, Tipton St John,Sidmouth EX10 0AX
✆ (0404) 813385   Mrs Kerstin Farmer

Higher Coombe offers comfortable farmhouse accommodation on a sheep and beef farm that lies east of Exeter (A3052/B3176), and only 4 miles from Sidmouth seafront. In this peaceful setting Mrs Farmer provides excellent food amidst a friendly and relaxed atmosphere. Cot, highchair, games and babysitting available. Bicton Park 6 miles. Otterton Mill and Crealy Park 8 miles

Open Mar-Dec.
3 bedrooms (1 double; 1 family; 1 single), 1🛏, 1WC.
🏠 ETB 👑 👑
Prices: B&B £16–17, weekly £91–98. EM £9. Weekly B&B plus EM £145–152.

Pinn Barton Farm, Peak Hill, Pinn Lane, Sidmouth
✆ (0395) 514004   Mrs Betty Sage

This 300-acre farm stands on the coast road between Sidmouth and the village of Otterton. In this Area of Outstanding Natural Beauty there are lovely walks around the farm and along the cliffs. There is so much to see and enjoy that most guests return to us: Sidmouth and Otterton Mill 2 miles, Bicton Park 3 miles, Donkey Sanctuary and Budleigh Salterton 5 miles.

Open all year
3 bedrooms (1 twin ens.🛁➘/WC;1 double ens.🛁➘/WC; 1 family ens.🛁➘/WC), 1WC.
🏠 🟊 ETB 👑 👑Commended

Prices: B&B from £17, weekly £112. ⚓ rates,🐕 £1 per night.

SOUTH MOLTON
Map 1 B2

Crangs Heasleigh, Heasley Mill, North Molton, EX36 3LE
✆ (05984) 268   Mary Yendell

This mixed beef and sheep farm lies within the National Park, 4 miles from the Tiverton-Barnstaple link road. The attractive Devon longhouse is a listed building, and offers a comfortable base from which to explore the area. The coast is easily accessible. Exmoor 2 miles. Barnstaple 12 miles.

Open all year
6 bedrooms (1 twin; 2 double; 2 family; 1 single), 1🛏, 2WCs.
⚓ 🐕 ETB 🏵 🏵
Prices: B&B £12.50–13.50, weekly £84.

Kerscott, Bishop's Nympton, South Molton EX36 4QG
✆ (0769) 550262

This 16th-century farmhouse, on a farm mentioned in the Domesday Book, stands in a peaceful elevated position with lovely views overlooking Exmoor. Kerscott is 3 miles from the village, and close to the Moor. The house has a fascinating old world interior and furnishings, and good farmhouse cooking is provided – with homemade bread and pies, 4-course dinners and hearty breakfasts. The farm has sheep and heifers. It is located on the B3227 (old A361) South Molton-Bampton route. South Molton 6 miles.

Open Mar-Oct.
3 bedrooms (1 twin; 1 double; 1 family), 1🛏, 2WCs.
⚓(8) ✂ ETB 🏵 🏵 Approved
Prices: B&B £13–14, EM £6.50. ⚓ rates.

North Newton Farm, Chittlehampton, Umberleigh EX37 9QS
✆ (0769) 540544   Mrs Margaret Thomas

This large traditional style farmhouse is on a 52-acre dairy farm west of South Molton, on the B3227, in lovely rolling countryside with extensive views. Mrs Thomas provides a warm welcome, a homely free atmosphere and plenty of excellent farmhouse food using own fresh produce. Cot available. Ideally situated for touring Exmoor and the North Devon coast. South Molton (Quince Honey Farm, Thursday market) 4 miles. Dartington Glass Factory 12 miles. Barnstaple 12 miles.

Open Jan-Nov.
3 bedrooms (1 twin; 1 double; 1 family), 1🛏, 1WC.
⚓ 🐕 ETB 🏵 🏵
Prices: B&B £13–15, weekly £90–95. EM £7–7.50. Weekly B&B plus EM £115–125. ⚓ rates.

Partridge Arms Farm, Yeo Mill, West Anstey, Nr South Molton
✆ (03984) 217

Formerly a country inn, Partridge Arms Farm is an old established family farm set in over 200 acres of land. We offer genuine hospitality and traditional farmhouse fare. Packed lunches on request. Licensed. Ground floor bedroom, cot and highchair available. The farm lies off the B3227 Bampton-South Molton road and is ideally situated for touring or walking in the National Park and the many local coastal beauty spots. Trout fishing and pony trekking 2 miles.

Open all year
7 bedrooms (2 twin inc. 1 ens. 🛁/WC; 3 double ens. 🛁/WC; 1 family; 1 single), 1🛏, 2WCs.
♿ ⚓ 🐕 ETB 🏵 🏵 Approved
Prices inc. VAT: B&B £17.50–20.50, weekly £122.50–143.50. EM £7.50. Weekly B&B plus EM £175–196. ⚓ rates.

TAVISTOCK
Map 1 B3

Langford Farm, Lamerton, Tavistock
✆ (0822) 612202   Mrs S. Dawe

A private beech lane leads to a quiet 500-year-old family farmhouse on a traditional mixed livestock farm with rare breed sheep. Afternoon teas and packed lunches on request. Cot and highchair available. Located 2 miles northwest of

Tavistock (B3362) there is a wide selection of places of interest close by. Dartmoor 3 miles. Morwellham Quay Working Museum 3 miles. Numerous historic country churches within 3 miles. Many N.T. properties within 7 miles.

Open April-Oct.
3 bedrooms (2 double; 1 family), 1🛏, 1WC.
🐕 ⚌ 🐓
Prices: B&B £11.50–13, weekly £85. 🐑 rates.

Rubbytown Farm, Gulworthy, Tavistock
✆ (0822) 832493

Guests are assured of every comfort in this lovely 17th-century character farmhouse overlooking the Tamar Valley. The house is furnished to a high standard, four poster beds and games room. You can enjoy good home cooking. Rubbytown Farm lies north of the A390 Tavistock-Liskeard road. In the immediate vicinity there are woodland walks and abundant wildlife. St Mellion golfcourse nearby.

Open all year
3 bedrooms (2 double ens. 🛁/WC; 1 twin ens. ⚌/WC), 1WC.
🐑(5) ⚌ ETB 🏵 🏵Highly Commended
Prices: B&B from £16. EM £10.

Wringworthy Farm, Mary Tavy, Tavistock PL19 9LT
✆ (0822) 810434

While modernised for comfort this mainly Elizabethan farmhouse, mentioned in the Domesday Book, retains many original features such as oak panelling, flagstone floors and studded doors. Cot available. This beef and sheep farm, entrance on the A386 between Mary Tavy and

Tavistock, lies in a quiet valley on the edge of Dartmoor National Farm. Dartmoor 1 mile, pony trekking, walking and golf within 3 miles. Convenient for touring all parts of Devon and Cornwall.

Open April-Oct.
3 bedrooms (1 twin ens. 🛁⚌/WC; 1 double; 1 family), 2🛏, 2WCs.
🐑 ETB Listed
Prices: B&B £14. 🐑 rates.

TIVERTON   Map 1 B2

Hensley Farm, Worlington, Crediton EX17 4TG
✆ (0884) 860346

Our 16th-century thatched farmhouse overlooks one of the prettiest villages in Devon, west of Tiverton (B3137, west of Witheridge). Guests are encouraged to join in on our dairy, beef and sheep farm, with dogs, cats and rabbits as well. We offer plenty of good farmhouse food, packed lunches and afternoon teas on request. Cot, highchair, games room, table tennis and darts all available. Ground floor bedroom if required. River walks and tennis close by. Riding and golf 1 mile. Dartmoor, Exmoor and the North Devon beaches are within easy reach.

Open April-Nov.
3 bedrooms (1 double; 1 family; 1 single), 🛏,
2WCs.
🐑 🐓 ETB Approved
Prices: B&B from £12. EM £6.50.

Quoit-at-Cross Farm, Stoodleigh, Tiverton EX16 9PJ
✆ (03985) 280   Mrs Linda Hill

A delightful 17th-century farmhouse, very comfortably furnished with log fires in winter, in the centre of the village of Stoodleigh, west of the A396 Tiverton-Bampton road. Quoit-at-Cross is a family-run mixed stock farm with lovely views in all directions. Here you will find delicious farmhouse fare and a welcoming atmosphere. Large garden, cot and highchair available. Knightshayes Court (N.T.) 5 miles. Tiverton Canal and

Castle 6 miles. Bickleigh Castle 10 miles. Killerton Gardens (N.T.) 15 miles.

Open May-Dec.
2 bedrooms (1 double ens. ⌂▽/WC; 1 family ens. ⌂/WC).
⌂ETB ♕ ♕ ♕
Prices: B&B £15, weekly £98. EM £8. Weekly B&B plus EM £155. ⌂ rates.

Weir Mill Farm, Willand, Cullompton EX15 2RE
✆ (0884) 820803   Mrs Rita Parish

Weir Mill is a working beef, sheep and arable farm of 105 acres. The farmhouse overlooks the fields beside the River Culm. TV and tea/coffee facilities in all rooms. From M5, Jct 27 take B3181 towards Willand (3 miles), 50 yards past the turning to Uffculme, turn left (hidden entrance) into Jaycroft for Weir Mill Farm. Cullompton 4 miles. Riding, swimming, golf and tennis all available locally. Childrens Adventure Park 1 mile. Exeter and South Devon seaside resorts 30 mins drive.

Open all year
3 bedrooms (2 double; 1 family ens.⌂/WC), 1➤.
⌂ ETB ♕ ♕Commended
Prices: B&B £13–15, weekly £89–103. EM £7, B&B plus EM weekly £130–144. ⌂ rates.

TOTNES   Map 1 B3

Berry Farm, Berry Pomeroy, Totnes TQ9 6LG
✆ (0803) 863231   Mrs Geraldine Nicholls

Come and be welcomed with comfort, good food and personal attention as featured in the Daily Telegraph Magazine. Our attractive Victorian farmhouse has spacious rooms, tastefully decorated. Berry Farm is in a quiet hamlet just a mile from Totnes off the A385. Famous Berry Pomeroy Castle is in walking distance. Torbay and South Hams both a short distance away.

Open all year
3 bedrooms (1 twin; 1 double; 1 family), 1➤, 1⌂, 1WC.
⌂ ⊱ ETB Listed Commended
Prices: B&B £13–15. EM (by arrangement) £8.50. ⌂ rates.

Bow Grange, Littlehempston, Totnes TQ9 6NO
✆ (0803) 812390   B.& S. Harris

Bow Grange is a Victorian farmhouse situated amongst Devon's rolling hills, midway between Newton Abbot and Totnes on the A381. We have a working mixed farm, well placed for touring the area. Totnes 4 miles. Torbay 5 miles. Buckfast Abbey 7 miles. Dartmoor 10 miles.

Open Jul-Sept.
3 bedrooms (2 double inc. 1 ens. ⌂/WC;1 family), 1➤, 2WC.
⌂ ⊱
Prices: B&B £11–15. ⌂ rates.

Great Court Farm, Weston Lane, Totnes TQ9 6LB
✆ (0803) 862326   Mrs Janet Hooper

Great Court is a large Victorian farmhouse overlooking the historic town of Totnes and surrounding countryside. This dairy and sheep farm covers 420 acres on the eastern side of Totnes (off Paignton Road) and runs down to the River Dart. Berry Pomeroy Castle is less than 3 miles away, Paignton and beaches 5 miles.

Open Feb-Nov.
3 bedrooms (1 double; 1 family; 1 twin), 2➤, 2WCs.
⌂ ⊱ETB ♕
Prices: B&B £12–15, weekly £84–100.⌂ rates.

Self-Catering

CHULMLEIGH   Map 1 B3
Manor Farm, Riddlecombe, Chulmleigh
✆ (07693) 335   Mrs M.E. Gay

Manor Farm is midway between Exeter and Barnstaple, west of the A377. You are assured a friendly welcome at our lovely farmhouse which has a very well equipped self-catering wing, sleeping 7/8. There are glorious views all around and a large garden to relax in. Guests are welcome to see the animals and watch the milking. Our superb games room caters for all ages. Gliding club and fishing lake close by. Golf 4 miles, Dartington Glass 8 miles.

Open all year
3 bedrooms (2 double; 1 family), 1➤, 1WC.

⚐ ⟟ ETB ♩♩♩♩Commended
Prices: weekly £110–320.

COLYTON   Map 2 A3

Smallicombe Farm, Northleigh, Colyton EX13 6BU

✆ (040483) 310   Mrs Margot Todd
✆ From spring 1993 (0404) 831310

For full farm description see p. 57. Accommodation is in 4 recently converted barns sleeping 2–8. One of the ground floor units has been designed and equipped for wheelchair users. A second ground floor unit is suitable for the partially disabled. Cots and highchair available. Brochure on request.

Open all year
♿⚐ ETB ♩♩ to ♩♩♩♩Commended
Prices: weekly £90–375. Off season shortbreaks from £75.

Higher Cownhayne Farm, Cownhayne Lane, Colyton EX13 6HD

✆ (0297) 552267   Mrs E. Pady

Higher Cownhayne is just off the A3052, 2 miles from Seaton. This is a working family farm with dairy, beef cattle and horse breeding, also chickens, dogs and cats. On the farm there is 1 mile of trout fishing fly, for rainbow and brown trout on River Coly. Colyton and Colyford both within walking distance. Lyme Regis 6 miles. Accommodation is offered in 3 apartments sleeping 4, 6 and 8 people, in our 16th-century farmhouse. Cot and highchair provided. Also 5 vans on holiday farm site.

Open all year ⚐
Prices (apartments): weekly £80–250.

CROYDE   Map 1 B2

Pickwell Barton, Georgeham, Braunton EX33 1LA

✆ (0271) 890987   Mrs Sheila Cook

Accommodation is available in 2 self-catering cottages, each sleeps 7/9, on this mixed farm, off the B3231 north of Braunton and Croyde. Ideal for a seaside holiday, there are beautiful coastal

walks with gorgeous views of Baggy and Morte Points. 20 minutes walk to the beach. Putsborough and Woolacombe sandy beaches close by. Ideal for surfing.

Open all year
⚐⟟ ETB♩♩Approved
Prices: weekly £100–300. Shortbreaks (3 nights) from £80.

HOLSWORTHY   Map 1 B2

Thorne Manor, Holsworthy EX22 7JD

✆ (0409) 253342   Mr & Mrs Clarke

Thorne Manor is a working dairy farm with 300 cows, located 1 mile from the Bude-Holsworthy road. There is a nature trail and nature reserve a mile away, and a fishing lake for children. Sandpit, swings and games room also provided. Accommodation is offered in 11 self-catering units from converted farm buildings, sleeping 4/5 in each unit. Licensed.

Open all year
⚐ ⟟ ETB ♩♩
Prices: weekly £100–290.

LYNTON   Map 1 B2

West Ilkerton Farm, Lynton EX35 6QA

✆ (0598) 52310   Mrs Victoria Eveleigh

West Ilkerton Farm is off the A39 Lynton-Barnstaple road, near Barbrook. This luxurious semi-detached cottage is on a secluded Exmoor hill farm with sheep, cattle and heavy horses. The farm is in Exmoor National Park and borders open moorland. Good walking direct from the farm on moorland, woodland and coastal paths. Riding stables and sea, coarse and fly fishing locally. Lynton and Lynmouth 3 miles. The large cottage sleeps 6 comfortably and is fully equipped. Cot, highchair, babybath, games and toys available. "Exmoor Farmer" holidays in winter.

Open all year
⚐ ✄⟟ ETB♩♩♩♩Approved
Prices: weekly £170–340.

KEY TO SYMBOLS

Bath	⚲
Shower	🛁
Bathroom	🛁
Disabled Guest Facilities	♿
No Smoking	✄
Children Welcome	⚐
Dogs by Arrangement	⟟

MORETONHAMPSTEAD   Map 1 B3

Budleigh Farm, Moretonhampstead TQ13 8SB

✆ (0647) 40835   Mrs J. Harvey

For full farm description, see p. 61. Self-catering accommodation is available in attractively con-verted barns. Six units in all, with 1–3 bedrooms, sleeping 2–6. One ground floor flat (sleeps 2–3) is suitable for disabled guests.

Open all year
&🛏 ETB↕/↕↕↕Commended
Prices: weekly £72–280.🛏 £7.50 per week.

DORSET

BLANDFORD FORUM
Map 2 A3

Manor House Farm, Ibberton, Blandford Forum DT11 0EN
✆ (0258) 817349   Mrs C.M. Old

This small 15th-century Manor House is now a farmhouse surrounded by a large colourful garden and situated in a quiet unspoilt village, 10 miles west of Blandford Forum via A350/A357, then 5 miles south of Shillingstone. Its position makes it an ideal base for exploring Thomas Hardy country. The farm covers 250 acres and comprises dairy and sheep. The Manor House was given by Henry VIII to his young queen and fifth wife, Katherine Howard. The oak beams and nail studded doors confirm its centuries old past. Cot and highchair provided. Milton Abbas 5 miles.

Open all year
3 bedrooms (1 twin; 2 double inc. 1 ens. ⋔/WC), 1🛏, 1WC. ⚸
Prices: B&B £12–15, weekly £70–90.🛏 £0.50 per night.

BRIDPORT
Map 2 A3

Frogmore Farm, Chideock, Bridport
✆ (0308) 56159   Mrs S.E. Norman

This traditional stone-built 17th-century farmhouse enjoys splendid sea views. Frogmore is a 90-acre hill farm adjoining National Trust land to the coast, 2 miles west of Bridport (off A35). Mrs Norman provides good home cooking and packed lunches on request. Cot, highchair and

games available. Seatown Beach 2 miles. West Bay 3 miles. Lyme Regis 9 miles. Parnham House 6 miles.

Open all year
3 bedrooms (1 twin; 1 double ens. ⋔/WC; 1 family ens. ⋔/WC), 1🛏, 1WC. ⚸ 🛏
Prices: B&B £13–15, weekly £88.00. EM £6. Weekly B&B plus EM £130. ⚸ rates.

DORCHESTER
Map 2 A3

Foxholes Farm, Littlebredy, Dorchester DT2 9HJ
✆ (0308) 482395   Mrs V.J. Fry

An opportunity to stay on a 200-year-old flint and slate farmhouse on a mixed family farm, milking a large dairy herd. The 380-acre farm is set in the Bride Valley 9 miles west of Dorchester (A35). Foxholes is well located for exploring the surrounding area and its many attractive beaches, Lulworth Cove, Durdle Door. Maiden Castle 9 miles. Weymouth 12 miles. Cot, highchair, swing, climbing frame and babysitting available.

Open Mar-Nov.
3 bedrooms (1 twin; 2 double), 2🛏, 2WCs. ⚸ 🛏
Prices: B&B £14, weekly £85. ⚸ rates.

Maiden Castle Farm, Dorchester DT2 9PR
✆ (0305) 262356   Mrs Hilary Hoskin

This large Victorian farmhouse lies off the A354 Dorchester-Weymouth road. The mixed family farm covers 1150 acres. In the middle of the farm stands the spectacular hill fort of Maiden Castle. Outstanding views and superb region for walking. Good farmhouse cooking and packed lunches on request. Licensed. Highchair and cot provided. Dorchester 1 mile. Weymouth 7 miles.

Open all year
4 bedrooms (1 twin/double ens. ⊟/WC; 2 family/double inc. 1 ens. ⊟/WC, 1 ens. ⋔; 1 family/twin priv. ⊟), 1🛏, 1WC.

ETB Commended
Prices: B&B £18–20. EM £10. rates.

GILLINGHAM — Map 2 A3

Huntingford Oak, Gillingham SP8 5QH
(0747) 860574 — Mr & Mrs A.H. James

The modern house of Huntingford Oak stands on a working farm amid the unspoilt Dorset countryside. Enjoy a peaceful atmosphere with marvellous views. Good farmhouse cooking with packed lunches on request. Groundfloor bedroom, highchair and playroom available. The farm lies under 2 miles from Mere (A303). NT Gardens Stourhead 4 miles. Shaftesbury 6 miles. Stonehenge 14 miles.

Open all year
3 bedrooms (2 twin inc. 1 ens. /WC, 1 ens. /WC; 1 family ens. /WC), 1, 2WCs.
ETB
Prices: B&B £21–25, weekly £110–130. EM £10.

Kington Manor Farm, Church Hill, Kington Magna SP8 5EG
(074785) 371 — Mrs G. Gosney

This newly-built stone farmhouse, attractively sited with views over Blackmore Vale, is located in a quiet and pretty village. The 30-acre farm has beef and pigs. Mrs Gosney provides good home cooking, tea/coffee facilities and TV in room. From Shaftesbury take A30 west for 6 miles, after West Stour turn right, signed Sandley, then follow signs to Kington Magna. Stourhead NT House 6 miles. Stourton Gardens and Shaftesbury 7 miles.

Open Jan-Nov.
1 twin bedroom ens. /WC.
ETB Listed
Prices: B&B £14, weekly £91. EM £7, weekly B&B plus EM £140. rates.

SHAFTESBURY — Map 2 A3

Culverhouse Farm, Motcombe, Shaftesbury SP7 9HU
(0747) 52273 — Mrs J. Menlove

This is an 80-acre stock rearing farm with 200 breeding ewes and 10 suckler cows and calves. The red-brick farmhouse has a large yard, farm buildings and a good sized garden. Magnificent views from the top of the farmland. Visitors' lounge with TV. Motcombe is north of the B3081 Shaftesbury-Gillingham road. Shaftesbury 3 miles. Stourhead NT 6 miles.

Open Apr-Sept.
3 twin bedrooms inc. 1 ens. /WC), 1, 1WC.
Prices: B&B £15, weekly £91. rates.

STURMINSTER NEWTON — Map 2 A3

Holebrook Farm, Lydlinch
(0258) 817348 — Sally & Charles Wingate-Saul

Guests are invited to relax in an informal family atmosphere at this Georgian farmhouse with delightfully converted stables. The accommodation is luxurious and ground floor bedrooms have access ramps etc. for disabled visitors. Cots, highchairs and games room with pool/table tennis table provided plus swimming pool and clay pigeon shooting. All accompanied by good home cooking and afternoon teas. The farm is all grass with beef cattle. Holebrook Farm is situated a mile south of the A357, 3 miles west of Sturminster Newton. Sherborne 10 miles. Milton Abbey 15 miles. Kingston Lacey, Dorchester and Longleat 20 miles.

Open all year
5 bedrooms (5 twin inc. 4 ens. /WC; 1 single), 1, 1WC.
ETB Listed Commended
Prices: B&B £19–22, weekly £133–147. EM £9.50–10. Weekly B&B plus EM £199.50–224. rates.

Lower Fifehead Farm, Fifehead St Quinton, Sturminster Newton

✆ (0258) 817335   Mrs J. Miller

Lower Fifehead Farmhouse is an exceptional listed building, part 16th- and part 17th-century, as its mullion windows testify. It stands on a 350-acre dairy farm in the heart of Hardy country. Cot and highchair are provided as well as a tennis court and farm tours. The farm is close to Fifehead Neville, which is 3 miles south of Sturminster Newton.

Open all year
2 bedrooms (1 twin; 1 double), 1🛏, 1WC.
⬧ ETB Listed
Prices: B&B £12.50–14. ⬧ rates.

Spire Hill Farm, Stalbridge, Sturminster Newton

✆ (0963) 62136   Mrs Carol Wallis

This large 18th-century farmhouse stands a mile north of Stalbridge (A357) with beautiful views over the surrounding Blackmore Vale. The farm has sheep and suckler cattle. Cot and highchair provided. Sherborne 8 miles. Stourhead 15 miles.

Open Apr-Oct.
3 bedrooms (2 adjoining twin rooms; 1 double), 1🛏, 1WC.
⬧ 🏕
Prices: B&B £13.50–15. ⬧ rates.

SWANAGE   Map 2 B3

Downshay Farm, Haycrafts Lane, Swanage BH19 3EB

✆ (0929) 480316   Mrs J. Pike

On a family-run dairy farm stands this delightfully situated Victorian Purbeck stone farmhouse overlooking Corfe Castle and the Purbeck Hills. Downshay Farm is 3 miles from Swanage, signposted from Harmans Cross on the A351 Wareham-Swanage road. Purbeck Steam Railway close by. Putlake Adventure Farm 2 miles. Sandy beaches and coastal path walks 3 miles. Cot and highchair available.

Open Apr-Oct.
2 bedrooms (1 double; 1 family), 2🛏, 2WCs.
⬧ ⚡ ETB Listed
Prices: B&B £12–14, weekly £85. ⬧ rates.

Knitson Old Farmhouse, Corfe Castle BH20 5JB

✆ (0929) 422836   Mrs Rachel Helfer

Knitson is a 200-acre family farm located 2 miles west of Swanage (A351). You will find a warm welcome and a relaxed informal atmosphere in this comfortable 15th-century farmhouse, built of Purbeck stone. Log fires and delicious home cooking. Water sports, golf, riding locally. Superb walks from farm linking coastal path. Studland 4 miles. Corfe Castle 3 miles.

Open all year
3 bedrooms (1 twin; 1 double; 1 family), 2🛏, 2WCs.
⬧ ETB Listed
Prices: B&B £13–15, weekly £90–100. EM £7–11. ⬧ rates.

WAREHAM   Map 2 A3

Chaldecotts, Swalland Farm, Kimmeridge, Wareham BH20 5PE

✆ (0929) 480936   Mrs C. Vearncombe

The Purbeck stone farmhouse is in a quiet location with views of the sea and the Purbeck Hills. The farm is mixed and has 2 miles of coastal paths as well as excellent hill walks. Packed lunches available. Take A35 Wareham-Swanage road, turn right before Corfe Castle and continue via Church Knole towards Kimmeridge. Corfe Castle 4 miles. Lulworth Cove, Durdle Door 5 miles. Wareham 5 miles.

Open Mar-Oct.
2 bedrooms (1 double; 1 family), 1🛏, 2WCs.
⬧(5) ETB Listed
Prices: B&B £12.50–15, weekly £80–100.

Hyde Woods, Hyde BH20 7NT

✆ (0929) 471087   Rosemary Shelton

This modernised spacious farmhouse stands in the heart of Thomas Hardy country. The farm has 37 acres with horses and sheep. Riding available, and guests can bring their own horses on holiday. Fishing nearby and golf course adjacent. Packed lunches on request. Groundfloor bedroom, highchair and children's games provided. Hyde lies north off the A352 Wareham-Wool road. Lawrence of Arabia's Cottage 2 miles. Corfe Castle 6 miles. Lulworth Cove 8 miles.

Open all year
3 bedrooms (1 twin; 1 family ens. 🛁/WC;

1 double ens. ☞/WC), 1🛏, 1WC.
🛆 🛏
Prices: B&B £14.50–19.50, weekly £115. EM
£7.50–9.50, weekly B&B plus EM £165.

Kimmeridge Farm House, Kimmeridge, Wareham BH20 5PE
☎ (0929) 480990   Mrs Annette Hole

In the heart of the Purbeck countryside stands this mixed farm and beautiful 16th-century farmhouse, which has views of the rolling hills and sea. The sandy beaches of Studland Bay and Swanage, entertainments of Bournemouth and Poole, all easily accessible. Packed lunches on request, cot and highchair available. Take A35 Wareham-Swanage road, turn right before Corfe Castle and continue via Church Knole to Kimmeridge.

Open all year
3 bedrooms (1 twin; 2 double inc. 1 ens.☞/WC), 1🛏. 🛆
Prices: B&B £15–17.50, weekly £105–122.50.

Luckford Wood House, East Stoke, Wareham BH20 6AW
☎ (0929) 463098

This friendly warm and spacious farmhouse is surrounded by the quiet and picturesque scenery of true Hardy country. There are many pleasant walks in and around the family run dairy farm, which is located south off the A352 Wareham-Wool road. Golf course and boating 4 miles. Lulworth beach and cove 5 miles. Wareham 3 miles.

Open all year
3 bedrooms (1 twin ens. ☞/WC; 1 double ens. ☞/WC; 1 family ens. ☞/WC), 2🛏.
🛆 🛏 ETB Listed
Prices: B&B £16–24, weekly £105–140. 🛆 rates.

Newlands Farm, West Lulworth, Wareham BH20 5PU
☎ (092941) 376

Newlands Farm has 700 acres of arable and sheep. The land goes to the cliff edge with several good footpaths. The farmhouse is 120 years old with large rooms and beautiful views of the Purbeck Hills. Cot, highchair and babysitting available. Packed lunches on request. The farm lies west of Wareham on the A352/B3070. The beach is 20 minutes walk from the house. Lulworth Cove 1 mile. Wareham 10 miles. Corfe Castle 12 miles. Dorchester 12 miles.

Open all year
2 bedrooms (1 double ens. ☞; 1 family ens. ☞), 1🛏,1WC.
🛆 ⚵
Prices: B&B £18–20, weekly £114–126. 🛆 rates.

WIMBORNE MINSTER   Map 2 A3

Homeacres, Homelands Farm, Three Legged Cross, Wimborne BH21 6QZ
☎ (0202) 822422

This 170-acre grass farm has beef, sheep and sweetcorn. It lies 4 miles from Ringwood, north of the A31 Ringwood-Wimborne Minster road. Homeacres provides good comfortable accommodation in an attractive rural location. Packed lunches on request. A country park with golf, children's steam train and adventure area is a mile's walk away. Riding available locally, fishing 4 miles.

Open all year
6 bedrooms (1 twin ens. ☞/WC; 1 double ens.☞/WC; 3 family ens. ☞/☞/WC; 1 single ens.☞/☞/WC), 1🛏, 1WC.
🛆 🛏 ETB 🐄 🐄Approved
Prices: B&B £14–19.50, weekly £84–105.🛆 rates.

Self-Catering

DORCHESTER   Map 2 A3

Eweleaze Farm, Tincleton, Dorchester DT2 8QR
☎ (0305) 848391   Mrs Rosemary Coleman

The working farm of Eweleaze lies 4 miles east of Dorchester (A35). Accommodation is in comfortably furnished cottages on the farm, sleeping maximum 4, 5 and 6 (2 and 3 bedrooms). One bungalow without stairs. Cot available. This is the place to choose if you want a relaxing holiday. Around Eweleaze you can enjoy a large garden, ducks, horses, tennis, fishing and forest walks. The beautiful coast is within easy reach. Hardy's Cottage 3 miles. Isle of Purbeck 10 miles.

Open all year
⚐ ETB ♪♪♪Commended
Prices: weekly £100–285. Also winter breaks with OAP reductions.

SHAFTESBURY   Map 2 A3
Hartgrove Farm, Hartgrove, Shaftesbury
✆ (0747) 811830   Mrs Susan Smart

Our 145-acre dairy farm is in an Area of Outstanding Natural Beauty with breathtaking views of glorious downland. A beautifully renovated cottage in the centre of the farm sleeps 5–6, with oak-fitted kitchen, beamed lounge, garden, laundry and games room. A self-contained unit in the farmhouse wing sleeps 2. Guests welcome to explore the farm, with abundant wildlife – badgers, deer, buzzards. Farm has cows, calves, sheep, chickens and horses. Farm produce available. Cot and highchair provided. Take A350 Shaftesbury-Blandford road south to Fontnell Magna, and turn left in village opposite garage, farm 2 miles further. Shaftesbury 4 miles.

Open all year ⚐
Prices: weekly £95–325.⚐ £10 per week.

STURMINSTER NEWTON   Map 2 A3
Holebrook Farm, Lydlinch
✆ (0258) 817348   Sally & Charles Wingate-Saul

For full farm description see p. 69. Accommodation is available in 4 units, each sleep 2, in a recently converted barn.

ETB ♪♪♪♪Highly Commended
Prices: weekly £130–225.

Lower Fifehead Farm, Fifehead St Quinton, Sturminster Newton
✆ (0258) 817335   Mrs J. Miller

For farm description see p. 70. Accommodation is available in 2 units, a cottage, sleeps 4–5, and a flat, sleeps 2–3.

Open May-Oct.
ETB♪♪♪Approved
Prices: weekly £80–195.

WAREHAM   Map 2 A3
Hyde Woods, Hyde BH20 7NT
✆ (0929) 471087   Rosemary Shelton

For full farm description see p. 70. Accommodation is available in two units, with 1 and 3 bedrooms, sleeping 2–3 and 4–6.

Open all year ⚐
Prices: weekly £125–375.

DURHAM

BARNARD CASTLE
Map 5 A1

West Roods Tourism, West Roods Farm, Boldron, Barnard Castle DL12 9SW
© (0833) 690116   Mrs R. Lowson

Our greystone roof farmhouse is over 100 years old. 2 miles south of Barnard Castle, the farm is in the foothills of the Pennines, with a spectacular view across 50 miles of countryside on a clear day. West Roods is a working farm standing in 59 acres of mainly pasture. There is also a small camp site (6 caravans, 10 tents) with facilities. Guests are welcome to walk the farm enjoying the wildlife, the birds and the stream which winds down to the River Tees. Water dowsing taught. Packed lunches and evening meals by arrangement. Raby Castle 6 miles.

Open Mar-Nov. **RAC**
3 bedrooms (1 double ens.⌂/WC;1 family ens.⌂/WC; 1 single), 2🛁, 3WCs.
⚘ ETB ♛ ♛ ♛
Prices: B&B £17–20, weekly £100–110. EM £7. Weekly B&B plus EM £147–154. ⚘ rates.

KEY TO SYMBOLS

Bath	🛏
Shower	⌂
Bathroom	🛁
Disabled Guest Facilities	♿
No Smoking	✄
Children Welcome	⚘
Dogs by Arrangement	🛏

CONSETT
Map 7 B3

Bee Cottage Farm, Consett DH8 9HW
© (0207) 508224   E. Lawson

This working farm is set in peaceful picturesque surroundings, off the A68, 15 miles north of Bishop Auckland. You can help with bottle feeding baby lambs or even learn to milk the goats. You can stay either in the farmhouse itself or in one of two bungalows on the farm. Wherever you stay, you can still enjoy our good home cooking, packed lunches and afternoon teas on request. Interesting walks in the area. Good centre for visiting Beamish Museum, Hadrian's Wall, Durham Cathedral and the Northumbrian coast.

Open all year
4 family bedrooms (2 twin; 2 double).
⚘ 🛏 ✄ in main farmhouse ETB Listed Commended
Prices: B&B £16–30. EM £10.50.

Willerby Grange Farm, Allensford, Castleside, Consett
© (0207) 508752   Mrs Ann Robson

The farm is in a secluded setting, but within a short distance of the A68 Tow Law-Corbridge road, turn right after Castleside. The farm keeps mainly horses and horse/pony trekking is available on site. Stabling and grazing provided for guests' horses. Ground floor bedrooms, cot and highchair available. Consett 3 miles. Hadrian's Wall, Durham City, Beamish Museum and Gateshead Metro Centre 10 miles.

Open all year
4 double/family bedrooms inc. 3 ens.⋒/WC, 1
ens. ☞⋒/WC).
⌂ ✝ ETB ♛ ♛
Prices: B&B £20–30, weekly £140–210.✝ £15
per week in kennels.

DURHAM CITY   Map 7 B3

Baxter Wood Farm, Crossgate Moor,
Durham DH1 4TG
✆ (091) 3865820

In a peaceful rural setting by the River Browney,
yet only 2 miles from the centre of Durham city,
stands Baxter Wood Farm, an attractive 17th-
century listed farmhouse. The farm is arable with
a horse livery yard, stabling available for guests'
horses. Take A1(M)/A167, then turning for Bear
Park. An ideal base for touring Northumberland
coast, Hadrian's Wall and N. Yorks Moors.

Open all year
1 twin bedroom ens. ☞/WC.
⌂(10) ✂ ✝
Prices: B&B £15–25.

WOLSINGHAM   Map 7 B3

Greenwell Farm, Nr Wolsingham, Tow
Law DL13 4PM
✆ (0388) 527248   Mrs Linda Vickers

Enjoy a real country holiday in this comfortable
300-year-old farmhouse, which stands on a traditional farm with cows, sheep, corn and breeds
of ornamental hens. Guests can follow the farm
walks and Nature Reserve trails with conservation areas. Mrs Vickers provides good farmhouse
hospitality with home cooking, afternoon teas
and packed lunches on request. Ground floor
rooms and highchair available. The farm lies 10
miles west of Durham off B6297 (A690 south to
Brancepeth, turn right and follow signs to Tow
Law). Beamish Museum 10 miles. High Force
Waterfall 20 miles.

Closed Xmas and New Year
3 bedrooms (1 twin ens. ☞/WC; 1 double ens.
⋒/WC; 1 family ens. ☞/WC), 1➡.
♿ ⌂ ✂ ✝ ETB ♛ ♛Commended

Prices: B&B £15–17.50, weekly £100–145. EM
£9, weekly £168–185. ⌂ rates,✝ £15 per week.

Self-Catering

BARNARD CASTLE   Map 5 A1

Wyse Hill Cottage, Startforth, Barnard
Castle
✆ (0325) 718372   Contact: Mrs G.E. Hodgson,
Fox Grove, East Layton, Richmond, N. Yorks
DL11 7PW

The cottage is on a livestock farm, with cattle and
sheep, a mile from Barnard Castle (south of River
Tees on the Startforth-Boldron road). The 2
bedroom cottage sleeps 4 and is well heated with
fully equipped kitchen. TV in sitting room. Bowes
Museum 1 mile. Yorkshire Dales 3 miles. Raby
Castle 6 miles.

Open Mar-Dec.
⌂(4) ✝ ETBↃↃApproved
Prices: weekly £75–150.

CONSETT   Map 7 B3

Bee Cottage Farm, Consett DH8 9HW
✆ (0207) 508224   E. Lawson

For full farm description see p. 73. Accommodation is offered in a bungalow, sleeps 5.
Equipped with ramps to aid partially disabled,
but not wheelchair-bound, guests.

Open all year
✂ ✝ ETB Listed Commended
Prices: weekly £265.

Willerby Grange Farm, Allensford,
Castleside, Consett
✆ (0207) 508752   Mrs Ann Robson

For full farm description see p. 73. Four self-
catering holiday apartments are available in stable conversions set around a courtyard. Each
sleeps 4, with a double bedroom and a double
sofa bed in lounge.

Open all year
✝ ETBↃↃↃCommended
Prices: weekly £100–200 low season, £200–300
high season. ✝ £15 per week in kennels.

DURHAM CITY   Map 7 B3

Baxter Wood Farm, Crossgate Moor,
Durham DH1 4TG
✆ (091) 3865820

For full farm description see above. On the farm
the old granaries have been converted into 2 self-
catering cottages, sleeping 2–4.

Open Feb-Dec.
🐕(10) ⛧ ETB♪♪♪♪Highly Commended
Prices: weekly £108–250.

WOLSINGHAM   Map 7 B3

Greenwell Farm, Nr Wolsingham, Tow Law DL13 4PM
✆ (0388) 527248   Mrs Linda Vickers

See p. 74. for full farm description. Self-catering accommodation is offered in two 2 bedroomed units sleeping 4–6.

Open all year
✄ ⛧ ETB♪♪♪♪Commended
Prices: weekly £150–285. ⛧ £15 per week.

See p. 74.

KEY TO SYMBOLS

Bath	🛁
Shower	🚿
Bathroom	🛀
Disabled Guest Facilities	♿
No Smoking	✄
Children Welcome	🐕
Dogs by Arrangement	⛧

EAST SUSSEX

BATTLE
Map 3 A3

Moons Hill Farm, The Green, Moons Hill, Ninfield TN33 9LH
✆ (0424) 892645   Mrs June B. Ive

The modernised farmhouse at Moons Hill stands on 10 acres in the centre of the village opposite the local pub. You will receive friendly personal attention, courtesy tray, and enjoy every comfort while using this as a base for exploring 1066 country. For Moons Hill, take the A269 to Ninfield from Bexhill. Bexhill and Battle Abbey 4 miles. Pevensey Castle 8 miles. Bewl Water and Michelham Priory 9 miles.

Open Jan.-Nov.
3 bedrooms (1 twin ens. ☕/WC;1 double ens. ☕/WC;1 family ens. ☕/WC;).
⚬(4) ⊁ ETB ♛ ♛
Prices: B&B £15–17.50, weekly £105–122.50.
⚬ rates, ⊁ £1 per day.

BURWASH
Map 3 A3

Woodlands Farm, Burwash, Etchingham TN18 7LA
✆ (0435) 882794   Mrs E. Sirrell

Woodlands Farm stands back from the A265, 4 miles east of Heathfield, surrounded by fields and woods. The peaceful and beautifully modernised farmhouse offers comfortable and friendly accommodation, one room even has a four poster bed. Excellent farm fresh food, including packed lunches on request. This is a mixed working farm of 55 acres, within easy reach of many places of interest. Batemans (NT) home of Rudyard Kipling 1 mile.

Open Easter-Oct.
4 bedrooms (2 twin inc. 1 ens. WC; 2 double inc. 1 ens. ☕/WC), 2☕, 2WCs.
⚬ ETB Listed
Prices:B&B £14–17.50. EM £8. ⚬ rates.

HARTFIELD
Map 3 A3

Stairs Farmhouse, High Street, Hartfield TN7 4RJ
✆ (0892) 770793   Mrs G. Pring

This carefully modernised 17th-century farmhouse and tea rooms, retaining various period features, has views over open countryside but is close to several pubs serving excellent bar and restaurant meals. Breakfast is from home bred and organic ingredients produced mainly on the farm. The farm is on the B2110, off the A22 and A26. Pooh Bridge 1 mile. Ashdown Forest 2 miles. Hever Castle 5 miles. Wakehurst Place, Chartwell and Penshurst Place 7 miles. Gatwick/M25 30 mins.

Open all year
3 bedrooms (1 twin; 1 double; 1 family), 2🛁, 3WCs.
🐾 ⅍ ETB Listed Commended
Prices: B&B £18–30.

HEATHFIELD   Map 3 A3
Little Stonehurst Farm, Pottens Mill Lane, Broad Oak, Heathfield TN21 8UA
✆ (0435) 862569

A comfortable old Sussex farmhouse on a 72-acre arable farm in the back of beyond, this is the place to come for a restful holiday. The surrounding countryside is peaceful and very picturesque. Little Stonehurst is situated north of the A265 at Broadoak, east of Heathfield, and its location makes it a good base for visiting historic sites in both Sussex and Kent. Batemans 6 miles. Eastbourne 18 miles. Bodiam Castle 15 miles. Sissinghurst Gardens 25 miles.

Open April-Sept.
3 bedrooms (2 twin; 1 single), 1🛁, 3WCs.
🐾 ⅍ 🐕(bitches only)
Prices: B&B £14.50, weekly £95. 🐾 rates.

LEWES   Map 3 A3
Camoys Farmhouse, Barcombe, Lewes BN8 5BH
✆ (0273) 400662   Mrs K. Cornwell

A warm welcome awaits you at this modern spacious farmhouse with outstanding views from every window. The farm is off the A26, north of Lewes in a quiet location. Disabled facilities include ramps, wide doors and handrails. Camoys has 860 acres, mainly dairy, with corn, blackcurrants and sheep. Lewes 4 miles. Bluebell Railway 5 miles. Ashdown Forest 8 miles. South Downs, Sheffield Park Gardens, Nymans within easy reach.

Open Jan-Nov.
3 bedrooms (1 twin ens. 🛁/WC; 1 double; 1 family), 1🛁, 2WCs.
♿ 🐾 ⅍ ETB 👑 👑
Prices: B&B £16–20, weekly £100–125. 🐾 rates.

ROBERTSBRIDGE   Map 3 A3
Parsonage Farm, Salehurst, Robertsbridge TN32 5PJ
✆ (0580) 880446   Mrs M. Hoad

Parsonage Farm stands in a quiet hamlet just off the A21, 6 miles north of Battle. The 15th-century farmhouse, with beams and panelling, is on a family run farm of 400 acres consisting of hops, arable and beef. Enjoy good home cooking in peaceful rural surroundings. Bodiam Castle 3 miles. Battle Abbey 5 miles. South Coast 12 miles.

Open Nov-Aug. Closed Xmas
2 bedrooms (1 twin; 1 double), 1🛁, 1WC.
🐾 ETB Member
Prices: B&B £14, weekly £92. EM £7. Weekly B&B plus EM £135. 🐾 rates.

Self-Catering
UCKFIELD   Map 3 A3
Brownings Farm, Blackboys, Uckfield, East Sussex TN22 5HG
✆ (0825) 890338   Alison Wright

This 350-acre farm stands on the edge of the High Weald Area of Outstanding Natural Beauty. Brownings is 3 miles east of Uckfield (B2102) and its position in the middle of East Sussex offers good access to the Sussex coast, the South Downs and Ashdown Forest as well as an attractive environment for a quiet farm holiday amidst the beautiful wooded countryside. Accommodation is in six self-catering cottages including a converted oast house and stables, sleeping 2 to 8 people. Cots, highchairs, games room, swimming pool and craft workshops available.

Open all year
♿ 🐾
Prices: £135–215 per week low season. £235–385 per week high season.

ESSEX

BRAINTREE
Map 3 A2

Spicers Farm, Rotten End, Wethersfield, Braintree CM7 4AL
✆ (0371) 851021   Mrs Delia Douse

Spicers is a mixed farm with arable crops and animals set in a quiet rural area designated of special landscape value. The attractive farmhouse provides comfortable accommodation, all rooms have TV, tea/coffee facilities and lovely views. From Braintree take B1053 to Shalford, then follow signs to Rotten End. Boydells Farm (open milking of sheep, goats and cows) 1 mile. Braintree and working silk museum 5 miles. Colne Valley Steam Railway 5 miles.

Open all year
3 bedrooms (2 twin inc. 1 ens. ⋔/WC; 1 double), 1🛏, 2WCs.
⌂(4) ETB 👑 👑
Prices: B&B £15–18, weekly £94.50–113. ⌂ rates.

CHIPPING ONGAR
Map 3 A2

Bumbles, Moreton Road, Chipping Ongar CM5 0EZ
✆ (0277) 362695   Mrs J. Withey

Bumbles is a large cottage built in the 18th century, located 2 miles north of Chipping Ongar off the B184. Modernised for comfort and warmth, we have retained oak beams, inglenook and log fires in winter. Bumbles is now run as a smallholding with free range hens, sheep and a livery yard. Close by is Greensted Church, the oldest wooden church in the world, and Northweald Airfield, which features Europe's largest outdoor market on Saturdays.

Open all year
3 twin bedrooms, 1🛏, 1 ⋔, 2WCs.
⌂(12) ⌯ ETB Listed
Prices: B&B £13–16, weekly £85–100.

FORDHAM
Map 3 B2

Kings Vineyard, Fordham, Nr Colchester CO6 3NY
✆ (0206) 240377   Mrs Inge Tweed

At Kings Vineyard you can relax in the peace and beauty of the Essex countryside. The farmhouse offers fine views across the Colne Valley. The farm, which supports a flock of rare sheep, lies 6 miles west of Colchester(A604). An excellent base for walking or touring, Essex Way is adjacent to the farm, Dedham Vale 10 miles, the ports of Harwich and Felixstowe 22 miles. Traditional or vegetarian breakfast provided. Cot available.

Open all year
3 bedrooms (1 twin; 1 double ens. ☞/WC; 1 family ens. ℍ/WC), 1➡, 1ℍ, 2WCs.
⌂ ETB ⚘ ⚘ Commended
Prices: B&B £16–20. ⌂ rates.

MARGARET RODING   Map 3 A2

Greys, Ongar Road, Margaret Roding, Nr Great Dunmow CM6 1QR
✆ (024531) 509

Formerly two farmworkers cottages, Greys is now an attractive beamed house with a large garden, pleasantly situated on the family arable and sheep farm. Just off the A1060, 8 miles from Chelmsford, the village is one of eight Roding villages. There is much to explore in the countryside among the winding streams and lanes around the Rodings: pretty villages Finchingfield and the Bardfields 15 miles, Thaxted, Saffron Walden, Greensted Church. Afternoon teas provided.

Open most of the year
3 bedrooms (1 twin; 2 double), 1➡, 2WCs.
⌂(10) ⚥ ETB Listed
Prices: B&B from £16.

SAFFRON WALDEN   Map 3 A2

Duddenhoe End Farm, Nr Saffron Walden
✆ (0763) 838258   The Foster Family

Duddenhoe End Farm is situated in a quiet rural area, a mile from the B1039 midway between Royston and Saffron Walden. The attractive farmhouse is 17th century and has a wealth of beams and inglenook fireplaces making it a delightful base for touring the area. Duxford Air Museum 6

> Reduced rates are sometimes available. Ask your host about weekend breaks.

miles. Wimpole Hall Home Farm Trust (Rare Breeds) 14 miles. Stansted Airport 12 miles.

Closed Xmas and New Year
3 bedrooms (1 twin ens. ☞/WC; 2 double inc. 1 ens. ℍ/WC, 1 ens. ☞/WC).
⌂(10) ⚥ ETB ⚘ ⚘Highly Commended
Prices: B&B £17.50–20.

Parsonage Farm, Arkesden, Nr.Saffron Walden
✆ (0799) 550306   Mrs D. Forster

This lovely Victorian farmhouse stands in the centre of a very attractive small village. Arkesden is southwest of Saffron Walden, off the B1038 Newport-Buntingford road. The house is surrounded by mature gardens with a hard tennis court. The farm is arable but a few pets are kept. A quiet setting for short breaks. Cot, highchair and children's games available. Audley End Mansion 5 miles. Duxford War Museum 8 miles. Saffron Walden 5 miles. Cambridge 18 miles.

Open all year
1 family suite (2 rooms ens. ☞/WC), 1➡, 1WC.
⌂ ⚥ 🐾 ETB ⚘ ⚘
Prices: B&B £15–18, weekly £100. ⌂ rates.

Rockells Farm, Duddenhoe End, Saffron Walden
✆ (0763) 838053

Rockells Farm is an arable farm, but with some farm animals, in a beautiful corner of Essex, off the B1039 5 miles west of Saffron Walden. Several footpaths and typical secluded rural villages close by make this a good area to explore at a leisurely pace. Rockells has a private lake for coarse fishing.

Open all year
3 bedrooms (1 twin ens. ☞/WC; 1 family ens. ℍ/WC; 1 single ens. ☞/WC).
♿ ⌂ 🐾 ETB ⚘ ⚘Approved
Prices: B&B £16–18. EM £6. ⌂ rates.

WIX

Map 3 B2

New Farm House, Spinnell's Lane, Wix, Manningtree C011 2UJ

✆ (0255) 870365
Fax (0255) 870837

Mrs H.P. Mitchell

Off the A120, 7 miles west of historic Harwich, stands New Farm. The extensive modern farm-house is part of a 50-acre arable farm, offering all the comforts of a hotel but combined with the delights of good home cooking. Packed lunches by request. Two ground floor rooms specially equipped for partially disabled. Cot, highchair, games and child's play area available. Centrally located, Wix offers easy access to the many points of interest in the region. Constable country 10 miles. Beth Chatto Gardens 7 miles. Colchester 12 miles.

Open all year
12 bedrooms (3 twin inc 2 ens. ⋔/WC;1 double ens. ⋔/WC; 5 family inc. 3 ens. ⋔/WC;3 single inc. 1 ens. ⋔/WC), 2➡, 3WCs.
& ⋒ ✝ ETB ♕ ♕ ♕Approved
Prices: B&B £17.50–21, weekly £110.25–132.30. EM £9.50. Weekly B&B plus EM £176.75–198.80. ⋒ rates. ✝ £0.50 per night.

GLOUCESTERSHIRE

BOURTON-ON-THE-WATER. Map 2 B2

Hill Farm, Little Rissington, Cheltenham
GL54 2ND
℃ (0451) 820380 Mrs E. Sweeting

The attractive Cotswold stone house of Hill Farm
is set in its own grounds of 3 acres. The retired
farmer keeps a market garden. Groundfloor
bedroom available, plus cot, highchair and children's games. The farm lies 2 miles east of Bourton-on-the-Water (A429) at Little Rissington.
Model Village, Car Museum and Bird Land 2
miles. Duck Valley and Rare Breeds Farm Park 7
miles.

Open all year
4 bedrooms (2 twin; 2 family inc. 1 ens. 🛁/WC),
2🛏, 2WCs.
🏠 ⛏ ETB 👑 👑
Prices: B&B £13–18. 🏠 rates.

Upper Farm, Clapton-on-the-Hill,
Bourton-on-the-Water GL54 2LG
℃ (0451) 820453

This 17th-century farmhouse on a 140-acre
mixed farm enjoys a beautiful hill position with
uninterrupted views across Windrush Valley. The
house has been lovingly restored with individually designed rooms. Upper Farm is situated off
the A429 south of Bourton. Bourton Birdland and
model village 2 miles. Northleach historic wool
town 4 miles. Stow 6 miles. Burford 8 miles.

Open Mar-Nov.
5 bedrooms (2 twin inc. 1 ens. 🛁/WC; 2 double

inc. 1 ens. 🛁/WC; 1 single), 2🛏, 2WCs.
🏠(5) ✂ ETB 👑 👑
Prices: B&B £14–17.50. 🏠 rates.

CHELTENHAM Map 2 B2

Butlers Hill Farm, Cockleford, Cowley,
Cheltenham GL53 9NW
℃ (0242) 870455 Mrs Bridget Brickell

A warm welcome awaits you at this modern spacious farmhouse. We are a working farm with
beef cattle and sheep in a peaceful location in the
Churn Valley, south of Cheltenham off the A435.
Good home cooking and log fires in winter. It is an
ideal centre for touring the Cotswolds. Chedworth Roman Villa 4 miles. Cheltenham 5 miles.
Cirencester 10 miles. Gloucester Cathedral 10
miles. Rare Breed Farm 14 miles.

Open all year
2 bedrooms (1 twin; 1 double), 1🛏, 1WC.
🏠(6) ETB 👑 👑
Prices: B&B £15. EM £7.

Hartbury Farm, Chedworth, Cheltenham
GL54 4AL
℃ (0285) 720350

Off the A429 north of Cirencester stands this attractive 17th-century farmhouse in peaceful
countryside. Enjoy good home cooking while you
explore the beautiful Cotswold villages. A Roman
Villa is just 2 miles along a footpath from the farm
(5 miles by road). Cot, highchair and games provided. One ground floor bedroom.

Open Apr-Oct.
4 bedrooms (1 twin ens. 🛁/WC; 1 double; 1
family; 1 single), 1🛏, 1WC.
🏠 ⛏ ETB Listed
Prices: B&B £12–13. EM £7.50. 🏠 rates.

See STOP PRESS
for more farms

The Original Yew Tree, Little Shurdington, Cheltenham GL51 5TY
✆ (0242) 862022 Geoffrey & Margaret Craven
Fax (0242) 862047

A couple of miles south of Cheltenham this Grade 2 listed farmhouse is found in a quiet hamlet, just below the Cotswold escarpment. With the location so peaceful and secluded, the hospitality warm and welcoming, the Original Yew Tree is a good choice for a touring base. Cirencester, Gloucester and the Malvern Hills all within easy reach.

Open all year
2 double bedrooms inc. 1 ens. 🛁/WC, 1 priv. 🛁/WC. 👪
Prices: B&B £17.50–20.

CIRENCESTER Map 2 B2

College Farm, Ampney St Mary, Nr Cirencester GL7 5SW
✆ (0285) 851382

Enjoy a stay on a friendly dairy farm, with cats dogs, horses, free range hens and chicks. Good farmhouse food is provided, as well as afternoon teas and packed lunches on request. Cot, swings, sand pit and toys for children. The farm is 4 miles east of Cirencester, take the A417 Fairford road and turn left past Ampney St Peter by the Red Lion. Bibury 3 miles. Cotswold Water Park 4 miles. Burford 12 miles.

Open all year
3 bedrooms (1 twin; 1 double; 1 family), 1🛁, 1WC.
👪(5) 🚭 ETB ♛♛
Prices: B&B £12.50, weekly £87.50. EM £7.50, weekly £140. 👪 rates.

DYMOCK Map 2 A2

Lower House Farm, Kempley, Dymock
✆ (053185) 301 Mrs G.M. Bennett

Less than 3 miles north of the M50, Jct3, Lower House Farm provides a haven of tranquility. The 130-acre dairy farm borders on a 1300-acre wood with a fishing lake and delightful walks. At the farmhouse, with authentic beams, you can enjoy good home cooking. You are welcome to watch the milking, collect eggs, or meander along footpaths and ride ponies. Golf course 2 miles. Vineyards, Falconry Centre, Butterfly Farm, Victorian Museum, all within 5 mile radius. Packed lunches and afternoon teas on request. Cot, highchair and play area.

Open Apr-Dec.
2 bedrooms (1 twin ens. 🚿/WC; 1 double ens. 🚿), 1🛁, 1WC.
👪 🐕
Prices: B&B £12.50–15. EM £8–10. 👪 rates.

GLOUCESTER Map 2 A2

Gilbert's, Gilbert's Lane, Brookthorpe, Nr Gloucester
✆ /Fax (0452) 812364 Mrs Jenny Beer

Gilbert's, in previous centuries a manorhouse, farmhouse and tenements, is now a listed building treasured for the quality of restoration as well as 400 years of history. The surrounding small organic farm with livestock, including bees, fruit and vegetables, demonstrate a sensitivity and commitment to the environment. Gilbert's is off the A4173 south of Gloucester, it lies beneath the dramatic Western escarpment of the Cotswold Hills in the Severn Vale, with views of the Forest of Dean. Fine walking country. All rooms have TV and telephone. Hot drinks readily available.

Open all year
4 bedrooms all ens. ♿/🛁/WC (1 twin; 2 double;
1 single).
♿ ETB ⚜ ⚜Highly Commended
Prices: B&B from £22, weekly £139. ♿ rates.

Hill Farm, Wainlode Lane, Norton, Gloucester GL2 9LN
℡ (0452) 730351

This 14th-century partially thatched farmhouse
offers every comfort and excellent food, packed
lunches and afternoon teas available on request.
Licensed. Hill Farm lies off the A38 Gloucester-
Tewkesbury road, and its central location makes
it ideal for exploring the Malvern Hills, Forest of
Dean, the Wye Valley and the Cotswolds.

Closed Xmas and New Year
4 bedrooms (1 twin; 3 doubles inc. 2 ens.
♿/WC),3WCs.
♿ETB ⚜ ⚜ ⚜
Prices: B&B £15–22.50, weekly £105–157.50.
EM £10. Weekly B&B plus EM £175–227.50. ♿
rates.

MORETON-IN-THE-MARSH   Map 2 B2

New Farm, Dorn, Moreton-in-the-Marsh
℡ (0608) 50782   Mrs C.M. Righton

This 250-acre dairy farm is in the quiet hamlet of
Dorn, a mile north of Moreton-in-the-Marsh on the
A429. In the farmhouse dining room, with its impressive Cotswold stone fireplace, you can taste
good country cooking and hot crispy bread. Well
placed for touring the Cotswolds. Bourton-on-
the-Water 10 miles. Chedworth Roman Villa 12
miles. Stratford 16 miles. Blenheim Palace 20
miles.

Closed Xmas
3 bedrooms (1 twin; 2 double ens. 🛁/WC), 3🐾,
3WCs.
♿(3) 🐾ETB Commended
Prices:B&B £15, weekly £98. EM £10. ♿ rates.

Park Farm, Blockley, Nr Moreton-in-the-Marsh GL56 9TA
℡ (0386) 700266

This 16th-century farmhouse has been carefully
modernised for full comfort, while retaining all its
old world charm. Here you can relax in the gardens and enjoy beautiful panoramic views.
Packed lunches on request. Cot, highchair, small
bed, swing provided. Park Farm is a mixed working hill farm of sheep and cattle. It stands off the
B4479, just west of Moreton-in-the-Marsh (A44).
Batsford Arboretum 2 miles. Hidcote Gardens 4
miles. Cotswold Farm Park 8 miles. Stratford 16
miles.

Open most of the year
4 bedrooms (1 twin; 1 double; 2 single), 1🐾,
2WCs.
♿ 🐾 ETB Listed
Prices: B&B £14, weekly £85. ♿ rates.

STOW-ON-THE-WOLD   Map 2 B2

Banks Farm, Upper Oddington, Moreton-in-the-Marsh GL56 0XG
℡ (0451) 830475   Mrs F.J. Adams

The farm is a working mixed farm. The Cotswold
farmhouse is situated in an elevated position in
the centre of the village of Oddington, 3 miles
east of Stow-in-the-Wold (A436). All rooms enjoy
lovely views over fields to the 11th-century
church. Banks Farm is centrally situated for
exploring the Cotswold villages. Bourton-on-the-
Water 7 miles. Sudeley Castle 14 miles. Blenheim
Palace 15 miles. Good English breakfast and
bedtime drink. Tea/coffee facilities in bedrooms.

Open April-Oct.
2 bedrooms (1 twin; 1 double), 1🐾, 1WC.
♿(10) ETB Listed Approved
Prices: B&B £15.75–17, weekly £105–110.

Eastern Hill Farm, Naunton, Nr Cheltenham GL54 3AF
℡ (0451) 850716

Relax in a traditional Cotswold farmhouse situated in its own gardens and lawns, in a peaceful
quiet location off the B4068 under 5 miles southwest of Stow-in-the-Wold. The farm is arable, with
stabling and grazing for horses. Afternoon teas
provided. Ground floor bedroom, cot and highchair available. Naunton Downs Golf Club (opening March 1993) 1 mile. Cotswold Farm Park 2
miles.

Open all year
3 bedrooms (1 twin/family; 2 double) 1🛁, 2🐾,
3WCs.

& ఉ ⚹ ETB Listed
Prices: B&B £16–17. ఉ rates.

STROUD
Map 2 A2

Down Barn Farmhouse, The Camp, Stroud GL6 7EY

✆ (0425) 812853 John & Anita Morley

Located in peaceful countryside off the B4070 4 miles south of the A417 Gloucester-Cirencester road, the farmhouse is on a smallholding with Pygmy goats and other small animals. The farm is in excellent walking country through NT woods and the Slad Valley, and its position puts all the attractions of the Cotswolds within easy reach. All accommodation at Down Barn Farm is on the ground floor and suitable for mobility disabled. Cot provided.

Closed December
3 bedrooms (2 twin; 1 double) 1➔, 1WC.
& ఉ ⚹ ETB Listed
Prices: B&B from £14.50. ఉ rates.

Elmtree Farm, Frocester, Nr Stonehouse GL10 3TG

✆ (0453) 823274 Mrs J. Pain

A warm welcome awaits you at this attractive 250-year-old farmhouse, with inglenook and beams. Elmtree is a 200-acre dairy farm in the small village of Frocester, west of Stroud (M5,Jct13), ideally sited for exploring the Cotswolds and the upper reaches of the River Severn. Slimbridge Wildfowl Trust 3 miles. Berkeley Centre 6 miles. Westonbirt Arboretum 6 miles.

Open April-Oct.
3 bedrooms (2 twin; 1 double), 1➔, 1WC.
ఉ(10) ✻ ETB ♔ ♔Commended
Prices: B&B £14–15 single. £25–26 double.

Nastend Farm, Nastend GL10 3RS

✆ (0453) 822300 Mrs Jackie Guilding

Nastend is a 41-acre mixed dairy farm lying west of Stroud off A419 (M5,Jct13). Guests are welcome to watch the farmwork. In the oakbeamed farmhouse Mrs Guilding provides excellent home cooking. Outside you can relax by the

swimming pool in the large garden. Packed lunches on request. Cot, highchair, swings available. Gloucester 8 miles. Slimbridge Wildfowl Trust 6 miles. Berkeley Castle 8 miles.

Closed Xmas and New Year
3 bedrooms (1 twin; 1 double; 1 family ens. ➔), 1➔, 1WC.
ఉ ETB ♔ ♔
Prices: B&B £13–15.50, weekly £91–108.50. EM £8. Weekly B&B plus EM £147–164.50. ఉ rates.

WINCHCOMBE
Map 2 B2

Postlip Hall Farm, Winchcombe GL54 5AQ

✆ (0242) 603351 Valerie Albutt

You will enjoy the warm and friendly atmosphere of Postlip Hall Farm, a family run farm of 270 acres comprising mainly beef and sheep. Located off the B4632, northeast of Cheltenham, this large comfortable farmhouse has panoramic views of the outstanding scenery from every window. Packed lunches on request. Ideal as a centre for touring the Cotswolds, Stratford, Bath and Warwick Castle. Sudeley Castle 2 miles. Golf course 1 mile.

Closed Xmas
3 bedrooms (1 twin;1 double; 1 family ens. ฿/WC), 2➔, 2WCs.
ఉ ✻ ETB ♔ ♔ Commended
Prices: B&B £14.50–20.

Sudeley Hill Farm, Winchcombe, Cheltenham GL54 5JB

✆ (0242) 602344 Mrs B. Scudamore

Sudeley Hill Farm, situated off the B4632, northeast of Cheltenham, has an attractive 15th-century listed farmhouse with log fires, a large garden and outstanding views across the countryside. This working mixed farm covers 800 acres. Sudeley Castle is only half a mile away, and all the attractions of the Cotswold Hills are within easy reach. Cot and highchair provided.

Closed Xmas
4 bedrooms (1 twin; 1 double; 1 family ens.

KEY TO SYMBOLS

Bath	฿
Shower	฿
Bathroom	➔
Disabled Guest Facilities	&
No Smoking	✻
Children Welcome	ఉ
Dogs by Arrangement	⚹

➿/WC; 1 single), 1🔧, 1WC.
🏡 ETB 🟣 🟣Highly Commended
Prices: B&B from £17.50.

WOTTON-UNDER-EDGE   Map 2 A2
Under-the-Hill House, Adey's Lane, Wotton-under-Edge GL12 7LY
✆ (0453) 842557   Mrs K.P.Forster

Under-the-Hill House, just ten minutes walk from the centre of Wotton-under-Edge, is a listed, predominantly Queen Anne, building. The small farm has suckler cows and calves, amongst which are some very rare Welsh Belted cattle and their calves (the ancient cattle of Wales). Cot and highchair provided. From this attractive base you can tour the Cotswolds, Cheltenham, Bath, Bristol and Gloucester. Berkeley Castle and Slimbridge Wildfowl Trust 10 miles.

Open Easter-Oct.
4 bedrooms (1 twin; 1 double ens. 🛁/WC; 1 family; 1 single), 1🔧, 1WC. 🏡
Prices: B&B £14.50–16.50, weekly £101.50. 🏡 rates.

Self-Catering
CIRENCESTER   Map 2 B2
Old Mill Farm, Poole Keynes, Cirencester GL7 6ED
✆ (0285) 821225   Contact: Mrs C Hazell, Ermin House Farm, Syde, Cheltenham GL53 9PN

Accommodation is available in 4 cottages, with 1–4 bedrooms, sleeping 2–7. The cottages are converted stone farm buildings set in the farmyard. Ground floor rooms, cot and highchair available. Old Mill Farm is mainly arable and sheep, close to the River Thames. Within a mile is the Cotswold Water Park with fishing, sailing, water-skiing, jet skiing, wind surfing and nature reserves. Leave Cirencester southwards by the Somerset Keynes road, turn off to Ewen. Old Mill Farm lies off the Ewen-Poole Keynes road, under 5 miles from Cirencester.

Open all year
🐾 ETB££££Commended
Prices: weekly £120–395.

STROUD   Map 2 A2
Ruscombe Farm, Stroud GL6 6EG
✆ (0453) 764780   Mrs L.S. Charley

Ruscombe Farm has a 17th-century Cotswold stone farmhouse and outbuildings (Grade 2 listed), with 2 self-catering units of 2 and 3 bedrooms, sleeping 4–5. The farm has beef cattle and horses and stands in a picturesque valley with a stream and small lake, 3 miles northwest of Stroud. An ideal base for a touring holiday of Bath, Cheltenham, Gloucester, Forest of Dean and Cotswold villages.

Open all year
🐾 ETB££££Commended
Prices: weekly £145–250.

HAMPSHIRE

CADNAM
Map 2 B3

Broad Oak Farm, School Lane, Minstead
✆ (0703) 812627

Take a holiday in the New Forest, and enjoy the tranquil atmosphere on this quiet friendly working animal farm. Broad Oak Farm lies 8 miles west of Southampton (M27, Jct 1/A31) at West Minstead. Beaulieu Motor Museum, Paultons Park and the cathedral towns of Winchester and Salisbury within easy reach.

Open all year
2 bedrooms (1 double; 1 family), 1🛏, 2WCs.
🐾 🛏
Prices: B&B £12.50, weekly £77. 🐾 rates.

Budd's Farm, Winsor Road, Winsor, Cadnam, Southampton SO4 2HN
✆ (0703) 812381

A warm welcome awaits you at our 18th-century thatched farmhouse, fully modernised for comfort but retaining its period charm. This working dairy farm is situated west of Southampton (M27, Jct1). Broadlands 5 miles. Southampton 8 miles. Beaulieu Motor Museum 10 miles. Winchester 18 miles. Salisbury 18 miles.

Open Apr-Oct.
2 bedrooms (1 twin; 1 family), 1 guest 🛏, 1WC.
🐾 ⚔ ETB 👑 👑
Prices: B&B £15-16. 🐾 rates.

DUMMER
Map 2 B3

Oakdown Farm, Dummer, Basingstoke RG23 7LR
✆ (0256) 397218   Mrs M. Hutton

Oakdown Farm Bungalow is in the yard of Oakdown Farm, with a direct line to the house. The farm produces sheep, a few cattle and combinable crops for seed. Easy access Heathrow, the farm is located off the A33 (M3, Jct7 then A30/ A33), a mile from Dummer village. Wayfarers Walk 200 yds. 2 Golf Courses within a mile.

Open all year
3 bedrooms (2 twin; 1 double), 1🛏, 2WCs.
🐾(10) ETB 👑
Prices: B&B £12.50–15, weekly £90–105. 🐾 rates.

NEW MILTON
Map 2 B3

Redwing Farm, Pitmore Lane, Sway SO41 6BN
✆ (0590) 683319   Mrs J. Dowson

Guest accommodation is in the original New Forest cottage section of the farmhouse, with beamed rooms and modern facilities. The farm has pedigree beef show animals. Redwing is less than 3 miles from Lymington. Good forest walks surround the farm. Beaulieu, Broadlands, Romsey Abbey, Salisbury and Winchester 30–35 miles.

Open all year
4 bedrooms (2 double; 2 single), 3🛏, 3WCs. ⚔
Prices: B&B £15, weekly £105.

Valesmoor Farm, Holmsley Road, Wootton, New Milton

✆ (0425) 614487   Mrs C. Marshallsay

This elegant pre-war house is set in its own attractive grounds, across the road from the New Forest. We offer generously sized bedrooms and a friendly informal service – as much like home as possible. Cot available. Valesmoor Farm is under 3 miles from New Milton, take A35 Lyndhurst-Christchurch road, then B3058 signed New Milton/Wootton. Sea 4 miles, yacht harbours Lymington and Christchurch 6–8 miles.

Open Apr-Sept.
4 bedrooms (1 twin; 1 double; 1 family; 1 single), 1🛁, 1WC. 🐕
Prices: B&B £14–16. weekly £88.20–100.80. EM by arrangement. 🐕 rates.

PETERSFIELD   Map 2 B3

The Bailiff's Cottage, Home Farm, Hollycombe, Liphook GU30 7LR

✆ (0428) 722171   Jim & Angela Jenner

There are beautiful views over the Millard valley from this 300-year-old tile hung cottage on the Hants/Sussex border. The 400-acre farm is arable, and sheep. Lambing is in March/April. The cottage is attractively furnished with every comfort, log fires in winter, tea/coffee facilities in rooms. Home Farm is under 2 miles from Liphook (A3 north of Petersfield). Numerous attractions within 25 miles – Chichester, Fishbourne Roman Palace, Arundel Castle, Goodwood Racecourse, Portsmouth.

Open all year
2 bedrooms (1 twin/double; 1 single), 1🛁, 1WC. 🐕 ⊁
Prices: B&B £14.50–16.50, weekly £93. 🐕 rates.

Coldhayes, Steepmarsh, Nr Petersfield

✆ (0703) 892114   Mr & Mrs B.L. Blacker

Coldhayes offers a comfortable stay and good farmhouse cooking in a large Victorian house. The surrounding farm is mainly grazing with beef cattle, and some arable, located 2 miles from Petersfield south off the A3. Winchester, Chichester, Goodwood Racecourse and Portsmouth 20 miles.

Open all year
3 bedrooms (1 twin adj. 🛁/WC; 2 double adj. 🛁/WC), 1🛁, 2WCs.
🐕 🐴
Prices: B&B £20, EM £10. 🐕 rates.

Mizzards Farm, Rogate, Petersfield GU31 5HS

✆ (0730) 821656   Mrs J.C. Francis

This large 16th-century farmhouse is set in 13 acres beside the River Rother. Interior is beautifully furnished, with a lovely vaulted dining room. Guests have use of large lounge, covered swimming pool and huge gardens. The varied countryside around Mizzards Farm, including the South Downs, provides a choice of excellent walks. The farm lies 4 miles from Midhurst, turn south off A272 Petersfield-Midhurst road at Rogate. Goodwood, Petworth House, Arundel and other historic houses close by. Polo at Cowdray Park.

Closed Xmas
3 bedrooms (1 twin ens. 🛁/WC; 2 double ens. 🛁/WC)
🐕(6) ⊁
Prices: B&B £20–34.

Twentyways Farm, Ramsdean, Petersfield GU32 1RX

✆ (073087) 606   Mrs Maureen M. Farmer

Twentyways Farm has 20 acres with a pedigree flock of Texel sheep, 3 horses, a donkey and cats and dogs. Accommodation is in a converted 17th-century barn. Take A272 west from Petersfield and turn left at Stroud for Ramsdean. Petersfield 2 miles. Queen Elizabeth Country Park 2 miles. Chichester 15 miles.

Open all year
2 twin bedrooms ens. 🛁/WC. ⊁
Prices: B&B £20, weekly £125–140.

RINGWOOD Map 2 B3

Dunain Farm, Hangersley, Ringwood BH24 3JN
✆ (0425) 472611 Mrs A. Griffin

You will find a friendly and homely atmosphere in this secluded ranch-style bungalow standing on a small working animal farm. Situated on high ground the farm has superb views and is only a short walk from open New Forest. Tea/coffee facilities and TV in bedrooms. Dunain Farm is 2 miles from Ringwood, take the A31 towards Southampton, turn off to Hangersley/North Poulner. Owl Sanctuary 1 mile. Breamore House, jousting and Heavy Horse Centre 5 miles.

Open Mar-Oct.
2 bedrooms (1 twin; 1 double), 1🛁, 1WC.
👪 🐕
Prices: B&B £12–16, weekly £72–96. 👪 rates.

ROMSEY Map 2 B3

Hatt Farm, Mottisfont, Romsey SO51 0LH
✆ (0794) 40237

This 700-acre working dairy and arable farm is set in beautiful countryside in the NT village of Mottisfont. Comfortable accommodation is available in the old and interesting farmhouse with use of the large pretty garden. Hatt Farm is 4 miles north of Romsey, on the B3084 (B3057). Brashfield-Hillier Arboretum and Gardens 3 miles.

Open all year
4 bedrooms (2 twin/family; 2 single), 2🛁, 2WCs.
👪 🐕 ETB Listed
Prices: B&B £13.50. 👪 rates.

Pyesmead Farm, Plaitford, Romsey
✆ (0794) 23386 Mrs C. Pybus

At Pyesmead our modern farmhouse is built to a traditional design. We are a family run stock farm, our main enterprise is beef, but with a few sheep. Our own lakes are stocked for coarse fishing. The New Forest is 100yds away, and with Romsey only 5 miles there are many places of interest within a short drive, eg. Broadlands House, Salisbury Cathedral.

Closed Xmas
2 bedrooms (1 twin; 1 double), 1🛁.
👪 🚭 ETB Listed
Prices: B&B £12–16, EM £6. 👪 rates.

SOUTHAMPTON Map 2 B3

Park Farm, Stoneham Lane, Eastleigh, Southampton
✆ (0703) 612960 Angela M. Fright

At Park Farm you will find a converted coaching stable in a lovely rural setting. Accommodation is very comfortable with tea/coffee facilities and TV in all rooms. Good home cooking, packed lunches on request and vegetarian and special diets catered for. There is coarse fishing in the farm's own secluded lake, adjacent to 200-year-old Capability Brown landscaped lakes, all well stocked. The farm is under 2 miles from Eastleigh, 800 yds from M27, Jct 5. Southampton, Winchester and Romsey 15 mins.

Open all year
4 bedrooms (1 twin ens. 🚿/🛁/WC; 1 double; 2 family), 4🛁, 2WCs.
👪 🐕 ETB Commended
Prices: B&B £15–17.50, weekly £77–90. EM £10. 👪 rates.

Self-Catering

PETERSFIELD   Map 2 B3

Woodside Farm Annexe, Gosport Road, Privett, Nr Alton GU34 3NJ
℡ (073088) 359   Miss Crisp & Mrs Newman

Accommodation is available in a 2 bedroomed annexe, sleeps 4, to the Georgian farmhouse on Woodside Farm. Guests are welcome to walk anywhere on the 208-acre ring-roaded farm. The annexe is well-furnished, fully equipped, comfortable and quiet. Cot and highchair available. Wheelchair access. The farm drive is off the A32, 4 miles north of A272 crossroads. Chawton, Petersfield and Alton 6 miles. Selbourne 8 miles.

Open Apr-Oct.
♿ ♞
Prices: weekly £120–210. ♞ £10.

HEREFORD AND WORCESTER

ALCESTER
Map 2 B2

Sambourne Hall Farm, Sambourne, Nr Redditch B96 6NZ
✆ (052785) 2151

Sambourne Hall Farm is in a peaceful village a mile from the A435, between Redditch and Alcester. The farm comprises 500 acres, mainly arable with some beef and horses. The attractive mid 17th-century farmhouse has retained original features such as the wealth of beams and log fires. Coughton Court (NT) 1 mile. Ragley Hall 3 miles. Stratford-upon-Avon 10 miles.

Open all year
2 bedrooms (1 family ens. ⌂/WC; 1 double ens. ⌂/WC), 1🛏.
⚗ 🛏 ETB ♛ ♛Commended
Prices: B&B £18–35.

BROADWAY
Map 2 B2

Manor Farm, Wormington
✆ (0386) 73302

This 15th-century Tudor house boasts leaded casements in the sitting room, a stone inglenook in the hall, slabs of Welsh slate on the floors, and even a cheese room surviving from its time as a dairy farm. Manor Farm has 300 acres of arable and beef off the B4632, between Broadway and Cheltenham, making it ideally situated for touring the Cotswolds. Broadway 4 miles. Stratford-on-Avon 18 miles.

Open all year
3 bedrooms (1 twin ens. ⌂; 2 double inc. 1 ens. ⌂/WC), 1🛏, 2WCs.
⚗🛏 ETB ♛ ♛Commended
Prices: B&B from £15 single person, from £28 double room. ⚗ rates.

See STOP PRESS
for more farms

BROMSGROVE
Map 2 B1

Home Farm, Mill Lane, Wildmoor, Bromsgrove B61 0BX
✆ (0527) 74964
Ray Lees

This pleasant farmhouse stands on a small-holding down a country lane in open country off the A491 near M5, Jct4. There are attractive views from the house and this quiet spot makes an excellent base for exploring the area. Ground floor bedroom available. Worcestershire Walk 2 miles. Country Park 2 miles. Canals 6 miles. Avoncraft Museum 4 miles. Black Country Museum 10 miles.

Open all year
6 bedrooms (3 twin inc. 1 ens. ⌂/WC; 1 double; 2 single), 3🛏, 4WCs. ⚗
Prices: B&B £12.50–15.

Lower Bentley Farm, Lower Bentley Lane, Lower Bentley, Bromsgrove B60 4JB
✆ (0527) 821286
Mrs C. Gibbs

A warm welcome awaits you at this Victorian farmhouse in peaceful countryside. An ideal base for a holiday, short break or business, a few minutes away from M5 and M42 between Droitwich, Redditch and Bromsgrove. All rooms have tea/coffee facilities, a comfortable lounge with TV and separate room. Cot and highchair provided. Lower Bentley Farm is close to Worcester, Stratford and Birmingham.

Open all year
2 bedrooms (1 double ens.☞/WC; 1 family), 1🛏,
1WC.
⚘ ETB ♨ ♨
Prices:B&B £13.50–20.⚘ rates.

BROMYARD
Map 2 A2

Hennerwood Farm, Pencombe, Bromyard
✆ (0885) 400245   Mrs Anita Thomas

Relax and unwind at our delightful 17th-century farmhouse. Hennerwood Farm is a 250-acre dairy and stock farm situated south of the A44, between Leominster and Bromyard. You are welcome to walk around the farm and see the animals, or just sit in the large enclosed garden. Table tennis, badminton and pool table available. We serve traditional farmhouse food using our own fresh produce and spring water. Cot and highchair provided. Packed lunches on request. Dinmore Arboretum, Stoke Lacy cider works 5 miles. Leominster 6 miles. Brockhampton (NT) 8 miles.

Open all year
2 bedrooms (1 double; 1 family), 1🛏, 1WC.
⚘ ✂ ETB Commended
Prices: B&B £14–16, weekly £90–100. EM £8–10. Weekly B&B plus EM £140–170. ⚘ rates.

DROITWICH
Map 2 A1

Orchard House, Berrow Hill Lane, Feckenham B96 6QT
✆ (0527) 821497   Mrs P. Housley

You will find a warm welcome at this peaceful Georgian country house, set in beautiful gardens and orchards with magnificent views. Breakfast and dinner by candlelight and log fires in the 16th-century dining hall. Packed lunches and afternoon teas on request. The farm is 6 miles east of Droitwich off B4090. This is prime hunting country and within 6 miles are Avoncroft Museum, Ragley Hall, Coughton Court and Hanbury Hall.

Closed Xmas
3 bedrooms (2 twin; 1 double), 1🛏, 2WCs.
⚘ ✂ ↟ ETB Listed Commended
Prices: B&B £17.50–20, weekly £122.50–140.
EM £7.50–15, weekly B&B plus EM £172–192/ 245. ⚘ rates, ↟ £5 in room, £2 in stable.

HEREFORD
Map 2 A2

Cwm Craig Farm, Little Dewchurch
✆ (0432) 840250   Mrs G.W. Lee

Our spacious Georgian farmhouse with large garden is surrounded by superb unspoilt countryside. We are situated 6 miles from Hereford (A49). The working farm covers 190 acres with arable and beef. Afternoon teas provided on request, and the games room is equipped with a billiards/snooker table. Cot and highchair available. There are excellent walks and trails to follow in all directions, and there is much to explore in our area: Symonds Yat, Goodrich Castle, Monmouth, Golden Valley, the Wye Valley, Forest of Dean and many historic churches. Ross-on-Wye 7 miles.

Open all year
3 bedrooms (1 twin; 1 double; 1 family), 2🛏, 2WCs.
⚘ ETB ♨ ♨Commended
Prices: B&B £13–14, weekly £80–86.⚘ rates.

Dinedor Court, Dinedor, Hereford HR2 6LG
✆ (0432) 870481   Rosemary Price

Dinedor Court is a 16th-century listed farmhouse on a family-run mixed farm in the Wye Valley. Set amidst cider orchards with beautiful views, this is a very peaceful place. The farmhouse rooms are spacious and furnished with antiques. The farm lies 3 miles out of Hereford, A49/B4399. The River Wye is just 200 yds away.

Open Mar-Nov.
2 bedrooms (1 twin; 1 double), 1🛏, 2WCs.
⚘(10) ↟ ETB ♨
Prices: B&B £15.

Lyston Smithy, Wormelow, Hereford HR2 8EL
✆ (0981) 540625

The Lyston Smithy stands on a soft fruit farm with 14 acres of gardens and paddocks, just outside the village of Wormelow. Packed lunches and afternoon teas provided. The Smithy is 6 miles south of Hereford (A466 Hereford-Monmouth road). Ross-on-Wye 8 miles.

Open all year
4 bedrooms (2 twin inc. 1 ens. ⌀/WC, 1 ens. ☞/WC; 1 double priv. ⌀/WC; 1 single priv. ⌀/WC), 1WC.
⚜(5) ETB ♛ ♛Commended
Prices: B&B £15–16.50, weekly £105. ⚜ rates.

Orchard Farm, Mordiford, Hereford HR1 4EJ
✆ (0432870) 253   Mrs M.J. Barrell

Situated in the Wye Valley, in an Area of Outstanding Natural Beauty, our attractive 17th-century farmhouse offers you a peaceful and relaxing stay. There are superb views and excellent home cooking in comfortable surrounds. Packed lunches on request. Licensed. The farm is south off the A438 Hereford-Ledbury road.

Closed Xmas
3 bedrooms (1 twin; 2 double), 2➡, 2WCs.
⚜(10) ETB ♛ ♛Commended
Prices: B&B from £15. EM £10.

Sink Green Farm, Rotherwas, Hereford
✆ (0432) 870223   D.E. Jones

This beautiful 16th-century farmhouse is set on a 180-acre livestock farm on the banks of the River Wye. The farm is 3 miles south of the city of Hereford on the B4399, 2 miles from the A49. Hereford Cathedral, museums and attractions are all within easy reach.

Open all year
3 bedrooms (1 twin ens. ⌀/WC; 2 double ens. ☞/WC).
⚜ ✂ ♞ ETB ♛ ♛
Prices: B&B £17–22, weekly £110–150. ⚜ rates.

Upper Newton Farmhouse, Kinnersley
✆ (0544) 327727

A delightful 17th-century country farmhouse situated in a peaceful location. An extensive garden surrounds the house and we are ideally placed for a wide range of activities based on walking and water, with airborne sports close by. This working mixed arable and stock farm of 280 acres is north of A438 Hereford-Brecon road, turn off at Letton. Black and White Village Trail encircles the farm. Black Mountains, Hay-on-Wye and Brecon Beacons 10 miles. Hereford 13 miles.

Open all year
3 bedrooms (1 twin; 1 double; 1 family), 1➡, 2WCs.
✂ ETB Listed
Prices: B&B £18–25, weekly £126–175.

KIDDERMINSTER   Map 2 A1

Clay Farm, Clows Top, Nr Kidderminster
✆ (029922) 421   Ella Grinnall

Clay Farm has a modern farmhouse surrounded by 98 acres of grass and woodlands, well stocked trout and coarse fishing pools. Instruction available if required. The farm lies west of Kidderminster, north of the A456. Witley Church 6 miles. Bewdley Safari Park 7 miles. Ludlow Castle 12 miles.

Open all year
3 bedrooms (1 twin; 2 double ens. ⌀/WC), 1➡, 2WCs.
⚜(6) ETB ♛ ♛Commended
Prices:B&B £15–18, weekly £88–114. ⚜ rates.

Planning a day out?
See RURAL ATTRACTIONS

LEDBURY
Map 2 A2

Moor Court Farm, Ledbury HR8 2TR
℗ (0531) 670408

Enjoy a relaxing holiday on a traditional working Herefordshire hop and livestock farm. Good farmhouse cooking with afternoon teas provided. Situated 6 miles from Ledbury, Moor Court is well-placed for touring the Malverns, the Wye Valley and Welsh borders.

Open Feb-Nov.
3 bedrooms (2 twin ens. ☞/WC; 1 double ens.☞/WC), 1WC.
⚘ ⚘ ETB Commended
Prices: B&B £14–16, EM £10. ⚘ rates.

Underhill Farm, Putley, Ledbury
℗ (0531) 670695   Mrs Anne Blandford

This is a warm, friendly family run arable farm with a 16th-century farmhouse set in a rural location at the foot of Marcle Ridge. Outstanding views from the Malverns, the Cotswolds to the Black Mountains. Packed lunches and afternoon teas provided. Underhill Farm is south of the A438 Ledbury-Hereford road. After Trumpet crossroads follow signs for Putley Common and Putley. The Hellens, Much Marcle 4 miles. Ledbury 7 miles. Hereford 9 miles.

Open Apr-Oct.
2 bedrooms (1 double; 1 family), 2☛, 2WCs.
⚘ ⚘ ETB Listed
Prices: B&B £13.50–15.50, weekly £150–170. ⚘ rates.

LEOMINSTER
Map 2 A1

The Hills Farm, Leysters, Leominster HR6 9HP
℗ (056887) 205   Jane Conolly

An arable farm set amidst the beautiful North Herefordshire countryside, The Hills has all the ingredients for a perfect break. Luxurious accommodation and panoramic views, especially from the Tigeen bedroom – a small converted barn offering the ultimate in privacy. Scrumptious food, traditional or vegetarian. This is superb walking country with wonderful views. The Hills lies off the A4112, 5 miles northeast of Leominster NT properties within 4 miles. Ludlow 8 miles. Hereford 16 miles.

Open Feb-Oct.
3 bedrooms (1 twin ens. ☞/WC; 2 double ens. ☞/WC).
⚘ by arrangement. ✝ ETB ♛ ♛ ♛Highly Commended
Prices: B&B £19–20, EM £14.

ROSS-ON-WYE
Map 2 A2

Aberhall Farm, St Owens Cross, Ross-on-Wye
℗ (098987) 256   Freda Davies

In this quiet secluded spot, on the B4521 off the A49 Ross-on-Wye-Hereford road, you can relax in our 17th-century farmhouse with lovely views over rolling countryside. We offer home from home comfort with a games room, tennis court and large gardens. Packed lunches on request. Come and savour the peace and tranquility. We are close to Symonds Yat, Goodrich Castle and the heart of the Wye Valley.

Open Mar-Oct.
3 bedrooms (1 twin; 2 double inc. 1 ens. ⚐/WC), 1☛, 1WC.
⚘ ETB ♛ ♛
Prices: B&B £14.50–16.

Rudhall Farm, Ross-on-Wye HR9 7TL
℃ (098985) 240 (evenings)

Relax and enjoy the comfort, peace and hospitality in our elegant 17th-century farmhouse set in a tranquil valley with millstream and lake. The house is tastefully furnished with antiques and has panoramic views across open countryside. Rudhall Farm lies off the B4221 (M50, Jct 4), 2 miles from Ross-on-Wye, gateway to the beautiful Wye Valley, the Forest of Dean and the Welsh marches. Golf, swimming and riding 2 miles.

Open Jan-Nov.
2 double bedrooms, 1🛁, 1WC.
🍴 ETB 🏅 🏅Highly Commended
Prices:B&B from £16.

Upper Pengethley Farm, Ross-on-Wye HR9 6LL
℃ (0989) 87687　　　　Mrs Sue Partridge

Our very attractive, comfortably furnished Georgian farmhouse stands on a mixed arable and stock rearing farm. We are convenient to major roads and motorways, the farm is off the A49 Hereford-Ross road, yet in a quiet situation. Ross-on-Wye 4 miles. Forest of Dean and Monmouth 10 miles.

Open Mar-Nov.
3 bedrooms (1 twin ens.🛁/🚻/WC; 2 double ens.🚻/WC).
🍴 🐕 ETB 🏅
Prices: B&B £15. 🐕 rates.

Wharton Farm, Weston-under-Penyard, Ross-on-Wye
℃ (0989) 750255

Wharton is a working arable and sheep farm, and the 17th-and 19th-century red sandstone farmhouse is situated on the edge of the Forest of Dean and the Wye Valley. From Ross-on-Wye take the A40 Gloucester road to Weston-under-Penyard, then turn south towards Cinderford. Numerous attractions within a few miles Falconry Centre, Symonds Yat, Farm Park. Ross-on-Wye 4 miles.

Open Jan-Nov.
2 double bedrooms priv. 🛁/🚻/WC.
🍴 ETB 🏅Commended
Prices: B&B £15.50-20, weekly £97.65-126. 🍴 rates.

TENBURY WELLS
Map 2 A1

Hunthouse Farm, Frith Common, Tenbury Wells WR15 8JY
℃ (0299) 832277　　　　Jane Keel

The 16th-century timber framed farmhouse is surrounded by breathtaking views. On our 180-acre arable and sheep farm we offer comfort, peace and hospitality in a relaxed friendly atmosphere from the moment you arrive, greeted with tea and homemade cake. Hunthouse Farm lies east of Tenbury Wells, south off the A456. Bewdley 5 miles. Severn Valley Railway, West Midlands Safari Park 7 miles. Worcester 15 miles.

Open Mar-Oct.
3 bedrooms (1 twin ens. 🛁/WC; 1 family ens. 🛁/WC; 1 double ens. 🚻/WC).
🍴(8) ETB 🏅 🏅Highly Commended
Prices:B&B £15-16.

UPTON-ON-SEVERN
Map 2 A2

Tiltridge Farm and Vineyard, Upper Hook Farm, Upton-on-Severn WR8 0SA
℃ (0684) 592906　　　　Mrs Sandy Barber

Tiltridge is an old family farmhouse on a quiet country road a mile outside Upton, easy access M5, Jct8. Fully renovated to a high standard we can offer you a well-cooked evening meal in pleasant surroundings accompanied by wine produced in our own vineyards. Wine tastings encouraged. Residential Licence. Animal and Bird Garden 1 mile. Malvern Hills and Spa 5 miles.

Open all year
2 bedrooms (1 double; 1 family), 1🛁, 2WCs.
🍴 🐕 ETB 🏅 🏅Commended
Prices: B&B £16-17.50, weekly £101.50-112. EM £8.50-12, weekly B&B plus EM £157.50-168. 🍴 rates.

WHITBOURNE
Map 2 A2

Upper Elmores End, Linley Green Road, Whitbourne WR6 5RE

☎ (0886) 21245   Mrs M.E. Simpson

The 16th-century half-timbered black and white farmhouse is set on a 50-acre farm with orchards, amid beautiful, unspoilt countryside. The farm lies approx. 9 miles west of Worcester off the A44. Good home cooking is offered. A cot is available. Malvern Hills and Worcester 10 miles. Hereford 19 miles.

Open Easter-Oct.
3 bedrooms (1 twin; 2 double), 1🛏, 2WCs.
🚭 ⚥ ETB ♛ ♛
Prices: B&B £14–15, EM £7–8.

WORCESTER
Map 2 A2

Chirkenhill, Leigh Sinton, Malvern

☎ (0886) 832205   Mrs S. Wenden

Chirkenhill is a small mixed farm in an elevated position with extensive views of the surrounding Elgar Countryside, where you can follow the well marked Elgar Trail or walk the Worcestershire Way. Cot, highchair and swimming pool available. Ideally sited for touring the area, Chirkenhill lies just beyond the village of Leigh Sinton off the A4103 Worcester-Hereford road. Malvern 4 miles. Worcester 5 miles. Knapp and Papermill Nature Reserve 1 mile.

Open all year
3 bedrooms (1 twin;1 double ens. 🛁;1 family ens. 🛁), 1🛏, 1WCs.
🚭 ⚥ ETB ♛ ♛
Prices: B&B £14–18. 🚭 rates.

Reduced rates are sometimes available.
Ask your host about weekend breaks.

Church House Farm, Shelsley Beauchamp, Nr Worcester WR6 6RH

☎ (08865) 393   Gill Moore

Our large 18th-century farmhouse is situated on the River Teme, 10 miles northwest of Worcester, off the B4197. We keep sheep and cattle on our 200-acre farm. Traditional farmhouse food is prepared from home and local produce. Cot and highchair available. Packed lunches on request. Several NT properties and gardens are close by. Baroque church 4 miles. Elgar's birthplace 7 miles. Bewdley Safari Park 8 miles. Severn Valley Railway 10 miles.

Open April-Oct.
2 twin bedrooms ens. 🛁/WC).
🚭 ⚥ ETB ♛ ♛
Prices: B&B £15–16, weekly £105. EM £9.50. Weekly B&B plus EM £171.50. 🚭 rates.

Self-Catering

BEWDLEY
Map 2 A1

Peacock House, Lower Park, Bewdley DY12 2DP

☎ (0299) 400149

This attractively restored 17th-century beamed coach house stands on the edge of the historic old town of Bewdley and the River Severn. The house has 2 bedrooms, sleeps 4–5. There is a private walled garden with patio and barbeque. Cot, highchair and children's games available. Bewdley is west of Kidderminster on the Ludlow road. Severn Valley Steam Railway 10 mins. West Midlands Safari Park 1 mile.

Open all year
ETB♫♫♫♫Commended
Prices: weekly £180–296.

BROMSGROVE
Map 2 A1

Valley Farm, Hanbury, Bromsgrove B60 4HJ

☎ (0527) 812678   Mrs Joyce Ulyet

The lovely old farmhouse at Valley Farm has recently been restored. Accommodation is offered in 3 self-catering cottages, sleeping 2–3. Cot and highchair provided. The house is south of Broms-grove on the B4091. The Jenny Ring Craft Centre, Hanbury Hall and the Avoncroft Museum are all within 4 miles.

Open all year
🐾 ETB𝄐𝄐&𝄐𝄐𝄐Commended
Prices: weekly £95–135.

BROMYARD
Map 2 A2

Blackhouse Farm, Suckley WR6 5DW
✆ (0886) 884234
Mrs G. Mansell

The attractive 16th-century barn conversion at Blackhouse Farm consists of 2 units sleeping 7 and 9. Each has a fully fitted kitchen and comfort-able lounge. The barn stands in large gardens amid peaceful surroundings. The working mixed farm covers 100 acres. Suckley is south of the A44 Worcester-Bromyard road. Bromyard 6 miles. Nature Reserve 2 miles. Malvern Hills and Worcestershire Way 6 miles. Worcester 8 miles.

Open all year
🛏 ETB𝄐𝄐𝄐
Prices: weekly £152–400.

HEREFORD
Map 2 A2

Lyston Smithy, Wormelow, Hereford HR2 8EL
✆ (0981) 540625

For full farm description see p. 92. Accommo-dation is available in a 2-bedroomed unit, sleeps 4. Cot and highchair provided.

Open all year
ETB𝄐𝄐𝄐Commended
Prices: weekly £125–265.

LEOMINSTER
Map 2 A1

Ashton Court Farm, Ashton, Leominster HR6 0DN
✆ (0584) 711245
Mrs Pam Edwards

Ashton Court Farm is east of the A49, 4 miles north of Leominster. Two spacious self-catering apartments, sleeping 4 and 9/10 respectively, comprise one end of the large brick-built farm-house, set in half an acre of lawns and garden. Table tennis and pool table in the barn, garden games available. The grassland farm has mainly sheep and is surrounded by a large wooded area offering peaceful walks. Berrington Hall (NT) is a short walk away. Croft Castle 6 miles. Burford House Gardens and Ludlow 7 miles.

Open all year
🐾 🛏 ETB𝄐𝄐𝄐𝄐
Prices: £75–170 weekly.

Bircher Hall, Leominster HR6 0AY
✆ (056885) 218

Accommodation is offered in the West Wing and Lodge of Bircher Hall. Please note the farms are some 4 miles distant. The West Wing sleeps 5, the Lodge which is suitable for disabled guests, sleeps 3. Cot available. Both have fully equipped kitchens, twin beds and TV. Bircher Hall is off the A49 Leominster-Ludlow road, a mile east of Croft Castle. The area offers a choice of NT properties to visit, fishing, riding, forestry reservations and excellent walking and rambling terrain.

Open all year
♿ 🐾 🛏
Prices: £60–180 per week.

Nicholson Farm, Docklow, Leominster
HR6 0SL
℗ (056882) 269   Mrs R.A. Brooke

At this 17th-century farmhouse, situated east of Leominster off the A44, there are 4 self-catering cottages sleeping 2–6. Two cottages take wheelchairs. Ideally placed for exploring the area. Carp lake fishing available. The Welsh hills, the Severn and Wye Valleys can be visited in a day. Ludlow, Hereford and Worcester within 40 minutes' drive.

Open all year
& ⚭ ⊁ ETB♪♪
Prices: weekly £40–178.

ROSS-ON WYE   Map 2 A2

Upper Pengethley Farm, Ross-on-Wye
HR9 6LL
℗ (0989) 87687   Mrs Sue Partridge

For full farm description see p. 94. Accommodation is offered in one unit, sleeps 2.

Open Mar-Nov.
Prices: weekly £100–140.

HUMBERSIDE

MARKET WEIGHTON — Map 5 B2

Arras Farmhouse, Arras, Market Weighton, York Y04 3RN
✆ (0430) 872404 — Mrs D.M. Stephenson

You will find a friendly family welcome and good food waiting for you in our large traditional farmhouse. The rooms are comfortable and spacious, the atmosphere is peaceful. Our arable farm covers 460 acres located on the A1079 at the crossroads 3 miles east of Market Weighton. Many good places to eat locally. Cot and highchair provided. Arras Farm is an ideal centre for touring the area. Beverley 7 miles. Water Lily Gardens 12 miles. Humber Bridge 15 miles. York 20 miles.

Open all year
3 bedrooms (1 twin; 2 double inc. 1 ens. 🚿/WC, 1 ens. 🛁/WC), 1🛁, 2WCs.
👪 🐕
Prices: B&B £14–18. 👪 rates.

POCKLINGTON — Map 5 B2

The Mohair Farm, Barmby Moor, Nr Pocklington, York Y04 5HU
✆ (07595) 308 — Lesley Scott

The Mohair Farm is on the A1079 York-Market Weighton road. The farm produces mohair and has a craft workshop. We usually also have a few pigs, ducks and hens, and rear calves and bulls. Ground floor access bedroom available. Situated between the Humber Bridge and York, both the moors and the coast are also within a reasonable distance.

Closed Xmas and New Year
3 bedrooms (1 twin; 1 double ens. 🛁/WC; 1 family), 1🛁, 1WC.
👪 🐕
Prices: B&B £14. 👪 rates.

ISLE OF WIGHT

BRIGHSTONE — Map 2 B3

Chilton Farm, Chilton Lane, Brighstone PO30 4DS
✆ (0983) 740338 — Mrs Susan Fisk

We are very much a working farm with 600 acres. Our dairy herd of Jerseys is the second oldest in the country, established in 1866. We milk 170 pedigree Jerseys and rear some beef cattle, Charollais or Belgian Blue, and grow 250 acres of corn. The beach is half a mile along a private road from the 18th-century farmhouse, a longer walk on the bridleway leads to the forest and Downs. Fishing by arrangement on our small lake stocked with trout and carp. Chilton Farm is a mile from Brighstone off B3399. Newport 7 miles.

Open Mar-Dec.
6 bedrooms (1 twin ens. 🚿/WC; 2 double ens. 🚿/WC; 3 family ens. 🚿/WC;).
👪 🚭
Prices: B&B £14.50–16.50, weekly £95–108.50. 👪 rates.

NEWPORT — Map2 B3

Briddlesford Lodge Farm, Wootton Bridge, Ryde PO33 4RY
✆ (0983) 882239 — Mrs Judi Griffin

This comfortable old farmhouse is centrally situated for all the island's attractions, walking, beaches and ferry terminal (2 miles). The farm is under a mile off the A3054 Ryde-Newport road at Wootton Bridge. Briddlesford Lodge is a 250-acre dairy farm with a Guernsey herd. Butterfly World half a mile. Steam Railway 2 miles. Beaches and Ryde 5 miles.

Closed Xmas
3 bedrooms (1 twin; 2 double), 1🛁, 1WC.
👪 🐕 ETB Listed
Prices: B&B £14–17. 👪 rates.

Cheverton Farm, Shorwell, Newport PO30 3JE
✆ (0983) 741017 — Mrs Sheila Hodgson

Cheverton is a 550-acre beef, sheep and arable farm. The listed farmhouse provides an attractive base for a relaxing holiday. Pony trekking and clay pigeon shooting on the farm. Exceptional downland walking and riding opportunities. Cot, highchair and large garden available. Tea/coffee in rooms. The farm is 4 miles from Newport, off B3323 Shorwell road.

Open Mar-Nov.
3 bedrooms (1 twin; 1 double; 1 single), 2🛁, 2WCs.
👪 🚭 ETB Listed
Prices: B&B £13.50–16, weekly £91–98.

Youngwoods Farm, Whitehouse Road, Porchfield, Newport PO30 4LJ
✆ (0983) 522170 — Mrs Judith Shanks

Youngwoods is a 80-acre grassland sheep farm, lambing in April. The 18th-century Island stone farmhouse has recently been renovated to provide every comfort, but retains its original character. Tea facilities in all rooms. The farm is 4 miles from Newport, north off the A3054 Yarmouth road. Newtown Nature Reserve 2 miles. Carisbrooke Castle 4 miles. Cowes 6 miles.

Open all year
2 twin bedrooms, 1🛁, 2WCs.
👪(5) 🚭 ETB Listed
Prices: B&B £14–16, weekly £91–105.

Planning a day out?
See RURAL ATTRACTIONS

SHANKLIN   Map 2 B3
Cliff Farm, Victoria Avenue, Shanklin
PO37 6QW
℃ (0983) 862107   Mrs Mavis H. Mew

Cliff Farm is a working farm of 100 acres with single suckled beef cows, situated on the outskirts of Shanklin (A3020 Godshill road) overlooking magnificent views of the countryside. Footpaths from the farm lead onto the Downs. Sandy beaches, golf course, horse riding all within 5 mins drive. TV and tea making facilities.

Open all year
2 bedrooms (1 triple room ens. ☞/WC; 1 double), 1➡, 1WC.
⚗(4) ✂ ETB Listed
Prices: B&B £15–20, weekly £90–112.

VENTNOR   Map 2 B3
Lisle Combe, Bank End Farm, Undercliff Drive, St Lawrence, Ventnor
℃ (0983) 852582   Hugh & Judy Noyes

The opportunity to stay in an Elizabethan style house on a coastal farm in an Area of Outstanding Natural Beauty. Cot provided. The farm maintains a small Friesian dairy herd. The Noyes have recently opened a Rare Breeds Survival Centre containing most rare breeds of British domestic farm animals. The farm is situated on the A3055, the island's southernmost coastal road. Ventnor Botanic Garden is half a mile away.

Closed Xmas and New Year
3 bedrooms (1 family; 1 double; 1 single), 1➡, 2WCs.
⚗ ✂ ETB Listed
Prices: B&B from £14.50.

YARMOUTH   Map 2 B3
Homestead Farm, Newbridge, Yarmouth
℃ (0983) 78270

Homestead Farm is a working dairy farm of 180 acres, situated in the charming unspoilt West Wight village of Newbridge, and within easy reach of Yarmouth (A3054). We also have sheep, pigs and chickens. There is a large picturesque pond with coarse fishing available. All bedrooms in the new wing are on the ground floor, cot and highchair available.

Open all year
2 bedrooms (1 twin ens. ☞/WC; 1 family ens. ☞/WC).
♿ ⚗
Prices: B&B £14.50–16, weekly £101.50–112.

Mattingley Farm, Wellow
℃ (0983) 760503

This stone farmhouse is in a quiet rural part of the West Wight in a wonderful walking area. Here you will find good home cooking and packed lunches provided on request. Mattingley was once a pig farm and is now a smallholding of 5 acres with goats, donkeys and ducks. The farm is 2 miles from Yarmouth (A3054/B3401). Choice of beautiful beaches 2 miles.

Open all year
2 bedrooms (1 twin; 1 family), 1➡, 1WC.
⚗ ✂
Prices: B&B £15.50, EM £9.

Self-Catering
BRIGHSTONE   Map 2 B3
Chilton Farm, Chilton Lane, Brighstone
PO30 4DS
℃ (0983) 740338   Mrs Susan Fisk

For full farm description see p. 99. There are seven courtyard cottages on Chilton Farm, with 1–3 bedrooms, sleeping 2–8. The cottages have been converted from the old stables and barns and are equipped to the highest standards. Children's play area, laundry and barbeque.

Open Mar–Dec.
Prices: weekly £170–399.

NEWPORT   Map 2 B3
Cheverton Farm, Shorwell, Newport
PO30 3JE
℃ (0983) 741017   Mrs Sheila Hodgson

For full farm description see p. 99. Accommodation is available in the self-catering wing to the farmhouse, 2 bedrooms, sleeps 4.

Open all year
⚓ ETB♫♫♫
Prices: daily £25–35, weekly £100–290.

YARMOUTH   Map 2 B3
Mattingley Farm, Wellow
℃ (0983) 760503

For full farm description see above. There are 2 self-catering units on the farm, each has 2 bedrooms, sleeps 4.

Open all year
Prices: weekly £135–390.

KENT

ASHFORD

Barnfield, Charing, Ashford TN27 0BN
✆ (0233) 712421   Mrs Pym

This charming Kent Hall farmhouse, built in 1420, has a wealth of history and character. It is a spacious and comfortable family home, with an attractive garden and wildfowl lake, on a 500-acre working farm. In these peaceful surroundings you can relax and enjoy some good home cooking. Cot, highchair, playroom and games available. Situated 4 miles west of Ashford, the farm is very convenient for Dover, Folkestone, Ramsgate and Sheerness. Nearby are Leeds Castle, Sissinghurst Castle and Canterbury.

Open all year
4 bedrooms (1 twin; 1 double; 2 single), 1🛌,
2WCs.
🐾 ✄ ETB Listed Commended
Prices: B&B £18–20, weekly £108–120. EM
£11.50. Weekly B&B plus EM £188.50–200.50.
🐾 rates.

CANTERBURY

Crockshard Farmhouse, Wingham CT3
1NY
✆ (0227) 720464   Mrs Nicola Ellen

You will receive a warm welcome at this spacious, traditional farmhouse set in beautiful gardens in the heart of the Kentish countryside amid orchards, pastures and winding lanes. At Crockshard you will find farmyard animals, sheep, home-produced eggs, preserves, fresh bread and the best quality farmhouse cooking. The farm lies off the B2046, north from the A2 Canterbury-Dover road, a convenient central location for exploring the whole of Kent. Canterbury 6 miles. Dover 13 miles.

Open all year
4 bedrooms (1 twin; 3 family inc. 1. ens. 🛁/WC),
2🛌, 2WCs.
🐾 ✕
Prices: B&B £15–17.50, weekly £90–105. EM
£7–10. Weekly £150–165. 🐾 rates.

Ripple Farm, Godmersham, Nr
Canterbury
✆ (0227) 730748

The 17th-century timber-framed farmhouse stands in lovely countryside on a small working mixed farm, which is farmed organically and approved by the Soil Association. The farm is located off the A28 between Canterbury and Ashford. The property is set within excellent walking and riding country (local riding stables). Wye 3 miles. Canterbury 9 miles.

Open all year
2 family bedrooms, priv.🛁/WC. 🐾
Prices: B&B £15.50. 🐾 rates.

CRANBROOK

Conghurst Farm, Hawkhurst
✆ (0580) 753331   Mrs Rosemary Piper

Conghurst is a 500-acre mixed farm on the Kent/Sussex border in unspoilt countryside. The Georgian farmhouse is very comfortable and you will enjoy good farmhouse cooking. The farm is situated south of Cranbrook, east of the A229, in beautiful walking country. There are many NT and private houses in the area, Sissinghurst, Bodiam Castle, Batemans and Hever Castle.

Open Mar-Nov.
2 bedrooms (1 twin ens. ☜/WC;1 double), 1🛏.
🐎 by arrangement. ⚡🛏 ETB ♛ ♛Highly Commended
Prices: B&B £16–19, weekly £112–122.50. EM £9–11.50. Weekly B&B plus EM £178.

Hallwood Farm House, Hallwood Farm, Hartley, Cranbrook TN17 2SP
✆ (0580) 713204   Mr & Mrs David Wickham

This 15th-century hall house is a listed building set on a farm devoted to apple production and grazing. Off the A229 south of Cranbrook, it is a good choice for touring the area. Sissinghurst and Scotney Castles 3 miles. Bedgebury Pinetum 4 miles. Great Dixter Gardens 5 miles. Leeds Castle 10 miles. Rye, Cinque Ports 15 miles.

Open Apr-Oct.
3 bedrooms (2 twin; 1 double), 1🛏, 1WC.
🐎 🛏 ETB Listed
Prices: B&B £18, EM £12. 🐎 rates.

DODDINGTON   Map 3 B3
Palace Farmhouse, Doddington, Sittingbourne ME9 0AU
✆ (079586) 820   Mr & Mrs Leake

The brick-built early Victorian farmhouse is set in the corner of a plum orchard on this fruit and arable farm. There are pleasant gardens to front and rear, log fires, and 2 bedrooms open onto a large balcony. We offer good country cooking, special diets, packed lunches and afternoon teas on request. Ground floor bedroom, cot and babysitting available. The house is on the edge of the village which runs along the pretty Newnham Valley. Doddington lies northwest of Faversham via M2, Jct5 or M20, Jct 8. Leeds Castle and Chilham 8 miles. Canterbury and Maidstone 12 miles.

Open all year
6 bedrooms (2 twin priv. ☜/WC; 1 double ens. 📷; 1 family; 2 single), 2🛏, 2WCs.
🛇 🐎 🛏
Prices: B&B £13–16, EM £8. Weekly B&B plus EM £137–158. 🐎 rates.

GRAVESEND   Map 3 A2
Nurstead Court Farm, Meopham, Nr Gravesend DA13 9AD
✆ (0474) 812121   Mr & Mrs Edmeades-Stearns

A 14th-century aisled hall house of great historical interest, this is a Grade 1 listed building, with an extension built in 1825. We have a pedigree Guernsey herd of milking cows, plus calves, sheep, goats and ponies. Packed lunches and afternoon teas provided on request. Croquet, tennis, billiards table, children's games, cot and highchair available. Lovely walks on the North Downs and woodland all around. The farm is located on Wealden Way, on the A227 Meopham-Gravesend road. Meopham Windmill and village green 2 miles. Rochester City, Castle and Dickens Centre 3 miles. Brands Hatch 4 miles.

Open all year
3 bedrooms (1 twin; 1 double with four poster ens. ☜/WC; 1 family ens. ☜/WC), 1🛏, 2WCs.
🐎🛏
Prices: B&B £12–15, weekly £84–105. 🐎 rates,🛏 £3 per night.

MAIDSTONE   Map 3 A3
Court Lodge, Court Lodge Farm, The Street, Teston, Maidstone ME18 5AQ
✆ (0622) 812570   Mrs R. Bannock
Fax (0622)814200

With magnificent views overlooking the Medway Valley and its hop gardens and orchard, set in a beautiful garden, our comfortably furnished 16th-century oakbeamed house offers you warm and friendly hospitality. Ideally situated 4 miles west of Maidstone (A26), with nearby access to M20, it is within easy reach of Leeds Castle, Ightham Mote, Sissinghurst, Knole House and Chartwell.

Fishing, swimming and tennis nearby. Six golf courses within 10 miles.

Open all year
3 bedrooms (2 twin inc. 1 ens. ⋔/WC; 1 double ens. ☜/WC), 1🛁, 2WCs.
💥ETB 👑 👑 👑
Prices: B&B £16–22.50 sharing, £22–28 single occupancy. Weekly terms negotiable.

MARDEN
Map 3 A3

Tanner House, Tanner Farm, Goudhurst Road, Marden TN12 9ND
✆ (0622) 831214   Mrs L.R. Mannington

This secluded Tudor farmhouse is on a working family farm where Shire horses are bred and worked. Tanner House offers every comfort, even a four poster bed, cot, highchair and good quality food. Packed lunches on request. Guests are welcome to walk the farm's attractive areas. Also a high quality touring caravan and camping park which includes facilities for disabled visitors. Tanner Farm is south of Maidstone (A229/B2079). Brattle Farm Museum 2 miles, Cranbrook Mill and Bewl Water 6 miles. Whitbread Hop Farm 8 miles.

Closed Xmas and New Year
3 bedrooms (2 twin ens. ⋔/WC;1 double ens. ⋔/WC).
💥ETB 👑 👑 👑
Prices:B&B £16.50–20, weekly £110–133. EM £12. Weekly B&B plus EM £190–212. rates.

TUNBRIDGE WELLS
Map 3 A3

Manor Court Farm, Ashurst, Tunbridge Wells
✆ (0892) 740279

A Grade 2 listed Georgian farmhouse with spacious rooms is at the centre of Manor Court's working farm, arable and sheep, plus several pets. Packed lunches by request, cot and highchair available. The farm, off the A264 5 miles west of Tunbridge Wells, is bounded by the River Medway and has lovely views over Kent and Sussex. Guests are welcome to explore all 350 acres of fields and woodland. Local pubs provide good food. The Wealdway and Sussex Border Paths cross the farm. Harrisons Rocks (climbing) 3 miles. Penshurst Place 4 miles.

Open all year
3 bedrooms (1 twin; 1 family; 1 single), 2🛁, 3WC.
🅿 🏋 ETB 👑 👑
Prices: B&B £16–18, rates.

WEST MALLING
Map 3 A3

Heavers Farm, Ryarsh, Nr West Malling ME19 5JU
✆ /Fax (0732) 842074   J.Edwards

Just 2 miles south of the M20(Jct4) amid peaceful countryside and woodland stands Heavers Farm, a 250-year-old house on a smallholding of 5 acres with sheep, poultry and bees. Plentiful supplies of good home cooking, packed lunches and afternoon teas on request. Cot, garden and swings available. Ideally sited for touring Kent, within 15 miles are Ightham Mote, Knowle House, Leeds Castle and Chatham Dockyard. Gatwick airport and Channel ports within easy reach.

Closed Xmas and New Year
3 bedrooms (1 twin; 1 double; 1 family), 2🛁, 2WCs.
🅿 💥 🏋
Prices: B&B £15–20, EM £7–12. rates.

Self-Catering

CANTERBURY
Map 3 B3

Ripple Farm, Godmersham, Nr Canterbury
✆ (0227) 730748

The 17th-century timber-framed farmhouse stands in lovely countryside on a small working mixed farm, which is farmed organically and approved by the Soil Association. The farm is located off the A28 between Canterbury and Ashford. Accommodation is offered in two fully equipped cottages, sleeping 4/5. The property is set within excellent walking and riding country (local riding stables). Wye 3 miles. Canterbury 9 miles.

Open all year
🐾 ♿
Prices: weekly £160–220.

MAIDSTONE   Map 3 A3
Owls Nest, Kingsnoad Farm, Pye Corner, Ulcombe ME17 1EG
✆ (0622) 858966

Owls Nest is a converted Victorian milking parlour in a secluded farm setting, half a mile along a farm track. The cottage is fully equipped and sleeps 4/6. Cot and highchair provided. Among its attractions is a large oak beamed withdrawing area and open fireplace. The cottage lies south of the A20, midway between Maidstone and Ashford. Leeds Castle 4 miles. Lenham 6 miles. Maidstone 10 miles. Tenterden 10 miles.

Open all year
🐾 ⚡ 🐴 ETBℐℐℐ Approved
Prices: weekly £130–275. 🐴 £10.

SEVENOAKS   Map 3 A3
Ash Place Farmhouse, Ash, Nr Sevenoaks TN15 7HD
✆ (0474) 872238   Mrs J. Scott
Contact: Ash Manor, Ash, Nr Sevenoaks TN15 7HD

Ash Place Farm is a Victorian farmhouse situated in a 600-acre working farm next to the Manor House, church and a bridlepath. The house has been converted into two luxury flats which have wonderful views over the rolling countryside of the North Downs. Each flat is full equipped for 4 people. Cot and highchair available. Ash Place lies east of the M20/A20 near New Ash Green. Easy access to London. Penshurst, Knole, Chartwell, Rochester and Leeds Castle all within a 20 mile radius.

Open all year
🐾 ETBℐℐℐℐ Commended
Prices: weekly £150–200.

STAPLEHURST   Map 3 A3
Brattle Farm, Staplehurst TN12 0HE
✆ (0580) 891222   Mr & Mrs Brian Thompson

Off the A229, 9 miles south of Maidstone, self-catering accommodation to sleep 5 is available in half of this 16th-century Wealden farmhouse, standing on a 140-acre working farm, mostly arable. The house is moated, so young children must be supervised. Ground floor bedroom and cot available. At the farm there is a rural museum including vintage cars, tractors, engines, cycles and domestic bygones.

Open all year
🐾 🐴
Prices: weekly £100–200.

LANCASHIRE

BURSCOUGH — Map 4 B2

Brandreth Farm, Brandreth Barn, Tarlscough Lane, Burscough, Nr Ormskirk L40 0RJ
✆ (0704) 893510

The Brandreth Barn is on a working farm 2 miles west of the A59, north of Ormskirk. It lies alongside Martin Mere Wildfowl Trust. In this beautiful West Lancashire countryside there are many places of historical interest and locally horse riding, fishing and choice of golf courses. The adjoining licensed restaurant offers a complete choice from the menu with home grown produce. Packed lunches and afternoon teas. Downstairs rooms designed to assist disabled guests.

Closed Xmas
7 bedrooms (5 twin ens. 🛁/WC;2 double ens. 🛁/WC).
♿ 👪 ETB 👑 👑 👑Approved
Prices: B&B from £18, weekly £126–210. EM £4.85–10.50. Weekly B&B plus EM £152.95–283.50. 👪 rates.

See STOP PRESS
for more farms

COLNE — Map 5 A2

Higher Wanless Farm, Red Lane, Colne BB8 7JP
✆ (0282) 865301 Mrs Carole Mitson

A warm welcome awaits you at this beautiful farmhouse. The farm lies just north of Colne off the A682, an ideal centre for both holidaymakers and business people visiting nearby Burnley, Blackburn or Nelson. Higher Wanless is luxuriously furnished, and nestles peacefully alongside one of the prettiest stretches of the Leeds-Liverpool Canal. Packed lunches and babysitting on request. The owners breed Shire Horses and sheep. A mile from Pendle Way, Bronte country 8 miles, Gawthorpe Hall 7 miles, Skipton 13 miles.

Open Feb-Nov.
2 twin bedrooms inc. 1 ens. 🚿/WC, 1🛁, 1WC.
👪(3) ETB 👑 👑 Commended
Prices: B&B £16–22, weekly £120–150. 👪 rates.

GARSTANG — Map 4 B2

Stirzakers Farm, Barnacre, Garstang, Preston
✆ (0995) 603335 Ruth Wrathall

Our old stone, beamed farmhouse lies in secluded countryside, south of Garstang off the B6430. At Stirzakers we have a milking herd of pedigree British Friesians. The Forest of Bowland 10 miles. Blackpool and the coast 12 miles. Lake District 30 miles. Cot and highchair available.

Closed Xmas and New Year
4 bedrooms (1 double; 1 family; 2 single), 2🛏,
2WCs.
⬧ ⚡ ETB Listed Highly Commended
Prices: B&B £12–14, weekly £72–84. ⬧ rates.

INGLETON   Map 4 B2

Stacksteads Farm, Tatterthorn road,
Ingleton, Carnforth LA6 3HS
✆ (05242) 41386

This grassland farm with sheep and poultry is by
the A65 between Kirkby Lonsdale and Settle. Although parts of the attractive stone-built farmhouse date back to the 17th century, it has been
modernised for full comfort. Situated in a picturesque location with panoramic views, Stacksteads Farm offers the opportunity for a relaxing
break with good home cooking and plenty to see
and admire. As well as walking and rambling
throughout the area and the Three Peaks, local
sights include Ingleton Waterfalls 1 mile and
White Scar Caves 3 miles. Packed lunches on
request. Cot and highchair provided.

Open all year
3 bedrooms (1 twin; 1 double ens. ⋔/WC; 1
family ens. ⋔/WC), 1🛏, 1WC.
⬧
Prices: B&B £13, EM £7. ⬧ rates.

ROCHDALE   Map 5 A2

Leaches Farm, Ashworth, Rochdale OL11
5UN
✆ (0706) 41116/7   Mrs Jane M. Neave
✆ (0706) 228520

Leaches is a beautiful 17th-century Pennine hill
farm, with beef and sheep, enjoying panoramic
views over four counties. This comfortable accommodation (cot available), with oak beams
and log fires, is off the beaten track (A680 northwest of Rochdale and beyond), yet only 4 miles
from Bury and Rochdale (M62 and M66), 10
miles from Manchester. Moorland walks, Rossendale Way through the farmland, the Valley of
Cheesden (Textile Heritage) on the farm boundary. Rossendale Ski Slope 3 miles. Rochdale
Pioneers Co-op Museum 4 miles.

Closed Xmas and New Year
3 bedrooms (1 twin; 1 double; 1 single), 1🛏,
1WC.
⬧ 🐕 ETB Listed
Prices:B&B £17. ⬧ rates.

Self-Catering

CARNFORTH   Map 4 B2

Brackenthwaite Farm, Yealand
Redmayne,Carnforth LA5 9TE
✆ (05395) 63276   Mrs Susan Clarke

Brackenthwaite is a beef and sheep farm situated off the A6, north of Carnforth. There are 3
cottages sleeping 4–6, attractively converted
from the old stables and barn. All fully equipped,
cot, highchair and ground floor bedrooms available. An Area of Outstanding Natural Beauty, it is
wonderful for walking with good access to Lakes,
coast and dales. Horse riding, fishing and golf
nearby. Facilities for your horse if required.

Open all year
⬧ 🐕 ETB💰💰💰Commended &💰💰💰Commended
Prices: weekly £80–300. Short breaks available
Nov-Easter.

KEY TO SYMBOLS

Bath	🛁
Shower	⋔
Bathroom	🛏
Disabled Guest Facilities	♿
No Smoking	⚡
Children Welcome	⬧
Dogs by Arrangement	🐕

LEICESTERSHIRE

CASTLE DONINGTON   Map 2 B1

High Barn Farm, Isley Walton, Castle Donington, Derby
✆ (0332) 810360   Mr J.C. & Mrs A.M. Bottomley

High Barn Farm is an 84-acre sheep farm in a peaceful rural setting just off the main A453 south of Castle Donington. The accommodation is in a newly converted barn and cottage. One twin adapted for wheelchaired guests. Cot and high-chair available. Donington Circuit under 2 miles. East Midland Airport 3 miles. Calke Abbey 5 miles. Nottingham 15 miles.

Open all year
9 bedrooms (6 twin inc. 2 ens. ᵐ/WC;1 double/family ens. ᵐ/WC; 2 single), 3🛏, 3WCs.
♿ ♨ 🦅 ETB Listed Commended
Prices: B&B £16–22. ♨ rates.

LEICESTER   Map 2 B1

Water Meadows Farm, Billington Road East, Elmesthorpe, Leicester LE9 7SB
✆ (0455) 843417   June & Peter Robinson

This attractive black and white Tudor farmhouse is surrounded by extensive gardens and wood-land. The Robinsons run a beef cattle and con-servation farm. The excellent farmhouse cooking is produced with organically grown farm pro-duce. Packed lunches on request. Water Mea-dows Farm lies off the A47 to Leicester, 3 miles from Hinckley. Bosworth Battlefield 5 miles. Shackerston Steam Railway 6 miles.

Open all year
3 bedrooms (1 twin; 1 double; 1 family), 1🛏, 1WC.
♨ ETB Member
Prices: B&B £13–16, EM £7. Weekly B&B plus EM £120–140. ♨ rates.

LUTTERWORTH   Map 2 B1

Manor House Farm, Bruntingthorpe, Lutterworth LE17 5QL
✆ (0533) 478347

Stay in a Georgian listed building on a working grass farm and savour the true delights of the country life. The house is furnished to the highest standard, and many original fittings have been retained. It is located in a small rural village, with duckpond and village church, west of the A50 Leicester-Northampton road (M1, Jct 20/A427). Good eating places locally. Packed lunches and afternoon teas provided on request. Naseby Battlefield 6 miles, Market Harborough 7 miles, Bosworth Field 12 miles.

Open all year
4 bedrooms (3 twin/double ens. ᵐ/🍽/WC; 1 single ens. ᵐ/🍽/WC).
ETB 👑 👑Commended
Prices: B&B £15–16, weekly £105.

Wheathill Farm, Church Lane, Shearsby LE17 6PG
✆ (0533) 478663

The opportunity to stay in a fine old Grade 2 listed house with original beams and inglenook fireplaces, set in a large garden with a small lake containing many fish (who love to be fed), and surrounded by rolling fields where our herd of Friesian cows graze. Convenient for motorways, off the A50 south of Leicester, yet quiet and unspoilt. Delightful local pub offers home cooked food (for vegetarians too). Ground floor bedroom and cot available. Packed lunches on request. Coarse fishing, Peter Welton's studio within walking distance. Foxton Locks, Welford gliding 3 miles. Stoney Cove diving 5 miles.

Closed Xmas
4 bedrooms (1 twin ens. 🛁; 1 double; 1 family ens. 🚿/WC; 1 single), 1🛏, 2WCs.
🐕 ⊁ ETB 🏵 🏵
Prices: B&B £18–20. 🐕 rates.

MARKET HARBOROUGH   Map 2 B1

The Wrongs, Welford Road, Sibbertoft, Market Harborough LE16 9UJ
✆ (0858) 880886

Set in the rural peace of the Northamptonshire Uplands, the 400-acre farm of Wrongs grows arable crops with a flock of 350 sheep and cattle. The spacious bungalow offers every comfort, cot available. Packed lunches on request. Carp lake on the farm. The farm is south of A427 Market Harborough-Lutterworth road (turn off at Husbands Bosworth). The farm is a mile before the village. Foxton Locks 6 miles. Market Harborough 7 miles.

Open all year
2 bedrooms (1 double; 1 single), 1🛏, 1WC.
🐕 ⊁ 🐴 ETB Listed
Prices: B&B £14, weekly £91. 🐕 rates, 🐴 £5 per night.

MELTON MOWBRAY   Map 2 A1

Home Farm, Asfordby Hill, Melton Mowbray LE14 3QX
✆ (0664) 812634   Mrs J. Spicer

Traditional farmhouse hospitality awaits you at Home Farm, a working dairy farm on the edge of a small village less than 2 miles from Melton Mowbray (A6006 Melton Mowbray-Rempstone road).

Relax in the secluded garden or visit the local attractions. Asfordby Mine is close by, Bell Foundry Museum and Loughborough 11 miles. Belvoir Castle 15 miles.

Closed Xmas
2 bedrooms (1 twin; 1 double/family), 1🛏, 2WCs.
🐕(4) ⊁ ETB Listed
Prices: B&B £13–15, weekly £85–100. 🐕 rates.

Home Farm, Church Lane, Old Dalby, Melton Mowbray
✆ (0664) 822622   Val Anderson

This peaceful Victorian farmhouse is set in an idyllic garden facing the church. Traces of the wealthy estate village take our guests back into the 18th century. Enjoy breakfast before a crackling fire on frosty mornings, packed lunches on request, then sample the food at the Routier Best Pub in Great Britain (1991) at the nearby Crown Inn. Old Dalby lies west of the A606 Nottingham-Melton Mowbray road. National Water Sports Centre 10 miles. Trent Bridge, Belvoir Castle 12 miles. Newstead Abbey 20 miles.

Open all year
5 bedrooms (2 twin; 1 family; 2 single ens. 🛁/WC), 2🛏/WC.
⊁
Prices: B&B £21.50–25 single, £33 twin.

WHITWICK   Map 2 B1

Talbot House Farm, Whitwick LE67 4NQ
✆ (0530) 222233   F.E. White

Talbot House Farm is a working dairy on the B1587, south of the A512, 3 miles east of Ashby-de-la-Zouch. The farmhouse was once a stopping point on the stage coach route and it has retained the large comfortable rooms and old world charm. Cot available, packed lunches on request. A good base for exploring the area, within 10 miles are Bradgate Park, Bosworth Bat-

tle Centre, Calke Abbey, Melbourne Hall and
Laugh Steam Railway.

Open all year
4 bedrooms (2 twin; 2 double), 2🛏, 3WCs. 🐾
Prices: B&B £15, weekly £99.50. EM £6, B&B
plus EM weekly £131.50. 🐾 rates.

LINCOLNSHIRE

EAST BARKWITH
Map 5 B2

The Grange, Torrington Lane, East
Barkwith, Lincoln LN3 5RY
✆ (0673) 8585249   Mrs Anne Stamp

Discover this welcoming Georgian farmhouse on
a wildlife and conservation award winning farm in
a quiet location, complete with Aga cooking,
candlelit dinners, care and comfort. Lawn tennis,
croquet and herb beds in the extensive grounds.
The Grange lies a mile off the A157 (A158) east of
Lincoln, close to the Lincolnshire Wolds. The Viking Way is a 10 minute drive. Horncastle, Lincoln,
Louth, Market Rasen Races, Cadwell Park 10–14
miles.

Open all year
3 bedrooms (2 double inc. 1 ens.⋔/⇌/WC,1
ens.⋔/WC;1 twin ens.⋔/WC).
⚶(7) ETB ♛ ♛ ♛De Luxe
Prices: B&B from £18, EM £10–12.

GRANTHAM
Map 5 B3

Sproxton Lodge, Skillington, Grantham
NG33 5HJ
✆ (0476) 860307   Mrs E.M. Whatton

A friendly welcome awaits you in these tranquil
rural surroundings on an arable farm with animals
in a small grass paddock and plenty of wildlife
and grass walks beside the fields. Sproxton
Lodge is south of Grantham, 3 miles west of the
A1. In the comfortable farmhouse, built between
1790–1810, you can enjoy good home cooking.
Packed lunches on request, vegetarians catered
for. Cot available. The farm runs alongside the
Viking Way. Rutland Water, Burghley House, Belvoir Castle and Belton House within 30 minutes
by car.

Closed Xmas and New Year
3 bedrooms (1 twin; 1 family; 1 single), 1🛁,
2WCs.
⚶ ETB Listed
Prices: B&B £13–14, EM £6.⚶ rates.

Sycamore Farm, Bassingthorpe,
Grantham NG33 4ED
✆ (047685) 274   Mrs Sue Robinson

A warm welcome and comfortable accommodation is assured at Sycamore Farm. Our large
peaceful Victorian farmhouse, with wonderful
views across the open countryside, stands on a
450-acre mixed farm, under 5 miles from the A1
southeast of Grantham. We offer a relaxed atmosphere, an open fire, piano and good farmhouse cooking. Ensuite facilities available from 1
April 1993. Packed lunches on request. Within
easy reach of many tourist attractions: Belton
House and Belvoir Castle 10 miles, Rutland
Water 12 miles, Burghley House 15 miles.

Open April-Oct. **RAC**
3 bedrooms (2 twin; 1 family), 1🛁, 1WC.
⚶(6) ⚥ ETB ♛

Prices: B&B £14–17, weekly £90–110. EM £7–8.50. rates.

HOLBEACH
Map 5 B3

Guy Wells Farm, Whaplode, Spalding PE12 6TZ
✆ (0406) 22239
Anne Thompson

Guy Wells Farm is a mixed arable and flower production farm with intensive glasshouses. Well placed for exploring the Wash Marshes with its abundant wildlife and the North Norfolk coast. It lies south of A151 in Eastgate by Whaplode St Catherine, just 5 miles east of Spalding, 2 miles west of Holbeach. Butterfly Farm and Springfield Gardens 4 miles.

Closed Xmas
3 bedrooms (1 twin; 2 double inc. 1 ens. ☞/WC), 1🚗, 2WCs.
(10)
Prices: B&B £16–18.50, EM £10–11. Weekly B&B plus EM £182. rates.

White House Farm, Colleys Gate, Lutton PE12 9HT
✆ (0406) 364125

White House Farm is situated a mile from Long Sutton off A17. Although not a working farm, there are a number of animals, dogs and horses, on the farm. Butterfly Park half a mile. Kings Lynn, Wisbech and Spalding all 10 miles.

Open all year
5 bedrooms (2 twin; 2 double; 1 family), 1🚗, 3WCs.
 ⋔
Prices: B&B £12, weekly £50. rates.

HORNCASTLE
Map 5 B2

Greenfield Farm, Minting, Nr Horncastle LN9 5RX
✆ (0507) 578457

Judy and Hugh invite you to stay at their comfortable farmhouse, set in a quiet location yet centrally placed for all major Lincolnshire attractions. We offer guests their own sitting room with wood burning stove. Forest walks border the farm

which is south of A158 Horncastle-Wragby road, 3 miles east of Wragby. The Wolds 4 miles. Cadwell Park 9 miles.

Open all year
3 bedrooms (1 twin ens. /WC; 2 double inc. 1 ens. /WC), 1🚗, 2WCs.
 ⋌ ETB 🏵 🏵
Prices: B&B £16–17, weekly £112. rates.

Stamford House Farm, Miningsby, Lincs PE22 7NW
✆ (0507) 588682

The farmhouse, built in 1870, stands on a 5-acre smallholding for poultry and rabbits. 5 miles from Horncastle, the smallholding is outside Miningsby village (south of A158 Horncastle-Skegness road. Fishing within easy reach. Snipe Dales Nature Reserve 2 miles. Bolingbroke Castle 4 miles. Tennyson's birthplace 6 miles.

Open all year
3 bedrooms (1 twin; 2 double priv. ☞), 1, 1WC.
 ⋌ ⋔ ETB Listed
Prices: B&B £13.50–15.50, EM £8.50. rates, ⋔ £1 per night.

LINCOLN
Map 5 B2

New Farm, Burton, Lincoln LN1 2RD
✆ (0522) 527326
Mrs P. Russon

We look forward to welcoming you to our spacious modern farm bungalow, with large lawns and log fires in season. This is a working dairy and arable farm of 328 acres just 3 miles northwest of Lincoln (A57). The attractions of the city are within easy reach: Cathedral, castle, museum, golf course. A Nature Reserve adjoins the farm. Whisby Nature Park 10 minutes' drive. Coarse fishing in private lakes available.

Open Mar-Oct.
2 twin bedrooms inc. 1 private ☞/WC. 1/WC
 & (5) ETB 🏵 🏵 Approved
Prices: B&B £14–20, weekly £95–130. EM £8. Weekly B&B plus EM £150–180.

LOUTH
Map 5 B2

The Grange, Grange Lane, Covenham, Louth LN11 0PD
✆ (0507) 363678
Mrs Phyl Shaw

Phyl and Jim welcome you to share the interests of their arable farm and the comfort of their old farmhouse, 8 miles north of Louth (A16) and a mile from Covenham village. Phyl serves a traditional farmhouse breakfast and can recommend local pubs etc. for evening meals. The Grange is an excellent base for the Humber Bridge, historic Lincoln, Lincolnshire Wolds and the coast.

Open all year
5 bedrooms (3 double; 2 single), 1🛁, 1WC.
🍴 ETB Listed
Prices: B&B from £12.50. 🍴 rates.

MARKET RASEN   Map 5 B2

Bleasby House Farm, Legsby, Market Rasen LN8 3QN
✆ (0673) 842383

On a 1200-acre mixed farm stands this welcoming Victorian farmhouse with flower-filled rooms, sun lounge, large garden and hard tennis court. Good home cooking provided with packed lunches and afternoon teas on request. Fly fishing available. The farm lies 4 miles south of Market Rasen, off B1202 to Linwood. Race course and golf 3 miles. Lincoln 12 miles.

Open all year
3 bedrooms (2 twin inc. 1 ens.🛁/🖙/WC, 1 ens. 🛁/WC; 1 single ens. 🛁), 1WC.
🍴 ⊁ ETB 👑 👑Highly Commended
Prices: B&B £15–17, EM £10. 🍴 rates.

East Farmhouse, Buslingthorpe, Market Rasen
✆ (0673) 842283   Mrs Gill Grant

This conservation award winning farm has a spacious farmhouse, built in 1757 and listed as being of special historic interest. With log fires, oak beams, good food, peace and relaxation your care and comfort are assured. The farm lies south of Market Rasen, 2 miles off the A46 Lincoln road. The Viking Way over the Lincolnshire Wolds is nearby. This is Tennyson country, with lots of lovely market towns and pretty villages, potteries and antique centres to be discovered. Lincoln 13 miles.

Open all year
2 bedrooms (1 twin private 🛁/WC; 1 double ens. 🖙/WC).
🍴 ETB 👑 👑Highly Commended
Prices: B&B £16–17, weekly £112. EM £10.
Weekly B&B plus EM £187. 🍴 rates.

Hainton Walk, Ludford, Lincoln LN3 6AP
✆ (0507) 313242

This beautiful Georgian stone farmhouse is situated on the Wolds in an Area of Outstanding Natural Beauty. The house is set in almost an acre of informal gardens on a smallholding with a few sheep. Good farmhouse cooking provided, with packed lunches on request. Cot, highchair and children's games available. Hainton Walk is 5 miles from Market Rasen (A631/B1225). Trout fishing 3 miles. Horse racing and golf 5 miles. Coast 18 miles.

Closed Xmas
3 bedrooms (1 double; 1 family; 1 single), 🛁, 1🛁, 1WC.
🍴 ⊁ ETB Commended
Prices: B&B £13, weekly £70. EM £6.50–8.50, weekly B&B plus EM £130. 🍴 rates.

SLEAFORD   Map 5 B3

Manor Farm, Leasingham, Sleaford NG34 8JN
✆ (0529) 302671

This 400-acre arable farm has an attractive 16th-century farmhouse, the bedrooms look out over a large garden. TV and tea facilities in rooms. Cot and highchair available. Manor Farm is 2 miles from Sleaford off A15 Lincoln road. Cranwell RAF College 2 miles. Tattershall Castle 12 miles. Lincoln Cathedral 15 miles.

Open all year
2 twin bedrooms, 1🛁, 2WCs.
🍴 ⊁ ETB Listed
Prices: B&B £13–18. 🍴 rates.

STURTON-BY-STOW   Map 5 B2

Gallows Dale Farm, Stow Park Road, Sturton-by-Stow, Lincoln
✆ (0427) 788387

This tastefully refurbished Grade 2 Listed farmhouse is set in 33 acres of grass paddocks. Beamed ceilings in TV lounge and dining room. Full English breakfast provided, bedrooms have tea making facilities. Excellent evening meals available in local pubs. The farm is a mile from the centre of the village (A15/A1500 from Lincoln). Bransby Home for Horses and Stow Minster 2 miles. Lincoln 9 miles.

Open all year
4 bedrooms (1 twin; 1 double; 2 single), 1🛁, 1WC.
♨(5) ✄
Prices: B&B £14–16. ♨ rates.

The Village Farm, Sturton-by-Stow, Lincoln LN1 2AE
✆ (0427) 788309

The farmhouse, built in 1845, stands in a large garden in the centre of the village and has been completely renovated. On the edge of the village the mixed farm has Limousin cattle and a large conservation area. Situated 9 miles from Lincoln (A57/B1241), the area appeals to a variety of interests: Stow Church and Bransby Home for Horses 1 mile, Red Arrows aerobatic team base 3 miles, Doddington Hall and Gainsborough Old Hall 9 miles.

Open Apr-Oct.
3 bedrooms (1 twin; 1 double ens. ℗/⬃/WC; 1 single), 1🛁, 2WCs.
♨(10)
Prices: B&B £15–18, weekly £100–120. ♨ rates.

WRAGBY   Map 5 B2
Skirbeck Farm, Benniworth LN3 6JN
✆ (0507) 313682   Kay Olivant

In the heart of the beautiful Lincolnshire Wolds, stands this attractive farmhouse, surrounded by the farm's own undulating green acres with game woods, a beck and fishing lakes. Tea/coffee facilities in rooms, cot and toys provided. Skirbeck is a working livestock and arable farm just outside Benniworth village. From Lincoln take A158/157 to East Barkwith, then follow signs to Panton and Benniworth. Easy access to Lincoln, coast, Market Rasen racecourse and Cadwell Park.

Open Easter-Nov.
2 bedrooms (1 twin ens.⬃/WC; 1 family ens.⬃/WC), 2🛁, 2WCs.
♨ ✄ ETB ♨ ♨
Prices: B&B £15–17.

Self-Catering

LOUTH   Map 5 B2
Willow Farm, Great Carlton, Louth LN11 8JP
✆ (0507) 338540

Accommodation is available on this fly and coarse fishing farm in a 3-bedroomed unit,

sleeps 5. Ground floor bedrooms available. The farm is south of the B1200, 9 miles east of Louth. Three golf courses within 10 miles.

Open all year
ETB♪♪♪
Prices: weekly £100–250.

SPILSBY   Map 2 B2
Northfield Farm, Mavis Enderby, Spilsby PE23 4EW
✆ (0507) 588251   Mrs C.A. Miller

Situated in a secluded rural area, there are two semi-detached Victorian cottages on Northfield Farm that offer an excellent base for a country holiday. The cottages are 3-bedroomed, sleep 4. Cot and highchair provided. The farm is 3 miles west of Spilsby (B1195). Country Park and Nature Reserve 1 mile. Bolingbroke Castle ruins 2 miles.

Open all year
🐂 ETB♪♪♪
Prices: weekly £125–255.

STAINTON-BY-LANGWORTH   Map 5 B2
Stainton Manor Farm Cottage, Stainton-by-Langworth, Lincoln LN3 5BL
✆ (0673) 62423   Mrs L.M.H. Bowser
Write to: Stainton Manor, Langworth, Lincoln

This tastefully decorated self-catering cottage stands in a quiet hamlet, off the A158 east of Lincoln. It is fully equipped for 5 people, cot and highchair provided. Fruit farm, trout fishing and adventure playground under 2 miles. 40-acre trout fishing reservoir 5 miles. Market Rasen and Lincoln 7 miles.

Open April-Oct.
♨ 🐂 ETB♪♪♪♪Commended
Prices: weekly £150–200.

WRAGBY   Map 5 B2
Skirbeck Farm, Benniworth LN3 6JN
✆ (0507) 313682   Kay Olivant

For full farm description see above. Lavender Cottage is in the village of South Willingham, just west of Benniworth. It has 2 bedrooms and sleeps 4–5.

Open all year
🐂
Prices: weekly £145–165.🐂 rates.

NORFOLK

EAST DEREHAM
Map 3 B1

Ivy House Farm, Welgate, Mattishall, East Dereham

℡ (0362) 850208   Mrs Betty Jewson

Ivy House Farm is a Grade 2 listed building, a fascinating mixture part Jacobean, part Georgian with Elizabethan influences. This working farm, located south off the A47, west of Norwich, consists of a flock of breeding ewes and approx. 3000 free range chickens. Mrs Jewson offers good home cooking and comfort. Packed lunches on request. East Dereham 4 miles. Rural Life Museum 4 miles. Norwich 12 miles. North Norfolk coast and various wildlife sanctuaries 30 miles.

Open all year
3 bedrooms (2 twin; 1 double), 1➡, 1WC.
⚒ ⊁
Prices: B&B £13, EM £6. ⚒ rates.

FAKENHAM
Map 3 B1

Old Coach House, Thursford, Fakenham NR21 0BD

℡ (0328) 878273

This peaceful Norfolk farmhouse in a parkland setting was converted from a 17th-century coach house and stables. Whilst it now has all modern comforts it still retains immense charm and character. The farm, midway between Fakenham and Holt on the A148, has a small herd of cows, a few sheep, ducks, chickens and household pets. Ground floor bedroom available. The Thursford

Collection (steam organs and Wurlittzer) is within walking distance. Pensthorpe Wildfowl Lakes 5 miles. Birdwatching at Titchwell 15 miles, Cley 10 miles and Blakeney Point 10 miles. Sandringham House 15 miles.

Open all year
4 bedrooms (3 twin inc. 2 ens.⊟/WC; 1 double), 1➡, 1WC.
& ⚒ ⊁ ETB Listed
Prices: B&B £15–18, weekly £100–120. EM £6–8. Weekly B&B plus EM £140–160. ⚒ rates.

THETFORD
Map 3 A1

East Farm, Barnham, Thetford IP24 2PB

℡ (0842) 890231   Mrs Margaret Heading

The farm is arable and sheep and beef. Our farmhouse is comfortable and spacious, set in a large garden in peaceful surroundings with superb views, just off the A134 south of Thetford. Our central position in East Anglia offers easy access to the coast and towns. Euston Hall 2 miles. Grimes Graves 6 miles. Bury St Edmunds 12 miles.

Open all year
2 bedrooms (1 twin ens.ℿ/⊟/WC;1 double ens.ℿ/⊟/WC).
⚒ ETB ♛
Prices: B&B £19–22. ⚒ rates.

Malting Farm, Blo Norton Road, South Lopham, Diss IP22 2HT
✆ (037988) 201   Mrs C. Huggins

Malting Farm is situated on the Norfolk/Suffolk border, on the A1066 midway between Thetford and Diss. It is a working dairy farm with an Elizabethan timber framed farmhouse, whose character remains intact assisted by some four poster beds and inglenook fireplaces and the fruits of the owner's keen interest in embroidery, patchwork and spinning. Guests are welcome to watch the cows being milked. Cot and highchair available. Thelnetham Windmill 3 miles. Blooms Gardens and Steam Museum Bressingham 3 miles.

Closed Xmas and New Year
3 bedrooms (1 twin; 1 double ens.🛏/WC; 1 family), 1🛏, 1WC.
🕅 ⅄ ETB 👑 👑
Prices: B&B from £15. 🕅 rates.

WYMONDHAM   Map 3 B1

Rose Farm, Suton, Wymondham NR18 9JN
✆ (0953) 603512

The family will all enjoy the opportunity to stay on this attractive smallholding situated close to the A11, between Wymondham and Attleborough. The poultry farm has ducks, geese and Bantam chickens, also donkeys which small children are welcome to ride. At Rose Farm you can sample good traditional farmhouse cooking. Packed lunches and afternoon teas on request. Ground floor bedrooms, cot and children's games available. Wymondham Abbey and Wicklewood Windmill close by. Banham Zoo and Craft Centre 8 miles. Norwich 10 miles.

Closed Xmas
4 bedrooms (1 double; 1 family; 2 single), 2🛏, 2WCs.
🕭 🕅 ⅄ ETB Listed
Prices: B&B £16–18, weekly £110–120. EM £8. Weekly B&B plus EM £160–180. 🕅 rates.

NORTHAMPTONSHIRE

BRACKLEY
Map 2 B2

Walltree House Farm, Steane, Brackley
✆ (0295) 811235   Richard & Pauline Harrison

In a courtyard adjacent to the farmhouse are grouped these comfortable and warm motel-type rooms. Breakfast is served in the farmhouse, packed lunches on request. Licensed. On this arable farm in the depths of the countryside you can enjoy peace and quiet in the woodlands and along the pleasant walks with which the area abounds. Walltree House Farm is under 2 miles from the A422, between Brackley and Banbury. Silverstone circuit 10 miles. Numerous NT properties 10–30 miles. Oxford, Blenheim, Stratford and Warwick 20 miles.

Closed Xmas and New Year
8 bedrooms (3 twin inc. 1 ens.🛁; 2 ens.☞/WC; 3 double ens.☞/WC; 2 family ens.☞/WC;), 1WC.
🐾 ETB ♛ ♛ ♛
Prices: B&B £18–26. 🐾 rates.

DAVENTRY
Map 2 B2

Barewell Fields, Prestidge Row, Moreton Pinkney, Daventry NN11 6NJ
✆ (0295) 760754   Margaret Lainchbury
Bakewell Fields is a comfortable, warm modern house tucked away amongst pleasing 16th- and 17th-century stone cottages in the peaceful village of Moreton Pinkney. Packed lunches and evening meals on request. Home Farm is 5 minutes' walk away. It is run by Margaret Lainchbury's son, Richard, and guests are always welcome to visit. This is a mixed farm, mainly

sheep and arable. The village is on the old B4525 Banbury-Northampton road.

Open Mar-Nov.
3 bedrooms (1 twin; 1 double; 1 single), 1🛏, 2WCs.
🐾(7) ETB Listed Highly Commended
Prices: B&B £15–18, weekly £100–120.

KETTERING
Map 5 A3

Dairy Farm, Cranford, Kettering NN14 4AQ
✆ (053678) 273   Audrey E. Clarke

The farmhouse at Dairy Farm is a 17th-century thatched Jacobean manor house, with an ancient dovecote in the grounds. A house of great character and typical of this area of Northamptonshire. Accommodation is in the farmhouse and the adjacent 2-bedroomed stable flat, which has full wheelchair access. There is good country cooking with home produce and a large garden to enjoy. This is a working arable farm, easily accessible from the new A14 (A604) near the village (A6 southeast from Kettering). The area has much to offer: Wichstead Park, Boughton House, Rockingham Castle, Coton Manor, Oundle, Burleigh House.

Open all year
5 bedrooms (3 twin inc. 2 ens. ᝐ/WC; 2 double inc. 1 ens. ᝐ/WC), 1🐾, 1🏠, 1WC.
🔥 🐾 ⵗ ETB ♛ ♛ ♛Commended
Prices: B&B £18–20, EM £10–12. 🐾 rates,ⵗ rates.

West Lodge Farm, Pipewell Road, Desborough NN14 2SH
℗ (0536) 760552   Mrs M. Edee

Stay in a spacious William the Fourth Farmhouse, on an arable farm where walks across the farmland provide sightings of abundant wildlife. 600 acres farmed, containing 80 acres of woodland and old iron stone quarries now reverting to wildlife havens. Packed lunches available. Sculpture courses given. The farm is 4 miles south of Market Harborough (A6/B669). Close by are numerous trout fisheries, sailing on 2 reservoirs and many stately homes.

Closed Xmas
2 bedrooms (1 twin ens. ᝐ/WC; 1 double ens. 🏠/WC).
🐾 ⵗ ETB ♛ ♛Commended
Prices: B&B £20, weekly £120. 🐾 rates.

NORTHAMPTON   Map 2 B1

The Elms, Kislingbury, Northampton
℗ (0604) 830326   Mr & Mrs D. Sanders

The Elms is a 450-acre mixed family run farm with a large Victorian farmhouse in the middle of Kislingbury village, 4 miles west of Northampton (A45/B452). All care is taken to make your stay an enjoyable one, packed lunches and afternoon teas provided, cot available. The Old Dairy Farm Centre 3 miles. Althorpe 4 miles. Sulgrave Manor 12 miles. M1, Jct16 2 miles.

Open all year
3 bedrooms (1 twin/family; 1 double; 1 single), 1🐾, 1WC.
🐾 ✂ ⵗ ETB Listed

Prices: B&B £17.50, weekly £105. 🐾 rates,ⵗ rates.

Quinton Green Farm, Quinton, Northampton NN7 2EG
℗ (0604) 862484   Mrs M. Turney

Quinton Green is a comfortable rambling 17th-century farmhouse with lovely views over its own land. We have a family run 1200-acre dairy and arable farm lying 6 miles south of Northampton (A508 then turning signed for Wootton and Quinton). Golf courses nearby. Excellent walks in Salcey Forest 1 mile. Canal Museum and Wootton Hall Park 4 miles. Towcester racecourse 8 miles.

Open all year
3 bedrooms (1 twin; 1 double; 1 single), 1🐾, 3WCs.
🐾 ⵗ ETB ♛ ♛Commended
Prices: B&B £15–18, weekly £105. 🐾 rates.

Wold Farm, Old, Northampton NN6 9RJ
℗ (0604) 781258   Mrs Anne Engler

The perfect choice for a break in the country. This 18th-century farmhouse stands on a 350-acre beef and arable farm, with delightful gardens and ornamental pheasants. The house is an attractive blend of comfort and beauty with oak beamed dining room, inglenook fireplace and snooker table. Home cooking, packed lunches on request. Ground floor bedroom, camping cot and highchair available. Wold Farm is north of Northampton between the A508 and the A43. Lamport Hall 2 miles. Brixworth Church (7th-century) 3 miles. Pitsford Reservoir (trout fishing, birdwatching and sailing) 4 miles. Kettering with new leisure village 6 miles. Northampton 10 miles.

Open all year
6 bedrooms (1 twin ens.🏠; 2 double inc. 1 ens.ᝐ, 1 ens.ᝐ/WC; 1 family ens. 🏠; 2 single ens.🏠/WC), 1WC.
🐾 ⵗ ETB ♛ ♛ ♛
Prices: B&B £18–21, EM from £10. Reductions for 3 nights or more. 🐾 rates,ⵗ £1 per night.

WELFORD
Map 5 A3

West End Farm, 5, West End, Welford
NN6 7HJ
✆ (0858) 575226

The farmhouse at West End was built in 1848, and stands on a sheep farm with 2 set-aside fields with access to public and fine views. The farm is 9 miles from Lutterworth (A427 east to Husbands Bosworth/A50 south to Welford). Cold Ashby Golf Club 2 miles. Naseby battlefield and Stanford Hall 3 miles.

Open all year
2 bedrooms (1 twin; 1 double ens. WC), 1🛏,
2WCs.
🐕 🚭 ETB ♛
Prices: B&B £15–20. 🐕 rates.

YARDLEY GOBION
Map 2 B2

Old Wharf Farm, Yardley Gobion NN12
7UE
✆ (0908) 542454
John Bowen

An historic farm and village wharf complex of Grade 2 listed buildings beside the Grand Union Canal. The smallholding is 10 acres and includes cattle, pigs and waterfowl. The wharf has a working dry dock where canal boats of all sorts are maintained. A rowing skiff can be borrowed for picnics, etc. Yardley Gobion is south of Northampton on the A508. Stoke Bruerne Canal Mu-

seum and Milton Keynes 3 miles. Towcester race course 6 miles. Silverstone circuit 8 miles.

Open all year.
3 bedrooms (1 double; 1 family; 1 single), 1🛏,
1🚿, 2WCs.
🐕 🐕 ETB Classified
Prices: B&B £17–20, weekly £100–120. 🐕
rates.

Self-Catering

NORTHAMPTON
Map 2 B1

Rye Hill Farm, Holdenby Road, East
Haddon, Northampton NN6 8DH
✆ (0604) 770990
Michael & Margaret
Widdowson

Accommodation is offered in five top quality, superbly equipped self-catering cottages, sleeping 2–6. Cot, highchair, sandpit, playroom and games provided. One cottage, sleeps 2, adapted for needs of disabled guests. Set in peaceful rolling countryside. Here you will find wonderful views, a charming atmosphere and friendly farm animals. Located off the A428 northwest of Northampton, Rye Hill Farm makes an excellent touring centre, Holdenby House 1 mile, Althorp House 2 miles, Cottes Brooke Hall 6 miles, Stoke Bruerne Canal Museum 15 miles.

Open all year
♿ 🐕 🐕 ETB♛♛♛♛Highly Commended
Prices: weekly £120–340.🐕 £15 per week.

KEY TO SYMBOLS	
Bath	🛁
Shower	🚿
Bathroom	🛏
Disabled Guest Facilities	♿
No Smoking	🚭
Children Welcome	🐕
Dogs by Arrangement	🐕

NORTHUMBERLAND

CHATHILL
Map 7 B2

Doxford Farm, Embleton, Chathill
℡ (066579) 235　　　　　A.D. Turnbull

Doxford Farm is situated centrally in 600 acres of unspoilt wooded countryside, 5 miles north of the market town of Alnwick. It is ideally placed for visiting other parts of Northumberland, being between the foothills of the Cheviots and the lovely heritage coastline. Good farmhouse cooking and packed lunches on request. Cot, highchair, playroom and tennis available. The sea 4 miles. Dunstanburgh Castle 5 miles. Alnwick Castle 7 miles. Chillingham Wild Cattle 7 miles.

Closed Xmas and New Year
4 bedrooms (1 twin; 1 double; 1 family ens. ⋔/☞/WC; 1 single), 1⇥, 1WC.
⚘ ⚡ ⋔ ETB ☽ ☽Approved
Prices: B&B £15–18, weekly £90–120. EM £8–9. Weekly B&B plus EM £140–180. ⚘ rates.

CORBRIDGE
Map 7 B3

Wallhouses Farm, Military Road, Corbridge NE45 5PU
℡ (0434) 672226　　　　Jean Patterson

Wallhouses is a working farm of cattle, sheep and arable land. Visitors are welcome to look around. It is an attractive period house situated on the Roman Wall, the garden is the Roman Ditch. The farm is 2 miles off the A69 west of Newcastle-upon-Tyne, well placed for exploring the area and sampling the variety of excellent pubs and restaurants in the area. Corbridge 4 miles.

Open April-Oct.
2 bedrooms (1 double; 1 family), 2⇥, 1WC. ⚘
Prices: B&B £15–16. ⚘ rates.

HALTWHISTLE
Map 7 A3

White Craig Farm, Shield Hill, Haltwhistle NE49 9NW
℡ (0434) 320565　　　Mrs R.A.C. Laidlow

Our very old ranch-style farmhouse is on a working sheep and rare breeds farm just a mile from Hadrian's Wall, east of Haltwhistle off the A69 Hexham road. Amid such magnificent scenery we offer every attention to your comfort in a friendly atmosphere. All rooms on the ground floor. Packed lunches on request. With excellent walks in every direction, this is a wonderful area for all country pursuits. Golf 3 miles.

Closed Xmas and New Year
3 bedrooms (2 double ens.⋔/WC; 1 twin ens.☞/WC).
⚡ ETB ☽ ☽ Highly Commended
Prices: B&B (per couple) £37–40, weekly £250.

HEXHAM-ON-TYNE
Map 7 B3

Allgood Farm, Simonburn, Hexham NE48 3BA
℡ (0434) 681359

This 18th-century farmhouse is set in a valley with magnificent open views. There is a large garden with walks over the farm's 520 acres, Hadrian's Wall only 10 mins away. Tea/coffee facilities and a separate lounge for guests use, evening meals and packed lunches available on request. The farm lies northwest of Hexham (A69 then B6318/B6320).

Open all year
2 bedrooms (1 twin; 1 double/family), 1➡, 1WC. 🌢 ⅍ ✝ ETB Listed Commended
Prices: B&B £13.50, EM £7. 🌢 rates.

Rye Hill Farm, Slaley, Nr Hexham NE47 OA4
✆ (0434) 673259   Elizabeth Courage

Come and stay in a warm and comfortable barn conversion on our small working livestock farm. We are noted for our friendly atmosphere and good food. Packed lunches on request. Licensed. Situated 4 miles south of Hexham on the B6306, we are surrounded by miles of beautiful countryside. Hadrian's Wall 8 miles. Metro Center 21 miles. Beamish Open Air Museum 15 miles.

Open all year
6 bedrooms (2 twin ens.🌢/�'WC; 2 double inc 1 ens.🌢/�'WC, 1 ens.🌢/WC; 2 family inc. 1 ens.🌢/WC, 1 ens.🌢/WC), 1➡, 2WCs. 🌢 ✝ ETB 🏅 🏅 🏅Commended
Prices: B&B £16.50-18.50, weekly £104-116.50. EM £9. 🌢 rates,✝ £1 per night.

Taylor Burn, Ninebanks, Hexham NE4 78DE
✆ (0434) 345343   Mr & Mrs C.P. Robson

Taylor Burn has a large comfortable farmhouse with outstanding views. On this working hill farm in the Pennine Dales Environmentally Sensitive Area you are welcome to join in the farm's activities – free range hens, sheep and cattle, walk the adjacent Alternative Pennine Way, or just enjoy the quiet and outstanding natural beauty. Good food and a warm welcome. The farm is 18 miles from Hexham, (A69 west, A686 south, then

signed to Ninebanks). Alston 6 miles. Hadrian's Wall 10 miles.

Open all year
3 bedrooms (2 double; 1 single), 1➡, 1WC. 🌢(7) ⅍ ✝
Prices: B&B £12-15, weekly £90-100. EM £5.50-8.50, weekly B&B plus £120-130. 🌢 rates,✝ rates.

MORPETH   Map 7 B3

East Farm, Eshott, Felton, Morpeth
✆ (0670) 787236   Mrs M. Pickard

This attractive farmhouse stands on a working mixed farm, arable and beef cattle. There is a large conservatory and south facing garden with tennis court. East Farm is west of A1 6 miles north of Morpeth. Many local attractions include Druridge Bay, Hadston Nature Reserve, Northumbrian Microlights at Eshote Airfield (instruction available), and Bywell Shooting Ground, the venue for international clay shooting events.

Open all year
2 bedrooms (1 twin; 1 double), 1➡, 2WCs. 🌢(12) ⅍ ✝ ETB Listed
Prices: B&B £14-16.

STOCKSFIELD-ON-TYNE   Map 7 B3

Wheelbirks Jersey Farm, Stocksfield-on-Tyne NE43 7HY
✆ (0661) 843378

This comfortable Victorian farmhouse stands on a 350-acre mixed farm, including dairy herd, sheep and forestry. The garden is worth exploring. Good country cooking, packed lunches and afternoon teas and in the evening high tea is served on request. The farm is east of the A68 and south of the A69, 12 miles west of Newcastle. This is good cycle touring country along by the Tyne Valley and Hadrian's Wall. Thomas Bewick's House 3 miles. Corbridge 5 miles. Keilder Water 30 miles.

Open May-Oct.
2 twin bedrooms, 1➡, 3WCs. 🌢(8) ETB Listed
Prices: B&B £16, weekly £110 (7 nights). EM £6. 🌢 rates.

See STOP PRESS
for more farms

WOOLER
Map 7 B2

Earle Hill Head Farm, Wooler NE71 6RH
℡ (0668) 81243   Mr & Mrs C.H. Armstrong

Earle Hill Head is a hill farm in 4000 acres of Northumberland National Park, with fantastic views from the farmhouse. Our home is very comfortable and everyone is made to feel welcome. Packed lunches and afternoon teas provided. We are situated off the A697 by Wooler. Within 30 minutes' drive you can choose the coast, castles or the Scottish Border.

Open April-Oct.
3 bedrooms (1 twin ens. ⋒/☞/WC; 2 double), 2🛏, 2WCs.
🏠(6) 🐦
Prices: B&B £15–17. 🏠 rates.

West Kirknewton Farm, Wooler NE71 6XF
℡ (06686) 227   Mrs E. Martin

This recently converted old mill gives comfortable and homely accommodation. We farm sheep and beef cows in the foothills of the Cheviot Hills on the edge of the Northumberland National Park. An ideal area for hillwalking. The farm is 6 miles northwest of Wooler, (A697 then B6351). Situated near the Scottish border within 3 mins are the historic towns of Berwick-upon-Tweed, Kelso and Jedburgh.

Open Apr-Sept.
2 bedrooms (1 twin; 1 family), 1🛏, 1WC.
🏠 ⚥
Prices: B&B £13–15, weekly £84–98. 🏠 rates.

Self-Catering

BELFORD
Map 7 B2

Greymare Farm, Belford NE20 7P9
℡ (0668) 213395

Two attractive cottages stand together not far from the farmhouse on this working sheep farm situated less than 3 miles north of Belford, outside the village of Detchant. The farm is quiet and secluded, part hill land, part grass, and has many lovely walks and views. Rose Cottage has 2 bedrooms, sleeps 4. Honeysuckle Cottage has 3 bedrooms, sleeps 6. Both are very well-equipped and cosy with open fires. Holy Island 8 miles. Berwick-upon-Tweed 12 miles.

Open all year
ETB𝄪𝄪𝄪 and 𝄪𝄪𝄪𝄪Commended
Prices: weekly £100–280.

Outchester and Ross Farm Cottages, Ross Farm, Belford NE70 7EN
℡ (0668) 213336   Mr & Mrs Sutherland

Our property is midway between Holy Island and Bamburgh, beside the Lindisfarne National Nature Reserve. An 18th-century farmhouse and 11 coastguard and farm cottages provide a choice of accommodation, ranging from 2–5 bedrooms, sleeping 4–11. The farm has breeding ewes, suckler cows with calves, and grows wheat and barley. At Ross Farm there is 3 miles of sandy beach. For Ross Farm, cross A1 from Belford and head northeast. For Outchester cross A1 from Belford and take B1342. Belford 3 miles. Lindisfarne Castle 5 miles.

Open all year
ETB𝄪𝄪𝄪/𝄪𝄪𝄪𝄪Approved-Commended
Prices: daily (Nov.-Easter only) £20–50, weekly £100–500.

CHATHILL
Map 7 B2

Tughall Grange, Chathill, Alnwick
℡ (066589) 239   Mrs S.M. Jordon

The mixed farm of Tughall Grange is just 2 miles from the coast, off the coastal road 3 miles south of Seahouses. The farm is arable with cattle, sheep and horses. Accommodation is available in the farm cottage, 3 bedrooms, sleeps 6. Cot, highchair, toys and cottage garden provided. Within 5 miles is a choice of beaches. Farne Islands 3 miles. Alnwick 11 miles. Holy Island 15–20 miles.

Open Apr-Oct.
🐦 ETB𝄪𝄪𝄪
Prices: weekly £180–250.

HALTWHISTLE Map 7 A3
White Craig Farm, Shield Hill, Haltwhistle
NE49 9NW
℡ (0434) 320565   Mrs R.A.C. Laidlow

Our very old ranch-style farmhouse is on a working sheep and rare breeds farm just a mile from Hadrian's Wall, east of Haltwhistle off the A69 Hexham road. We have converted the smithy and other farm buildings into four very comfortable self-catering cottages, sleeping 3–8. With excellent walks in every direction, this is a wonderful area for all country pursuits. Golf 3 miles.

Closed Xmas and New Year
🐾 ⊁ ETB♪♪♪♪ Highly Commended
Prices: weekly £90–310.

MORPETH Map 7 B2
Gallowhill Farm, Whalton, Morpeth
℡ (0661) 881241   Mr & Mrs A.P. Coatsworth

On Gallowhill Farm accommodation is available in two spacious stone semi-detached cottages, recently modernised to the highest standard, with grassed gardens front and back. The cottages have 2 and 4 bedrooms, sleeping 4 and 6. The very tidy mixed working farm has cereals, cattle and sheep. Gallowhill Farm is situated 10 miles west of Morpeth (B6524). Bolam Lake 2 miles. Belsay Castle 4 miles. Wallington House 6 miles.

Open May-Oct.
ETB♪♪♪♪♪Highly Commended
Prices: weekly £180–375.

WOOLER Map 7 B2
Branxton Moor Farm, Cornhill-on-Tweed
TD12 4QF
℡ (089082) 246

Accommodation is available in a large well-equipped cottage, sleeps 6, on this working sheep and corn farm. There are also goats. The farm is in lovely open countryside under 2 miles south of A697 Newcastle-Edinburgh road, between Wooler and Coldstream. Branxton Moor Farm stands beside Flodden Field, Coldstream 8 miles.

Open all year
ETB♪♪♪
Prices: weekly £90–155.

Firwood Bungalow and Humphrey's
House, Nr Middleton Hall, Wooler NE71 6RH
℡ (0668) 81243   Contact: Mrs S. Armstrong, Earle Hill Head Farm, Wooler NE71 6RH

Firwood Bungalow and Humphrey's House stand in well maintained gardens at the foot of the Cheviot Hills near Middleton Hall in the National Park 2 miles south of Wooler, just off A697. Both are furnished to a very high standard. Firwood sleeps 9–11, Humphrey's sleeps 6. We assure you of every comfort, central heating, log fires and Highland cattle in the field. You are welcome to walk the 4000 acres of Earle Hill Farm which extends to the foot of the Cheviot itself. Fishing by prior arrangement. Cross-country skiing in winter.

Open all year
ETB♪♪♪♪Highly Commended
Prices: weekly £190–460.

NORTH YORKSHIRE

AMPLEFORTH

Carr House Farm, Ampleforth YO6 4ED
✆ (03476) 526   Mrs Anna Taylor
✆ From February 1993 (0347) 868526

Our 16th-century farmhouse stands on a family
run mixed farm in peaceful Herriot countryside, to
add to the atmosphere there is even a romantic
four poster bed. Our hospitality has been recommended by the Sunday Observer and Yorkshire Life. We are situated in undulating
pastureland in the Hambleton Hills north of York,
halfway between Ampleforth and the tiny hamlet
of Wass (south of the A170). Byland Abbey 1
mile. Newburgh Priory, Shandy Hall 2 miles. Gill-
ing Castle 4 miles. Helmsley Castle 5 miles. Rievaulx Abbey 7 miles.

Closed Xmas and New Year
3 double bedrooms ens. ⋔/WC).
⚜(7) ⚥ ETB ♛ ♛
Prices: B&B £12.50–15, EM £7.50.

BAINBRIDGE

High Force Farm, Bainbridge, Leyburn
✆ (0969) 50379   Mrs M. Iveson

My spacious farmhouse is warm and welcoming.
The surrounding 470-acre farm consists of 40
milking cows and 500 sheep. During April the
farm is open in the afternoons for visitors to watch
the lambing and feed pet lambs. High Force
Farm is located south of the A684 Kendal-
Leyburn road, in wonderful walking country. Lake
Semer Water is 5 minutes from the farm. Aysgarth
Falls 4 miles.

Open all year
3 bedrooms (1 twin; 1 double; 1 family), 2♛,
2WCs.
⚜ ⚥ ETB Listed
Prices: B&B £12.50–14, weekly £87–98. ⚜
rates.

BEDALE

Ainderby Myers Farm, Bedale DL8 1PF
✆ (0609) 748668   Mrs Valerie Anderson

Step back in time in this fascinating manor house
with origins dating back to the 10th century.
Once farmed by the monks of nearby Jervaulx
Abbey, the 420-acre mixed working farm now lies
west of the A1, southeast of Richmond. In this
peaceful area there is pony trekking, fishing,
walks across farmland or on open moorland and
plenty of excellent inns serving good food.
Packed lunches on request, cot and highchair
provided. Within 10 miles are Castle Bolton, Aysgarth Falls, local market towns and Rare Breed
Centres.

Open all year
4 bedrooms (1 twin; 1 double; 1 family; 1 single),
2♛, 2WCs.
⚜ ⚥ ETB ♛ ♛Approved
Prices: B&B £14–15, EM £8.50. Weekly B&B
plus EM £157–178. ⚜ rates.

KEY TO SYMBOLS

Bath	☶
Shower	⋔
Bathroom	♛
Disabled Guest Facilities	♿
No Smoking	⚥
Children Welcome	⚜
Dogs by Arrangement	☍

HELMSLEY
Map 5 A1

Barn Close Farm, Rievaulx, Helmsley YO6 5HL
© (04396) 321
Joan Milburn

This hill farm is set in a wooded valley with outstanding views, close to Rievaulx Abbey and old Byland. The farmhouse cooking, with fresh baked bread a speciality, comes highly recommended. Packed lunches on request. Ground floor bedrooms available. Cot and highchair provided. A rewarding area for walking or riding, the scenery is magnificent. Situated north off the A170 Thirsk-Pickering road. Helmsley Castle 5 miles. Castle Howard 15 miles.

Open all year
2 bedrooms (1 double ens. ⋔/WC; 1 family), 1🛏,
3WCs.
🐾 ETB 👑 👑 👑
Prices: B&B £14–18, EM £10. Weekly B&B plus EM £175–196. 🐾 rates.

Cringle Carr Farm, Hawnby, Helmsley YO6 5LT
© (04396) 264
Susan Garbutt

We offer a warm welcome and all the comforts of home to our guests. Our dairy farm stands amid scenic surroundings on the B1257, north off the A170 Thirsk-Pickering road. Good home cooking provided in a friendly atmosphere. Rievaulx Abbey 2 miles. Helmsley 5 miles.

Open Mar-Nov.
2 bedrooms (1 twin; 1 double), 1🛏, 1WC.
ETB 👑
Prices: B&B £14–15, weekly £98. EM £9.
Weekly B&B plus EM £161. Winter rates.

Hill End Farm, Chop Gate, Bilsdale TS9 7JR
© (04396) 278
Brenda Johnson

Hill End Farm is a 17th-century farmhouse with beautiful views of Bilsdale. We provide good farmhouse fare, packed lunches on request. Cot and highchair available. This is a stock rearing farm and guests are welcome to look around. The farm lies 9 miles north of Helmsley (B1257). Rievaulx Abbey 5 miles. Stokesley 9 miles. Great Ayton (Captain Cook country) 11 miles. York and Whitby 30 miles.

Open Easter-Nov.
2 bedrooms (1 double; 1 family ens. 🖙/WC),
1🛏, 1WC.
🐾 ETB 👑 👑
Prices: B&B £14–16. EM £9. 🐾 rates.

Laskill Farm, Hawnby, Nr Helmsley
© (04396) 268
Mrs S. Smith

Relax in this attractive stone-built farmhouse with its own secluded walled garden and lake in the heart of James Herriot country. The farm has 600 acres of sheep and beef cattle. The house is lovingly cared for throughout. We offer a high standard of cuisine using home grown produce as much as possible. Packed lunches on request. Ground floor bedrooms, cot and highchair available. Laskill Farm is 6 miles north of Helmsley off the B1257. A walker's paradise, with many places of historic interest nearby. Pony trekking locally.

Closed Xmas
8 bedrooms (3 twin inc. 2 ens.⌂/☐/WC; 3 double inc. 2 ens.⌂/☐/WC; 1 family; 1 single), 1🛏, 2WCs.
🐾 ✝
Prices: B&B £15.50–20, weekly £118.50–140. EM £10.50. Weekly B&B plus EM £195.50–217. 🐾 rates.

Wether Cote Farm, Bilsdale, Helmsley
✆ (04396) 260　　　　　　　　Winnie Wood

Wether Cote Farm is a working farm lying 7 miles north of the market town of Helmsley (B1257). We offer good home cooking and a welcoming atmosphere. All around us there are beautiful views of the sensational scenery. Ideally placed for walking, pony trekking or touring. Within easy reach are Rievaulx Abbey, Wunnington Hall, Castle Howard, Duncombe Park and much more.

Open Mar-Nov.
3 bedrooms (1 double; 1 family; 1 single), 1🛏, 1⌂, 2WCs.
🐾 ✝ ETB Listed
Prices: B&B £13, EM £8. 🐾 rates.

INGLEBY GREENHOW　　　　Map 5 A1
Manor House Farm, Ingleby Greenhow, Great Ayton TS9 6RB
✆ (0642) 722384　　　　　Dr & Mrs M. Bloom

This delightful stone-built farmhouse, parts of which date from circa 1760, stands on a 164-acre grass and arable farm in North Yorkshire Moors National Park and has an open view over the hills. Rare breed animals and wildlife surround the farmhouse which is approached via a half-mile wooded drive. Accommodation is of the highest standard with fine evening dinners and wines. Licensed. Packed lunches on request. Manor House Farm lies southeast of Middlesborough, off the B1365/1257. Captain Cook Country 5 miles. James Herriot Country 15 miles. Ryedale Folk Museum, Rievaulx Abbey 20 miles.

Closed Xmas
3 bedrooms (2 twin; 1 double), 3🛏, 3WCs.
🐾(12) ⚡ ✝ ETB ♨ ♨Commended
Prices from: B&B £21–24. EM £10. Weekly B&B plus EM £210–235.

INGLETON　　　　　　　　　Map 4 B1
Langber, Tatterthorne Lane, Ingleton, via Carnforth LA6 3DT
✆ (05242) 41587　　　　　　　Mrs Mollie Bell

This large and comfortable Victorian residence with panoramic views is attached to a 60-acre smallholding with sheep and lambs. Mrs Bell provides wholesome home cooking and baking. Located off the A65 between Kirkby Lonsdale and Settle, Langber is a good centre for visiting the Cumbrian Lakes, Yorkshire Dales and Lancashire coast. Kirkby Lonsdale 8 miles.

Closed Xmas
7 bedrooms (2 twin inc. 1 ens. ⌂/WC; 2 double ens. ☐/WC; 2 family; 1 single), 1🛏, 1⌂, 3WCs.
🐾 ✝ ETB ♨ ♨
Prices: B&B £13.95–15.50, weekly £93–104. EM £5.50–6.75. Weekly £119–131. 🐾 rates,✝ £1.50 per night.

Langber End Farm, Ingleton, Carnforth LA6 3DT
✆ (05242) 41776

Langber End Farm is a comfortable and warm old beamed house with an informal and welcoming atmosphere. Located off the A65 Kirkby Lonsdale-Settle road, in beautiful walking country, it is in an ideal position for exploring the Yorkshire Dales, Ribble Valley, Huddar Valley, and the Three Peaks area as well as the Lakes.

Open Feb-Dec.
4 bedrooms (1 twin; 2 double inc. 1 ens. ⌂/WC;1 single), 1🛏, 1WC.
⚡
Prices: B&B £12–14, weekly £74–87.50.

Nutstile Farm, Ingleton, via Carnforth LA6 3DT

✆ (05242) 41752   Mrs C. Brennand

The warm and comfortable farmhouse at Nutstile makes a perfect base for a holiday exploring this scenic area. Packed lunches provided on request, tea/coffee facilities in rooms. Nutstile is a typical Dales farm consisting of a dairy herd and sheep. Guests are invited to watch milking and other farm activities. Situated 2 miles from Ingleton, off A65 Settle road, the local attractions include a waterfall walk, show caves, golf course, fishing, swimming and tennis. Settle-Carlisle railway 10 miles.

Open all year
3 bedrooms (1 twin; 1 double; 1 family), 2🛏,
2WCs.
🐾✄
Prices: B&B £13, weekly £87.50. 🐾 rates.

KILBURN   Map 5 A1

Church Farm, Kilburn, York YO6 4AH

✆ (03476) 318   Mrs C. Thompson

You will be welcomed warmly at this large farm-house surrounded by a well-sized garden in the centre of Kilburn, southeast of Thirsk off the A170. Mrs Thompson provides good home cooking and packed lunches on request. Cot, children's games and swing available. White Horse landmark 1 mile. Rievaulx Abbey 7 miles. Helmsley Castle 12 miles.

Open Feb-Nov.
2 bedrooms (1 twin; 1 family), 1🛏, 1🗟.
🐾🕱
Prices: B&B £13, weekly £85. EM £7. Weekly B&B plus EM £130. 🐾 rates.

KIRKBYMOORSIDE   Map 5 A1

Sinnington Common Farm,
Kirkbymoorside, York YO6 6NX

✆ (0751) 31719   Felicity Wiles

Spacious ground-floor accommodation, one room suited to wheelchair users, with separate outside entrances has recently been built on to this working family farm. The animals include sheep, cattle, poultry and pet pigs. Delicious home cooking served, cot, highchair and games available. The farm is situated on the A170 west of Pickering. Ryedale Folk Museum, North Yorkshire Moors 2 miles. Flamingo Land, Nunnington Hall 5 miles. Castle Howard 10 miles. East coast 25 miles.

Open all year
2 bedrooms (1 twin ens.🗟/WC; 1 double ens.🗟/WC).
🖧 🐾 🕱 ETB 🏆 🏆Commended
Prices: B&B £15.50–16.50, weekly £108.50. EM £7.50. Weekly B&B plus EM £160.50. 🐾 rates.

NUNNINGTON   Map 5 A1

Sunley Court, Nunnington, York YO6 5XQ

✆ (04395) 233   Mrs J. Brown

Sunley Court is a modern farmhouse with open views in a quiet secluded area. The farm is arable with sheep and horses. You can enjoy good country cooking, packed lunches on request. Located 20 miles north of York, off the B1257, there is much to explore in the area. Moors 8 miles. Castle Howard 10 miles. Scarborough, Whitby 30 miles.

Open Mar-Oct.
4 bedrooms (2 twin inc. 1 ens.🗟/WC; 2 single),
1🛏, 1WC.
🐾(5) 🕱 ETB 🏆 🏆
Prices: B&B £12.50–15, EM £8.

PATELEY BRIDGE   Map 5 A1

Nidderdale Lodge, Felbeck, Pateley Bridge, Harrogate

✆ (0423) 711677

A warm welcome awaits you at this spacious and comfortable farm bungalow, set off the B6265 at Pateley Bridge, northwest of Harrogate. Nidderdale Lodge is a mixed working farm in attractive surroundings. Brimham Rocks 2 miles. Fountains Abbey 5 miles. Emmerdale Farm 10 miles. Herriot Country 15 miles.

Open Apr-Oct.
3 bedrooms (1 twin ens.🗟/WC; 1 double; 1 family), 2🛏, 3WCs.

👪(5)
Prices: B&B £13, weekly £90. 👪 rates.

PICKERING — Map 5 B1

Seavy Slack Farm, Stape, Pickering YO18 8HZ
✆ (0751) 73131 — Anne Barrett

Seavy Slack is a family run dairy farm on the edge of the North York Moors offering comfortable accommodation and good farmhouse cooking. Located 6 miles north of Pickering, home of the North York Steam Railway. Castle Howard 20 miles. York, Yorkshire coast 25 miles.

Open Easter-Oct.
2 bedrooms (1 double; 1 family), 1🛁, 1WC.
👪 🐕ETB Listed
Prices: B&B £12–16, EM £8–10.

White House Farm, Great Barugh, Malton YO17 0XB
✆ (065386) 317

This attractive large 17th-century farmhouse lies in a peaceful rural area, south off the A170, west of Pickering. Here you can enjoy a relaxing break and sample traditional farmhouse cooking using own farm produce. Castle Howard 4 miles. North Yorkshire Moors 4 miles. York 18 miles.

Open May-Oct.
2 bedrooms (1 twin ens.🛁/WC;1 double ens.🛁/WC).
👪(10) ETB ♛♛♛Commended
Prices: B&B £16–17, weekly £110–115. EM £9.

RICHMOND — Map 5 A1

Wilson House, Barningham, Richmond DL11 7EB
✆ (0833) 21218 — Mr & Mrs C. Lowes

This 450 acres mixed, working family farm is 5 miles south of Barnard Castle, a mile from the A6 at Greta Bridge. With magnificent views, the accommodation wing is beautifully furnished to match the charming old farmhouse. Twin room has access for wheelchairs, qualified nursing available. For children: cot, highchair, games, farm walks, nature trail and even (under supervision) ponies. Enjoy good home cooking while exploring the many local attractions. Raby Castle 6 miles. Richmond Castle 10 miles. High Force, England's highest waterfall 15 miles.

Open all year.
5 bedrooms (1 twin ens.🚿/WC;2 double inc. 1 ens.🚿/WC; 1 family ens.🚿/WC; 1 single), 1🛁, 2WCs.
♿ 👪
Prices: B&B £10–15, weekly £70–100. EM £6. Weekly B&B plus EM £112–140. 👪 rates.

RIPON — Map 5 A1

The Curlews, Winksley Banks, Nr Ripon HG4 3NS
✆ (0765) 658439 — Mrs A. Bancroft

Our large bungalow and garden is surrounded by fields and woodland. We operate a registered smallholding with a variety of livestock. We offer good country cooking, packed lunches on request. All bedrooms ground floor. Cot and highchair provided by arrangement. The Curlews is off the B6265 Ripon-Pateley Bridge road. Fountains Abbey 2 miles. Ripon 4 miles. Harrogate 12 miles.

Open Mar-Oct.
2 bedrooms (1 twin; 1 double ens.🚿/WC), 1🛁, 1WC.
♿ 👪 🐕 ETB Listed
Prices: B&B £13–14.50, weekly £85–95. EM £6–7. Weekly B&B plus EM £120–160 👪 rates.

St George's Court, Old Home Farm, High Grantley, Ripon HG4 3EU
✆ (0765) 620618 — Mrs Sandra Gordon

Peace and tranquility are our passwords. At St George's Court you can sleep in comfortable accommodation in renovated farm buildings, then breakfast in our beautiful 17th-century farmhouse. All rooms ground floor. We are 200 yards from any road, and in this secluded spot we have a third acre pond where natural wildlife and flora are encouraged. Located off the B6265 south-west of Ripon, we are surrounded by marvellous walking country, with the moors less than a mile away. Fountains Abbey 2 miles. Brimham Rocks 2 miles.

Open all year
5 bedrooms (1 twin ens.⊖/WC;3 double ens.⊖/WC;1 single ens.⊖/WC).
⅏ ⚘ ETB Approved Listed
Prices: B&B £17.50–22.50, weekly £120. EM £7.50.⚘ rates.

SCARBOROUGH
Map 5 B1

Tofta Farm, Staintondale, Scarborough YO13 0EB
✆ (0723) 870298
Mrs D. Dobson

There are glorious views of both sea and country-side from this modernised 300-year-old farm-house with extensive landscaped gardens. Tofta Farm stands on the edge of the North Yorkshire Moors, just off the A171 north of Scarborough, ideally situated for walkers – Cleveland Way 1 mile. Staintondale Shire Horse Farm 1 mile. Coastal villages of Ravenscar and Robin Hoods Bay nearby. Whitby, York and Castle Howard within easy reach.

Open all year
4 bedrooms (1 twin; 3 double inc. 1 ens.ffl/⊖/WC), 1➡, 2WCs.
⚘ ᛊ
Prices: B&B £12.50–17.50, EM £7.50. ⚘ rates.

Whitestone Farm, Downdale Road, Staintondale, Scarborough YO13 0EZ
✆ (0723) 870612
Mrs Patricia Angus

Whitestone Farm has a spacious stone-built farmhouse with panoramic views over sea and countryside, in the North York Moors National Park, off the A171 7 miles north of Scarborough. This is a working farm, all grassland with cows and sheep, adjoining Hayburn Wike Nature reserve and the Heritage Coast. Good farm-house cooking is provided, cot and highchair available. Pony trekking 2 miles. Cleveland Way Footpath 1 mile. Sea Life Centre 6 miles. Dalby

Forest 5 miles. East Ayton Honey Farm 9 miles. Whitby 13 miles.

Closed Xmas
3 bedrooms (1 twin; 2 double), 1➡, 2WCs.
⚘ ᛊ ᛉ
Prices: B&B £12.50–13, EM £7.

SKIPTON
Map 5 A2

Bondcroft Farm, Embsay, Skipton BD23 6SF
✆ (0756) 793371
C. Clarkson

Bondcroft Farm is a stock and sheep farm in the beautiful Yorkshire Dales. Mrs Clarkson is renowned for her excellent cooking and you are guaranteed all you need for a quiet holiday in peaceful surroundings. The farm is 2 miles north-east of the market town of Skipton, off the A59. Skipton has a golf course, castle and indoor pool. Within 30 minutes by car are Bolton Abbey, Mal-ham, Grassington, Embsay Steam Railway and Bronte country.

Open Easter-Oct.
3 bedrooms (1 twin; 2 double), 1➡, 2WCs.
ᛉ ETB Listed Approved
Prices: B&B £14.50, EM £6.50.

Miresfield Farm, Malham, Skipton BD23 4DA
✆ (0729) 830414

Situated 7 miles north of the A65 Skipton-Settle road at Gargrave, Miresfield Farm offers comfort-able accommodation and home cooking, packed lunches on request. This is a working farm of 30 acres, guest rooms are in converted farm buildings connected to the main farmhouse. Ground floor bedrooms, cot and highchair avail-able. Malham Cove in walking distance, Gordale Scar under 2 miles. Settle-Carlisle railway 7 miles.

Open all year
14 bedrooms (6 twin inc. 5 ens.ffl/WC;6 double inc. 5 ens.ffl/WC; 2 family ens.ffl/WC), 2➡ 3WCs.
⅏ ⚘ ᛊ ETB ♛ ♛ ♛Commended

Prices: B&B £18–20, weekly £119–133. EM £8. Weekly B&B plus EM £175–189. ⚘ rates.

SLINGSBY
Map 5 A1

Beech Tree House Farm, South Holme, Slingsby YO6 7BA
℡ (0653) 628257 Mrs C.M. Farnell

A spacious Victorian farmhouse surrounded by a large garden and 260 acres of arable land with cattle, sheep and pigs. There is good home cooking, comfortable rooms, log fire and snooker/games room, plus a safe play area for children. We are situated in a peaceful valley northeast of York (A64/B1257). Castle Howard 5 miles. Flamingo Land 10 miles. North Yorkshire Moors 10 miles. York 20 miles.

Closed Xmas.
5 bedrooms (1 twin; 1 double; 1 family; 2 single), 2🛏, 2WCs. ⚘
Prices: B&B £12.50, weekly £85. EM £6.50. Weekly £125. ⚘ rates.

STAMFORD BRIDGE
Map 5 A1

High Catton Grange, Stamford Bridge, York
℡ (0759) 71374 Mrs Sheila Foster

This 300-acre mixed working farm offers accommodation of a high standard in a peaceful rural setting. Ample parking. In a good position for touring the region's many attractions, the historic

city of York, Castle Howard and the Yorkshire Dales.

Open Feb-Nov.
3 bedrooms (1 twin; 1 double; 1 single), 1🛏, 2WCs.
⚘ 🐈
Prices: B&B £14. ⚘ rates.

THIRSK
Map 5 A1

High Paradise Farm, Boltby, Thirsk YO7 2HT
℡ (0845) 537353 Mr & Mrs J. Stephenson

High Paradise is an interesting old hill farmhouse built of local stone. The house and farm buildings totally enclose a square courtyard. The farm is small with sheep, cattle, horses, geese and hens, and the limestone meadowland has many flowers. Lunch and afternoon teas are available. Ground floor bedroom and cot provided. The farm lies 6 miles northeast of Thirsk via the A170. Rievaulx Abbey 6 miles. White Horse Hill 6 miles. Helmsley 9 miles. Fountains Abbey 15 miles.

Open Mar-Oct.
3 bedrooms (2 twin inc. 1 ens.🛁/WC; 1 double ens.🛁/🚿/WC), 1🛏, 1WC.
⚘ ⚜ 🐈
Prices: B&B £13.50–15, weekly £85–95. EM £8.50. Weekly B&B plus EM £140–150. ⚘ rates.

Thornborough House Farm, South Kilvington, Thirsk YO7 2NP
℡ (0845) 522103 Mrs Tess Williamson

A warm welcome awaits you in our 200-year-old farmhouse home set in lovely Herriot country. The rooms are well-appointed and very comfortable. You can relax before a log fire after sampling some good farmhouse cooking. Cot and high-chair available. We are a working farm with 206 acres, off the A168 north of Thirsk just after South Kilvington village. Fountains Abbey 15 miles. Rievaulx Abbey 17 miles. York 23 miles. Castle Howard 24 miles.

Open all year.
3 bedrooms (1 twin; 1 double; 1 family ens. 🛁/ WC), 1🛌, 1WC.
🐕 🚭 ✝ ETB ♛ ♛
Prices: B&B £12–17, weekly £84–112. EM £7. Weekly B&B plus EM £120–150. 🐕 rates.

WHITBY   Map 5 B1

Dale End Farm, Green End, Goathland, Whitby
✆ (0947) 85371   Mrs Marion Cockrem

Guests often return to this 500-year-old stone-built farmhouse with its olde worlde atmosphere amid the oak beams, log fires and antiques. Good country cooking served, packed lunches on request. Ground floor room available. The farm keeps unusual animals, Vietnamese pot bellied pigs, poultry, cows, sheep and goats. Dale End Farm is situated 2 miles from the A169, 6 miles southwest of Whitby.

Open all year
3 bedrooms (1 double; 2 family), 1🛌, 1WC. 🐕 ✝
Prices: B&B £12–13, EM £5–6, Weekly B&B plus EM £119–126. 🐕 rates.

YORK   Map 5 A2

Ivy House Farm, Kexby. York YO4 5LQ
✆ (0904) 489368   K.R. Daniel

Ivy House Farm is a dairy and mixed farm of 132 acres having been in the family for 100 years. Situated on the A1079 5 miles east of the historic city of York, it offers easy access to the Yorkshire Wolds, North Yorkshire Moors, Bronte Country, Yorkshire Dales and the East Coast. Cot and highchair available.

Closed Xmas Day   RAC
4 bedrooms (1 twin; 1 double; 1 family; 1 single), 1🛌, 2WCs. 🐕
Prices: B&B £12.50–15, weekly £84–94.50. 🐕 rates.

Treble Sykes Farm, Helperby, York YO6 2SB
✆ (0423) 360667

Our large farmhouse is peacefully situated on a working farm. We have an extensive garden with an unspoilt panoramic view over the Vale of York. Cot, highchair and children's games provided. It is a 15 minute walk beside the River Swale to the villages of Brafferton and Helperby where village inns provide evening meals. Situated west of the A19 York-Thirsk road, Treble Sykes Farm is well placed for visiting the North Yorkshire Moors and Dales. York 12 miles. Harrogate 13 miles.

Open Mar-Oct.
3 bedrooms (1 twin; 2 family), 2🛌, 2WCs. 🐕 ✝ ETB Listed
Prices: B&B £13–14, weekly £90. 🐕 rates.

KEY TO SYMBOLS	
Bath	🍶
Shower	🛁
Bathroom	🛁
Disabled Guest Facilities	♿
No Smoking	🚭
Children Welcome	🐕
Dogs by Arrangement	✝

NOTTINGHAMSHIRE

MANSFIELD
Map 5 A2

Blue Barn Farm, Langwith, Mansfield
NG20 9JD
✆ (0623) 742248 Mrs Ibbotson

This mixed arable family run farm of 450 acres stands in quiet countryside on the Werbeck Estate, within a short drive are many places of interest to suit all ages. The redbrick Victorian farmhouse has a garden, guest dining room and TV lounge. Tea/coffee facilities in rooms. The farm lies 8 miles north of Mansfield, (A60/A616). Sherwood Forest and Hardwick Hall 7 miles. Peak district 20 miles.

Closed Xmas
3 bedrooms (2 twin inc. 1 ens. 🛁/WC; 1 double), 1🛏, 1WC.
🐾 ETB ♛ ♛Approved
Prices: B&B £15–20, weekly £90–120. 🐾 rates.

NEWARK
Map 5 A3

Manor Farm, Laxton, Newark NG22 0NU
✆ (0777) 870417

Manor Farm is a mixed dairy and arable farm of 137 acres in the last remaining open field village in England. It lies northwest of Newark between the A1 and A616. Good home cooking provided. Cot and highchair available. Sherwood Forest 6 miles. The Dukeries 10 miles.

Closed Xmas and New Year
3 bedrooms (1 double; 2 family), 1🛏, 1WC.
🐾 ETB Listed
Prices: B&B £12–14, weekly £84. EM £7. 🐾 rates.

New Manor Farm, Greaves Lane,
Edingley, Newark NG22 8BJ
✆ (0623) 883044

This Victorian farmhouse offers comfortable accommodation and delicious 3-course evening meals. For children: cot, highchair and games.

Situated west of Newark between the A617 and B6386, New Manor Farm is well placed for visiting the local attractions. White Post Modern Farm 3 miles. Southwell Minster 3 miles. Southwell all weather racetrack 5 miles. Robin Hood Visitors Centre 10 miles.

Open all year
2 bedrooms (1 twin; 1 family), 1🛏, 1WC.
🐾 🐴
Prices: B&B £12.50–15, EM £8.

NOTTINGHAM
Map 5 A3

Home Farm, Cropwell Bishop,
Nottingham NG12 3BU
✆ (0602) 892598

Home Farm stands opposite the village church in Cropwell Bishop. The 300-acre farm is arable with a hunter livery yard. The 30-year-old farmhouse provides comfortable accommodation, with attractive walks along Grantham Canal. The farm is 10 miles east of Nottingham (A52/A46 south, turn off into village of Cropwell Bishop). Belvoir Castle 10 miles.

Open all year
2 bedrooms (1 twin; 1 double), 1🛏, 1WC.
🐾(3) ✄ ETB Listed
Prices: B&B £14, weekly £90. 🐾 rates.

Self-Catering

MANSFIELD
Map 5 A2

Blue Barn Farm, Langwith, Mansfield
NG20 9JD
✆ (0623) 742248 Mrs Ibbotson

For full farm description see above. Self-catering is available in the cottage that was the original stonebuilt farmhouse, 4 bedrooms, sleeps 8.

Open all year
🐴 ETB♪♪♪♪Commended
Prices: weekly £325–375.

SOUTHWELL   Map 5 A3

The Flat, Norwood Park, Southwell
℗ (0636) 812762   Lady Starkey, Norwood Park, Southwell

Combine a farm holiday with sightseeing. Accommodation is offered in a first floor flat, sleeps 3, in a wing of a stately home. Norwood Park is on the outskirts of Southwell (A612 from Nottingham). The estate comprises the house, park, orchards and woodland. The farm deals in apples and soft fruit. Cycles can be hired to explore the park, enclosed 12th-century, landscaped 18th-century. The house dates from 1763, originally a hunting lodge now a family home. Open to the public Sundays in summer. Local attractions include Sherwood Forest, Southwell Minster and Newstead Abbey.

Open all year
⌂ ⊁ ⋔
Prices: weekly £70–140.

OXFORDSHIRE

ABINGDON
Map 2 B2

Willowbrook Farm, Hanney Road, Steventon, Abingdon OX13 6BE
✆ (0235) 868188 Mrs E.S. Walker

Willowbrook Farm is a spacious and comfortable modern stone house surrounded by farmland, adjacent to a bridle path and old canal walk. This arable and mixed farm lies 2 miles east off the A338 Oxford-Wantage road. Steventon village 3 miles. Didcot Railway Centre 6 miles. Farm Craft Centre 6 miles. Abingdon 6 miles. White Horse Hill, Uffington 11 miles.

Open all year
1 twin bedroom ens.🛁/WC, 1WC.
ETB 👑👑
Prices: B&B £34–36, weekly £238.

BAMPTON
Map 2 B2

The Farmhouse Hotel, University Farm, Lew, Nr Bampton OX18 2AO
✆ (0993) 850297 Mrs Mary Rouse
Fax (0993) 850965

This 17th-century Cotswold stone farmhouse while modernised for comfort, has retained its original character with such features as inglenook fireplaces and oak beamed ceilings. It stands on a working dairy farm with a large herd of Friesians in 216 acres of rolling countryside. The dining room sets high standards in cooking the best traditional farmhouse food using the freshest ingredients. Licensed. Situated on the edge of the Cotswolds, 2 miles southwest from Witney on the A4095 Bampton road. Cogges Farm Museum 3 miles. Burford Wild Life Park 4 miles. Blenheim Palace, Woodstock 9 miles. Oxford 10 miles.

Open all year
6 bedrooms (2 twin inc. 1 ens.🚿/WC,1 ens. 🛁/WC;2 double ens.🚿/🛁/WC;2 family ens.🚿/WC), 2WCs.
♿ 👪(5) ETB 👑👑👑👑Commended
Prices: B&B £25–35. EM £13.75–17.25.👪 rates.

BANBURY
Map 2 B2

New House Farm, Brailes, Banbury OX15 5BD
✆ (060875) 239 Helen Taylor

This three storey red brick Georgian house with 480 acres has everything for your comfort, golf course 200 yds. Cot and highchair provided. Tea/coffee facilities. Situated off the B4035 west of Banbury, New House Farm lies in an area of outstanding natural beauty within easy reach of the Cotswolds. Upton House Gardens 6 miles. Hidcote Gardens, Braighton Castle 8 miles. Warwick Castle 16 miles.

Open all year
3 bedrooms (1 twin; 1 double ens.🚿/WC;1 family ens.🚿/WC), 1🛁, 2WCs.
👪 🐕 ETB 👑👑
Prices: B&B £14–16.👪 rates.

Planning a day out?
See RURAL ATTRACTIONS

BICESTER
Map 2 B2

Manor Farm, Poundon, NrBicester OX6 0BB

℗ (0869) 277212   Mrs J. Collett

This comfortable and spacious 400-year-old farmhouse stands on the edge of a peaceful rural village amidst lovely countryside. The family run arable and livestock farm is 6 miles from Bicester, east off A421 Buckingham road towards Poundon. Clayon House 4 miles. Golf course 6 miles. Brill Windmill 8 miles. Local pleasure flights 10 miles. Quainton Steam Railway Museum 12 miles.

Open all year
3 bedrooms (1 double; 1 family; 1 single), 2🛁, 2WCs.
🐾 ⚡ 🦃 ETB Listed
Prices: B&B £15–17, weekly £105–119. 🐾 rates.

BLETCHINGTON
Map 2 B2

Stonehouse Farm, Weston Road, Bletchington OX5 3CA

℗ (0869) 50585   Mrs P.M. Hedges

Southwest of Bicester, well off the beaten track between the A34 and A4260, stands the 560 acres of Stonehouse Farm. The 17th-century farmhouse, with a garden to relax in, makes an ideal touring centre for Oxford 15 mins, Blenheim Palace 10 mins, Banbury 17 miles, and Warwick and Stratford-on-Avon.

Closed Xmas.
4 bedrooms (1 twin; 1 double; 1 family; 1 single), 2🛁, 2WCs.
🐾 ETB Listed
Prices: B&B £15–20.

CHARLBURY
Map 2 B2

Banbury Hill Farm, Enstone Road, Charlbury OX7 3JH

℗ (0608) 810314

The Cotswold stone farmhouse at Banbury Hill Farm overlooks the beautiful Evenlode Valley. The atmosphere is warm and friendly, the standard of food is high, licensed dining room, and packed lunches and afternoon teas are available on request. Daytime access. Small animals for the children to see. Ideal for all the family. The farm is on the B4022, 2 miles from A44 at Enstone, north of Oxford. Bleinheim Palace 6 miles. Burford 9 miles.

Open all year
4 bedrooms (1 twin; 1 double; 1 single; 1 family ens. 🚿/WC), 1🛁, 1WC.
🐾 ⚡ ETB 🛏️ 🛏️
Prices: B&B £16–20, EM from £7.50. Weekly B&B £112–140. 🐾 rates.

FARINGDON
Map 2 B2

Ashen Copse Farm, Coleshill, Faringdon SN6 7PU

℗ (0367) 240175   Mrs Pat Hoddinott

Ashen Copse Farm is situated off the B4109 northeast of Swindon. The 580-acre National Trust farm, set in beautiful peaceful countryside, is ideal for exploring the Cotswolds, Thames Valley villages, Oxford, Bath, Stratford and Windsor. Plenty of tourist information kept at the house to help you plan your days. Pet lambs and calves usually near the farmyard. Cot, highchair and games available. Great Coxwell Tithe Barn (NT) 2 miles. Buscot House (NT) 4 miles. River Thames 5 miles. Kelmscot Manor 6 miles. M4 11 miles. Oxford, Avebury 20 miles.

Open all year
3 bedrooms (1 twin; 1 family ens. ⋔/WC; 1 single), 1🛏, 1WC.
🦽 ⊁ ETB ⚘ ⚘
Prices: B&B £16–19. 🦽 rates.

Bowling Green Farm, Stanford Road, Faringdon SN7 8EZ
✆ (0367) 240229   Mrs D. Barnard

In the Vale of the White Horse this attractive 18th-century period farmhouse offers you every comfort and maximum convenience for the perfect country holiday. Packed lunches on request. Cot provided. Situated on the A417 a mile south of Faringdon, Bowling Green Farm breeds horses and cattle. Horse riding 2 miles. Golf and fishing 5 miles.

Open all year
2 family bedrooms inc. 1 (ground floor) ens. ⋔/WC, 1 ens. ⊟/WC).
🦽 ⊁ ETB ⚘ ⚘
Prices: B&B £36–40 per double. 🦽 rates.

HENLEY-ON-THAMES   Map 2 B2

Little Parmoor Farm, Frieth, Henley-on-Thames RG9 6NL
✆ (0494) 881600   Frances Emmett

Little Parmoor Farm has a 17th-century brick and flint farmhouse with oak beam interior, open fires in winter, on a 200-acre mixed farm in an Area of Outstanding Natural Beauty. Cot, highchair, playroom and garden swing available. The farm lies north off the A4155 Henley-Marlow road. You can enjoy refreshing country walks by the River Thames and in the attractive beech woods nearby. Easy access to Heathrow, Windsor, Marlow and Henley-on-Thames. Good pub and restaurant food locally.

Open all year
3 bedrooms (2 twin; 1 double), 1🛏.
🦽 ETB Listed Commended
Prices: B&B £16–20, weekly £110–140. 🦽 rates.

HORTON-CUM-STUDLEY   Map 2 B2

Studley Farm House, Horton-cum-Studley OX33 1BP
✆ (0865) 351286   Mrs Jean Hicks

Studley farmhouse dates back to the 16th century and provides spacious and comfortable accommodation in a peaceful rural setting. Ground floor bedroom available. Situated off the B4027 northeast of the A40 Oxford bypass, it is well placed for exploring the Oxford area. Waterperry Gardens 4 miles. Oxford 7 miles. Blenheim

Palace 10 miles. Cotswolds and London within easy reach.

Open all year
3 bedrooms (2 twin/single ens. ⊟/WC; 1 double ens. ⊟/WC), 1🛏, 2WCs. ⊁
Prices: B&B £20–30, weekly £140–210.

MINSTER LOVELL   Map 2 B2

Hill Grove Farm, Minster Lovell OX8 5NA
✆ (0993) 703120   Mrs Katharine Brown

Hill Grove Farm is a 300-acre mixed working farm situated in a picturesque setting overlooking the Windrush Valley. Relax in a friendly family atmosphere, and enjoy the peaceful walks through the farm to Minster Lovell ruins and the very pretty village by the river. Packed lunches and afternoon teas on request. Cot and highchair provided. The farm is located off the B4047 west of Witney. Cogges Farm Museum 2 miles. North Leigh Roman Villa 6 miles. Burford 6 miles. Blenheim Palace, Woodstock 10 miles.

Closed Xmas
2 bedrooms (1 double priv. ⋔/WC; 1 twin ens. ⊟/WC), 1WC.
🦽 ⊁ ETB ⚘Highly Commended
Prices: B&B £32–38 per double. 🦽 rates.

OXFORD   Map 2 B2

Mead Close, Manor Farm, Forest Hill, Oxford OX33 1DY
✆ (0865) 872248

This warm friendly farmhouse provides good home cooking, packed lunches on request, and a relaxing atmosphere. The farm comprises 375 acres, milking 90 cows. Forest Hill is 5 miles east of Oxford, signed from A40 London road. Nearby are Waterperry Gardens, Blenheim Palace and Waddesdon Manor.

Open all year
3 bedrooms (1 twin; 1 double; 1 single), 1🛏, 1WC.
🦽 ⊁
Prices: B&B £15–20, weekly £105–140. EM from £7.

THAME
Map 2 B2

Upper Green Farm, Manor Road, Towersey, Thame OX9 3QR
✆ (0844) 212496   Evan & Marjorie Aitken

Bed and breakfast accommodation is available both in the attractive 15th-century thatched farmhouse and across the lawned farmyard in Paradise Barn, which has been sumptuously renovated and equipped with all modern comforts. Ground floor bedroom available. Antique furnishings throughout. The farm supports pedigree sheep and poultry. There are many excellent eating places in Thame. The farm lies south of the A4129 Thame-Princes Risborough road. Waddesdon Manor 15 minutes. Within 30 minutes: Oxford, Blenheim Palace, Marlow and Henley.

Open all year
9 bedrooms (2 twin inc.1 ens.ffi/⊜/WC, 1 ens.ffi/WC;5 double inc. 3 ens. ffi/⊜/WC, 1 ens.ffi/WC; 2 single inc. 1 ens. ffi/WC), 1➡, 2WCs.
⚓(14) ✂
Prices inc. VAT: B&B £35–50 per double.

WANTAGE
Map 2 B2

Lyford Manor Farm, Lyford, Wantage OX12 0EG
✆ (0235) 868204   Mary & Richard Pike

A welcome opportunity to stay in a 15th-century stone built manor house nestling on the banks of the River Ock in a peaceful rural setting. Breakfast in the conservatory overlooking the large garden beyond which lies the 400-acre dairy farm. Packed lunches on request. Ground floor bedrooms available. Lyford Manor Farm is north of Wantage, west of the A338. Ridgeway walking and White Horse 7 miles. Oxford 12 miles. Cotswolds and various NT properties within 20 miles.

Open all year
4 bedrooms (2 twin inc. 1ens.ffi/WC,1 ens.⊜/WC; 1 double ens. ffi/WC; 1 single ens. ffi/WC).
⚓✂ETB ♨ ♨Highly Commended
Prices: B&B per double £36, weekly £220.

WOODSTOCK
Map 2 B2

Burleigh Farm, Bladon Road, Cassington, Witney, Oxford OX8 1EA
✆ (0865) 881352   Mrs Jane Cook

Manor Farm is a working dairy farm on the Blenheim estate. The 18th-century listed stone farmhouse is spacious, warm and comfortable with a friendly family atmosphere. Hospitality trays in rooms. Well-placed for touring the Cotswold villages, the farm lies 3 miles south of Woodstock, A44/A4095 via Bladon and follow signs to Cassington. Bleinheim Palace 3 miles. Oxford 6 miles. Cogges Manor Farm Museum 7 miles.

Open all year
2 bedrooms (1 twin ens. ffi/⊜/WC; 1 double/ family ens. ffi/⊜/WC), 1➡, 1WC.
⚓✂ETB ♨ ♨
Prices: B&B £17.50–19.50. ⚓ rates.

Self-Catering
BICESTER
Map 2 B2

Pimlico Farm, Tusmore, Bicester OX6 9SL
✆ (0869) 810306

Pimlico Farm is a 370-acre beef, sheep and arable farm on the borders of Oxfordshire, Northants and Bucks. Accommodation is in 4 cottages in a converted 18th-century Cotswold stone barn. The cottages have 1–3 bedrooms, sleeping 2–6. One cottage is specifically equipped to meet the needs of disabled guests. Fishing on farm. Ideal as a touring base, the farm is 5 miles south of Brackley off the A43 Oxford road. Blenheim Palace 14 miles. Cotswolds 20 miles.

Open all year
♿ ⊁ ETBⵌⵌⵌⵌHighly Commended
Prices: weekly £133–375.

Reduced rates are sometimes available. Ask your host about weekend breaks.

CHARLBURY
Map 2 B2

Banbury Hill Farm, Enstone Road,
Charlbury OX7 3JH
℗ (0608) 810314

For full farm description see p. 134. Accommodation is also offered in 2 one-bedroomed units, each sleeps 2.

Open all year
Prices: weekly £185–250.

KEY TO SYMBOLS

Bath	☕
Shower	⌂
Bathroom	🛁
Disabled Guest Facilities	♿
No Smoking	⚊
Children Welcome	⚮
Dogs by Arrangement	ⵟ

SHROPSHIRE

BUCKNELL
Map 2 A1

Bucknell House, Bucknell SY7 0AD
✆ (05474) 248 Mrs Brenda Davies

Bucknell House is a large spacious creeper-clad old Georgian vicarage – listed 1817 – on the fringe of a picturesque village in a tranquil rural corner of South Shropshire, on the B4367 west of Ludlow (A49/4113). The house overlooks the peaceful Teme Valley in the legendary Marches, amidst rolling wooded hillsides. All rooms have TV and tea/coffee facilities. Offa's Dyke Walk 4 miles. Medieval Ludlow, Black and White villages 12 miles.

Open Mar-Nov.
3 bedrooms (1 twin; 1 double; 1 family), 1🛁, 2WCs.
(12) ETB ♛♛ Highly Commended
Prices: B&B £15–17.50, weekly £105–115. £0.50 per night.

The Hall, Bucknell SY7 0AA
✆ (05474) 249 Mrs Christine Price

The Hall is a Georgian farmhouse standing on a 200-acre mixed farm, where you can enjoy good home cooking in quiet rural surroundings. All rooms well-equipped including tea/coffee facilities and TV. Bucknell lies west of Ludlow on the B4367 (A49/4113). Offa's Dyke 5 miles. Ludlow 12 miles. Shrewsbury, Hereford 30 miles.

Open Mar-Nov.
3 bedrooms (1 twin ens./WC; 2 double), 1🛁.
(7) ETB ♛♛ Commended
Prices: B&B from £15, EM £8.

CHURCH STRETTON
Map 2 A1

Acton Scott Farm, Acton Scott, Church Stretton SY6 6QN
✆ (0694) 781260 Mrs Mary Jones

This mixed working farm covers over 300 acres, lying west off the A49 Shrewsbury-Ludlow road, 3 miles south of Church Stretton. The peaceful 17th-century farmhouse has warm, comfortable and spacious rooms, an ideal base for exploring the region. 2 minutes walk from an historic working farm. Cardingmill Valley, Long Mynd Hills 3 miles. Stokesay Castle 5 miles.

Open Feb-Nov.
3 bedrooms (1 twin; 1 double; 1 family), 1🛁, 1WC.
ETB Listed Approved
Prices:B&B £12–15. rates.

Glenburrell Farm, Horderley, Craven Arms
✆ (0588) 672318 S. Jones

Guests are free to wander around our stock rearing farm, conveniently situated 3 miles from Craven Arms on the A489 Newtown-Welshpool road. This is excellent walking country with Ironbridge, Ludlow, Shrewsbury and Church Stretton all within easy reach.

Open all year
2 bedrooms (1 twin ens./WC; 1 double ens./WC).
Prices: B&B £12–15.

Strefford Hall, Strefford, Craven Arms SY7 8DE
✆ (0588) 672383 Mrs Caroline Morgan

Strefford Hall is an imposing stonebuilt Victorian farmhouse surrounded by its 360 acres of working farmland in the picturesque hamlet of Strefford, nestling at the foot of the Wenlock Edge. Situated off the A49 north of Craven Arms, this makes a good choice as a base for touring the region. Packed lunches provided on request.

Stokesay Castle and Acton Scott Historic Working Farm 3 miles. Church Stretton Hills 5 miles. Ironbridge Gorge Museum and Severn Valley Railway 20 miles.

Open April-Oct.
3 bedrooms (2 double ens. 🛁/WC, 1 twin priv. 🛁/WC), 1WC.
🏡 ⚒ ✝ ETB ♛ ♛Commended
Prices:B&B £15–16. 🏡 rates.

CLUN   Map 2 A1
Hurst Mill Farm, Clun, Craven Arms SY7 0JA
✆ (05884) 224   Joyce & Roy Williams

A friendly welcome awaits you at this attractive stone farmhouse and gardens amid delightful surroundings of woodland and river. Home cooking provided and packed lunches on request. This is a working farm with activities. Pony riding available. Hurst Mill Farm is on the B4368, 8 miles west of Craven Arms (A49). Offa's Dyke, Bury Ditches 3 miles. Stiperstones 13 miles. Ludlow 15 miles.

Open all year
3 bedrooms (1 twin; 2 double), 2🛏, 2WCs.
🏡 ✝ ETB ♛ ♛
Prices: B&B £12–15, weekly £84–91. EM £6–7. Weekly B&B plus EM £126–150. 🏡 rates.

Newhouse Farm, Clun, Craven Arms SY7 8WJ
✆ (0588) 638314

This peaceful and isolated 18th-century farmhouse is set in Clun's Hills near the Welsh border on a mixed farm of 215 acres and a sheep hill which includes an Iron Age hill fort. The rooms are large and comfortable, furnished to a high standard, with scenic views. Tea/coffee facilities. Comprehensive selection of books and newspaper articles. The farm is 4 miles from Clun, west off A488 Clun-Bishop's Castle road at Colehatch. Prime hill walking region: Shropshire Way close by, Offa's Dyke 1 mile, Kerry Ridgeway 3 miles.

Closed Xmas and 4 weeks Mar-Apr.
4 bedrooms (1 twin ens. 🛁/WC; 1 double; 1 family; 1 single), 1🛏, 🛁, 2WC.
🏡 ✝ ETB ♛ ♛Commended
Prices: B&B £14.50–16, weekly £100–110. EM £8.50, weekly B&B plus EM £160–170. 🏡 rates, ✝ rates.

See STOP PRESS
for more farms

LUDLOW   Map 2 A1
The Barn Farm, Leinthall Starkes, Nr Ludlow SY8 2HP
✆ (056886) 388   Sylvia Price

The Barn Farm is set on the edge of a peaceful valley. A warm welcome and plenty of good food await you on this 140-acre mixed farm with beef, sheep and corn. Cot and highchair available. The farm is 5 miles southwest of Ludlow, a mile from Wigmore Castle. Croft Castle 5 miles.

Open Mar-Nov.
3 bedrooms (1 twin; 2 double ens. 🛁/WC), 1🛏, 1WC.
🏡 ✝ ETB ♛ ♛
Prices: B&B £14–19, EM £10. Weekly B&B plus EM £150–185. 🏡 rates.

Haynall Villa, Little Hereford, Nr Ludlow SY8 4BG
✆ (058472) 589   Mrs Rachel Edwards

A warm welcome awaits guests at our early 19th-century farmhouse which is set in a large garden away from the farm buildings. The surroundings are both picturesque and quiet, and you can sample our award winning freshly prepared evening meals. Situated a mile off the A456, 6 miles southeast of Ludlow, there is much to see and visit in the vicinity. River and pool fishing available. Burford House Garden, Tenbury Wells 4 miles. Leominster 7 miles. Croft Castle, Black and White villages trail 8 miles.

Closed Xmas
3 bedrooms (1 twin ens. 🛁/🚿/WC; 1 double; 1 family), 1🛏, 2WCs.
🏡(6) ✝ ETB ♛ ♛Commended
Prices from: B&B £14–17, EM £10. Weekly B&B plus EM £155–175. 🏡 rates. ✝ £3 per night.

MARKET DRAYTON   Map 2 A1
Stoke Manor Stoke-on-Tern, Market Drayton TF9 2DU
✆ (063084) 222   J.M. Thomas

Stoke Manor's 18th- and 19th-century farmhouse is set in 2 acres of gardens. Situated south of Market Drayton, 2 miles off the A53, the arable farm covers 250 acres, with a farm trail and an interesting collection of vintage tractors and cast iron implement seats. Licensed. Hodnet Hall Gardens 2 miles. Ironbridge Museums 11 miles. Weston Park 15 miles. Shrewsbury 16 miles.

Open Jan-Nov.
3 bedrooms (1 twin ens. 🛁/🚿/WC;1 double ens. 🛁/🚿/WC;1 family ens. 🛁/🚿/WC), 1WC.
🏡 ETB ♛ ♛Commended
Prices: B&B £20–25. 🏡 rates.

OSWESTRY Map 4 B3

Bwlch-y-Rhiw Farmhouse, Llansilin, Oswestry
✆ (069170) 261

A large early Victorian farmhouse of considerable charm, attractively restored to provide modern comforts whilst retaining its original character. Breakfast is served in a period oak dining room with inglenook fireplace and original breadoven. The farm is a 120-acre sheep farm, just over 4 miles west of Oswestry on the B4580, perched high above the Tanat Valley just outside Llansilin. Chirk Castle 8 miles. Llanrhaeadr Waterfall and Llangollen 12 miles. Powys Castle 20 miles.

Open April-Oct.
3 bedrooms (1 twin ens. 🚿/🛁/WC;1 family ens.🚿/WC;1 double ens.🛁/WC).
👪(7)
Prices per double: B&B £32–35, weekly £215. 👪 rates.

TELFORD Map 2 A1

Church Farm, Rowton, Telford
✆ (0952) 770381

A large country breakfast and a warm welcome awaits you in this 300-year-old farmhouse set in a peaceful hamlet north of Telford, a mile west of the A442. Cot, highchair and children's games available. Packed lunches provided on request. Easy motorway access (M54, Jct6) an advantage. Ironbridge 12 miles. Shrewsbury 10 miles.

Open all year
4 bedrooms (1 twin; 1 double ens.🚿/WC; 1 family ens.🚿/WC; 1 single), 1🛁, 2WCs.
👪🐕 ETB ♛♛
Prices: B&B £13.50–16. Holiday caravans available weekly £60–160. 👪 rates.

Church Farm, Wrockwardine, Wellington, Telford TF6 5DG
✆ (0952) 244917 Mrs Jo Savage

Enjoy the friendly atmosphere of our Georgian village farmhouse standing on medieval manor house foundations, visible in the cellar and sunken garden. We have delightful bedrooms, delicious farmhouse cooking, oak beams and log fires. May we tempt you with a brochure? Located a mile north of M54, Jct7, within 30 minutes are many NT and English Heritage properties, Ironbridge Gorge Museum, Severn Valley Railway, Weston Park and much more.

Open all year
5 bedrooms (2 twin inc. 1 ens.🚿/WC; 3 double inc. 2 ens.🛁/WC), 1🛁, 3WCs.
ETB ♛♛♛Commended
Prices: B&B £19–23, EM £13.

Planning a day out?
See RURAL ATTRACTIONS

WEM Map 2 A1
Lowe Hall Farm, Wem
℃ (0939) 32236 Mrs E.A. Jones

Lowe Hall is a historically famous 16th-century listed farmhouse, once the country residence of Judge Jeffreys (1648–89). There is a splendid Jacobean staircase and Charles II fireplace. Situated just a mile from the Welsh border this working dairy farm lies north of Shrewsbury (A528/B5476), a mile from Wem, making it an ideal touring centre. Convenient for Ironbridge, Llangollen and Chester. Hawkstone Golf Course within 5 miles.

Open all year
3 bedrooms (1 twin; 1 double; 1 family), 2🛁,
2WCs.
🕮 ETB ♛ ♛
Prices: B&B £16, weekly £98.

WHITCHURCH Map 4 B3
Bradeley Green Farm, Tarporley Road, Whitchurch SY13 4HD
℃ (0948) 3442 Ruth Mulliner

Bradeley Green Farm has much to offer, the large Georgian farmhouse is on a working dairy farm and waterfowl sanctuary, with water gardens and 3 acres of pools stocked with fish and 100 species of wild waterfowl and geese. The house provides comfortable accommodation, open fires and good home cooking. Packed lunches on request. The farm is located 2 miles north of Whitchurch on the A49. Cholmondeley Park 2 miles. Stapeley Water Gardens, Bridgemere Garden World and Nantwich 10 miles. Llangollen and Chester 20 miles.

Open all year
3 bedrooms (2 twin ens.🕮/WC; 1 double ens.🖎/🕮/WC).
🕮 ETB ♛ ♛Commended
Prices:B&B £18, weekly £115. EM £8.50.
Weekly B&B plus EM £174. 🕮 rates.

Self-Catering
WHITCHURCH Map 4 B3
Bradeley Green Farm, Tarporley Road, Whitchurch SY13 4HD
℃ (0948) 3442 Ruth Mulliner

For full farm description see entry above. Up a lane adjacent to the farm stands a 150-year-old brick farmworkers' cottage. 2 bedrooms, sleeps 4, ideal for families.

Open all year
Prices: weekly £90–150.

SOMERSET

BRIDGWATER
Map 2 A3

Blackmore Farm, Cannington, Bridgwater TA5 2NE
✆ /Fax (0278) 653442

Blackmore Farm's Grade 1 listed 14th-century manor house retains many period features, including a four poster and oak bedsteads. The accommodation is comfortable, with cot, high-chair and children's games available. Afternoon teas are served. The 650-acre dairy and arable farm is on the A39 west of Bridgwater, well placed for touring. Quantock Hills 3 miles. West Somerset coast 8 miles.

Open all year
3 bedrooms (2 double ens.⬒/WC; 1 twin ens. ⬜), 1🛁, 1WC.
⬔ ⤬ ETB ♚Commended
Prices: B&B £15–20, weekly £98–126. ⬔ rates.

Cokerhurst Farm, 87 Wembdon Hill, Bridgwater TA6 7QA
✆ (0278) 422330   Mr & Mrs D. Chappell

The 16th-century farmhouse overlooks the 100-acre arable and soft fruit farm. There is a swimming pool and a large peaceful garden. TV in all rooms. Cokerhurst Farm is just west of Bridgwater on the A39, within easy striking distance of the M5. Fyne Court and Quantock Hills 6 miles. Burnham-on-Sea 8 miles. Dunster Castle and Cheddar Caves 20 miles.

Open Easter-Oct.
3 bedrooms (1 twin; 1 double ens.⬜/⬒/WC; 1 family), 1🛁, 1WC.
⬔ ⤬ 🐴 ETB ♚ ♚
Prices: B&B £16–20. Weekly £100.80–126. ⬔ rates.

CHEDDAR
Map 2 A3

Tor Farm, Nyland, Cheddar BS27 3UD
✆ (0934) 743710   Mr & Mrs Ladd

This working farm is on the Somerset Levels and has open views from every window. Some rooms have private patio, one has a four poster. All have tea/coffee facilities. We are licensed and evening meals are available using fresh farm produce. Also packed lunches. The farm is 3 miles from Cheddar Gorge (A37 towards Wells, then Nyland turning). Easy access to Wells, Glastonbury, Bath and the coast.

Open all year
9 bedrooms (2 twin inc. 1 ens. ⬜/WC; 1 family ens.⬜/WC; 5 double inc. 1 ens. ⬜/WC, 2 ens. ⬒/WC; 1 single), 2🛁, 1WC.
⬔ ETB Commended/Listed
Prices: B&B £15–21.50, weekly £100.80–135.45. EM a la carte.

See STOP PRESS
for more farms

142

CHISELBOROUGH Map 2 A3

Manor Farm, Chiselborough, Stoke-sub-Hamdon TA14 6TQ
☎ (0935) 881203   Mrs E.E.L. Holloway

This gracious Victorian Manor House offers every comfort. The mixed farm of 460 acres lies in a picturesque village, situated east of the A356 (A303), in excellent walking country. Well-placed for exploring the region, Ham Hill Country Park is close by. Montacute House 3 miles. Yeovilton Air Museum 8 miles. Lyme Regis and coast 20 miles.

Open April-Oct.
4 bedrooms (1 twin; 2 double; 1 family), 2🛏,
2WCs.
🔖 ETB ✿ ✿Commended
Prices: B&B £16–18, weekly £103–110. 🔖
rates.

DUNSTER Map 1 B2

Burnells Farm, Knowle Lane, Dunster
☎ (0643) 821841

A warm welcome awaits you in this modern farmhouse on a small farm in the Avill Valley on the edge of the moors. Good farmhouse cooking and packed lunches by request. Located in magnificent walking country, Burnells Farm is just off the A396 south to Tiverton from Dunster.

Open all year
3 bedrooms (1 twin; 1 double; 1 single), 2🛏,
2WCs.
🔖(8) ⅍ ✝
Prices: B&B £15. Weekly B&B plus EM £129.50.

Higher Rodhuish Farm, Rodhuish, Minehead TA24 6QL
☎ (0984) 40253

Dating back to the 16th century, Higher Rodhuish Farm offers comfortable accommodation and good home cooking. A working farm with beef, sheep and arable enterprises situated in the hamlet of Rodhuish surrounded by unspoilt countryside. On the edge of Exmoor National Park, this is an ideal centre for touring coast and moors, walking, riding, hunting, fishing, birdwatching, sailing, golf, painting and just relaxing.

The farm is south off the A39 Minehead-Williton road at Withycombe. Minehead 6 miles. Dunster 4 miles.

Open all year
2 bedrooms (1 double priv. ♒/WC; 1 twin ens. ♒/WC), 1🛏, 2WCs.
🔖 ✝ ETB ✿ ✿Commended
Prices: B&B £14–16, weekly £93–106. EM £6–8.50, B&B plus EM weekly £135–163. 🔖
rates.

Wood Advent Farm, Roadwater, Dunster TA23 0RR
☎ (0984) 40920   Diana Brewer

This spacious listed farmhouse, set in 360 acres of working farm in the Exmoor National Park, offers fresh country cuisine, rooms with delightful views, woodburner in inglenook, large garden, tennis court and heated swimming pool. Guests are welcome to take part in farm life or just relax in the gardens. Further options include horse riding, fishing, rough and clay pigeon shooting. For walkers well marked footpaths run over the farm. Packed lunches, Sunday lunch provided on request. Wood Advent Farm lies south off the A39 between Dunster and Williton.

Open all year
5 bedrooms (2 twin inc. 1 ens.♒/WC, 1 ens.♒/WC; 2 double ens.♒/WC; 1 family ens.♒/WC), 2🛏, 2WCs.
🔖 ✝ ETB ✿ ✿Commended

Prices: B&B £15.50–19.50, weekly £100–125. EM £10–12. Weekly £165–200. 🐾 rates.

EXMOOR Map 1 B2

Hindon Farm, Nr Minehead TA24 8SH
✆ (0643) 705244

Guests are welcome to participate on our working hill sheep farm with lots of animals. We offer good farmhouse cooking, packed lunches by request. Enjoy the fun and friendly atmosphere in our lovely 18th-century NT farmhouse, superbly situated in our own valley south of the A39 Minehead-Porlock road. Direct access to the moors for wonderful walks, wildlife and riding. Stabling and grazing, fishing available. Minehead, West Somerset Steam Trains 3 miles. Dunster Castle and watermill 5 miles.

Open Easter-Oct.
4 bedrooms (1 twin; 1 double; 1 family, 1 single), 1🛁, 1WC.
🐾 ⊁ ETB Listed Commended
Prices: B&B £14–18, EM £10–12. 🐾 rates, 🐴 rates.

Little Brendon Hill, Wheddon Cross, Exmoor National Park TA24 7DG
✆ (0643) 841556 Mr & Mrs L.J. Maxwell

Enjoy the true peace of the countryside in this beautifully appointed farmhouse in a quiet location on a smallholding keeping mainly sheep, where ducks, chickens and other fowls roam freely. The farm is within Exmoor National Park, an Area of Outstanding Natural Beauty on the doorstep. Little Brendon Hill is on the B3224 south of Minehead (A396).

Open all year
3 bedrooms (2 twin; 1 double), 2🛁, 2WCs.
🐾 ⊁ ETB Listed Highly Commended
Prices: B&B £14.50–16.50, weekly £96–110. EM £8. Weekly B&B plus EM £150–163.

Little Quarme Farm, Wheddon Cross, Exmoor TA24 7EA
✆ (0643) 841249 Mr R.B. Cody-Boutcher

This lovely old farmhouse stands amid 18 acres and beautiful gardens in the heart of Exmoor National Park. The large sun lounge has panoramic southerly views. Relax in the friendly family atmosphere and enjoy the traffic free tranquility. Little Quarme is a sheep and horse farm, located southwest of Minehead (A396, just beyond B3224 junction at Wheddon Cross) near Dunkery Beacon, the highest point in Somerset. Porlock and Dunster 5 miles.

Open May-Sept.
3 bedrooms (1 twin; 1 double; 1 family), 2🛁, 2WCs.
🐾 ⊁ ETB Listed
Prices: B&B £15–16, weekly £100.

Springfield Farm, Dulverton TA22 9QD
✆ (0398) 23722 Mrs P. Vellacott

Springfield is a working stock farm of 270 acres, supporting a herd of beef suckler cows and a flock of breeding ewes. Wildlife including red deer, foxes, rabbits, badgers and buzzards are frequently seen on the farm. The modern farmhouse is south facing and overlooks the River Barle with magnificent moorland and woodland views. We offer good home cooking using home grown ingredients whenever possible. Situated north of Tiverton (A396) and just 4 miles west of Dulverton (B3223), the farm is within easy reach of coastal resorts. Horse riding, fishing available locally.

Open Easter-Oct.
3 bedrooms (1 twin priv. 🛁/WC; 1 double; 1 single), 1🛁.
🐾 🐴 ETB ⚫ ⚫Commended
Prices: B&B £15–19, weekly £100. EM £10. Weekly B&B plus EM £165. 🐾 rates, 🐴 £2 per night.

GLASTONBURY Map 2 A3

Cradlebridge Farm, Glastonbury BA16 9SD
✆ (0458) 31827 Mrs H. Tinney

Cradlebridge Farm is a 200-acre working dairy farm on the Somerset Levels. The accommodation is in a recently converted barn. Ground floor bedroom and cot available. Glastonbury Abbey and the famous Tor are 2 miles from the farm, which lies just south on the A39. Wells Cathedral 8 miles. Wookey Hole Caves 10 miles. Cheddar Gorge and Caves 15 miles.

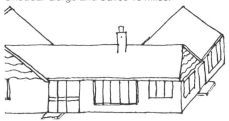

Closed Xmas
4 bedrooms (2 twin ens.⌐/WC;2 family ens.⌐/WC).
⌐ ⌐ ⌐ ETB ♛
Prices: B&B £16–17.50, weekly £96–105.

HENSTRIDGE   Map 2 A3

Quiet Corner Farm, Henstridge, Templecombe BA8 0RA
✆ (0963) 63045   Brian & Patricia Thompson

This 18th-century stone farmhouse is aptly named as it nestles in its garden and orchard with sheep and Shetland ponies on the edge of the village. Off the A357/A30 junction midway between Shaftesbury and Yeovil, it is wonderfully situated for exploring the host of NT houses and gardens within a 20 mile radius. Packed lunches and afternoon teas on request. Cots and highchair available.

Closed Xmas Day
3 bedrooms (1 family; 2 double ens.⌐/WC), 1⌐, 2WCs.
⌐ ETB ♛ ♛Commended
Prices: B&B £16–18.50 supplement single occupancy. ⌐ rates.

Planning a day out?
See RURAL ATTRACTIONS

HIGHBRIDGE   Map 2 A3

Laurel Farm, Markcauseway, Nr Highbridge TA9 4PZ
✆ (027864) 1216   Mrs B.M. Puddy

Laurel Farm is over 300 years old with milking cows and 120 acres. There are old beams inside, a large sitting room with TV, and log fires out of season. The farm is on the B3139 Wells-Burnham-on-Sea road, 2 miles from M5, Jct 22. Highbridge 2 miles. Burnham-on-Sea 5 miles. Wells and Cheddar 12 miles.

Open all year
4 bedrooms (2 double; 1 family; 1 single), 2⌐, 1⌐, 3WCs.
⌐ ⌐
Prices: B&B £13–14, weekly £87.50. ⌐ rates.

SOMERTON   Map 2 A3

Lower Farm, Kingweston, Somerton TA11 6BA
✆ (0458) 223237   David & Jane Sedgman

The attractive listed house at Lower Farm was formerly a coaching inn, and now successfully combines old world charm with modern comfort. This working farm is set in a conservation area south of Glastonbury off the A39/B3151/3. Lytes Cary 2 miles. Glastonbury 5 miles. Wells and Wookey Hole 10 miles. Cot and highchair available.

Open all year
3 bedrooms (1 twin ens.⌐/⌐/WC;1 double

ens.♒/☞/WC;1 single ens.♒/☞/WC).
♒ ⊁ ⋔ ETB ☙Commended
Prices: B&B from £18.50, weekly £111. ♒ rates.

TAUNTON   Map 2 A3

Parsonage Farm, Stoke-St-Gregory, Taunton TA3 6ET
℗ (0823)'698205   Mrs M.E. House

This spacious Georgian farmhouse with a large garden overlooks the Somerset Levels. The farm is a working dairy farm of 120 acres, with good coarse fishing on the farmland. Well placed for touring both north and south coasts, Parsonage Farm is 9 miles east of Taunton (A358), north off the A378. Altheny, famed for King Alfred and the burnt cakes, is within walking distance. Glastonbury Abbey 10 miles. Wells 12 miles.

Open all year
4 bedrooms (2 twin; 1 double; 1 family), 1➡,
2WCs.
♒ ⋔ ETB Listed
Prices: B&B £12-50-15, weekly £80–85. ♒
rates.

Prockters Farm, Westmonkton, Taunton
℗ (0823) 412269   Dianne & Henry Besley

Prockters Farm is a lovely 17th-century farmhouse full of old world charm with exposed oak beams and log fires, surrounded by a family run farm. Welcomed by tea and cake, your stay will be an enjoyable one. Packed lunches provided on request. One ground floor twin room equipped for disabled guests. Cot, highchair and children's games provided. Located northeast of Taunton off the A361, the farm is ideally placed for touring Exmoor, the Quantock Hills and the coast.

Open all year
4 bedrooms (1 twin ens.♒/WC; 2 double inc. 1 ens.♒/WC; 1 family), 1➡, 1♒, 1WC.
♿ ♒ ⋔
Prices: B&B £15–19, weekly £100–130. ♒
rates,⋔ £1 to charity.

Slimbridge Station Farm, Bishops Lydeard, Taunton TA4 3BX
℗ (0823) 432223   Mrs Ann Pattemore

Slimbridge is an attractive Victorian house on a dairy farm of 120 acres. It stands next to the terminus of the West Somerset Railway, Britain's longest privately owned steam railway (operating Mar-Oct, no night trains). Situated on the A358 northwest of Taunton, both north and south coasts are within comfortable driving distance as are many stately homes, ruins and the caves of Cheddar and Wookey Hole.

Closed Xmas
3 bedrooms (1 twin; 1 double; 1 single), 1➡,
2WCs.
♒ ⊁ ⋔ ETB ☙ ☙Commended
Prices:B&B £15–17. ♒ rates.

Volis Farm, Hestercombe, Taunton TA2 8HS
℗ (0823) 451545   Mrs Diana Taylor

This 300-acre working dairy and arable farm is 400ft up the southern slopes of the Quantock Hills, commanding magnificent views of the Vale of Taunton. Volis Farm offers total tranquility but, situated off the A38 between Taunton and Bridgwater, it is within 15 minutes of M5, Jct25, and the centre of Taunton. The farmhouse dates from the 16th century and has a magnificent hall, as well as an oak panelled dining room with inglenook. Cot and highchair provided. Hestercombe Gardens are under a mile away. Easy access to Exmoor, Brendon Hills and the north coast.

Open Mar-Oct.
3 bedrooms (2 twin; 1 double), 1➡, 1WC.
♒ ⊁ ETB Registered/Listed.
Prices: B&B £16. ♒ rates.

WELLINGTON   Map 2 A3

Pinksmoor Farm, Pinksmoor, Wellington TA21 0HD
℗ (0823) 672361

Pinksmoor Farm is a family run dairy farm based in the mill house adjoining the old mill and leat. A Somerset Farming and Wildlife Award Winner, there is an abundance of wildlife and scenic walks, the haunt of kingfisher, mallard and snipe. Comfortable surroundings, personal service and home grown produce combine to make a rural retreat just south of the A38 at Wellington, west of Taunton. Highchair provided. Wellington 3 miles. Blackdown Hills 5 miles. Taunton 9 miles.

Open all year
3 bedrooms (1 twin priv. ♒/☞/WC;1 family ens.♒/☞/WC;1 double ens.♒/WC).

⚙ ↟ ETB ♨ ♨ ♨Commended
Prices: B&B £16–19.50, weekly £105–129.50.
EM £10.50. Weekly B&B plus EM £178.50–203.
⚙ rates.

WELLS   Map 2 A3

Manor Farm, Old Bristol Road, Upper
Milton, Wells BA5 3AH
✆ (0749) 673394   Mrs Janet Gould

This listed Grade 2 Star Elizabethan manor house
is superbly situated on the southern slopes of the
Mendip Hills. It has a large garden surrounded
by a 130-acre working farm, a mile north of Wells
off the A39. Wookey Hole 1 mile. Glastonbury 4
miles. Cheddar 5 miles. Longleat and Weston-
super-Mare 17 miles.

Closed Xmas
3 bedrooms (1 twin; 1 double; 1 family), 1🛁,
2WCs.
⚙ ETB ♨
Prices: B&B £13–15, weekly £87–93. ⚙ rates.

Whitnell Farm, Binegar, Emborough, BA3
4UF
✆ (0749) 840277

We welcome guests to our mixed family farm, a
manor house with unique character set in beautiful gardens amid peaceful countryside. The atmosphere is relaxed and friendly. Just off B3139
Wells-Bath road, it is an excellent base for touring
the west country towns, villages, parks, caves
and castles. Mendip Golf Course and Chewton
Mendip cheese-making dairies 2 miles. Wells 4
miles. Wookey Hole Caves 5 miles. Cheddar
Gorge 6 miles.

Open all year
3 bedrooms (1 twin; 1 double; 1 family), 1🛁,
1WC.
⚙ ✂ ETB Member
Prices: B&B £16–18.

WINCANTON   Map 2 A3

Lower Church Farm, Rectory Lane,
Charlton Musgrove, Wincanton BA9 8ES
✆ (0963) 32307   Mrs Alicia Teague

This 18th-century farmhouse provides a pleasant
homely atmosphere complete with beamed room
and inglenook fireplaces. It is on a 60-acre dairy
farm set in lovely countryside bordering on Wiltshire and Dorset, on the B3081 north of the A303
at Wincanton. Packed lunches on request. Within
a comfortable driving distance lie Bath, Glastonbury, Cheddar, Salisbury, Longleat, Tintinhull
(NT) and Montacute House (NT).

Closed Xmas and New Year
3 bedrooms (1 twin ens.🛁/WC; 2 double ens.🛁/
WC).
⚙(6) ✂ ↟ ETB ♨ ♨
Prices: B&B £12–14. ⚙ rates.

Self-Catering

DUNSTER   Map 1 B2

Higher Rodhuish Farm, Rodhuish,
Minehead TA24 6QL
✆ (0984) 40253

For full description see p. 143. Accommodation
is available in a 3-bedroomed unit, sleeps 6.

Open all year
Prices on application.

EXMOOR   Map 1 B2

Hindon Farm, Nr Minehead TA24 8SH
✆ (0643) 705244

For full farm description see p. 144. Self-catering
accommodation is also available. One unit, 2
bedrooms, sleeps 5.

Open Easter-Oct.
↟
Prices: weekly £150–375.↟ rates.

WELLS

Map 2 A3

Whitnell Farm, Binegar, Emborough, BA3 4UF

✆ (0749) 840277

For full farm description see p. 147. The farm has 2 holiday homes, 2–3 bedrooms, sleeping 4–8. Each has its own character and is spacious and well-equipped. Cot and highchair available. The larger unit is suitable for disabled guests.

Open all year
♿ ETB Member
Prices: £100–290.

KEY TO SYMBOLS

Bath	🍺
Shower	🚿
Bathroom	🛁
Disabled Guest Facilities	♿
No Smoking	🚭
Children Welcome	🧒
Dogs by Arrangement	🐕

SOUTH YORKSHIRE

HATHERSAGE
Map 5 A2

Lane End Farm, Abney, Hathersage, via Sheffield S30 1AA
℡ (0433) 650371   Mrs Jill Salisbury

This dairy and sheep farm was nominated for the Tourist Board's England For Excellence 1992 Award. With stunning views, charmingly decorated rooms, hearty breakfasts, tea/coffee facilities, nature trail and country walks on the doorstep. Stabling and grazing provided for guests' horses. Cot available. Packed lunches on request. Abney is west of the B6001 from Hathersage (3 miles). Derwent Reservoirs 6 miles. Castleton Caverns 9 miles. Chatsworth and Haddon Halls 11 miles. Edale and Kinder Scout 12 miles.

Closed Xmas
3 bedrooms (1 twin; 2 double inc. 1 ens. 🛁/WC), 1🛏, 1WC.
♿ ETB Listed Highly Commended
Prices: B&B £15–22. ♿ rates.

HATHERSAGE
Map 5 A2

Lane End Farm, Abney, Hathersage, via Sheffield S30 1AA
℡ (0433) 650371   Mrs Jill Salisbury

See above entry for farm description. Self-catering accommodation also available in a one bedroomed unit, sleeps 4 with sofa bed.

Closed Xmas
Prices: weekly £100–150.

STAFFORDSHIRE

CODSALL
Map 4 B3

Moors Farm & Country Restaurant,
Chillington Lane, Codsall, Nr
Wolverhampton WV8 1QH
℮ (0902) 842330 Mrs D.E. Moreton

This 200-year-old farmhouse with modern additions is set on a working livestock farm in a quiet valley. There are lovely views from all the rooms and a particularly cosy lounge for guests. Home produced vegetables etc. are used in the farmhouse kitchen. Licensed. Packed lunches on request. The farm is situated off the A41 west of Wolverhampton. Weston Park, Cosford Aerospace Museum 3 miles. Shrewsbury 30 miles.

Open all year **RAC**
6 bedrooms (2 twin; 2 double inc. 1 ens.⋔/WC; 2 family inc. 1 ens.⋔/WC), 2➡, 4WCs.
⋔(4) ETB ♛ ♛ ♛
Prices: B&B £19–28. EM £9–14. ⋔ rates.

LEEK
Map 5 A3

Back Lane Farm, Winkhill, Leek ST13 7PJ
℮ (0538) 308273 Mrs Menga Bentley

Back Lane Farm is set in 20 acres of pastureland. The stone built farmhouse is 18th-century with original oak beams and open fires. Good breakfasts and evening meals provided, packed lunches on request. Situated off A523, 5 miles southeast of Leek, Alton Towers 4 miles, Potteries 15 miles.

Open Mar-Dec.
4 bedrooms (1 twin priv. ⋔/WC; 2 double inc.

1 ens. ⋔/WC; 1 single ens. ➡/WC), 1➡, 2WCs.
⋔ ETB ♛ ♛ ♛Highly Commended
Prices: B&B £15.75–18.50, weekly
£110.25–116.55. EM £10–10.50, weekly
£180.25–186.55. ⋔ rates.

Brook House Farm, Cheddleton, Leek
ST13 7DF
℮ (0538) 360296 Elizabeth Winterton

Brook House Farm is a 180-acre dairy farm situated in a picturesque valley, with many pleasant walks. Guests can sleep in the farmhouse or a comfortably converted cowshed, and eat in an attractive conservatory looking out on magnificent country views. Packed lunches on request. Ground floor bedroom, cot, highchair and children's games are available. The farm is off the A520, south of Leek. Cheddleton Flint Mill and Railway Museum 1 mile. Wedgewood and Royal Doulton 7 miles. Grange Gardens 9 miles.

Open all year
5 bedrooms (1 twin ens. ⋔/WC; 1 double ens. ⋔/WC;3 family ens.⋔/WC).
⋔ ⊁ ETB ♛ ♛ ♛and Commended
Prices: B&B £14–16, weekly £98. EM £8.
Weekly B&B plus EM £154. ⋔ rates.

Fairboroughs Farm, Rudyard, Nr Leek
ST13 8PR
℮ (02606) 226341

Just off the A523 northwest of Leek this large 16th-century stone farmhouse makes an extremely comfortable retreat. There is a separate lounge and dining room with spectacular views. Guests are welcomed with a cup of tea on arrival, and another is offered on retiring to bed. Packed lunches and evening meals supplied on request, and children can use a cot, highchair and games provided. Peak District 1 mile. Rudyard Lake (Coarse fishing) and Tittlesworth reservoir (trout fishing) 2 miles. Pony trekking 5 miles. Alton Towers 10 miles.

Open April-Dec.
3 bedrooms (1 twin; 1 double; 1 family), 1🛏,
2WCs.
⚙ ⋔ ETB 🏵 🏵
Prices:B&B £12–14, EM £8.50.

Pool Hall Farm, Bradnop, Nr Leek ST13 7LZ
✆ (0538) 382774

Pool Hall Farm is an 18th-century farmhouse set
on a 95-acre dairy farm. Good breakfasts, cot
and highchair provided. The farm lies just over a
mile outside Leek off the A523 Leek-Ashbourne
road.

Open Apr-Nov.
3 bedrooms (1 twin; 1 double ens. 🛁/WC; 1
family), 1🛏, 2WCs.
⚙(2) ETB 🏵 🏵
Prices: B&B £12–13. ⚙ rates.

Swainsley Farm, Butterton, Nr Leek
✆ (0298) 84530   Mr & Mrs Chris Snook

Swainsley Farm is surrounded by some of the
most magnificent scenery in the Peak District
National Park. The area is criss-crossed with footpaths and cycle tracks, ideal for exploring the
many pretty villages. Cot and highchair provided. Butterton is off the B5054 (north of A523
Leek-Ashbourne road, 10–12 miles from Leek,
Buxton, Ashbourne and Bakewell.

Open all year
1 family bedroom, priv.🛁/🚿/WC.
⚙ ⋔ ETB Listed
Prices: B&B £15 first night, £13.50 thereafter.
Weekly £96. ⚙ rates.

STOKE-ON-TRENT   Map 5 A3

Tenement Farm, Three Lows, Ribden, Nr Oakmoor, Stoke-on-Trent ST10 3BW
✆ (0538) 702333   Mrs Joyce Miller

Come and enjoy our traditional country hospitality. Tenement Farm is in the Staffordshire moorlands south of the B5417/A52, east of
Stoke-on-Trent. Perfectly placed for both walking
and sightseeing. Dovedale Valley, Manifold Valley and Alton Towers are all within 3 miles. This is

a working farm with pedigree Charolais cattle
and sheep. Cot, highchair and games available.
Open Mar-Oct.
3 bedrooms (2 double ens.🛁/🚿/WC; 1 family
ens.🛁/🚿/WC), 3🛏, 4WCs.
⚙ ⋔ ETB 🏵 🏵
Prices: B&B £15–17.50, weekly £105–122.60.

Self-Catering

CAULDON   Map 5 A3

Limestone View Farm Cottage, Cauldon, Nr Waterhouses, Stoke-on-Trent ST10 3JP
✆ (0538) 308288

This farm cottage, set in a pretty garden, is on a
typical Staffordshire dairy farm with sheep, pigs
and poultry and overlooks open hay meadows.
Fresh flowers, open fires and a tea tray await your
arrival. A place where guests keep returning. Accommodation comprises 2 bedrooms, sleeps
max. 6 and a cot. The farm lies north of the A52,
Stoke-Ashbourne road, 7 miles from Ashbourne.
Manifold Valley 2 miles. Alton Towers 3 miles.
Dovedale 4 miles.

Open all year
ETB♫♫♫Commended
Prices: weekly £90–180. ⋔ £6 per week.

Park View Farm, Stoney Lane, Cauldon, Nr Waterhouses, Stoke-on-Trent ST10 3EP
✆ (0538) 308233   Mrs M. Burndred

The 3-bedroomed cottage, sleeps 6, adjoins a
pleasant redbrick farmhouse on this dairy and
sheep farm. Cot, highchair and games provided.
Scenic drives and ample walks in the Dales,
moors and valleys. Cauldon is 7 miles from Leek,
turn off A523 Ashbourne road at Waterhouses.
Manifold Valley and cycle hire 2 miles. Ashbourne and Leek 7 miles.

Open all year
ETB♫♫♫♫Highly Commended
Prices: weekly £100–225.

IPSTONES   Map 5 A3

Clough Head Farm, Shay Lane, Ipstones, Stoke-on-Trent ST10 2LZ
✆ (0538) 266259   Mrs Sheila Leeson

Clough Head Farm is a working dairy farm in a
quiet, secluded spot about 1 mile from village
shops and pubs. Accommodation is offered in a
recently converted barn which comprises the
Stable, which has one bedroom, sleeps 5, and
the Cartshed, 3 bedrooms, sleeps 6. The farm is

7 miles south of Leek, A523/B5053. Alton Towers and Peak District 5 miles.

Open all year
🐾 ETB♬♬Commended
Prices: weekly £100–210.

LEEK
Map 5 A3

Lower Berkhamsytch, Bottom House, Nr Leek ST13 7QP
✆ (0538) 308213   Edith & Alwyn Mycock

Self-catering accommodation is offered in the ground floor cottage which adjoins this dairy and pig farm. It sleeps 6 with 2 bedrooms and sofa bed in lounge. Cot available. Lower Berkhamsytch is 5 miles southeast of Leek off A523 Ashbourne road. Local pubs and cafe within walking distance. Peak district 5 miles, Alton Towers 6 miles. Potteries 15 miles.

Open all year
🐾 ETB♬♬Approved
Prices: weekly £90–150. 🐾 £5.

Swainsley Farm, Butterton, Nr Leek
✆ (0298) 84530   Mr & Mrs Chris Snook

For full farm description see p. 151. The Coach House and Haybarn have been converted from two former estate farm buildings. Both are full of character, furnished to the highest standard with all modern facilities. Coach House sleeps 6 in 3 bedrooms, 2 of which are suitable for wheelchair users. It is rated Category 1 for the disabled. The Haybarn has 2 bedrooms, sleeps 4–5. Cot available.

Open all year
♿ 🐾 ETB♬♬♬Highly Commended
Prices: weekly £200–425.

RUGELEY
Map 5 A3

Priory Farm, Blithbury, Rugeley WS15 3JA
✆ (088922) 269

Priory Farm is 185-acre dairy farm set in a picturesque and secluded situation alongside the River Blythe (off the B5014 northeast of Rugeley, via B5013/5234). The accommodation in a converted 18th-century fishing house incorporates a large lounge/bedroom for up to 4 people and a modern kitchen and shower room. Abbots Bromley, ancient village, 2 miles. Cannock Chase 3 miles.

Open all year
🏠 🐾 ETB♬♬♬
Prices: weekly £110.

SUFFOLK

BRAMFIELD
Map 3 B1

Broad Oak Farm, Bramfield
☎ (098684) 232　　　　Mrs Patricia Kemsley

Broad Oak Farm is a dairy farm on the A144, off the A12 north from Saxmundham. The spacious 16th-century farmhouse has been carefully modernised and is surrounded by meadowland and an attractive garden with a tennis court. A separate sitting room and dining room are provided for guests, who are greeted with afternoon tea on arrival and treated to good home cooking during their stay.

Open all year
3 bedrooms (2 twin inc. 1 ens.⌂/WC;1 double), 1🛏, 2WCs.
⚸ 🛉 ETB ♛ ♛ Commended
Prices: B&B £12–15, weekly £84. EM £8. Weekly B&B plus EM £140. ⚸ rates.

BURY ST EDMUNDS
Map 3 A1

Brighthouse Farm, Melford Road, Lawshall, Bury St Edmunds IP29 4PX
☎ (0284) 830385

Brighthouse farmhouse is a homely 200-year-old timbered building set in a tranquil, beautiful 3-acre garden. There is a TV in the lounge and log fires in winter. Packed lunches on request. Cot available. The surrounding arable farm is off the A134, 7 miles south of Bury St Edmunds, and includes a large well-kept camping and caravan site. Lavenham 5 miles. Constable country 7 miles.

Open Jan-Nov.
3 bedrooms (1 twin; 2 double ens.⌂/WC), 1🛏, 2WCs.

⚸ ETB ♛ ♛Commended
Prices: B&B £14–20, weekly £112.⚸ rates.

HINTLESHAM
Map 3 B2

College Farm, Hintlesham, Ipswich IP8 3NT
☎ (047387) 253　　　　Mrs R. Bryce

This 15th-century farmhouse is set in a quiet rural position on a 600-acre arable and beef farm on the A1071 west of Ipswich. The house belonged to Cardinal Wolsey and is comfortably furnished in keeping with the venerable age of the building. There is a large log fire and TV in the guest lounge. Golf courses, riding school nearby. Constable Country 10 miles. Lavenham 16 miles.

Open mid Jan-mid Dec.
3 bedrooms (1 double ens.⊡/WC; 1 family; 1 single), 1🛏, 1WC.
⚸(5) ETB ♛ ♛Highly Commended
Prices: B&B £15–17. ⚸ rates.

LAVENHAM
Map 3 B2

Weaners Farm, Bears Lane, Lavenham, Sudbury CO10 9RX
☎ (0787) 247310　　　　Mrs H. Rhodes

Weaners Farm is a comfortable modern farmhouse on a mixed farm set in a peaceful location off the A1141/134, south of Bury St Edmunds. It is just a mile from Lavenham, a fine medieval Suffolk wool town with magnificent timbered buildings.

Open all year
3 bedrooms (2 twin; 1 double), 1🛏, 2WCs.
ETB Listed
Prices: B&B £15–17.

SURREY

DORKING
Map 3 A3

Bulmer Farm, Holmbury St Mary, Dorking RH5 6LG
✆ (0306) 730210   Mrs Gill Hill

This is a 30-acre beef farm lying in the picturesque Surrey Hills, southwest of Dorking (A25/B2126). The farmhouse is 17th-century with beamed rooms and inglenook fireplaces. Guests can also stay in the tastefully converted barn which adjoins the house. There is a woodland walk to a lake, ideal for birdwatching. Homemade preserves are a speciality and there is a wealth of good pubs locally. Within 30 minutes by car: NT properties of Polesden Lacy, Hatchlands, and Clandon Park, as well as Wisley RHG.

Open all year
8 bedrooms (5 twin inc. 2 ens.⋔/WC;3 double ens.⋔/WC), 2🛁, 2WCs.
🐕 (12) ⊁ ETB 👑 👑
Prices: B&B £15–18.

Crossways Farm, Raikes Lane, Abinger Hammer, Dorking RH5 6PZ
✆ (0306) 730173   Mrs Sheila Hughes

Crossways is a beef and arable farm situated off the A25, 4 miles west of Dorking. The farmhouse is a 17th-century listed building full of beams and inglenook log fires in large comfortable rooms. Packed lunches on request, cot and highchair available. Leith Hill 2 miles. Box Hill 5 miles.

Open all year
3 bedrooms (1 suite of twin, double,🛁/WC; 1 family),1🛁, 2WCs.
🐕 ETB 👑 👑 👑
Prices:B&B £14–18, weekly £98–175. EM (2 courses) £7. Weekly B&B plus EM £140–154. 🐕 rates.

Sturtwood Farm, Partridge Lane, Newdigate, Dorking
✆ (0306) 631308   Bridget Mackinnon

This is a working family farm which specialises in beef, sheep and chickens. Evening meals can be provided by arrangement. The farm lies 5 miles from Dorking, Reigate and Crawley. Zoo and Aviaries 2 miles. Gatwick 6 miles. Brighton 25 miles.

Open all year
2 bedrooms (1 twin ens.⋔/WC; 1 single), 1🛁, 1WC.
🐕 ETB 👑 👑
Prices: B&B £17–18, EM £8.50–10. 🐕 rates.

SMALLFIELD
Map 3 A3

Chithurst Farm, Chithurst Lane, Horne, Smallfield, Nr Horley RH6 9JU
✆ (0342) 842487   Mrs G.E. Tucker

Chithurst is a working dairy farm in a truly rural location yet within easy distance of M23, M25, Gatwick, London and the coast, just northeast of Crawley and M23, Jct9. The 16th-century farmhouse has great character and is set in half an acre of attractive garden. The comfortable sitting/dining room has an inglenook fireplace and all the spacious bedrooms have lovely rustic views. Babysitting, cot and highchair available. Ashdown Forest and Gatwick Zoo 5 miles. North Downs 6 miles. Hever Castle 8 miles. Chartwell 10 miles.

Open Feb-Nov.
3 bedrooms (1 double; 1 family; 1 single), 1🛁, 1WC.
🐕 ⊁ ETB Listed
Prices: B&B £13.50–18, weekly £90–120. 🐕 rates.

SURREY

Self-Catering

DORKING
Map 3 A3

Bulmer Farm, Holmbury St Mary, Dorking RH5 6LG

© (0306) 730210
Mrs Gill Hill

This is a 30-acre beef farm lying in the picturesque Surrey hills, southwest of Dorking (A25/B2126). The farmhouse is 17th-century with beamed rooms and inglenook fireplaces. Accommodation is offered in 2 self-catering units sleeping 2 and 4. The smaller is equipped to meet the needs of disabled guests. There is a woodland walk to a lake, ideal for birdwatching, and a wealth of good pubs locally. Within 30 minutes by car: NT properties of Polesden Lacy, Hatchlands, and Clandon Park, as well as Wisley RHG.

Open all year
& ஃ ✝ ETB♫♫♫Commended & ♫♫♫♫Commended
Prices: weekly £110–165 (2 person unit)
£190–250 (4 person unit)

KEY TO SYMBOLS

Bath	☞
Shower	⌐
Bathroom	⇟
Disabled Guest Facilities	&
No Smoking	⅍
Children Welcome	ஃ
Dogs by Arrangement	✝

EWHURST
Map 3 A3

Westland Farm, Ockley Road, Ewhurst GU6 7SL

© (0483) 277270
Fax (0483) 267216

Two delightful 2-bedroomed cottages set within the gardens of the 18th-century farmhouse on a 38-acre farm, which includes an ancient wood with wild deer bordered by a stream. Highchair, cot, tennis court and swimming pool provided. The Cottage sleeps 5, the Stables sleeps 4. No cats or dogs. Westland Farm is a mile outside Ewhurst (A24/B2126/2127 from Dorking). Clandon Park 9 miles. Polesden Lacey 12 miles. Petworth House 20 miles.

Open all year
ETB♫♫♫♫ and ♫♫♫♫♫Commended
Prices: weekly £175–265.

155

WARWICKSHIRE

COVENTRY Map 2 B1

Camp Farm, Hob Lane, Balsall Common, Coventry, West Midlands CV7 7GX
✆ (0676) 33804 Mrs Evans

Camp Farm is a mixed farm 7 miles from M6, Jct4. The farmhouse is about 200 years old and gets its name from when Cromwell used the site for a camp when besieging nearby Kenilworth. Packed lunches and afternoon teas can be provided on request, also cot and highchair. Berkswell Mill, built 1826, is a short walk from the farmhouse. Kenilworth 3 miles. Coventry 6 miles. NEC 7 miles. Warwick 12 miles.

Open all year
4 bedrooms (2 twin; 2 double), 1 bath, 2WCs.
Prices: B&B £14.50–19, EM £8–9. rates.

Park Farm, Barnacle, Shilton, Coventry CV7 9LG
✆ (0203) 612628 Mr & Mrs Grindal

Despite its convenient access to the M6, Jct2, and M69 just 3 miles away, Park Farm is quiet and secluded. The farm is a working dairy farm and the house is a listed building of considerable historical interest. It was originally moated and offers spacious, comfortable accommodation with TV and tea/coffee facilities. Golf course 2 miles. Riding stable 3 miles. Coventry 5 miles. Arbury Hall 6 miles. Warwick Castle 16 miles.

Open all year
2 bedrooms (1 twin; 1 double), 1 bath, 1WC.
(12) ETB Commended
Prices: B&B £17.50, EM £10.

HENLEY-IN-ARDEN Map 2 B1

Irelands Farm, Irelands Lane, Henley-in-Arden B95 5SA
✆ (056479) 2476 Pamela & Colin Shaw

A farmhouse welcome and a peaceful night's sleep are offered by the Shaws. Their capacious late Georgian house has large airy rooms overlooking the 220-acre working arable farm, set in the rolling Warwickshire countryside. Irelands Farm is situated a mile north of Henley-in-Arden off the A3400 Stratford-Birmingham road. Long boats at Hatton Lock. Sailing, golf, fishing, gliding, swimming and cycling, all in the vicinity. Warwick 12 miles. Stratford-on-Avon 14 miles.

Open all year
3 bedrooms (1 twin ens. shower/WC; 2 double priv. bath/WC).
ETB Commended
Prices: B&B £17–20.

See STOP PRESS for more farms

KENILWORTH   Map 2 B1

Oldwych House Farm, Oldwych Lane,
Fen End, Nr Kenilworth CV8 1NR
℃ (0676) 33552   Ann & John Beaman

This 14th-century, timber-framed, redbrick farm-house was the ancestral home of the Shake-speare family long before their association with Stratford. The house is surrounded by cows, horses, poultry and even peacocks. There are two ponds in the grounds. Art courses and exhi-bitions in the converted barn in summer months. Tea/coffee facilities. Oldwych House Farm is 4 miles from Kenilworth, head west off A452 Birm-ingham road at Balsall Common. NAC 5 miles. NEC 6 miles. Warwick 8 miles. M42, Jct5 4 miles.

Open 11 Jan-Nov.
2 double bedrooms ens. 🖫/🖘/WC.
🏠(10) 🍴ETB 🏅 🏅Commended
Prices: B&B £19–20, weekly £105–126. 🏠 rates.

LEAMINGTON SPA   Map 2 B1

Crandon House, Avon Dassett,
Leamington Spa CV33 DAA
℃ (0295) 770652   Deborah Lea

Crandon House offers luxurious accommodation and an especially warm welcome. Set in a peace-ful spot overlooking traditional farmland south-east of Leamington Spa (M4, Jct12/B4100), the farm specialises in rare breeds of cattle, sheep and poultry. Guests have a separate sitting room and dining room and are plied with good food.

Warwick (town and castle) 11 miles. Leamington Spa 12 miles. Stratford-on-Avon 14 miles.

Open all year
3 bedrooms (2 twin inc. 1 ens.🖫/WC, 1 ens.🖘/WC; 1 double ens.🖘/WC).
🏠(8) 🐓 ETB 🏅 🏅Highly Commended
Prices:B&B £17–22, weekly £115–145. EM £11–12. Weekly B&B plus EM £180–224. 🏠 rates. Credit cards accepted.

Hill Farm, Lewis Road, Radford Semele,
Leamington Spa CV31 1UX
℃ (0926) 337571   Mrs Rebecca Gibbs

Guests' needs are a priority in this comfortable friendly farmhouse set in 350 acres of mixed farmland. The bedrooms are tastefully furnished with tea/coffee facilities and there is a guest lounge. Packed lunches and evening meals by arrangement. Cot and highchair available. The farm is 2 miles from Leamington Spa, off A425 Southam road. Warwick Castle 3 miles. Stratford-upon-Avon 10 miles. Cotswolds 30 mins drive.

Closed Xmas
5 bedrooms (2 twin inc. 1 ens. 🖫/WC; 3 double inc. 2 ens. 🖫/WC), 1🛏, 2WCs.
🏠 🍴ETB 🏅 🏅
Prices: B&B £15–17, EM £12. 🏠 rates.

Snowford Hall, Snowford Hall Farm,
Hunningham, Leamington Spa CV33 9ES
℃ (0926) 632297   Mrs Rudi Hancock

Snowford Hall is a picture book Georgian house set in quiet surroundings overlooking unspoilt countryside. The farm is mainly arable and lies west of the A423, east of Royal Leamington Spa. Packed lunches on request, cot and highchair available. Warwick Castle, Kenilworth and Coventry 7 miles.

Open all year
3 bedrooms (2 twin inc. 1 ens.🖫/WC, 1 ens.🖫; 1 double), 1🛏, 2WCs.
🏠 ETB 🏅 🏅Commended
Prices: B&B from £15. 🏠 rates.

OXHILL
Map 2 B2

Nolands Farm and Country Restaurant, Oxhill CV35 0RJ
✆ (0926) 640309

Nolands Farm is to be found off the A422 a mile east of Pillerton Priors, in a tranquil valley surrounded by woods and walks. There is a lake for fishing nearby. Accommodation is offered in attractively converted stables grouped around the stable yard. Several of the bedrooms are on the ground floor and two have romantic four posters. The restaurant is licensed. We offer clay pigeon shooting, bicycles for hire and riding nearby. Stratford-on-Avon 7 miles.

Open 15 Jan-15 Dec.
9 bedrooms (1 twin; 5 double inc. 2 ens.♿/WC, 3 ens.♿/WC; 3 family inc. 2 ens.♿/WC, 1 ens.♿/WC), 1🛁, 2WCs.
♿ ♿(7) ETB ♛ ♛ ♛
Prices:B&B £15–22, EM from £14.

RUGBY
Map 2 B1

Manor Farm, Willey, Nr Rugby CV23 0SH
✆ (0455) 553143   Mrs Helen Sharpe

This comfortable old farmhouse offers every amenity needed to make a stay delightful. The farm is a 93-acre sheep farm 3 miles west of Lutterworth, just off the A5. It is tucked into a tranquil village on the borders of Warwickshire, Northamptonshire and Leicestershire. An ideal base for touring or complete relaxation. National Organic Garden Centre 8 miles. Mallory Park 12 miles. NAC, Warwick Castle, Bosworth Battlefield and Althrop 15 miles.

Closed Xmas
3 bedrooms (2 twin; 1 double ens. ♿), 1🛁, 1WC.
✂ ETB ♛ ♛Commended
Prices: B&B from £16.

Marton Fields Farm, Marton, Nr Rugby
✆ (0926) 632410   Pamela Dronfield

Marton Fields is a 240-acre working farm offering a mile of private course fishing, good farm walks, a large garden with croquet lawn and the beauty of the surrounding countryside to entertain their

guests. Water colour tuition is another attraction. Separate dining room and sitting room for visitors. Coffee/tea facilities in rooms. Packed lunches and afternoon teas with homemade bread and preserves a speciality. The farm lies a mile off the A423 9 miles southwest of Rugby, 30 mins drive from the NEC Coventry and NAC 9 miles. Warwick 10 miles. Nidcote Manor Gardens and the Cotswolds within easy reach.

Open all year
4 bedrooms (1 twin; 1 double; 2 single), 1🛁, 1WC. ✂
Prices: B&B £18, weekly £105.

SHIPSTON-ON-STOUR
Map 2 B2

Ascott House Farm, Ascott, Whichford, Nr Long Compton, Shipston-on-Stour CV36 5PP
✆ (0608) 84655   Janet R. Haines

Ascott House is a 500-acre arable and sheep farm situated midway between Stratford-upon-Avon and Oxford, east of the A3400. The listed farmhouse is built of Cotswold stone and is a suitable focus for the surrounding Area of Outstanding Natural Beauty. There is a swimming pool and a snooker room with darts. Cot and highchair available. Rollright Stones 2 miles. Chipping Norton 5 miles. Upton House 9 miles. Banbury Cross and Stow-on-the-Wold 10 miles. Broadway, Blenheim Palace and Burford Wildlife Park 14 miles.

Closed Xmas and New Year
3 bedrooms (1 twin; 1 double ens. ⋔/WC;1 family ens. ⋔/WC), 2⬚, 2WCs.
⬚ ⋔ ETB ⬚ ⬚
Prices: B&B £14–17, weekly £98–105. ⬚ rates.

Manor Farm, Great Wolford, Shipston-on-Stour CV36 5NQ
✆ (0608) 74247

or Farm

This 17th-century listed farmhouse is set on a 270-acre arable farm with sheep and horses on the edge of an Area of Outstanding Natural Beauty. The comfortable rooms have lovely views. Cot and highchair provided, and packed lunches on request. Ideal for exploring the Cotswolds. Manor Farm is 4 miles from Moreton-in-the-Marsh, north of A44 Chipping Norton road. Stratford-upon-Avon 12 miles. Blenheim Palace 15 miles.

Open Mar-Oct.
2 bedrooms (1 twin; 1 double), 1⬚, 1WC.
⬚ ETB Listed
Prices: B&B £14–18, weekly £98.

STRATFORD-ON-AVON   Map 2 B2

Church Farm, Dorsington CV37 8AX
✆ (0831) 504194   Mrs M.J. Walters
✆ (0789) 720471

Church Farm is a 130-acre working farm with lakes and walks for guests to explore, as well as an equestrian cross country course. The comfortable well-equipped bedrooms are situated in the converted stable block of the Georgian farmhouse. Cot and highchair provided. The farm lies south of A439 Stratford-Evesham road, via Welford-on-Avon. Stratford and Cotswolds 6 miles. Warwick House 14 miles.

Open all year
7 bedrooms (2 twin ens. ⬚/WC; 3 double; 2 family ens. ⬚/WC), 3⬚, 2WC.
⬚ ⬚ ETB ⬚ ⬚Commended
Prices: B&B £13–17.

Church Farm, Long Marston, Stratford-upon-Avon CV37 8RH
✆ (0789) 720275   Mrs P.A. Taylor

A very warm welcome awaits you at our 17th-century farmhouse with a high level of comfort, surrounded by lovely countryside to explore. Fresh farm eggs a speciality. Packed lunches available. Cot and highchair supplied. Long Marston lies 6 miles southwest of Stratford-upon-Avon (A3400/B4632). Cotswold Hills 2 miles. Warwick Castle 12 miles. NEC 40 mins drive. NAC 30 mins.

Open all year
2 bedrooms (1 twin ens. ⋔/WC; 1 double/family priv. ⋔/⬚/WC), 1WC.
⬚ ⋔ ETB ⬚ ⬚Commended
Prices: B&B £15–19.50, weekly £90.

Sandbarn Farm, Hampton Lucy, Warwick CV35 8AU
✆ (0789) 842280   Mrs H. Waterworth

This beautifully renovated 16th-century farmhouse is set in very tranquil open countryside, yet it is only a few minutes away from Stratford-upon-Avon. Hampton Lucy is off A439 Warwick road, 3 miles from Stratford and Warwick Castle. Cotswolds, NEC and NAC under 30 mins drive.

Closed Xmas
5 bedrooms all ens. ⋔/🚿/WC (1 twin; 2 double; 2 family), 1🛁, 1WC.
🌳(5) ETB 🏵 🏵Commended
Prices: B&B £20–25.

Whitchurch Farm, Wimpstone, Stratford-on-Avon
✆ (0789) 450275   Mrs Joan James

Whitchurch Farm was built in 1725 and is set in park-like surroundings in the valley of the River Stour. The farm is a working farm of 220 acres, mainly sheep and cereals, located 5 miles south of Stratford-on-Avon, off the A3400. The separate dining and sitting room for guests has log fires in winter. Cot and highchair available. A 10th-century church is within walking distance. Hidcote Gardens 3 miles. Warwick Castle 8 miles.

Closed Xmas Day
3 bedrooms (1 twin ens.⋔/WC; 2 double inc. 1 ens.⋔/WC), 1🛁, 1⋔, 1WC.
🌳 ETB Listed
Prices: B&B £14–17, EM £8.50.🌳 rates.

Wootton Park Farm, Wootton Wawen, Solihull, Nr Statford-on-Avon B95 6HJ
✆ (0564) 792673   Mrs J.S. McCall

This family-run dairy and arable farm of 340 acres is situated off the A3400, 6 miles northwest of Stratford-on-Avon. Guests are welcome in the farmyard and milking parlour. The farmhouse is a charming 16th-century half-timbered building with lots of beams and character. Cot, highchair and children's games provided. Wootton Park Farm is in the centre of Shakespeare country. Ragley Hall 6 miles. Warwick Castle 10 miles. NEC 12 miles.

Open all year
4 bedrooms (1 twin; 1 double ens.⋔/🚿/WC; 2 family), 1🛁, 2WCs.
🌳 ETB 🏵 🏵Approved
Prices:B&B £16–22, weekly £96–120. 🌳 rates.

WARWICK   Map 2 B1

The Croft Guesthouse, Haseley Knob, Warwick CV35 7NL
✆ (0926) 484447   David & Pat Clapp

The Croft Guesthouse is situated on a small-holding 6 miles north of Warwick, off A4177. All meals available on request, cot and highchair provided. There is also a self-catering mobile home.

Open all year
5 bedrooms (1 twin ens. ⋔/WC; 1 double ens. ⋔/WC; 2 family ens. ⋔/WC;1 single ens. ⋔/WC), 2🛁, 2WCs.
🌳 ✄ 🐾 ETB 🏵 🏵Commended
Prices from: B&B £18.50, EM £8.🌳 rates.

Shrewley House and Cottages, Shrewley, Nr Warwick
✆ (092684) 2549

You can sleep in a king-size four poster in this 17th-century farmhouse, set in 2 acres of gardens and surrounded by fields. The house is beautifully furnished and decorated. Cot and highchair available. The farm is 4 miles northwest of Warwick, A4177/B4439. NAC 9 miles. NEC and Stratford 11 miles.

Open all year
3 bedrooms (2 double ens. 🚿/WC; 1 family ens. 🚿/WC), 1WC.
🌳 🐾 ETB 🏵 🏵 🏵Highly Commended
Prices: B&B £30–37. 🌳 rates,🐾 rates.

WELLESBOURNE   Map 2 B2

Little Hill Farm, Wellesbourne, Warwick CV35 9EB
✆ (0789) 840261   Charlotte Elizabeth Hutsby

Little Hill Farm has 300 acres of arable and beef land just north of Wellesbourne on the A429. The large rambling farmhouse exudes a warm and friendly atmosphere and shows its 300 years in the abundance of beams throughout. The rooms are furnished with antiques and there is a log fire in the drawing room on cold days. Packed lunches and afternoon teas available on request. Cot, highchair and children's games provided. Charlecote House 2 miles. Warwick Castle, Shakespeare's birthplace and Royal Leamington Spa 6 miles. Kenilworth 9 miles.

Closed Xmas and New Year
2 bedrooms (1 twin ens. ⋔/⊟/WC; 1 family ens. ⋔/⊟/WC).
⋔ ✝ ETB ♚ ♚
Prices:B&B £22 (single) £32 (couple), weekly £210–350 (couple). EM £10. ⋔ rates.

Self-Catering

COVENTRY
Map 2 B1

Cheshire Farm, Church Lane, Corley, Coventry CV7 8BA
℡ (0676) 40289/42269
Mrs Sheila Sykes

Cheshire Farm is 5 miles from Coventry, off B4098 to Tamworth. Accommodation is offered in 3 units converted from barns set around a courtyard and gardens adjacent to the large farmhouse. There are resident chickens and goats and sheep in the fields. Each unit has 2 bedrooms, sleeps 5, cot available. NEC 7 miles. NAC 10 miles. Warwick Castle 15 miles.

Open all year
ETB♪♪♪Commended
Prices: daily £50, weekly £125–250.

HENLEY-IN-ARDEN
Map 2 B1

Irelands Farm, Irelands Lane, Henley-in-Arden B95 5SA
℡ (056479) 2476
Pamela & Colin Shaw

For full farm description see p. 156. Accommodation is offered in 4 delightful oak beamed cottages, sleeping 2 and 4 persons, in a sheltered

courtyard setting. One cottage equipped for disabled guests.

Open all year
♿ ⋔ ✝
Prices: weekly £100–200 (2 person cottage), £150–350 (4 person cottage)

LEAMINGTON SPA
Map 2 B1

Blackdown Farm Cottages, Blackdown, Leamington Spa CV32 6QS
℡ (0926) 422522
Mrs R. Solt

Blackdown Farm has not been a working farm since the 1920s. Accommodation is available in two cottages converted from a cowbarn and stables. The cottages have 1 and 2 bedrooms, sleeping 2 and 4. Blackdown Farm lies off A452, 2 miles from Leamington Spa. Kenilworth Castle 4 miles. Warwick Castle 5 miles.

Open all year
ETB♪♪♪Approved
Prices: weekly £100–270.

WARWICK
Map 2 B1

Shrewley House and Cottages, Shrewley, Nr Warwick
℡ (092684) 2549

For full farm description see p. 160. Three self-catering units have been converted from the farm's old stables. Furnished with every modern requirement, they retain their exposed beams and character. All units have 2 bedrooms, sleeping 4–6 people.

Open all year
✝ ETB♪♪♪♪-♪♪♪♪♪Commended
Prices: weekly £195–295. ✝ £10.

WEST SUSSEX

HENFIELD — Map 3 A3

Great Wapses Farm, Henfield
✆ (0273) 492544 Mrs E. Wilkin

To find Great Wapses Farm turn west off the A23 onto the B2116 Henfield-Albourne road. The Grade 2 listed farmhouse is part Tudor, part Georgian, set in peaceful rural surroundings. There are horses in the paddock and a tennis court in the garden. Ground floor bedroom, cot and highchair available. Hickstead Showjumping Course 3 miles. Brighton 10 miles. Gatwick 15 miles.

Open all year
4 bedrooms (1 twin ens.🚿/WC;3 double inc. 2 ens.🛁/WC; 1 ens.🚿/WC).
👪 🐕
Prices: B&B £17–25.

Sparright Farm, Rackham, Pulborough RH20 2EY
✆ (0798) 872132

This 17th-century listed farmhouse complete with inglenook fireplace makes an ideal base for touring. Surrounded by peaceful woods, it is located west of the A283 between Pulborough and Storrington. There is a great choice of pub food to sample within a 3 mile radius. Parham House and Gardens with maze, and Amberley Wild Brooks 1 mile. Arundel Castle 7 miles.

Closed Xmas and New Year
2 bedrooms (1 double; 1 family), 1🛁, 1🚿, 2WCs.
👪 🚭 🐕 ETB Listed
Prices: B&B £13–14. 👪 rates.

HORSHAM — Map 3 A3

Swallows Farm, Dial Post, Horsham RH13 8NN
✆ (0403) 710385

Swallows Farm has been in the same family for over 60 years. It is a 210-acre mixed farm of beef, sheep, horses and arable crops. At the Georgian farmhouse, you will find an inglenook fireplace in the visitors lounge, generous, well-equipped rooms, and good home cooking. The farm is situated just off the A24 at Dial Post. Within 25 miles you have a choice of country houses, gardens, castles, race courses, open air museums and golf courses.

Open Mar-Nov.
3bedrooms (1 twin; 2 double), 1🛁, 1🚿, 2WCs.
👪(10) ETB ♛♛
Prices: B&B £15–25, EM £8.50–12.

STORRINGTON — Map 3 A3

Greenacres Farm, Washington Road, Storrington RH20 4AF
✆ (0903) 742538

Greenacres Farm stands at the foot of the Sussex Downs, surrounded by fields yet central for touring. There is a heated swimming pool for guests. Cot and highchair provided. Packed lunches and evening meals supplied on request. Greenacres is off the A283 Storrington road, west of A24. Golf, horse riding, bowls and tennis all within 8 miles. Amberley Chalk Pits 3 miles. Worthing 8 miles. Arundel Castle 10 miles.

Open all year
7 bedrooms (2 twin ens. 🚿/WC; 3 double inc. 2 ens. 🚿/WC, 1 ens. 🛁/WC;1 family ens. 🛁/WC; 1 single ens. 🛁/WC).
👪 🐕 ETB ♛♛♛Commended
Prices: B&B £18–25, EM £5–7.50, weekly B&B plus EM £220–250. 🐕 £2 per night, £12 per week.

Self-Catering

STORRINGTON   Map 3 A3

Greenacres Farm, Washington Road,
Storrington RH20 4AF
✆ (0903) 742538

For full farm description see previous entry. Accommodation is also offered in 4 one bedroom chalets, sleeping 3–5.

Open Feb-Nov.
ETB✓✓✓/✓✓✓✓ Commended
Prices: daily £30–45, weekly £150–260. ↖ £2 per night, £12 per week.

Reduced rates are sometimes available. Ask your host about weekend breaks.

WEST YORKSHIRE

BINGLEY
Map 5 A2

March Cote Farm, Cottingley, Bingley BD16 1UB

✆ (0274) 487433   George & Jean Warin

Lots of repeat bookings testify to the fact that guests at March Cote Farm are beautifully looked after. The 17th-century farmhouse has oak beams and charming mullioned windows, but has been fully modernised to a high degree of comfort. Top quality farmhouse cooking, mainly from home grown produce, is served in a delightful dining room. Cot and highchair available. The farm stands a mile from the A650 Bradford-Keighley road. Bradford 4 miles. Haworth, Bronte country 6 miles. Skipton, the Dales 12 miles.

Closed Xmas and New Year
3 bedrooms (1 twin ens. ⋔/WC; 2 double inc. 1 ens.�/WC), 1🛏, 2WCs.
♨ ⊱ ETB Listed Commended
Prices: B&B £15–17, weekly £105–119.♨ rates.

Self-Catering

HAWORTH
Map 5 A2

Westfield Farm, Tim Lane, Haworth BD22 7SA

✆ (0535) 644568   Mrs W. Carr

Half a mile from the famous village of Haworth stands Westfield Farm, a hill farm with sheep and suckler cows. Five delightful self-catering cottages, adjacent to the owners' farmhouse, offer accommodation for 2–6 people. One 2-person cottage is specifically designed for disabled visitors. As well as cot and highchair, there is a special play area for children with sand pit, swing and climbing frame. To reach the farm take the B6143 to Oakworth from Keighley. Pennine Way 2 miles. Skipton 8 miles.

Open all year
& ♨ 🛏 ETB♪♪♪ to ♪♪♪♪Commended
Prices: weekly £100–250.

WILTSHIRE

BOX
Map 2 A2

Hatt Farm, Fiveways, Box, Nr Bath SN14 9DJ
℡ (0225) 742989   Carol & Michael Pope

The Popes warmly invite you to enjoy the peace and comfort of their family home. Hatt Farm was built in the 18th century and overlooks magnificent views of the Wiltshire countryside. Situated only 6 miles northeast of the Georgian city of Bath, off the A365/B3109 junction, it is ideally placed for visiting many NT properties, Lacock 8 miles, picturesque villages and historic sites, Avebury 15 miles. Cot and children's games available.

Open Jan-Nov.
2 bedrooms (1 twin ens.⌾/WC; 1 family priv.⌾/WC).
⌂ ETB Listed Commended
Prices: B&B £15–20, weekly £100–140.

Saltbox Farm, Drewetts Mill, Box, Nr Bath SN14 9PT
℡ (0225) 742608

Saltbox Farm is a family run dairy farm bordering Bybrook in an enticingly steep valley between the villages of Colerne and Box. Enjoy excellent country walking and wildlife, only 6 miles from the centre of Bath. The farmhouse is a listed 18th-century building with a cosy comfortable atmosphere, situated just off the A4 midway between Chippenham and Bath. Packed lunches on request and cot available. Working watermill 500 yds. Brunel (Box) Tunnel 1 mile. Stone Quarry Museum 3 miles.

Open Mar-Dec.
2 bedrooms (1 twin; 1 double), 1⌂, 1WC.
⌂ ⌘ ⌂ ETB ⚜Commended
Prices: B&B £15–20, weekly £98. ⌂ rates.

BRADFORD-ON-AVON
Map 2 A3

Dog Kennel Farm Cottages, Iford, Nr Bradford-on-Avon BA15 2BB
℡ (0225) 723533

Set on a 200-acre working dairy farm 7 miles south of Bath off the A36, these cottages offer a home from home atmosphere with TV and tea/coffee facilities in all rooms. The setting is idyllic, quiet and beautiful with the River Frome only 150 yds away. Iford Manor, with Italian Gardens, 500

yds. Bradford-on-Avon 2 miles. Longleat Safari Park 10 miles. Cheddar Caves 15 miles.

Open all year
4 bedrooms (3 family; 1 single), 2🛏, 1🛏, 2WCs. 🐕(2) 🐾
Prices: B&B £12–15, weekly £75–90. 🐕 rates.

CORSHAM   Map 2 A2

Boyds Farm, Gastard, Corsham SN13 9PT
✆ (0249) 713146   Mrs D. Robinson

This arable working farm lies in the peaceful rural setting of Gastard, south on the B3353 from Corsham. The attractive farmhouse is 16th-century and the atmosphere welcoming. Babysitting is offered, and cot and highchair provided. Packed lunches on request and a cup of tea welcomes you on arrival. Good pub food close by. Corsham Court 1 mile. Sheldon Manor 2 miles. Lacock 3 miles. Bowood House and Castle Combe 5 miles.

Open all year
3 bedrooms (1 twin; 1 double; 1 family), 2🛏, 2WCs.
🐕 ⅃ ETB 👑 👑Commended
Prices: B&B from £14.50. 🐕 rates.

Pickwick Lodge, Corsham SN13 0PS
✆ (0249) 712207

This Grade 2 listed farmhouse is just 8 miles northeast of Bath, off the A4. The rooms are spacious, well furnished and fully equipped with all modern conveniences. Guests are welcome to relax in the large garden. Delicious home cooking, packed lunches on request. Highchair available. Lacock 5 miles. Castle Combe 6 miles. Bath 8 miles. Longleat Safari Park and Avebury 15 miles.

Open Mar-Nov.
3 bedrooms (1 twin priv.🛁/WC; 2 double priv. ⬗/WC).
🐕 ⅃ ETB Listed Commended
Prices: B&B from £15. 🐕 rates.

DEVIZES   Map 2 B3

Easton Farmhouse, Bishops Cannings, Devizes SN10 2LR
✆ (0380) 860228   Mrs Ann Horton

Easton Farmhouse is very quietly situated at the end of a lane, a mile from Bishops Cannings which is 3 miles north of Devizes, south off the A361. The 600-acre mixed farm runs from the house up onto the Wiltshire Downs, through the ancient Wansdyke. It makes a convenient base for visiting Bath, Salisbury, Lacock (10 miles) and Avebury (6 miles), or a peaceful retreat to relax and unwind. Cot and highchair available.

Open Jan-Dec.
2 bedrooms (1 twin; 1 double), 1🛏, 3WCs. 🐕
Prices: B&B £16–18. 🐕 rates.

Higher Green Farm, Poulshot, Devizes SNW 1RW
✆ (0380) 828355   Marlene Nixon

Higher Green is a 140-acre working dairy farm a mile south of the A361 Devizes-Trowbridge road. The listed 17th-century timbered farmhouse faces south onto the village green, very close to a traditional inn. The rooms are comfortable and there is a separate lounge for guests. Devizes 3 miles. Lacock 5 miles. Bath 20 miles. Salisbury 21 miles.

Open Feb-Dec.
4 bedrooms (1 twin; 1 double; 2 single), 2🛏, 2WCs.
🐕 ⅃🐾 ETB Listed
Prices: B&B £14. 🐕 rates.

Lower Foxhanger Farm, Rowde, Devizes SN10 1SS

✆ (0380) 828254 Colin & Cynthia Fletcher

This early 18th-century farmhouse is in a quiet, calm setting by the Kennet and Avon Canal. It is 300 yds from the A361, 2 miles west of Devizes. The Caen Hill flight of locks (29), the longest in the country, is 200 yds from the farm. Lacock 6 miles. Avebury 10 miles. Bath 14 miles. Cot and high-chair available.

Open Easter-Oct.
3 bedrooms (1 twin; 1 double; 1 family), 2🛁, 3WCs.
⚘ ⛨ ETB 👑 👑
Prices: B&B £14–18, weekly £95. ⚘ rates.

MALMESBURY Map 2 B2

Manor Farm, Corston, Malmesbury SN16 0HF

✆ (0666) 822148 John & Ross Eavis

This Grade 2 listed Cotswold stone farmhouse is 300 years old, situated on a 436-acre mixed dairy and arable farm. Cot, tea/coffee facilities available. Corston makes a marvellous base for exploring the Cotswolds as well as Bath, Castle Combe, Bristol, Tetbury and Cirencester. The farm is on A429 3 miles south of Malmesbury.

Open all year
5 bedrooms (2 twin; 1 double; 1 family; 1 single), 2🛁, 3WCs.
⚘ ETB 👑 👑Commended
Prices: B&B £14–20. ⚘ rates.

Oakwood Farm, Upper Minety, Malmesbury SN16 9PY

✆ (0666) 860286 Mrs Katie Gallop

A friendly farming couple welcome you to their dairy farm close to the quiet village of Upper Minety. The village is 7 miles east of Malmesbury, just north of the B4040. Guests have a separate lounge/dining room. Cot available. The farm is ideally placed for touring the Cotswolds and surrounding NT properties. Cotswold Water Park 3 miles. Malmesbury Abbey 7 miles. Cirencester 8 miles.

Open all year
3 bedrooms (1 twin; 2 double), 1🛁, 1WC.
⚘ ⛨ ETB Listed Commended
Prices: B&B £13, weekly £90. ⚘ rates, ⛨ £2.

Olivemead Farm, Olivemead Lane, Dauntsey, Nr Chippenham

✆ (0666) 510205

This is an 18th-century farmhouse situated on a working dairy farm in Dauntsey Vale. Children are made welcome in a large garden with climbing frames, swing and sandpit, inside there are toys, games, highchair and cot. For the farm, from M4 Jct17 take B4069 via Sutton Benger, then follow the Dauntsey signs over the motorway. Malmesbury 6 miles. Bowood 10 miles.

Open Jan-Nov.
3 bedrooms (1 twin; 1 double; 1 family), 1🛁, 1WC.
⚘ ⛨ ETB 👑
Prices: B&B £12–15, weekly £84–105. ⚘ rates.

Stonehill Farm, Charlton, Malmesbury SN16 9DY

✆ (0666) 823310

Stonehill is a 180-acre dairy and sheep farm reached by the B4040, off the A429. The 15th-century Cotswold stone farmhouse offers every comfort in a peaceful rural setting. Cot available. Malmesbury Abbey 3 miles. Cotswold Water Park 7 miles. Cirencester 12 miles.

Open all year
3 bedrooms (2 twin inc 1 ens.🛁/WC; 1 double), 1🛁, 2WCs.
⚘ ⛨ ETB Listed
Prices: B&B £13–17.50. ⚘ rates.

Widleys Farm, Sherston, Malmesbury SN16 0PY
℗ (0666) 840213   Mrs Mary Hibbard

This is a 300-acre dairy and arable working farm located off the B4040, 6 miles west of Malmesbury, the oldest borough in England. The Grade 2 listed Cotswold stone farmhouse provides a relaxing atmosphere. Packed lunches on request, cot and highchair available. Westonbirt Arboretum 3 miles. Castle Combe 6 miles. Berkley Castle and Slimbridge within easy driving distance.

Open Mar-Nov.
3 bedrooms (1 twin; 1 double; 1 family), 2🛁, 2WCs.
🦽 ETB 👑Approved
Prices: B&B £15, EM £7. Weekly B&B plus EM £120. 🦽 rates.

MARLBOROUGH   Map 2 B2
Bayardo Farm, Clatford Bottom, Marlborough SN8 4DU
℗ (0672) 515225   Mrs Shirley Bull
℗ (0672) 515116

The farm is southwest of Marlborough off the A345, and comprises 255 acres of arable land with some beef cattle. The house is particularly charming, built of brick and Sarcen stone in the 18th century and set in a beautiful garden. Packed lunches available on request, and children's games. Good country walks locally. Kennet and Avon Canal 2 miles. The Ridgeway Path 3 miles. Avebury 5 miles.

Open Mar-Nov.
3 bedrooms (1 twin; 1 double; 1 family), 1🛁, 2WCs.
🦽(8) ⅄ ETB 👑 👑Commended
Prices: B&B £15-18, weekly £105-120.

MELKSHAM   Map 2 A3
Frying Pan Farm, Melksham Lane, Broughton Gifford, Melksham SN12 8LL
℗ (0225) 702343

This stock rearing farm lies off the B3107/A350 west from Melksham. The farmhouse is a Grade 2 listed building, offering guests every comfort and attention. Lacock 3 miles. Bradford-on-Avon 4 miles. Bath 12 miles.

Closed Xmas and New Year
2 bedrooms (1 twin; 1 double ens.🚿/WC), 1🛁, 1WC.
🦽(2) ⅄ ETB 👑 👑
Prices: B&B £15-17.

SALISBURY   Map 2 B3
Vale View Farm, Slab Lane, Woodfalls, Salisbury SP5 2NE
℗ (0725) 22116   Mrs Barker

Vale View Farm is situated south of Salisbury on the A338, turning east onto the B3080. The farmhouse is modern, set in a large and peaceful garden on a small working farm with beef cows and pigs. It is particularly interesting to visit when the cows are calving (March-May). Ground floor bedroom and cot available. Vale View is an ideal base for exploring the region, with plenty of good walking. New Forest 1 mile. Bremore House 3 miles. Salisbury Cathedral 8 miles. Stonehenge 12 miles.

Open Mar-Nov.
3 bedrooms (1 double priv.🗠/WC; 1 single; 1 twin priv.🚿/WC), 1🛁, 1🗠 2WCs.
🦽 ⅄ ETB 👑 👑Commended
Prices: B&B £15-20, weekly £105-120. 🦽 rates.

SWINDON   Map 2 B2
Little Cotmarsh Farm, Broad Town, Wootton Bassett, Swindon SN4 7RA
℗ (0793) 731322   Mary A. Richards

This charming 17th-century farmhouse is situated in the quiet hamlet of Cotmarsh, 4 miles south of the M4, Jct16, off the B4041 from Wootton Bassett. The farmhouse has three cosy bedrooms full of character. A highchair is available in the guests' dining room which has the original flagstone floor. Avebury 6 miles. Marlborough 10 miles. Bath, Oxford and the Cotswolds 29 miles.

Open all year
3 bedrooms (1 twin; 1 double ens.🛁/WC; 1 family), 1🛏, 1WC.
🐾 ⚘ ETB Listed
Prices: B&B £14–17, weekly £98–105. 🐾 rates.

TROWBRIDGE   Map 2 A3

Spiers Piece Farm, Steeple Ashton, Trowbridge BA14 6HG
✆ (0380) 870266   Mrs P.J.Awdry

Take the A350 south from Melksham turning east at Ashton Common to find Spiers Piece Farm, a Georgian farmhouse nestling peacefully under the Wiltshire Downs with fantastic views across the countryside. This is an arable and beef family run concern. Afternoon teas served, cot and highchair available. Within easy reach of Bath (13 miles), and many tourist attractions, the farm makes a good base for touring the area. Bradford-on-Avon and Lacock 6 miles. Longleat Safari Park 10 miles. Stonehenge 12 miles.

Open Feb-Nov.
3 bedrooms (1 twin; 2 double), 1🛏, 2WCs.
🐾 ⚘ ETB 👑 👑Commended
Prices: B&B £13–15. 🐾 rates.

Self-Catering

CALNE   Map 2 B2

Home Farm, Heddington, Nr Calne SN11 0PL
✆ (0380) 850523   Mrs Janet Tyler

Home Farm is found 3 miles south of Calne off the A4 or A3102 in the centre of the village. Two attractive self-catering units have been converted

from a barn and a stable, sleeping 5 and 2 respectively, on this large dairy and arable farm. Highchair and cot available. Downland walks, riding school and golf course adjoin. The farm has a private lake. Bowood House 2 miles. Avebury, Marlborough and Bath all within 15 mile radius.

Open all year
🐾 ⚘ ETB ♪♪♪♪Commended (both properties)
Prices: weekly £150–325.

MALMESBURY   Map 2 A2

Stonehill Farm, Charlton, Malmesbury SN16 9DY
✆ (0666) 823310

Stonehill is a 180-acre dairy and sheep farm reached by the B4040, off the A429. Farm buildings attached to the 15th-century Cotswold stone farmhouse have been converted into 2 self-contained units, each sleeping 2/3. Cot available. Malmesbury Abbey 3 miles. Cotswold Water Park 7 miles. Cirencester 12 miles.

Open all year
🐾 ⚘ ETB ♪♪♪ Commended
Prices: weekly £100–230.

SCOTLAND

BORDERS

BROUGHTON
Map 7 A2

South Mains Farm, Skirling, by Biggar, Lanarkshire ML12 6HF
✆ (08996) 226   Mrs Rosemary Harper

A warm welcome is assured at this cosy, well furnished farmhouse, which enjoys good views across the countryside. An excellent breakfast starts the day which ends with an evening cup of tea, scones and cake. South Mains is a working family farm on the B7016 between Biggar and Broughton. An excellent 'resting place when travelling between north and south, and a good base for a holiday touring the Borders. 2 miles from Broughton Gallery, John Buchan Centre, golf, boating lake and puppet theatre.

Open all year
3 bedrooms (2 double; 1 single), 2➡, 2WCs.
⚿ �
Prices: B&B £10–11. ⚿ rates.

COLDSTREAM
Map 7 B2

Lochton, Coldstream, Berwickshire TD12 4NH
✆ (0890) 830205   Mrs J. Aitchison
Fax (0890) 830210

Lochton is a 600-acre arable and sheep farm off the A698 a mile north of Birgham. The cosy refurbished traditional farm cottage sleeps 5 people. Cot provided. From this delightfully peaceful spot there are wonderful views across the Tweed Valley to the Cheviot Hills. Locally: fishing on the Tweed, golf packages available. Kelso 4 miles.

Open all year
⚿ STB ♛ ♛ ♛Commended
Prices: B&B £12.50.

See STOP PRESS
for more farms

DUNS
Map 7 A2

Broomhouse Mains, Duns, Berwickshire
✆ (0361) 83665   Simon & Tracey Ashby

On this 230-acre arable farm, the farmhouse has just been completely refurbished and offers a high standard of comfort and facilities. The evening meal is first class cuisine. Privately owned trout and salmon fishing facilities. The farm is 2 miles from Duns off A6112. Locally Manderston House and Whiteadder River. Coast 10 miles.

Open all year.
3 bedrooms, all ens. ℔/WC (1 twin; 1 double; 1 family), 1➡, 2WCs.
⚵ STB ♛ ♛ ♛Highly Commended
Prices: B&B £16–24, EM £8–11.

Cockburn Mill, Duns, Berwickshire TD11 3TL
✆ (0361) 82811   Mrs A.M. Prentice

This small farm lies within sight and sound of the River Whiteadder. The farm offers well-equipped accommodation and evening meals by arrangement, home baking and farm produce. It is surrounded by abundant plant and wildlife. Trout fishing, and donkeys, hens, ducks and pet lambs to play with. Cockburn Mill lies north of Duns on the B6355. Close to Southern Upland Way, Border castles and keeps, abbeys and mills, fishing villages and fine sandy beaches.

Open Mar–Nov.
2 twin bedrooms ens.☞/WC.
⚿ STB ♛
Prices: B&B £16–18, EM £8. ⚿ rates.

EARLSTON
Map 7 A3

The Smithy, Legerwood, Earlston TD4 6AS
✆ (089684) 518

This renovated smithy is in a quiet rural area surrounded by farmland to which the smithy belonged. It is 4 miles from Earlston, east of A68 Earlston-Lauder road. Packed lunches available.

Cot and highchair provided. All bedrooms are groundfloor and there are special facilities for disabled guests. Farm trail on the doorstep. Kelso and Galashiels 12 miles.

Open Apr-Oct.
4 bedrooms (1 twin; 1 double; 2 single), 1🛁, 1🚿, 1WC.
♿ ⌂ 🐎 STB Member
Prices: B&B £13.50, weekly £85. EM £7.50, weekly B&B plus EM £135. ⌂ rates.

HAWICK   Map 7 A2

Carlenrig Farm, Teviothead, Nr Hawick, Roxburghshire TD9 OLH
✆ (045085) 218

Carlenrig is a large comfortable farmhouse, situated in beautiful Teviotdale. A traditional working hill farm extending to 1300 acres, it is ideal for walks, picnics or relaxing in the rambling country garden. It lies 10 miles south of Hawick on the A7. Convenient for riding, cycling and golf. Afternoon teas and children's facilities available.

Open May-Oct.
2 bedrooms (1 double; 1 family), 1🛁, 1WC.
⌂ ⤬ 🐎
Prices: B&B £12-14, weekly £70. ⌂ rates.

Crumelknowes Farm, Hawick, Roxburghshire
✆ (0450) 72251

Half a mile from the A7, close to Hawick, this modern bungalow farmhouse stands high on a hill overlooking the Teviot Valley with splendid views. This is the heart of the Border country, with its great tradition of knitwear, and a chance to visit the many specialist cashmere and tweed mill shops in Hawick.

Open Mar-Oct.
1 double bedroom ens. 🚿/WC. ♿
Prices: B&B £12.50, weekly £84.

Wiltonburn Farm, Hawick, Roxburghshire
✆ (0450) 72414   Mrs Sheila Shell
✆ (0450) 78000

This working hill farm of 400 acres is situated 2 miles from Hawick off the B711 (A7). The charming 200-year-old farmhouse is set in a sheltered valley with lovely views of hills and fields. A small stream runs by the peaceful garden. The farm is an excellent base for all kinds of outdoor activities – walking, riding, golf, fishing, tennis and swimming. Packed lunches on request and cot available. Craik Forest 7 miles. Kielder Water 20 miles. A wide choice of castles, abbeys and stately homes: Floors, Hermitage, Manderston, Bowhill and Abbotsford, within easy reach.

Open all year
3 bedrooms (2 double; 1 family ens. 🚿/🚿/WC), 2🛁, 2WCs.
⌂ 🐎 STB Listed Commended
Prices: B&B £13-14, weekly £84-91. ⌂ rates.

INNERLEITHEN   Map 7 A2

Traquair Bank, Innerleithen, Peebles-shire
✆ (0896830) 425

The attractive farmhouse of Traquair Bank has a mellow friendly atmosphere. Children are made particularly welcome with toys, safe garden, cot and highchair provided, as well as all the family pets, kittens, dogs, horses and lambs to be played with. Good home cooking served and packed lunches on request. To find the farm take the B709 south of Innerleithen to Traquair. Traquair House gates are 300 yds from Traquair Bank.

Open April-Feb.
3 bedrooms (1 twin; 2 double), 2🛁, 2WCs.
⌂ 🐎 STB Commended
Prices: B&B £14. EM £6. ⌂ rates.

KELSO   Map 7 A2

Cliftonhill Farm, Ednam, Kelso, Roxburghshire TD5 7QE
✆ (0573) 225028   Archie & Maggie Stewart
Fax (0573) 226416

Cliftonhill is a mixed working farm with cows, sheep, horses, hens, geese and arable. The spacious farmhouse is set amid breathtaking scenery. Full and continental breakfasts are available. The farm lies 2 miles north of Kelso (B6461). Floors Castle 2 miles. Mellerstain House 6 miles. Berwick-upon-Tweed 16 miles

Open all year
3 bedrooms (2 twin; 1 family ens. ☞/WC), 1🐾,1WC.
🐕 STB ♛ ♛ ♛
Prices: B&B £15–16, weekly £120. EM (Mon-Thurs only) £10. 🐴 £5 per night.

Houndridge, Ednam, Nr Kelso, Roxburghshire TD5 7QN
✆ (05737) 283

Houndridge is an arable and horticultural farm offering B&B in a cottage on the farm. Continental breakfasts, cot and highchair provided. It lies 3 miles north of Kelso (B6461). Hume Castle 2 miles. Floors Castle 3 miles.

Open all year
3 bedrooms (2 twin; 1 double ens.☞/WC), 1🐾, 1WC.
Prices: B&B £14–20. 🐕 rates,🐴 £6 per week.

MELROSE   Map 7 A3
Halidean Mill, Nr Bemersyde, Melrose
✆ (089682) 2341   Mrs Diana Wood

This mixed arable, cattle and sheep farm also has a small pony stud with Welsh ponies. Packed lunches provided on request. Climbing frame, swings, cot and highchair available. The farm is by Scotts View, 3 miles from Melrose, east of A68 at Newstead. Dryburgh Abbey 1 mile. Abbotsford 3 miles.

Open all year
2 bedrooms (1 double; 1 family), 4🐾, 2WCs.
🐕 ✂ 🐴
Prices: B&B £15. 🐕 rates.

PEEBLES   Map 7 A2
Langhaugh, Kirkton Manor, Peebles
✆ (0721) 740226   Mrs A. Campbell

This large modernised farmhouse is situated on a 2000-acre hill farm in picturesque Manor valley and makes an excellent base for hill walking. Fishing and cycling opportunities on the doorstep. Swimming 7 miles. Packed lunches, evening meals, cot and highchair available. The farm is 8 miles from Peebles, follow signs to Manor Head off A72 Glasgow road.

Open all year
3 bedrooms (1 twin ens. ☞; 1 double ens. ☫/WC; 1 family ens. ☫/WC), 1🐾, 2WCs.
🐕 🐴
Prices: B&B £15.50–20, weekly £135–150. EM £10–12, weekly B&B plus EM £200–230. 🐕 rates, 🐴rates.

SELKIRK   Map 7 A2
Oakwood Farm, Ettrickbridge, Selkirk TD7 5HJ
✆ (0750) 52245   Mrs S. Nixon

The owners of this spacious comfortable farmhouse aim to make it a home from home. The farm is mixed with sheep, horses and some arable land. It lies on the B7009 (Ettrickbridge road) 4 miles from Selkirk. Bowhill Country Park and Riding Centre 2 miles. Selkirk glass factory 4 miles.

Open all year
3 bedrooms (1 twin; 2 double), 1🐾, 1WC.
🐕 ✂ 🐴
Prices: B&B £11–12.50, weekly £77. 🐕 rates,🐴 £1.

Self-Catering

COLDSTREAM   Map 7 B2
Lochton, Coldstream, Berwickshire TD12 4NH
✆ (0890) 830205   Mrs J. Aitchison
Fax (0890) 830210

For full description see p. 170. The farm cottage is also available for self-catering, sleeps 5, cot provided.

Open all year
🐕 STB ♛ ♛ ♛Commended
Prices: weekly £100–200.

DUNS
Map 7 A2

Broomhouse Mains, Duns, Berwickshire
© (0361) 83665　　Simon & Tracey Ashby

For full farm description see p. 170. Accommodation is also available in a self-catering unit, 2 bedrooms, sleeps 4.

Open all year.
Prices on application.

Cockburn Mill, Duns, Berwickshire TD11 3TL
© (0361) 82811　　Mrs A.M. Prentice

For full description see p. 170. The warm and well-equipped self-catering cottage sleeps 5. Barbecue and inner tubes available.

Open all year
⚷ ⋔ by arrangement STB ♕ ♕
Prices: weekly £100–170.

KELSO
Map 7 A2

Cliftonhill Farm, Ednam, Kelso, Roxburghshire TD5 7QE
© (0573) 225028　　Archie & Maggie Stewart
Fax (0573) 226416

For full farm description see p. 171. Accommodation is also available in Rose, and Clematis, (above) and Craggs (below) farm cottages. All are fully equipped, having 2–3 bedrooms, sleeping 4–7. Cot available.

Open all year
⋔ ETB Commended
Prices: weekly £75–300. ⋔ £10 per week.

Houndridge, Ednam, Nr Kelso, Roxburghshire TD5 7QN
© (05737) 283

For farm description see p. 172. Accommodation is available in 5 well-equipped self-catering cottages, 1–3 bedrooms, sleeping 2–6.

Open all year
Prices: weekly £95–350.⋔ £6 per week.

Kerchesters, Kelso, Roxburghshire TD5 8HR
© (0573) 224321　　Mrs J. Clark

These welcoming terraced cottages are on a mixed farm which grows grain and potatoes, and rears sheep and cattle. There are 2 cottages sleeping 5 and 7 people. Kerchesters is 3 miles from Kelso. Take the B6350 to Sprouston, turn off by church. Farm lies a mile outside the village. Well-placed for touring Scottish Borders and Northumbria. Golf, fishing and swimming locally.

Open all year
⋔ STB ♕ ♕ ♕ ♕Commended
Prices: weekly £100–280.

PEEBLES
Map 7 A2

Langhaugh, Kirkton Manor, Peebles
© (0721) 740226　　Mrs A. Campbell

For full farm description, see p. 172. Accommodation is available in a 3-bedroomed unit, sleeps 8 people.

Open Apr-Sept.
Prices: weekly £300–500. ⚷ rates, ⋔ £10.

CENTRAL

CUMBERNAULD
Map 7 A2

Bandominie, Walton Road, Castlecary, Bonnybridge FK4 2HP
✆ (0324) 840248 Jean Forrester

This working farm rears a beef suckler herd. Cot and highchair provided. The farm lies 2 miles east of Cumbernauld. Antonine Wall 2 miles. Stirling Castle, Wallace's Monument 12 miles.

Open all year
2 bedrooms (1 twin; 1 double), 1🛌.
⚐ STB Listed Commended
Prices: B&B £13–14.

DOUNE
Map 6 B1

Inverardoch Mains Farm, Doune, Dunblane FK15 9NZ
✆ (0786) 841268 Mrs Joyce Anderson

This is a working farm set in beautiful countryside looking over to Doune Castle. The farmhouse is traditional in style, with a Doo'Cot tower attached. The rooms are spacious and comfortable. Cot, highchair and children's games available. The farm is located off the B824 (M9, Jct 11). Motor Museum 2 miles. Stirling Castle 8 miles. Callander, Rob Roy Centre 9 miles. Safari Park close by.

Open April-Oct.
3 bedrooms (1 twin; 1 double; 1 family ens.🛁), 1🛁/WC.
⚐ ➤ STB Member
Prices: B&B £13–16. ⚐ rates.

PORT OF MENTEITH
Map 6 B1

Inchie Farm, Port of Menteith, Stirling FK8 3JZ
✆ (08775) 233

This traditional farmhouse is set in a 170-acre arable, beef and sheep farm on the shores of the Lake of Menteith (A873/B8034 from Stirling. Good farmhouse cooking is provided. Cot and highchair available. A mile from the farm is the ancient Inchmahome Priory. Stirling 15 miles.

Open Apr-Oct.
2 bedrooms (1 twin; 1 family), 1🛌, 1WC.
⚐ ⚒ STB 🏅 🏅Commended
Prices: B&B £12–14, EM £7.⚐ rates.

Reduced rates are sometimes available. Ask your host about weekend breaks.

DUMFRIES & GALLOWAY

AUCHENCAIRN
Map 6 B3

Rascarrel Cottage, Rascarrel Farm, Auchencairn, Castle Douglas DG7 1RJ
✆ (055664) 214 Mrs Ellice Hendry

Bed and breakfast is offered in a beautiful cottage overlooking this 400-acre dairy, beef and sheep farm on the Solway coast. Ground floor bedrooms available. The farm is situated less than 2 miles off the A711 at Auchencairn, and just 500 yds from the sea. Coastal and forest walks of varying lengths can be taken from the farm. Bird watching, golf and fishing all locally. Good meals available at local village. Threave Gardens (NT) 9 miles.

Open Mar-Oct.
3 bedrooms (2 twin inc. 1 priv. 🛁; 1 double), 1🛁, 1WC.
STB 🏅 🏅Highly Commended
Prices: B&B from £15.

BORELAND
Map 7 A3

Nether Boreland, Boreland, Lockerbie, Dumfriesshire DG11 2LL
✆ (05766) 248 Mrs Rae

Nether Boreland is a 200 acre sheep and cattle farm on the B723, north of Lockerbie, in a quiet unspoilt village nestling in the Boreland Hills. Here you will find warm hospitality, log fires and country cooking. With over 20 golf courses in the region, and fishing available in lochs, rivers and reservoirs within a 12 mile radius of the farm, there is much to occupy the visitor. This is an ideal base for touring southern Scotland's fascinating abbeys and castles, tweed mills and the wide variety of scenery.

Open April-Oct.
3 bedrooms (1 twin ens.⌂/WC; 2 double inc. 1 ens.⌂/WC, 1 priv.⌂/WC).
⚶ STB ♨ ♨Commended
Prices: B&B £18–20, weekly £105–120.

CANONBIE   Map 7 A3
Caulside Head, Canonbie, Dumfriesshire DG14 0RT
✆ (03873) 71452   Mrs Ruth Williams

This traditional crofters cottage is set in large gardens with beautiful views over the Border Country. There is a comfortable lounge for guests with log fire and oak beams. All bedrooms are ground floor. Packed lunches available. Cot, highchair, slide and swings available. Fishing, golf, riding and tennis locally. Caulside Head is on B6357 (east of Canonbie, A7 north of Carlisle). Gretna Green 12 miles.

Open all year
3 bedrooms (1 twin; 1 double; 1 family ens.⌂/WC), 1🛁, 2WCs.
⚶ ⭲ STB ♨ ♨Commended
Prices: B&B £12.50–14.50, weekly £84–98. ⚶ rates.

CASTLE DOUGLAS   Map 6 B3
Balannan Farm, Ringford, Castle Douglas
✆ (055722) 221   Mrs Dawn Millar

This is a working beef and sheep farm which guests are welcome to explore. Large enclosed garden with play area for young children, cot, highchair and games also available. Packed lunches on request. The farm is deep in the Galloway countryside, off the A75 Castle Douglas-Stranraer road, 6 miles from Castle Douglas, Kirkudbright and Gatehouse of Fleet.

Closed Xmas and New Year
2 bedrooms (1 double; 1 family suite priv.⌂/WC), 1⌂, 1WC.
⚶ ✄
Prices: B&B £12.50–15, weekly £77–95. ⚶ rates.

Bluehill Farm, Auchencairn, Castle Douglas, Kirkcudbrightshire DG7 1QW
✆ (055664) 228

This beautifully appointed, whitewashed farmhouse is decorated to a high standard. Tea facilities in all the large bedrooms. Lovely views of country and sea. Ideal for walking and birdwatching. NT gardens, castles and abbeys all within easy distance. Auchencairn is 9 miles south of Castle Douglas on A711.

Open Easter-Sept.
3 bedrooms (1 twin priv. WC; 2 double inc. 1 ens. ⌂/WC, 1 priv. ⌂/WC).
STB ♨ ♨De Luxe
Prices: B&B £17–20.

MOFFAT   Map 7 A2
Corehead, Annanwater, Moffat DG10 9LT
✆ (0683) 20973

This 2500-acre hill farm is nestled in the Devil's Beef Tub, 5 miles north of Moffat, off A701. Packed lunches and evening meals available on request.

Open Easter-Oct.
2 bedrooms (1 twin ens. ⌂/WC; 1 double ens. ⌂/WC).
⚶(7) ✄ ⭲ STB Highly Commended
Prices: B&B £20–22, weekly £140. EM £12, weekly B&B plus EM £224. ⚶ rates.

Longbedholm Farm, Beattock, Nr Moffat, Dumfriesshire DG10 9SN
✆ (06833) 414   Mrs Val Wilson

This mainly sheep farm, 37 acres, is set in a valley with salmon and trout fishing available in the river. Ideal for birdwatching. Pony trekking and golf nearby. Packed lunches and evening meals available on request. Cot and children's games provided. The farm is 2 miles south of Moffat off A74.

Closed Xmas
3 bedrooms (2 twin; 1 double), 1🛁, 1WC.
⚶ ⭲ STB ♨
Prices: B&B £15–25, weekly £100–150. EM £8–10, weekly £150–165.

See STOP PRESS
for more farms

NEWTON STEWART   Map 6 B3

Auchenleck Farm, Minnigaff, Newton Stewart, Wigtownshire DG8 7AA
✆ (0671) 2035

This is a stock rearing farm with beef cattle and blackface sheep. The turreted farmhouse was originally built as a shooting lodge in 1863 by the Earl of Galloway. Furnished in keeping with its character, it is comfortable and homely. Cot available. Auchenleck Farm lies 5 miles northeast of Newton Stewart through Minigaff on an unmarked lane between A712 and back road to Glentrool, in Kirroughtree Forest, at the centre of the Glentrool National Park area where red, roe and fallow deer abound. Hill climbing, forest walking, river, loch and sea fishing in the vicinity.

Open Easter-Oct.
3 bedrooms (1 twin priv.◿/WC; 2 double inc. 1 priv.◿/WC, 1 ens. ▥/WC). ⚐
Prices: B&B £16, weekly £105. ⚐ rates.

THORNHILL   Map 7 A3

Waterside Mains, Thornhill, Dumfriesshire
✆ (0848) 30405

This is a working dairy and arable farm overlooking the River Nith with a panoramic view over Nith Valley. The river has salmon and sea trout in season. Packed lunches and evening meals

available on request. Thornhill (A76 north of Dumfries) is an ideal centre for exploring Galloway and Border valleys and hills. The farm is a mile north of Thornhill, off A76.

Open Mar-Nov.
3 bedrooms (1 twin; 1 double; 1 family), 2⇥, 2WCs.
⚐ STB ♛ ♛Commended
Prices: B&B £12.50, weekly £87.50. EM £7.50, weekly B&B plus EM £140. ⚐ rates.

WHITHORN   Map 6 B3

Baltier Farm, Whithorn, Newton Stewart, Wigtownshire DG8 8HA
✆ (09886) 665   Mrs E.C. Forsyth

The farmhouse of this dairy/mixed farm is a spacious stone building with a sunlounge overlooking the large garden, countryside and Isle of Man in the distance. Separate dining room for guests. Cot available. Archaeological dig in progress at Whithorn. Sailing, sea and river fishing, 5 miles. Monteith 8 miles. The farm is off B7004 Whithorn-Garlieston road, west of Wigtown Bay.

Open all year
2 bedrooms (1 twin; 1 double/family), 1⇥, 1WC.
⚐ STB Listed Commended
Prices: B&B £14, EM £8.50. ⚐ rates.

Self-Catering

CASTLE DOUGLAS   Map 6 B3

Balannan Farm, Ringford, Castle Douglas
✆ (055722) 283   Mrs Dawn Millar

For full farm description see p. 175. The cottage, sleeps 6, is set in its own grounds, surrounded by the farm.

Open all year
⚓STB ♛ ♛ ♛ ♛Commended
Prices: weekly £150–300.

KIRKCUDBRIGHT · Map 6 B3
High Kirkland Cottages, Kirkcudbright
© (0557) 30684
Contact: Mrs Dunlop, Cannee Farm,
Kirkcudbright DG6 4XD

Self-catering accommodation is available in two traditional stone Galloway cottages which have been newly reconstructed. The cottages have 4 and 3 bedrooms, sleeping 6–8. The cottages are a mile from Kirkcudbright (off B727). The picturesque local area has sandy beaches, fishing boats at the harbour, pony trekking, 18-hole golf course and a wildlife park.

Open all year
STB ♛ ♛ ♛ Commended
Prices: weekly £100–260.

FIFE
AUCHTERMUCHTY · Map 7 A1
Arodhoille Farmhouse, Dunshalt, Nr Auchtermuchty
© /Fax (0337) 28414

The farmhouse is spacious, warm and well-appointed with superb views of the Lomand Hills. A large guest lounge, delicious 'Taste of Scotland' breakfasts, 4-course dinners, lovely walks in woods and fields make guests feel pampered and relaxed. For children there are ponies to ride, games and a playroom. Cot and highchair provided. Packed lunches on request. The farmhouse is on the B936 south of Auchtermuchty. Golf course and tennis courts locally. Well placed for exploring the Fife fishing villages. Royal Palace of Falkland (NT) under 2 miles.

Open all year RAC
3 twin bedrooms inc. 2 ens. ⬚/WC, 1 ens.☞.
⬚
Prices: B&B £22–27, weekly £160. EM £16.
Weekly B&B plus EM £260. ⬚ rates.

CUPAR · Map 7 A1
Easter Lumbennie Farm, Newburgh, Cupar KY14 6ET
© (0337) 40368 · Mrs Margaret Ferguson

A working arable and stock farm set in quiet scenic surroundings with interesting country walks. The early 19th-century farmhouse has spacious bedrooms, lounge and dining room, all with splendid views. Packed lunches and tea available. Abundance of golf courses nearby. The farm is north of Auchtermuchty, A91/B936, 8 miles west of Cupar.

Open May-Sept.
2 bedrooms (1 twin/family; 1 double/family), 1⬚,
2WCs.
⬚ ⬚ ⬚
Prices: B&B £13–15, weekly £84–98. ⬚ rates.

Myrecairnie Farm, Cupar KY15 4QD
© (0334) 53266 · Mrs Lilias Smith

A large, comfortable and friendly farmhouse with Highland Cattle grazing beside the well-maintained garden. Packed lunches on request. 50 golf courses within 35 mile radius. The farm lies 2 miles from Cupar on the Rathillet road.

Open all year
3 twin bedrooms, 2⬚, 2WCs.
⬚ ⬚
Prices: B&B £16–20, weekly £120–140. ⬚ rates.

Ninewells Farm, Woodriffe Road, Newburgh, Cupar KY14 6EY
© (0337) 40307 · Mrs Barbara Baird

This traditional stone farmhouse is set on a working stock and arable farm. Magnificent views over the River Tay from Dundee to the mountains. Afternoon tea available. The farm is midway between Perth and Cupar (10 miles), with easy access M90, Jct 9. An ideal touring centre. Many golf courses within easy distance.

Open Apr-Sept.
3 bedrooms (2 twin; 1 double), 2🛁. 🐾
Prices: B&B £13.50–16, weekly £91–105. EM £5.🐾 rates.

Scotstarvit Farm, Ceres, by Cupar KY15 5PA
✆ (0334) 53591   Mrs Morna Chrisp

Nestled beside the 16th-century Scotstarvit Tower with the Hill of Tarvit Mansion House close by. The farm lies off the A916 south of Cupar. It is a traditional Scottish working family farm rearing cattle and sheep. The Victorian farmhouse is furnished to a high standard with spectacular views over the beautiful Howe of Fife to the Grampians. With St Andrews only 10 minutes, away the farm is ideal for golfers.

Open all year
1 double bedroom, private facilities. ⅟
Prices: B&B from £16.

Templelands Farm, Falkland KY7 7DE
✆ (0337) 57383

A small mixed farm perched on the hillside with panoramic views. Tea/coffee facilities, separate lounge and dining room. Packed lunches and evening meals available. Cot, highchair and children's games provided.The farm is a mile south of Falkland (A912), southwest of Cupar. Falkland Palace (NT) 1 mile. Deer centre 5 miles. Numerous golf courses.

Open Easter-Oct.
2 bedrooms (1 double; 1 family), 2🛁, 2WCs.
🐾 ⚲ STB ♨ ♨Commended
Prices: B&B £14.50–15, weekly £100. EM £7.50, weekly B&B plus EM £150.🐾 rates.

DUNFERMLINE   Map 7 A2
Bowleys Farm, Dunfermline KY12 0SG
✆ (0383) 721056   Mrs E.M. Fotheringham

This is a working livestock farm situated 800 feet above sea level. The farmhouse is early 19th century with many antique features and spacious accommodation. Packed lunches on request. Cot, highchair and games available. The farm is 4 miles north of Dunfermline, M90 Jct 4, B914. Knockhill Racing Circuit 2 miles. Water Ski Centre 3 miles. Undersea World, North Queensferry 8 miles.

Open Apr-Nov.
2 family bedrooms, 1🛁, 1WC.
🐾 ⅟
Prices: B&B £14–16, weekly £90. 🐾 rates.

ST ANDREWS   Map 7 A1
Greigston, Peat Inn, Cupar
✆ (033484) 284   Mrs M. Grant

This is a family run cattle and sheep farm with a 17th-century farmhouse of great character, a typical Scottish laird's house. Children are welcome to help on the farm, all farming questions willingly answered. East Neuk fishing villages and sandy beaches close by. The farm is 6 miles from St Andrews and Cupar (A915/B940 southwest of St Andrews).

Open Apr-Oct.
2 bedrooms (1 twin; 1 double ens. ⌲/WC), 1🛁, 1WC.
🐾 ⅟ 🐕 STB ♨ ♨Commended
Prices: B&B £14–17. 🐾 rates,🐕 rates.

GRAMPIAN
ABERCHIRDER   Map 9 B2
Skeibhill Farm, Aberchirder, Huntly,Aberdeenshire AB54 5TT
✆ (0466) 780301   Mrs E. Gregor

This traditional stone farmhouse stands on a family-run mixed farm of beef cattle, sheep and grain. Packed lunches and evening meals available. The farm lies a mile from Aberchirder off the Netherdale road. Plenty of golf courses nearby. Coast 10 miles. Whisky Trail 12 miles.

Open all year
2 family bedrooms inc. 1 ens. ⌲/WC, 1🛁, 1WC.
🐾 🐕 STB Commended Listed
Prices: B&B £11–12, weekly £75–80. EM £5–6, weekly B&B plus EM £110–125. 🐾 rates.

ABERLOUR
Map 9 A3

Kinermony Farm, Aberlour, Banffshire AB38 9LX
✆ (0340) 871818   Mrs Agnes Thom

This traditional whitewashed farmhouse stands on a sheep farm which also rears suckler cows. Packed lunches and evening meals available. Kinermony Farm is on the Whisky Trail and the Speyside Way, a mile from Aberlour (A95). Several golf courses within easy reach.

Open all year
3 bedrooms (2 twin; 1 family), 2🛏.
🐕 🛏
Prices: B&B £11.50, weekly £70. EM £7.50, weekly B&B plus EM £122.50. 🐕 rates.

BANFF
Map 9 B2

Bankhead Croft, Banff

A delightful modern country cottage offering good home cooking. Lunches and evening meals available. The house is on one level and has disabled facilities. Cot and highchair can be provided. Tea facilities. Bankhead Croft is a few miles from the quaint fishing villages of the north-east, close to the Whisky Trail, many castles, bird sanctuaries, golf and fishing. From Banff take A98 Fraserburgh road, signs after 6 miles. Pennan 4 miles.

Open all year
4 bedrooms (2 twin inc. 1 ens.🛁/WC, 1 ens. 🚽/WC; 1 double; 1 family), 1🛏, 1WC.
♿ 🐕 🛏 STB 🏵Commended
Prices: B&B £11, weekly £77. EM £6, weekly B&B plus EM £112. 🐕 rates.

Clayfolds Farm, Alvah, Banff AB45 3UD
✆ (02616) 288

This traditional farmhouse offers home cooking and the scenic countryside of Deveron Valley on a mixed farm concentrating on beef production. Friendly personal attention at all times. Tea/coffee facilities. Seaside with lovely beaches 3 miles. The farm is 3 miles from Banff, Alvah is signed off A97 Banff-Aberchirder road.

Open Mar-Oct.
3 bedrooms (1 twin; 1 double; 1 family), 1🛏, 1WC.
🐕 ✂ 🛏 STB Listed Commended
Prices: B&B £12–14, weekly £84–98. EM £7, weekly B&B plus EM £130–145. 🐕 rates.

ELLON
Map 9 B3

Sunnybrae Farm, Gight, Methlick, Ellon, Aberdeenshire AB41 0JA
✆ (0651) 806456   Mrs C. Staff

This is a traditional Scottish farmhouse with superb views set in a quiet location on a beef, sheep and arable farm. Packed lunches available. The farm is 9 miles northwest of Ellon, off B9005 Fyvie road. Fyvie Castle 5 miles. Haddo House 6 miles.

Open all year
3 bedrooms (1 twin ens. 🚽/WC; 1 double ens. 🚽/WC; 1 single).
🐕 🛏 STB 🏵Approved
Prices: B&B £15–18, weekly £105–126. 🐕 rates.

FORRES
Map 9 A2

Woodside, Kinloss, Forres, Moray IV36 0UA
✆ (0304) 690258   Mrs Alma Rhind

This 18th-century farmhouse set in a mixed arable and stock farm has been tastefully modernised to provide every comfort. Ground floor bedrooms, cot, highchair and children's games available. Woodside is 3 miles from Forres. Beach with sailing 2 miles. Golf 3 miles.

Open Apr-Oct.
3 bedrooms (1 twin; 1 double; 1 family), 2🛏, 2WCs.
🐕 🛏 STB 🏵 🏵Commended
Prices: B&B £12–13.

HUNTLY
Map 9 B2

Faich-Hill, Gartly, Huntly, Aberdeenshire AB54 4RR
✆ (046688) 240   Mrs Margaret I. Grant

This traditional family farmhouse is set in tranquil surroundings on a 500-acre beef and arable farm. It has been the repeated winner of the Scottish Farmhouse of the Year award. Home cooking using local produce a speciality. The farm is 4 miles south of Huntly (A97), on the fringe of Castle and Whisky Trails.

Open all year
2 bedrooms (1 double priv. 🚽/WC; 1 twin ens. 🛁/WC).
🐕(4) STB 🏵 🏵 🏵Commended
Prices: B&B £15, EM £7.

INVERURIE — Map 9 B3

East Blairdaff Farm, Kemnay, Inverurie, Aberdeenshire AB51 9LT
✆ (04677) 339 — Mrs Heather Duncan

East Blairdaff is a mixed farm of mainly cattle and sheep, plus a few pigs, ducks, hens, geese and a peacock. Guests have a separate sitting room in the warm and comfortable farmhouse. Cot and children's games available. Southwest of Inverurie, the farm is reached from the B994 to Kemnay, via A96 from Aberdeen. At the farmhouse there is a display of watercolours and silk paintings of farm animals, wildlife and local scenes. Thainstone Agricultural Centre and Mart 6 miles. Alford Farm Heritage Centre and Transport Museum 12 miles.

Open all year
3 bedrooms (1 double; 2 family), 2🛁, 2WCs.
👪 🐕
Prices: B&B £12–13, weekly £80–85. 👪 rates.

KEITH — Map 9 B2

The Haughs Farm, Keith AB55 3QN
✆ (05422) 2238 — Mrs Jean Jackson

The Haughs is a traditional mixed farm engaged in rotational cropping and cattle and sheep production. The spacious old farmhouse has a light cheerful dining room with excellent views. Tea/coffee facilities. Ground floor bedroom, cot and highchair provided. The farm is just outside Keith, off the A96 Inverness road. Nearby are the Whisky Trail, Castle Trail, Baxters Food Factory shop and restaurant. Falconry Centre 8 miles.

Open Apr-Oct.
4 bedrooms (1 twin ens. 🚿/WC; 1 family ens. 🚿/WC;2 double inc. 1 ens. 🚿/WC, 1 ens. 🛁/WC).
👪(2) STB 👑 👑 👑Commended
Prices: B&B £13.50–15.50, EM £8–9. 👪 rates.

OLD RAYNE — Map 9 B3

Mill Croft Guest House and Woodcraft Centre, Lawrence Road, Old Rayne, Aberdeenshire AB52 6RY
✆ (04645) 210 — Dorothy & Peter Thomson

This is a working croft in the heart of the Grampian countryside with highland cattle and pet goats on 5 acres of parkland bordering the River Urie on the edge of Old Rayne village (A96 Aberdeen-Inverness road). The homely cottage offers comfortable accommodation, good country cooking and a friendly welcome. One bedroom equipped to meet the needs of disabled guests, (A2 graded and classified), access, shower room grabrails etc. Woodcraft courses available, fishing locally. Ideal hill walking country.

Open all year
3 bedrooms (1 double priv. 🚿/WC; 1 twin priv.🛁/WC; 1 family ens.🚿/WC).
♿ 👪 🚭 STB Listed Commended
Prices: B&B £12–14, EM £6–8. 👪 rates.

TOMINTOUL — Map 9 A3

Milton Farm, Tomintoul, Ballindalloch, Banffshire
✆ (0807) 580288 — Mrs C. McIntosh

On this small beef farm the 200-year-old farmhouse provides a welcoming and friendly family atmosphere. Packed lunches and afternoon teas available. Milton Farm is just outside Tomintoul on the Dufftown road. Pony trekking, ranger guided walks, ski centre and Whisky Trail all local.

Open all year
2 bedrooms (1 double; 1 family), 1🛁, 1WC.
👪 🚭 🐕 STB Commended Listed
Prices: B&B £12–14, weekly £77–91. 👪 rates.

TURRIFF — Map 9 B2

Silverwells, St Mary's Well, Turriff, Aberdeenshire AB53 8BS
✆ (0888) 62469 — Mrs Jenny Rae

There are sheep, cattle, pigs, cats, dogs and a horse on this secluded 100-acre farm. The old farmhouse has splendid views over the surrounding countryside. Silverwells is just over 3 miles south of Turriff, off A947. Castle and Whisky Trails close by. Golf 2 miles. Fishing, pony trekking and the coast 3 miles.

Open all year
3 bedrooms (2 twin; 1 double), 1🛏.
⌂ (4) ✗ ✗ STB ♨ Commended
Prices: B&B £12–15, weekly £72–90.

Self-Catering

CRUDEN BAY   Map 9 B2

North Aldie, Cruden Bay, Peterhead
✆ (077984) 256   Mr & Mrs A.P. Taylor

This compact well-equipped 2-bedroomed cottage, sleeps 4, stands in its own garden on a 100-acre farm, mainly grass, which visitors are welcome to wander over. Cot and highchair supplied. The farm is secluded but not remote. River and loch fishing locally. Rock climbing and cliff walking close by. Cruden Bay and beach 4 miles. Peterhead and fish market 6 miles.

Open Apr-Sept.
STB ♨ ♨ ♨ ♨Commended
Prices: weekly £200–250.

HUNTLY   Map 9 B2

Faich-Hill, Gartly, Huntly, Aberdeenshire
AB54 4RR
✆ (046688) 240   Mrs Margaret I. Grant

For full farm description see p. 179. The farm cottage is 200 yards from the main farm building, in its own garden. The cottage has 3 bedrooms, sleeps 6.

May-Oct.
✗ STB ♨ ♨ ♨Commended
Prices: weekly £120–180.

OLD RAYNE   Map 9 B3

Strathorn Farm, Pitcaple, Inverurie,
Aberdeenshire AB51 9EJ
✆ (04645) 204

These 2 semi-detached cottages stand in their own gardens on a beef and arable farm which also has an equestrian centre for riding and carrige driving. Both units sleep 6 in 3 bedrooms. The farm is 8 miles north of Inverurie, a mile out-

side the village of Old Rayne (A96 Aberdeen-Inverness road). Fyvie Castle 9 miles.

Open May-Sept.
STB ♨ ♨ ♨ ♨Approved
Prices: weekly £200–300.

STRATHPEFFER   Map 9 A2

Scatwell Farm, Comrie, Contin,
Strathpeffer, Ross-shire
✆ (09976) 234   C.F. Cuthbert

This is a livestock hill farm rearing sheep and cattle with some arable land as well. The farm stands amid beautiful scenery with abundant wildlife. The farm is off the A835 at Contin, 12 miles west of Dingwall, by the River Conon, salmon fishing available. The three self-catering units have 2–3 bedrooms, sleeping 5–9 people. Cot and ground floor bedrooms available.

Open Apr-Oct.
✗ STB ♨ ♨Approved and Commended
Prices: weekly £100–250. ✗ £10.

HIGHLAND

BEAULY   Map 9 A2

Rheindown Farm, by Beauly, Inverness-
shire IV4 7AB
✆ (0463) 782461   Mrs S.M.M. Ritchie

Rheindown Farm is a small livestock farm of 70 acres with beef cattle, sheep and poultry, offering a holiday for all the family to enjoy. There are pet lambs to feed and eggs to collect, also games, cot and highchair available. The farm is a mile from Beauly (A862), which has an ancient priory. Golf course 2 miles. Hill walking, loch fishing (pike), deer farm with pets and rare animals, 3 miles.

Open Easter-Oct.
1 family bedroom, 1🛏.
⌂ ✗ STB ♨Commended
Prices: B&B from £13.50, EM £6.50. ⌂ rates.

Wester Moniack Farmhouse, Kirkhill,
Inverness IV5 7PQ
✆ (046383) 237

This small friendly farmhouse stands on a beef, cattle and arable farm of 600 acres. Excellent home cooking and baking a speciality. Packed lunches and afternoon teas on request. The farm is 9 miles from Inverness (A862 to Beauly). Moniack Castle Wineries 500 yds. Soap Factory 2 miles. Loch Ness 6 miles.

Open all year
2 bedrooms (1 double; 1 family), 1🛏, 1WC.

KEY TO SYMBOLS

Bath	🛁
Shower	🚿
Bathroom	🛁
Disabled Guest Facilities	♿
No Smoking	✗
Children Welcome	⌂
Dogs by Arrangement	✗

⚶ ⚕ STB Commended Listed
Prices: B&B £12.50–13, weekly £85–90. EM
£6–7, weekly £126–140. ⚶ rates.

BRORA   Map 9 A2

Clynelish Farm, Brora, Sutherland KW9 6LR
✆ (0408) 621265   Mrs Jane Ballantyne

This 300-year-old family run farm is situated on
the coast overlooking the Moray Firth, a mile
north of Brora (A9). There are suckler cows and
calves, ewes and lambs. The farmhouse was
built in 1865 and has a spacious secluded garden. Packed lunches and evening meals available by arrangement. Cot and highchair
provided. Sandy beaches and whisky distillery
within a mile. Dunrobin Castle 5 miles.

Open Easter-Oct.
3 bedrooms all ens. ⋔/WC (1 twin; 1 double; 1
family), 2⚘, 2WCs.
⚶ ⭢ STB ♛Commended
Prices: B&B £13.50–15, weekly £90–100. EM
£7.50, weekly B&B plus EM £140–150. ⚶ rates.

DRUMNADROCHIT   Map 9 A3

Allanmore Farm, Drumnadrochit IV22 2JB
✆ (04562) 247   Mrs E. Paterson

This farmhouse is 500 years old. It stands on a
beef cattle and sheep farm just outside the village of Drumnadrochit (A82) by Loch Ness.
There is a large garden for children to play in, and

locally the Loch Ness Monster Exhibition, hill
walking and fishing. Urquhart Castle 2 miles.

Open Apr-Oct.
3 bedrooms (1 twin; 2 double), 1⚘, 1WC.
⚶ STB Commended Listed
Prices: B&B £12.50–13, ⚶ rates.

GAIRLOCH   Map 8 B2

Cnoc Donn, Badfearn, Aultbea, Ross-shire IV22 2JB
✆ (0445) 731485   Mrs Anne Jones

Cnoc Donn is a new bungalow with an open coal
fire in the lounge. Set on a working croft with
sheep in good hill walking country and a choice
of lovely safe beaches. Packed lunches provided. Aultbea is off A832 north of Gairloch and
Poolewe, 85 miles west of Inverness. Inverewe
Gardens (NT) 7 miles.

Open Easter-Nov.
3 bedrooms (1 twin; 2 double ens. ⋔/WC), 1⚘.
⚶ ⚕
Prices: B&B £12–14, weekly £77–91. EM £7,
weekly B&B plus EM £126–140. ⚶ rates.

Duisary, Strath, Gairloch
✆ (0445) 2252   Miss L.M. Mackenzie

This is a modernised croft house which has
excellent views of the sea and hills, looking over
Loch Gairloch. Gairloch is on the A832, 60 miles
west of Dingwall. Sandy beaches 1 mile. The
croft is mostly used for grazing cattle and sheep.

Open Apr-Oct.
3 bedrooms (1 twin; 1 double; 1 family), 2⚘,
3WCs.
⚶ ⭢ STB ♛ ♛Commended
Prices: B&B £13.

Balaggan Farm, Culloden Moor, by Inverness IV1 2EL
✆ (0463) 790213   Mrs P. Alexander

A warm welcome is found at this comfortable
farmhouse with good food, home baking and
open fire in the sitting room. Packed lunches on
request. The 90-acre farm rears stock and crops
for winter feed. Fishing in the River Nairn, Clava

Cairns, Culloden Battlefield and Cawdor Castle close by. The farm is off B9006 from Inverness (7 miles).

Open Apr-Oct.
2 bedrooms (1 twin; 1 family), 1🛁, 1WC.
⌖ ⚲ STB Listed Commended
Prices: B&B £13–14, weekly £91. EM £8, weekly B&B plus EM £145. ⌖ rates.

Culdoich Farm, Culloden Moor, Inverness-shire
✆ (0463) 790268   Elizabeth M.C. Alexander

Culdoich Farm makes an ideal base for touring the Highlands. This working farm is situated off the B9006 7 miles east of Inverness. The 18th-century farmhouse is well-furnished, and offers the opportunity to enjoy some good home cooking in quiet and peaceful surroundings. Cot and highchair provided. Clava Standing Stones within walking distance. Culloden Battlefield 2 miles.

Open May-Oct.
2 bedrooms (1 double; 1 family), 1🛁, 1WC.
⌖STB ♛ ♛ Commended
Prices: B&B £13–14, EM £8–8.50. ⌖ rates.

Easter Dalziel Farm, Dalcross, Inverness IV1 2JL
✆ (0667) 462213

Easter Dalziel is a 210-acre farm breeding cattle and growing grain, there is also a flock of breeding sheep. The farm is to be found between the A96 and B9039, east of Inverness. The early Victorian farmhouse is charmingly furnished with separate guest lounge and roaring log fires on colder evenings. Castle Stuart 1 mile. Fort George and Culloden Battlefield 5 miles. Cawdor Castle 6 miles. Loch Ness 12 miles. Brodie Castle 15 miles.

Open Mar-Nov.
3 bedrooms (1 twin; 2 double), 2🛁.

⌖ ⚲ ⚲ STB ♛ ♛Highly Commended
Prices: B&B £14–16, weekly £91. EM £9. ⌖ rates.

LATHERON   Map 9 A1
Upper Latheron Farm, Latheron, Caithness KW5 6DT
✆ (05934) 224   Mrs Camilla Sinclair

Upper Latheron Farm, 20 miles south of Wick on the A9, has outstanding views of the coast and is an excellent base for touring the Highlands. The farm is surrounded by a wealth of animal life from puffins to ponies and sheep dogs (trials to watch). Day trips to Orkney are easy to arrange, and visits to highland games. The atmosphere at Upper Latheron is relaxing, guests well looked after with packed lunches and afternoon teas available on request. Clan Gunn Centre, Dunbeath Heritage Centre approx. 2 miles. John O'Groats 35 miles.

Open May-Sept.
3 bedrooms (1 twin; 1 double; 1 family), 1🛁, 2WCs. ⌖
Prices: B&B £12, EM £6.

MUIR-OF-ORD   Map 9 A2
Gilchrist Farm, Muir-of-Ord, Ross-shire IV6 YRS
✆ (0463) 870243   Mrs Ann B.G. Fraser

This mixed arable farm grows barley and crops for winter feed. There is a flock of Cheviot ewes with a friendly collie and farm cats. The house has an attractive garden. Good home cooking, Taste of Scotand selected. No EM at weekends. Packed lunches available. Cot and highchair provided. The farm is 14 miles from Inverness (A9/A832/A862), just outside Muir-of-Ord. Many beautiful walks on Black Isle peninsula. 18-hole golf course and Ord distillery under a mile away. Pony trekking 5 miles.

Open April-Oct.
2 bedrooms (1 twin; 1 double), 1🛁, 1WC.
⌖ STB ♛Commended
Prices: B&B £13–15, weekly £84. EM £8–10, ⌖ rates.

PLOCKTON
Map 8 B2

Achnahenich Farm, Plockton, Ross-shire IV52 8TY
✆ (059984) 238   Mrs B. Townend

The croft house was built in 1900 and has been comfortably modernised. Situated in a secluded glen, the farm is 4 miles from Plockton. This is a friendly working farm with beef cattle and sheep. Isle of Skye 6 miles. Eileen Donan Castle 10 miles.

Open Apr-Oct.
3 bedrooms (2 twin, 1 family triple ens. ⋔/WC), 1 ⊷.
⌂ STB Listed
Prices: B&B £12–14, EM £5. ⌂ rates.

Craig Highland Farm, Plockton, Ross-shire IV52 8UB
✆ (059984) 205   Mrs Patricia Heaviside

This converted croft house is on an open rare breeds farm where you can feed sheep, goats, pigs, poultry, waterfowl and even a llama. There are wonderful views over Loch Carron and a private coral beach. Children's games, toys and cot available. Packed lunches provided on request. The farm is midway between Plockton and Stromeferry on the shore road west of the A890. Small boats, canoes and bicycles for hire in Plockton, 3 miles, and a good selection of restaurants. The area also provides good fishing, hill walking, bird and seal spotting.

Open all year
3 bedrooms (2 double; 1 family), 1 ⊷, 1WC.
⌂ ⊩
Prices: B&B £12.50–14, weekly £80. ⌂ rates.

SPEAN BRIDGE
Map 8 B3

Old Pines, Gairlochy Road, Spean Bridge, Inverness-shire PH34 4EG
✆ (039781) 324   Niall & Sukie Scott

This is a Scandinavian style log built house quietly set in 30 acres with breathtaking views towards Aonach Mor and Ben Nevis. All bedrooms are on the ground floor, 3 are specially equipped for wheelchairs. Old Pines is a paradise for children with bikes, rope swings and other children to play with. Cot, highchair and babysitting available. Packed lunches and afternoon teas on request. The guest house is a mile north of Spean Bridge (B8004/A82).

Open all year
8 bedrooms (2 twin ens. ⋔/WC;2 double ens. ⋔/WC; 2 family ens. ⋔/WC; 2 single ens. ⋔/WC), 1 ⊷.
& ⌂ ⊁ ⊩ STB ♨ ♨ ♨Commended
Prices: B&B £20. EM £12.50. Weekly B&B plus EM £200–225. ⌂ rates.

ULLAPOOL
Map 6 B2

Clisham, Rhue, Ullapool, Ross-shire IV26 2TJ
✆ (0854) 612498

The croft house stands on 10 acres of arable land, 3 miles northwest of Ullapool (A835). The local area has boat trips, fishing, an interesting museum and many pleasant walks.

Open May-Oct.
2 family bedrooms, 1 ⊷, 1WC.
⌂(3) STB ♨Commended
Prices: B&B £12.50, ⌂ rates.

> Planning a day out?
> See RURAL ATTRACTIONS

Self-Catering

BRORA
Map 9 A2

Clynelish Farm, Brora, Sutherland KW9 6LR
✆ (0408) 621265 Mrs Jane Ballantyne

For full farm description see p. 182. Accommodation is offered in one 2-bedroomed unit, sleeps 4–5.

Open Easter-Oct.
✝ STB ➳Commended
Prices: weekly £140–160.

INVERNESS
Map 9 A2

Easter Dalziel Farm, Dalcross, Inverness IV1 2JL
✆ (0667) 462213

For full farm description see p. 183. The farm also has available 3 traditional stonebuilt cottages for self-catering holidays. The cottages are well-equipped, 3-bedroomed and sleep 4–6.

Open all year
STB ➳ ➳ ➳Highly Commended
Prices: weekly £160–340.

MUIR-OF-ORD
Map 9 A2

Gilchrist Farm, Muir-of-Ord, Ross-shire IV6 YRS
✆ (0463) 870243 Mrs Ann B.G. Fraser

For full farm description see p. 183. Accommodation available in a comfortably furnished, very well-equipped 3-bedroomed house, sleeps 6, set in its own garden in a quiet location.

Open April-Oct.
STB ➳ ➳ ➳Commended
Prices: weekly £115–220.

NAIRN
Map 9 A2

Broomton, Auldearn, Nairn
✆ (03094) 223 D. Ker

Broomton is a mixed arable farm with views over the Moray Firth. The farm has a self-catering cottage available, 2 bedrooms, sleeps 4–5. Cot provided. Standing 7 miles from Nairn, the cottage is 2 miles outside Auldean village. Good beaches all along the coast close by. Brodie Castle 3 miles. Cawdor Castle 6 miles.

Open all year
✝ STB ➳ ➳ ➳Commended
Prices: weekly £110–250. ✝ £8 per dog.

LOTHIAN

HADDINGTON
Map 7 A2

Ballencrieff Farm, Longniddry, East Lothian
✆ (08757) 362 Mr & Mrs G. Playfair

This is a typical 19th-century East Lothian farmhouse standing on an arable farm of 200 acres, with barley, wheat, potatoes and oilseed rape. Cot and highchair available. The farm is 3 miles north of Haddington (A1/A6137/B1377). Motor museum 1 mile. Sandy beaches 4 miles. 14 golf courses within 15 miles.

Open Mar-Nov.
3 bedrooms (1 twin; 1 double; 1 family ens. ⌂/WC), 1🛏, 1⌂, 2WCs.
⌂ ✝ STB ➳ ➳Approved
Prices: B&B £13–15, weekly £84–98.⌂ rates.

Barney Mains Farm, Haddington, East Lothian EH41 3SA
✆ (062088) 310 Mrs Katie Kerr
FAX (062088) 639

Barney Mains lies half a mile east of Haddington, off the A1. The farm is mostly arable, but there is also a suckler herd of cross Hereford-Friesians (which calve April-May) and a few hens. The beautiful Georgian farmhouse is traditionally furnished and has magnificent views over lovely open countryside. A cot, highchair and safe play area are available. Within 10 minutes drive are fine sandy beaches, selection of golf courses, castles, country houses and heather-covered hills.

Open April-Oct.
3 bedrooms (2 twin; 1 double), 1🛏, 1🛁.
⚘STB Listed Commended
Prices: B&B £12–17, weekly £80–110. ⚘ rates.

Long Newton Farm, Gifford, Haddington, East Lothian EH41 4JW
✆ (062081) 210

This 17th-century farmhouse has all modern comforts. The mixed arable farm has ponies, a suckler herd and fattening cattle. River fishing and lovely beaches nearby. Cot and highchair available. The farm is off the B6355 Edinburgh road 3 miles from Gifford village (B6369 south of Haddington). Ideal for touring the stately homes of the Border country and only 20 mins from Edinburgh.

Open Feb-Nov.
3 bedrooms (1 twin; 1 double; 1 family ens.🛁/🖘/WC), 1🛏, 1WC.
⚘ STB 👑 👑Highly Commended
Prices: B&B £14–16, ⚘ rates.

Tanderlane Farmhouse, Garvald, Haddington, East Lothian EH41 4LL
✆ (062083) 224   Mrs Jean D. Waddell

This stone farmhouse has spacious rooms. In a quiet rural setting on a 950-acre mixed farm, with cereals, sheep and beef cattle, it is only 30 mins drive to Edinburgh. 17 golf courses within a 15 mile radius. Packed lunches on request. From Dunbar (A1) take B6970 to Garvald (8 miles). Glenkinchie Distillery 8 miles. Bass Rock Bird Sanctuary 12 miles.

Open May-Oct.
3 bedrooms (1 twin; 1 double; 1 family), 3🛏.
⚘ 🐾 STB Commended and Listed
Prices: B&B £14, weekly £91–98. EM £7, weekly B&B plus EM £140–147. ⚘ rates.

LINLITHGOW   Map 7 A2

Belsyde House, Belsyde, Linlithgow
✆ (0506) 842098

The listed farmhouse on this 106-acre sheep farm dates from 1788. Cot and highchair avail-

able. The farm lies under 2 miles southwest of Linlithgow, on A706. Fishing and golf 1 mile. Hopetoun House 7 miles.

Open all year
4 bedrooms (1 double; 1 family ens. 🛁/WC; 2 single).
⚘ 🐾 STB 👑 👑Commended
Prices: B&B £15–18. ⚘ rates.

Woodcockdale Farm, Lanark Road, Linlithgow EH49 6QE
✆ (0506) 842088   Mrs W. Erskine

Woodcockdale Farm has a comfortable modern farmhouse set on a dairy and sheep farm which also rears Highland cows. Cot and highchair available. Less than 2 miles from Linlithgow (A706 Lanark road). Binns House 5 miles.

Open all year
4 bedrooms (1 twin; 2 family; 1 double ens.🛁/WC), 2🛏, 1WC.
⚘ ✂ 🐾
Prices: B&B £13, weekly £86. ⚘ rates.

PENICUIK   Map 7 A2

Peggyslea Farm, Nine Mile Burn
✆ (0968) 60930   Annette Noble

This is a modern bungalow on a 100-acre farm, mostly arable with some pigs and Clydesdale sheep. Afternoon tea and packed lunches available on request. The farm is situated on the A702, 4 miles southwest of Penicuik. Edinburgh Crystal Factory 4 miles. Edinburgh City Centre 10 miles.

Open all year
3 bedrooms (1 twin; 2 double), 2🛏, 2WCs.
⚘ 🐾
Prices: B&B £11–12, weekly £70–77. ⚘ rates.

Self-Catering

DUNBAR   Map 7 A2

Aikengall, Innerwick, Dunbar EH42 1SG
✆ (03684) 249   Mrs K.S. Macdonald

This self-catering cottage is set on a hill farm with views over the hills. 2 bedrooms, sleeps 5. Cot provided. The cottage is 8 miles south of Dunbar (A1 to Innerwick). Edinburgh 35 miles.

Open Mar-Oct.
🐾 STB 👑 👑 👑Commended
Prices: weekly £145–160.

See STOP PRESS
for more farms

ORKNEY ISLANDS

STROMNESS
Map 8 A1

Howe Farm, Stromness, Orkney KW16 3JU
✆ (0856) 850302

Accommodation is available at Home Farm in four 2-bedroomed semi-detached cottages (sleep 4). The cottages are on a working dairy farm with Friesian and Holstein cows and young stock. Free fishing. Golf and horse riding 2 miles. The farm is 2 miles from Stromness.

Open all year
STB ☺ ☺ ☺Commended
Prices: weekly £70–150.

STRATHCLYDE

AIRDRIE
Map 6 B2

Easter Glentore Farm, Greengairs, Airdrie, Lanarkshire ML6 7TJ
✆ (0236) 830243

This early 18th-century ground floor farmhouse is set on a 245-acre stock farm with panoramic views. The tasteful, comfortable rooms have tea/coffee facilities. Homemade shortbread and home baking are offered in the lounge in the evenings. Packed lunches and afternoon teas available. Best B&B Award Winner. The farm is 5 miles from Airdrie off B803 (east of A73 Airdrie-Cumbernauld road).

Open all year
3 double bedrooms inc. 1 ens. ⌂/WC, 1☺.
☺(5) STB ☺ ☺Commended

KEY TO SYMBOLS	
Bath	☺
Shower	⌂
Bathroom	☺
Disabled Guest Facilities	☺
No Smoking	☺
Children Welcome	☺
Dogs by Arrangement	☺

Prices: B&B £16–20, weekly £105–133. EM £9–10, weekly B&B plus EM £168–196.

AYR
Map 6 B2

Fisherton Farm, Dunure, Ayr KA7 4LF
✆ (029250) 223

A traditional Scottish farmhouse set on a working dairy, beef and arable farm with lovely sea views. Cot and ground floor bedrooms available. The farm is 5 miles south of Ayr, off A719 coast road. Wonderwest World 2 miles. Robert Burns Cottage 5 miles. Culzean Castle 6 miles. Midway between Troon and Turnberry Golf Courses.

Open Mar-Nov.
2 twin bedrooms ens. ☺/⌂/WC).
☺ ☺ STB Listed Commended
Prices: B&B £11.50–13.

Gadginth Mains Farm, Nr Annbank, Ayr
✆ (0292) 520721   Mr Iain Hendry
Write to: Gadginth Cottage, Gadginth Mains Farm, Nr Annbank Ayr KA6 5AJ

Four cottages gathered around a cobbled courtyard have been imaginatively converted from barns, stables and haylofts. The cottages have 1–2 bedrooms, sleeping 2–4, and are also available as self-catering. Breakfast and lunch can be supplied. Gadginth Mains is 6 miles from Ayr (A70/B742) and within a few miles are championship golf courses, sailing and other water sports, theatres and fine restaurants. Fishing, shooting and riding can be arranged. Beautiful river walks on the doorstep.

Open all year
☺ STB ☺ ☺ ☺ ☺Highly Commended
Prices: B&B £12.50, weekly £87.50.

BARRHEAD
Map 6 B2

East Uplaw, Uplawmoor, Glasgow
✆ (050585) 383   J. & J. Macleod

East Uplaw is a dairy and beef unit with 100 cows and calves. Here you can enjoy good home cooking, packed lunches and afternoon teas provided on request. The farm is 6 miles from Barrhead, M8 Jct 26/A736 south to village. Golf course under a mile. Glasgow 20 mins.

Open all year
4 bedrooms (1 twin; 2 double; 1 family ens.☞/ WC), 2🚻.
🐾 ✝ STB Listed & Commended
Prices: B&B £12–15, EM £8.50. 🐾 rates.

BEITH
Map 6 B2

Meikle Auchengree, Glengarnock, Beith, Ayrshire KA14 3BU
✆ (0294) 832205

This is a 250-acre dairy farm with a large farmhouse in a lovely setting with views of the loch. There is a big games room with indoor bowling mat, pool table and table tennis. Packed lunches on request. Cot and ground floor bedrooms provided. The farm is north of A737 Beith-Dalry road. Beith 2 miles. Plenty of golf courses, nearest 2 miles. Boating and skiing on lochs 5 miles.

Open all year
4 bedrooms (2 double inc. 1 ens.🛁/WC; 2 twin inc. 1 ens.☞/WC), 1🚻, 2WCs.
🐾 ✝ STB 👑 👑Commended
Prices: B&B £13.50–16.50. 🐾 rates.

Shotts Farm, Beith, Ayrshire KA15 1LB
✆ (05055) 2273

Shotts Farm is a working dairy farm set in beautiful open countryside, just off the B706 south of Beith. The rooms are comfortable and well equipped, with lovely views from the dining room. Cot, highchair and ground floor bedroom available. All meals are offered, including packed lunches and afternoon teas. Local working mill 5 miles. Championship golf course, Troon 12 miles. Burns country 20 miles.

Open all year
2 bedrooms (1 double; 1 family), 2🚻.
🐾 STB Registered
Prices: B&B £12, weekly £84. EM £6, weekly £126.🐾 rates.

BIGGAR
Map 7 A2

Biggarshiels Farm, Biggar, Lanarkshire ML12 6RE
✆ (0899) 20545

This recently renovated charming old farmhouse is set in 200 acres of beautiful open countryside. Good hill walking area. Packed lunches available on request. The farm is off B7016 just over a mile north of Biggar, where there are museums, golf course, puppet theatre and a selection of eating places.

Open Apr-Oct.
3 bedrooms (1 twin; 1 double; 1 family), 2🚻, 2WCs.
🐾 ✝
Prices: B&B £12.50, weekly £77. 🐾 rates.

Craighead Farm, Abington, Biggar, Lanarkshire ML12 6SQ
✆ (08642) 356   Mrs Mary Hodge

Craighead is a working mixed farm of 600 acres southwest of Biggar, off the A74/M74 on Crawford John Road. The attractive farmhouse is well equipped, offering a homely, well-run atmosphere and good country cooking. Packed lunches on request. Cot and highchair available. The farm is well placed for touring the region with the Clyde Valley, Biggar, Lanark and Leadhills nearby.

Open April-Nov.
3 bedrooms (1 twin; 1 double; 1 single), 1🚻, 1WC. 🐾
Prices: B&B £12.50–13.50, weekly £87.50. EM £6.50–7.50. Weekly B&B plus EM £130. 🐾 rates.

Dunsyre Mains, Dunsyre, Carnwath, Lanarkshire
✆ (089981) 251   M. Armstrong

Dunsyre Mains is a 400-acre beef and sheep farm situated in a very picturesque area 8 miles from Biggar, off the A702, ideal for hill walking and birdwatching. The cosy farmhouse is stone built, dating back to the 1700s. Packed lunches available on request. Cot and highchair provided. New Lanark 14 miles. Peebles (Traquair House) 14 miles.

Open all year
3 bedrooms (1 twin; 1 double; 1 family), 1🚻, 1🛁, 1WC.

❁ 🕆 STB ♻ ♻Commended
Prices: B&B £13, weekly £85. EM £8, weekly
B&B plus EM £140. ❁ rates.

Hillridge Farm, Biggar, Lanarkshire ML12 6LY
℡ (0899) 20332   Mrs M. Carrel

A lovely old farmhouse set on a 400-acre sheep
and cattle farm. Fantastic views, excellent home
cooked food and a warm friendly atmosphere
welcome everyone. Cot, highchair and games
available. Hillridge Farm is a mile from Biggar,
past Burnbraes Park. Biggar has 4 museums.
New Lanark World Heritage site 12 miles.

Open all year
3 bedrooms (1 double; 1 family; 1 single), 1🛁,
1WC.
❁ 🕆 STB ♻ ♻Commended
Prices: B&B £13.50–14.50, weekly £94.50. EM
£6.50, B&B plus EM weekly £140. ❁ rates.

Howburn Farm, Elsrickle, Biggar, Lanarkshire ML12 6QZ
℡ (089981) 276   Mrs A. Barrie

This traditional 18th-century farmhouse has a
warm and friendly atmosphere. TV in rooms. The
farm covers 830 acres, comprising mainly beef
cattle and sheep, and is located 4 miles northeast of Biggar on the A721. The oldest surviving
rural gasworks, now part of Biggar Museum, is a
unique local landmark and stands only 4 miles
from the farm. New Lanark 12 miles.

Open all year
2 bedrooms (1 twin/double; 1 single/double),
1🛁, 1WC.
♿ ❁ ✄ 🕆
Prices: B&B £12. ❁ rates.

Ormsary Farm, Southend, Campbeltown, Argyll PA28 6RN
℡ (058683) 665   Mrs Inez Ronald

Ormsary Farm is situated 8 miles south of Campbeltown in 200 acres, a combined dairy farm with
60 Ayrshire cows and 200 blackfaced sheep. In
this truly rural setting the stone built farmhouse
provides every comfort and good country cooking. Ground floor bedroom and cot available. St
Columba's Footsteps 3 miles. Mull of Kintyre
Lighthouse 7 miles.

Open April-Sept.
3 bedrooms (1 twin; 1 double; 1 family), 1🛁.
❁ 🕆 STB Listed Commended
Prices: B&B £12–13, EM £6. ❁ rates.

Walston Mansions Farmhouse, Walston Carnwath, Lanark ML11 8NF
℡ (089981) 338

A real home from home. The guest lounge has a
log fire and tea/coffee facilities. Farmhouse cooking offered with home produced meat, eggs and
organic vegetables. Packed lunches on request.
5 miles of Biggar (A702/A721 and take Walston
turning after Elsrickle). Heritage village of New
Lanark and spectacular Falls of Clyde 14 miles.

Open all year
3 bedrooms (1 twin; 1 family ens. 🛁/🛁/WC; 1
double ens. 🛁), 2🛁.
❁ 🕆 STB ♻ ♻ ♻Commended
Prices: B&B £11–13, EM £6.50–7.❁ rates.

CAMPBELTOWN   Map 6 A2

Mains Farm, Carradale, Campbeltown, Argyll
℡ (05833) 216   Mrs D. MacCormick

This comfortable farmhouse is set on a sheep
and beef farm with lovely views of the beach and
forest. Separate dining and sitting room, log and
coal fires, and home cooking. Evening meals on
request. Cot and highchair available. A mile from
the farm is a picturesque fishing harbour looking
across to the Isle of Arran. Good beach and forest walks 5 mins from the farm. Carradale is
northwest of Campbeltown on B842.

Open Apr-Oct.
3 bedrooms (1 family; 1 double; 1 single), 1🛏,
1WC.
🐾 ⊁ STB Commended/Listed
Prices: B&B £12.50, weekly £87.50. EM £4.50,
weekly £119. 🐾 rates.

DALMALLY
Map 6 B1

Rockhill Farm and Guest House,
Ardbrecknish, Argyll PA33 1BH
✆ (08663) 218

Rockhill is a 200-acre Hanoverian horse stud and
sheep farm with a long shoreline on the south
side of Loch Awe. On the loch there is free fishing, boating and bathing. On the farm there are
show mares and foals, a miniature Shetland pony
and donkey. The farm is on the B840, off the A819
south of Dalmally. The farmhouse is licensed,
and food cooked from fresh home grown produce including organic beef and lamb, salmon
and trout from the Loch Awe, and local venison
and game – five course set dinner. Packed
lunches on request. Ground floor bedrooms
available.

Open mid May-Sept.
5 bedrooms (1 twin ens.🚽/WC;1 double
ens.🚽/WC; 3 family ens.🚽/WC).
🐾(12) ⊁ STB 🏅 🏅
Prices: B&B plus EM £35-45. (Minimum
booking 2 nights)

DARVEL
Map 6 B2

Auchenbart Farm, Priestland by Darvel,
Ayrshire
✆ (0560) 20392   Mrs E. Seton

Auchenbart is a working dairy farm of 145 acres a
mile off the A71 east end of Darvel. The modern
spacious farmhouse has lovely views over the
Irvine Valley and is very well equipped for your
comfort. Tea/coffee facilities in all rooms. Cot
available. Convenient for Kilmarnock, Ayr and
Prestwick. Golf course 4 miles.

Open Easter-Oct.
3 bedrooms (1 twin; 1 double; 1 family), 1🛏, 1🛁.
🐾 ⊁ STB Listed/Commended
Prices: B&B from £14. 🐾 rates.

DOUGLAS
Map 6 B2

West Glespin Farm, Glespin, Douglas,
Lanark
✆ (0555) 851349

This is a stock rearing farm with beef cattle set in
the Douglas Valley with excellent views. The
peaceful farmhouse was built in 1818. Cot available. The farm is 2 miles southwest of the historic
village of Douglas (A70 Lanark-Holmhead road).
Lanark market town and New Lanark 14 miles.

Open June-Sept.
3 bedrooms (1 twin; 1 double; 1 family), 1🛏. 🐾
Prices: B&B £14-15.50. 🐾 rates.

GIRVAN
Map 6 B3

Ardwell Farm, Girvan, Ayrshire
✆ (0465) 3389

This farmhouse overlooks the Firth of Clyde and 2
bedrooms have sea views. Tea facilities and separate guest lounge. This is a sheep and beef farm
with many hill and shore walks. Safe, sandy
beach 100 yds. The farm is 3 miles south of Girvan on the A77 Stranraer road. Fishing harbour at
Girvan and golf 3 miles. Culzean Castle 9 miles.

Open all year
3 bedrooms (1 twin; 2 double), 1🛏.
🐾 ⊁
Prices: B&B £12-14, weekly £80-95. 🐾 rates. ⊁
£5.

Burnfoot Farm, Colmonell, Girvan,
Ayrshire
✆ (046588) 220/265   Mrs Grace B. Shankland

A warm welcome awaits you at Burnfoot, a family
run sheep and beef farm of 157 acres on the
south side of the beautiful Stinchar Valley, amid
the lovely unspoilt scenery of this non-industrial
river, famous also for its salmon fishing. The farm
is south of Girvan (A765). Good home cooking
and packed lunches on request. Cot and highchair available. Burnfoot is only a short distance
from beaches, golf courses, pony trekking, horse
racing, hill walking, river, loch and sea fishing.

Open Mar-Oct.
1 twin bedroom, 1 family suite, 1🛏, 1WC.
🐾 ⛪ STB ♛ ♛Commended
Prices: B&B £12–13, weekly £80–91. EM £7.
Weekly B&B plus 6 EM £122. 🐾 rates.

Glengennet Farm, Barr, Girvan, Ayrshire KA26 9TY
✆ (046586) 220   Mrs V. Dunlop

This spacious Victorian farmhouse was formerly a shooting lodge. It is set on a 500-acre sheep farm and has glorious views over the Stinchar Valley. Glengennet Farm lies off the B734 east of Girvan near the conservation village of Barr and Galloway Forest Park. Packed lunches available on request. Ayrshire coast 10 miles. Culzean Castle Country Park 15 miles.

Open May-Oct.
2 bedrooms (1 twin priv.🖘/WC; 1 double), 1🛏, 1WC.
🐾(10) STB ♛ ♛Commended
Prices: B&B from £15.

Hawkhill Farm, Old Dailly, Girvan, Ayrshire KA26 9RD
✆ (046587) 232

This spacious comfortable farmhouse was a former 16th-century coaching inn, and is set on a 220-acre arable and stock farm. There is a separate lounge and dining room for guests and an attractive garden. Cot available. Hawkhill Farm is 3 miles from Girvan (B734 to Old Dailly). Golf 2 miles. Coast 3 miles. Pony trekking 5 miles. Galloway Forest Park 8 miles..

Open Mar-Oct.
2 bedrooms (1 double ens.🖻/WC; 1 twin ens.🖘/ WC).
🐾⛪ STB ♛ ♛Highly Commended
Prices: B&B £16–18, weekly £112. EM £10. 🐾 rates.

Maxwelston Farm, Dailly, Nr Girvan, Ayrshire KA26 9RH
✆ (046581) 210

This working beef and sheep farm of approx. 1500 acres is situated on the B734 Girvan-Barr road, in excellent walking country. The beautiful listed farmhouse is warm and tastefully decorated. Home baking and fresh produce are always available with packed lunches on request. Children can play in the large garden. New Brunston Castle Golf Course opposite farm. Girvan and Turnberry beach 5 miles. Burns country, Galloway forest, Culzean Castle and Ayr within easy reach.

Open April-Oct.
2 bedrooms (1 twin; 1 double), 1🛏.
🐾⛪ STB ♛ ♛Commended
Prices:B&B £13–13.50, EM £8.

ISLE OF ARRAN   Map 6 B2

Glenscorrodale Farm, Ross Road, Lanlash KA27 8NX
✆ (077087) 241

This stone farmhouse, built in 1780, offers quiet accommodation with good cooking and open fires. It is on a sheep farm with its own salmon fishing rights. Packed lunches, evening meals, cot and highchair provided. The farm is 4 miles west of Lanlash on the Ross road. Local cheese making 5 miles. Arran Museum 8 miles.

Open May-Oct.
5 bedrooms (2 double; 1 family; 2 single), 2🛏, 2WCs.
🐾 ⛪ STB Listed/Commended
Prices: B&B £14, EM £5. 🐾 rates.

Rosebank Farm, Corriecravie KA27 8PD
✆ (077087) 228   Mrs Pat Adamson

This is a modernised farmhouse on a hill sheep farm set in a very quiet rural area with splendid views of Mull of Kintyre and the Antrim hills of Ireland. Log fires and home baking welcome you. Packed lunches and afternoon teas available. Cot and highchair provided. The farm is on the southwest coast of the island, 3 miles south of Blackwaterfoot.

Open Jan-Nov.
3 bedrooms (1 twin; 1 double ens.🖻/WC; 1 single), 1🛏, 2WCs.

  STB ★ ★Commended
Prices: B&B £14–17.  rates.

ISLE OF ISLAY   Map 6 A2

Octofod, Port Charlotte, Isle of Islay, Argyll
© (049685) 225

A modern luxury bungalow with beautiful views over Lochindool, it stands on a working dairy farm, with some sheep. Packed lunches and dinner available. Cot provided. The farm is 3 miles from Port Charlotte on the Portnahaven road, A847. Easy access to a number of sandy beaches, birdwatching and fishing all over the island. Museum of Islay Life 3 miles. Pony trekking 10 miles.

Open Apr-Sept.
3 bedrooms (1 twin; 1 double; 1 family), 3🚿, 1WC.
  ⁄
Prices: B&B £15, EM £10.

ISLE OF MULL   Map 6 A1

Antuim Farm, Dervaig, Isle of Mull
© (06884) 230   Mrs Lorna Boa

Situated in the north of the island west of Tobermory on the Dervaig-Salen road, this farm of 2000 acres is mainly given to sheep and cattle. The surroundings offer a magnificent combination of sea, loch and countryside. A cot and babysitting service are offered in the comfortable old farmhouse. Mull Little Theatre within walking distance. Dervaig village 1 mile. Calgary beach 4 miles. Boat trips 8 miles.

Open May-Oct.
3 bedrooms (1 twin; 1 double; 1 family), 1🚿, 1WC.  
Prices on application.   rates.

Kentallen Farm, Aros
© (0680) 300427   Mrs C. Stephens

This large family farmhouse has outstanding views from all rooms of the Sound of Mull. The 800-acre family run farm rears beef cattle and sheep. The farm is 6 miles from Tobermory, from the ferry terminal take the Tobermory road via Salen village. Boat trips to Staffa 8 miles. Torosay and Duart Castles 17 miles.

Open May-Sept.
2 double bedrooms inc. 1 ens.  /WC, 1 ens.  /WC, 1🚿, 1WC.
  ⁄ STB ★ ★Highly Commended
Prices: B&B £16.50–20, weekly £105–130.

KILBARCHAN   Map 6 B2

Gladstone Farmhouse, Kilbarchan. by Johnstone, Renfrewshire PA10 2PB
© (05057) 2579

A charming rural farmhouse with wonderful views, and less than 10 mins from Glasgow airport. Fresh milk from the dairy herd. The farm also has calves, chickens, pony and dogs. Tea/coffee facilities and TV in rooms, cot provided, all bedrooms on ground floor. 3 miles from Johnstone (M8 Jct 29/A761). Easy access M8, makes this a good stopover for trips to Loch Lomond and beyond. The area has beautiful walks through quiet countryside, boating, windsurfing etc all local.

Open all year
2 bedrooms (1 twin; 1 family), 1🚿.
  🐗
Prices: B&B £14, EM £7.   rates.

Pannell Farm, Kilbarchan Road, Bridge of Weir, Renfrewshire PA11 3RN
© (0505) 612480   Mrs J. McIntyre

Milking can be viewed twice daily on this working dairy and sheep farm. There are also calves and lambs in season. The comfortable house was built in 1826. Cot, highchair and games provided. The farm is 10 miles from Glasgow, M8 Jct 29/A761 via Kilbarchan. Near the farm are golf courses, antique shops, cycle tracks on disused railway lines, and NT Weavers Cottage in Kilbarchan. Caravans and tents also on site.

Open all year
3 bedrooms (1 double ens. ⋔/WC; 1 family; 1 single), 1🛏.
⬤ 🏃
Prices: B&B £13.50–16. ⬤ rates.

KILMARNOCK   Map 6 B2

Auchencloigh Farm, Galston, Ayrshire
KA4 8NP
✆ (0563) 820567   Mrs Jessie Bone

A warm welcome and good food awaits the holidaymaker at this 240-acre beef and sheep farm in rural Ayrshire with scenic views and walks all around. The farm has been in the same family for 5 generations. Packed lunches available on request. Cot provided. The farm is on the B7037 south off A71 Kilmarnock-Darvel raod, 10 miles from Kilmarnock. Burns Cottage and Burns country 10–16 miles.

Open Easter-Oct.
3 bedrooms (2 twin; 1 double), 1🛏.
⬤ ✂ STB Listed Commended
Prices: B&B £14–16, weekly £95–110. EM £7.50–10. ⬤ rates.

Reduced rates are sometimes available.
Ask your host about weekend breaks.

Hillhouse Farm, Grassyards Road,
Kilmarnock, Ayrshire
✆ (0563) 23370   Mrs Mary Howie

This spacious and comfortable farmhouse with sun lounge and garden is set on a 500-acre working dairy farm. Afternoon tea available. The farm is 2 miles from Kilmarnock. Centrally placed for touring and in good walking countryside. Numerous golf courses within a 10 mile radius. Glasgow 20 miles.

Open all year
3 bedrooms (1 twin; 2 family), 1🛏, 2WCs.
⬤ STB 🏆 🏆Commended
Prices: B&B £12–14, ⬤ rates.

Laigh Langmuir Farm, Kilmaurs,
Kilmarnock, Ayrshire
✆ (0563) 38270

Laigh Langmuir is a picturesque 18th-century farmhouse with all modern amenities in a peaceful rural setting. Home made preserves and baking a speciality, farm produce used in all cooking. Visitors are welcome to wander around the farm and relax by a log fire in the evening. Packed lunches and afternoon teas on request, ground floor bedroom, highchair and cot available. The farm is just outside Kilmaurs on the Irvine road (A77/B751 from Kilmarnock). Dean Castle 3 miles. Island of Arran, 12 miles to boat at Ardrossan. Kilmarnock 3 miles. Irvine 5 miles.

Open all year
4 bedrooms (1 twin; 1 double; 1 family ens.⋔/WC; 1 single), 1🛏, 2WCs.
♿ ⬤ 🏃 STB 🏆 🏆Commended
Prices: B&B £12.50–15, weekly £77. ⬤ rates.

Laigh Todhill Farm, Rowallan Castle
Estate, Fenwick, Kilmarnock KA3 2LW
✆ (0563) 40354

Laigh Todhill is a working farm with many rare breeds, including horses, sheep and pigs. The period farmhouse offers panoramic views and a warm friendly welcome from humans and animals alike. There is stabling for 3 horses. Packed lunches and afternoon teas on request. Cot, highchair and games room available. The farm is 3 miles north of Kilmarnock, A77/B751. Rowallan Castle 500 yds, own trout fishing available. Dean Castle, Country Park and Riding Stables 3 miles. Coast 6 miles.

Open Mar-Oct.
2 bedrooms (1 twin; 1 family), 2🛏, 2WCs.
🍴 ⚓
Prices: B&B £13–15, weekly £147–175. EM £7, weekly B&B plus EM £196–224. 🍴 rates.

Muirhouse Farm, Gatehead, Kilmarnock, Ayrshire KA2 0BT
✆ (0563) 23975   Mrs Martha S. Love

Muirhouse Farm is a working dairy farm of 170 acres, carrying a herd of Friesian cows with some beef cattle. It is situated off the A759, from the A71/A77 west of Kilmarnock. The traditional stone built farmhouse is welcoming and comfortable. Mrs Love offers good home cooking and packed lunches on request. Cot and highchair available. Dean Castle and Park 3 miles. Troon Championship Golf Course 4 miles.

Open all year
3 bedrooms (1 twin; 1 double; 1 family ens.🚿/WC), 2🛏.
🍴 ⚓ STB 👑 👑Commended
Prices: B&B £13–17, EM £7.50–8. 🍴 rates.

LANARK   Map 7 A2
Hillhouse Farm, Sandilands, Lanark, Lanarkshire
✆ (055588) 661   Mrs J. Lamb

This 17th-century farmhouse has a warm and comfortable atmosphere. Hillhouse is a working farm, mainly beef and sheep, situated south of Lanark off the A70 near Douglas Water. The farm also has a stud of Clydesdale Horses. Packed lunches provided on request, cot and highchair available. New Lanark and the Falls of Clyde 6 miles.

Open all year
2 bedrooms (1 double; 1 family), 1🛏, 1WC.
🍴 ⚓

Prices: B&B £12, weekly £80. EM £6. Weekly B&B plus EM £122.

Jerviswood Mains Farm, Lanark ML11 7RL
✆ (0555) 663987

This 18th-century farmhouse has been in the same family for over a century and has considerable character. The farm stands midway between Edinburgh and Glasgow, a mile from Lanark on A706 heading northwards. New Lanark, World Heritage site, 2 miles.

Open all year
3 bedrooms (1 twin; 2 double), 2🛏.
🍴 ⚓ STB 👑 👑Commended
Prices: B&B £14–18. 🍴 rates.

LARGS   Map 6 B2
South Whittlieburn Farm, Brisbane Glen, Largs, Ayrshire KA30 8SN
✆ (0475) 675881   Mrs Mary Watson

Mrs Watson offers a friendly homely atmosphere with comfortable accommodation, TV and tea/coffee facilities in rooms. The farm is an attractive working sheep farm set in the lovely Brisbane Glen, 2 miles northeast of Largs. Children are made especially welcome with fields to play in, lambs to feed and sheep and horses on the farm. Cot available. Largs seafront and pier 2 miles. Golf courses, horseriding, fishing, sailing, diving and hillwalking – all in the local area.

Open all year
3 bedrooms (1 twin; 1 double ens.🚿/🛁/WC; 1 family), 2🛏, 2WCs.
🍴 STB 👑 👑Commended
Prices: B&B from £14. 🍴 rates.

MAYBOLE   Map 6 B2
Three Thorns Farm, Straiton, Nr Maybole KA19 7QR
✆ (06557) 221   Mrs H.R. Henry

This 18th-century stone farmhouse is set in a large garden on a mixed farm. Tea facilities, cot and highchair provided. The farm is 6 miles southwest of Maybole, off B7023. Good hill walking area, Straiton Conservation Village 1 mile. Loch Doon and Culzean Castle 8 miles.

Open all year
4 bedrooms (1 double ens.🛁/WC; 1 family ens. 🛁/WC; 1 twin ens.🛁; 1 single ens.🛁), 1🛁, 2WCs.
⚘ 🐎
Prices: B&B £14.50, weekly £98. EM £7, weekly B&B plus EM £147.

Self-Catering

AYR
Map 6 B2
Fisherton Farm, Dunure, Ayr KA7 4LF
✆ (029250) 223

For full farm description see p. 187. Self-catering is available in one 3-bedroomed unit, sleeps 6–8.

Open Mar-Nov.
🐎 STB Listed
Prices: weekly £120–240.

Gadginth Mains Farm, Nr Annbank, Ayr
✆ (0292) 520721   Mr Iain Hendry
Write to: Gadginth Cottage, Gadginth Mains Farm, Nr Annbank Ayr KA6 5AJ

The four cottages, for full description see p. 187, are also available as well-equipped self-catering accommodation.

Open all year
🐎 STB 👑 👑 👑 👑Highly Commended
Prices: daily £30–45, weekly £100–330.

BIGGAR
Map 7 A2
Hillridge Farm, Biggar, Lanarkshire ML12 6LY
✆ (0899) 20332   Mrs M. Carrel

For full farm description see p. 189. Two cottages are available for self-catering, with 1 and 2 bedrooms, sleeping 2 and 5.

Open all year
🐎 STB 👑 👑 👑 & 👑 👑 👑 👑Commended
Prices: weekly £150–250.

DALMALLY
Map 6 B1
Rockhill Farm and Guest House, Ardbrecknish, Argyll PA33 1BH
✆ (08663) 218

For full farm description see p. 190. A cottage and a bungalow are offered for self-catering holi-

days. The cottage is a traditional stone built building, and the bungalow is a capacious cedarwood bungalow. Both sleep up to 6.

⚘ 🐎 STB 👑 👑
Prices: weekly £220–285. 🐎 £6 per week.

GIRVAN
Map 6 B3
Ardwell Farm, Girvan, Ayrshire
✆ (0465) 3389

For full farm description see p. 190. Accommodation is also available in a 3 bedroomed unit, sleeps 6.

Open all year 🐎
Prices: weekly £100–200.🐎 £5.

ISLE OF MULL
Map 6 A1
Kentallen Farm, Aros
✆ (0680) 300427   Mrs C. Stephens

For full farm description see p. 192. The farm has 4 self-catering units with 1–4 bedrooms, sleeping 2–7.

Open Mar-Nov.
🐎 STB 👑 👑 👑 👑Commended
Prices: weekly £95–400.

KILMARNOCK
Map 6 B2
Auchencloigh Farm, Galston, Ayrshire KA4 8NP
✆ (0563) 820567   Mrs Jessie Bone

For full farm description see p. 193. Accommodation is available in a 3-bedroomed unit, sleeps 6–7.

Open all year
STB 👑 👑 👑 👑Commended
Prices: weekly £180–250.

Hillhouse Farm, Grassyards Road, Kilmarnock, Ayrshire
✆ (0563) 23370   Mrs Mary Howie

For full farm description see p. 193. Accommodation is available in two fully equipped 3-bedroomed units, sleeping 6–9.

Open all year
🐎 STB 👑 👑Commended
Prices: weekly £130–290.

TAYSIDE

ARBROATH   Map 7 A1

Grange of Conon, Arbroath, Angus DD11 3SD
✆ (02416) 202

A spacious farmhouse set in a beautifully land-scaped garden on a working mixed arable farm. Excellent home cooking, tea/coffee facilities, ground floor bedroom, games room with snooker table, table tennis and exercise equipment, shooting and fishing are all offered. Grange of Conon is 4 miles northwest of the fishing town of Arbroath (west off A933 at Colliston village). Ideally situated for touring the surrounding Angus Glens, and only a short drive from Glamis Castle and Royal Deeside.

Open all year
3 bedrooms (2 twin; 1 family), 2🛏.
🏠(3) STB 👑 👑Highly Commended
Prices: B&B £22.50–30.

Templeton Farm, Nr Letham Grange, by Arbroath DD11 4RP
✆ (024189) 220   Mrs Mary Soutar

This is a large and comfortable farmhouse set on an arable farm with Letham Grange Golf Course next door. The farm stands 4 miles north of Arbroath.

Open Apr-Oct.
3 bedrooms (1 twin; 1 double; 1 family), 2🛏, 2WCs. 🏠
Prices: B&B £12. 🏠 rates.

BLAIRGOWRIE   Map 7 A1

Easter Tullyweddie, Clunie, by Blairgowrie
✆ (0250) 884281
Contact: Mrs H. Wightman, Bankhead, Clunie, Blairgowrie PH10 6SG

This is a family run mixed farm of 215 acres, with cows, sheep, cereals, potatoes and raspberries. All accommodation ground floor, in a self-contained unit. Packed lunches available on request. The farm is 4 miles from Blairgowrie off the A923

Dunkeld road. A good centre for touring, Loch of Lowes Nature Reserve 6 miles. Several golf courses nearby.

Open all year
2 bedrooms (1 twin; 1 family), 1🛏.
🏠 ⚡ STB 👑Commended
Prices: B&B £13. 🏠 rates.

Newmill of Kinloch, Clunie, Blairgowrie, Perthshire PH10 6SG
✆ (0250) 884263

The stone farmhouse is adjacent to a cottage, farmsteading and disused mill, surrounded by trees and open farmland. The eel farm uses the old mill race to catch the eels. There are also sheep and hens. Packed lunches available. Cot, highchair and games room provided. The farm is 3 miles from Blairgowrie on the A923 Dunkeld road. Many beautiful walks, Lochs Clunie and Marlee close by. Loch of Lowes Nature Reserve (Osprey Nesting site) 5 miles.

Open all year
2 bedrooms (1 twin; 1 double), 1🛏, 1WC.
🏠 ⚡
Prices: B&B £13. 🏠 rates.

BRECHIN   Map 7 A1

Blibberhill Farm, Brechin, Angus DD9 6TH
✆ (030783) 225 ✆ From April 1993: (0304) 830225

A warm welcome awaits you at this spacious well-appointed farmhouse set in peaceful surroundings. The farm is 300 acres of arable and stock rearing and lies between Angus Glens and the coast, 5 miles southwest of Brechin off the B9134. Good home cooking and baking is offered with homemade marmalade and jams a speciality. Pictish Stones at Aberlemno 2 miles. Brechin Cathedral and Round Tower 5 miles. House of Dun 8 miles. Angus Folk Museum and Glamis Castle 12 miles.

Open all year
3 bedrooms (2 twin inc. 1 ens.🛁/WC, 1 ens.🚿/WC; 1 double), 1🛏, 1WC.
⚡ STB 👑 👑 👑Highly Commended
Prices: B&B from £13, EM £8.50.

See STOP PRESS
for more farms

Briarton, Little Brechin, Brechin, Angus
✆ (0356) 624682   Mrs Nancy Cruickshank

Briarton is an 8-acre smallholding in a quiet, secluded position midway between Aberdeen and Dundee. Ground floor bedroom available. Off the Kirkton of Menmuir road 2 miles northwest of Brechin, it is very convenient for the Angus Glens. Montrose beach 15 miles.

Open Easter-Oct
2 bedrooms (1 twin; 1 double), 1🛁, 1WC.
🐕(3)
Prices: B&B £12. 🐕 rates.

CALLANDER   Map 6 B1
Leny Estate, Callander, Perthshire FK17 8HA
✆ (0877) 31078
Leny House

The family run estate is set in Leny Park and surrounded by acres of farmland in the Leny Hills just north of Callander (A84). There is a small goat herd and the private Leny Glen which visitors may explore is full of wildlife, deer, fox, pheasant, badger and hawk. Rock plunge pool in Leny burn for use of visitors. Leny House is a spacious country house offering comfortable accommodation in historic surroundings.

Open all year
3 bedrooms (1 family ens. 🛁/WC; 1 twin priv. 🛁/WC; 1 double), 1🛁, 1WC.
🐕 🐾
Prices: B&B £17–19, 🐕 rates.

CLEISH   Map 7 A1
Ardgairney Farm, Cleish, Kinross
✆ (0577) 850233

Ardgairney Farm is a 540-acre farm with 180 milking cows, some crops and sheep. It is situated off the B9097, west of M90, Jct 5. Children are made specially welcome at the farmhouse with their own games and playroom as well as cot and highchair being provided. All bedrooms sited on ground floor. Packed lunches and afternoon teas available on request. St Andrews, Stirling, Edinburgh, Perth, Fife all within 25 miles.

Open all year
3 bedrooms (1 twin; 2 double inc. 1 with priv.🛁), 1🛁, 1🛁.
🐕 🐾
Prices: B&B £12.50, weekly £85. EM £3–5. Weekly B&B plus EM £105. 🐕 rates.

CRIEFF   Map 7 A1
Concraig Farm, Crieff, Perthshire
✆ (0764) 3237   Mrs Anne Scott

Concraig Farm is an arable farm, peacefully situated just south of Crieff (A822). The farmhouse is comfortable with spacious rooms and stands a short distance from Drummond Castle Gardens. Glenturret Distillery 2 miles. 5 golf courses nearby, Gleneagles 7 miles.

Open Apr-Oct.
3 bedrooms (1 twin; 2 double), 1🛁.
🐕 STB Approved
Prices: B&B £12.50–13.50, weekly £84–90. 🐕 rates.

DUNKELD   Map 7 A1
The Coppers, Inchmagrannachnan, Dunkeld PH8 0JS
✆ (0350) 727372   J.L. Mathieson

The farm is 3 miles north of Dunkeld (A9/B898). Trout fishing close by. NT properties 3 miles. Caravan also available on site.

Open all year
2 bedrooms (1 twin ens.🛁/WC; 1 double), 1🛁, 1WC. ✂
Prices: B&B £13–16, EM £6.50–7.

Tirchardie Farm, Glen Quaich, Amulree, by Dunkeld, Perthshire PH8 0DE
✆ (0350) 725266

This is an old-fashioned farmhouse with sheep, hens and ducks. Packed lunches on request, cot, highchair, ground floor bedrooms and play area provided. The hill farm offers lovely walks, water sports at Loch Tay and Kenmore 6 miles. Amulree is on A822 Crieff-Aberfeldy road. Crieff and Aberfeldy 16 miles.

Open all year
4 bedrooms (1 twin; 1 double; 1 family; 1 single), 2🛏, 2WCs.
🐾 🐕
Prices: B&B £12.50, weekly £70. EM £5.50. Weekly B&B plus EM £100. 🐾 rates.

FORFAR   Map 7 A1

Wemyss Farm, Montrose Road, Forfar, Angus DD8 2TB
✆ (0307) 62887   Mrs Deanna Lindsay

Wemyss farm is a 190-acre mixed family run farm with a wide variety of animals, situated on the B9113 less than 3 miles east of Forfar. All bedrooms have views over the surrounding countryside. Home cooking and a friendly welcome make this a relaxing place to stay. Cot, play area and children's games available. Packed lunches on request. Golf, fishing (Rescobie Loch) and attractive walks nearby. Glamis Castle 7 miles.

Open all year
2 bedrooms (1 double; 1 family), 2🛏, 2WCs.
🐾 🐕 STB Commended and Listed
Prices: B&B from £12, EM £7. Single supplement £3.

West Mains of Turin Farmhouse, Rescobie, Forfar, Angus DD8 2TE
✆ (030783) 229   Mrs C.L. Jolly

This is a family run stock farm with a panoramic view over Rescobie Loch. The farmhouse is warm and welcoming, with croquet in the large garden and snooker for evening entertainments. Excellent home cooking is another bonus. Cot and children's games provided. The farm is east

of Forfar (B9113). Rescobie and Balgavies Lochs are close by and fishing permits can be arranged. Hill walking, golfing, etc., are well catered for in the area. Restenneth ancient priory and standing stones at Aberlemno are only a short distance from the farm. Glamis Castle and House of Dun 10 miles.

Open Mar-Oct.
3 bedrooms (1 double ens.🍲/WC; 1 family priv.🍲/WC; 1 single),1🛏, 1WC.
🐾 STB 👑 👑Commended
Prices: B&B £12–15, EM £7–7.50.🐾 rates.

KIRRIEMUIR   Map 7 A1

Purgavie Farm, Lintrathen, Nr Kirriemuir, Angus
✆ (05756) 213   Mrs Moira Clark

Purgavie Farm is composed of 470 acres of mixed farm and 206 acres of hill. The farmhouse is over 100 years old and has a comfortable, welcoming atmosphere. There is a lounge and dining room for guests, and good quality home cooking. Packed lunches on request, cot available. The farm is at the foot of Glen Isla near the lovely Lintrathen Loch, 7 miles west of Kirriemuir (B951). Ideal base for touring, hillwalking, fishing, downhill skiing, cross country skiing and pony trekking. Barrie's birthplace 6 miles. Glamis Castle 10 miles.

Open all year
2 bedrooms (1 double priv.🍲/🚿/WC; 1 family ens.🍲/WC).
🐾 🐕 STB 👑 👑 👑Commended
Prices: B&B £12–15, weekly £7. 🐾 rates, 🐕 £.0.50 per night.

KEY TO SYMBOLS	
Bath	🍲
Shower	🍲
Bathroom	🛏
Disabled Guest Facilities	♿
No Smoking	🚭
Children Welcome	🐾
Dogs by Arrangement	🐕

LOCHEARNHEAD Map 6 B1

Monachyle Mhor Farmhouse Hotel, Balquhidder, Lochearnhead, Perthshire FK19 8PQ
✆ (08774) 622
Fax (08774) 305

This is a 2000-acre sheep and cattle hill farm. Packed lunches, afternoon teas and evening meals served. Licensed. The farm is 17 miles from Callander, west off A84 at Kinghouse. An ideal base for touring central Scotland, home of Rob Roy MacGregor, battle site of Robert the Bruce 5 miles.

Open all year
5 bedrooms (1 twin ens. 🚿/🛁/WC; 4 double ens. 🚿/🛁/WC), 3WCs.
♿ STB ♛♛♛Commended
Prices: B&B £19.50–21, EM £12.50–17.50.

PERTH Map 7 A1

Craighall Farm, Forgandenny, Bridge of Earn, Perth
✆ (0738) 812415 Mary Fotheringham

Craighall Farm is by the B935, between the A9 and M90, Jct 9. This 1000-acre mixed farm has cattle, sheep, outdoor pigs, goats and hens. The house is modern, warm and very comfortable with some ground floor bedrooms suited to the requirements of disabled guests. Afternoon tea is offered, cot and highchair available. This peaceful farmhouse is ideally placed for touring the region. Rhynd Castle, Huntingtower Castle, Scone Palace, Branklyn Gardens and Cherry Bank Gardens 6 miles.

Open all year
5 bedrooms (2 twin ens. 🚿/WC; 1 double; 1 family ens. 🚿/WC; 1 single), 2🛁, 1WC.
♿ 🚸 STB ♛♛♛Highly Commended
Prices: B&B £12.50, EM £8. 🚸 rates.

Letham Farm, Bankfoot, Perth PH1 4EF
✆ (0738) 87322 Mrs Dorothy McFarlane

Letham Farm is situated a mile from the A9, north of Perth. It comprises 300 acres of mixed arable and 20 acres of raspberries. The house is well equipped and warm with delicious free teas in the hall served complete with scones and cakes. The farm lies within easy reach of all the golf courses.

Open Mar-Oct.
3 bedrooms (2 twin; 1 double), 1🛁, 2WCs.
🚭 STB ♛♛
Prices: B&B £12–13.

Stanley Farm, Stanley, By Perth PH1 4QQ
✆ (0738) 828334 Mrs Sheena Howden

This 200-acre farm is mixed arable, sheep and cattle. There is a play area for children and a separate dining room and lounge. Tea/coffee facilities. Afternoon tea and evening meals served. Stanley is 7 miles north of Perth (A9/B9099).

Open Apr-Dec.
2 bedrooms (1 double; 1 family), 2🛁, 2WCs.
🚸 🚭
Prices: B&B £12.50–15, weekly £80–95. EM £8–10, weekly B&B plus EM £130–160. 🚸 rates.

PITLOCHRY Map 7 A1

Auchnahyle Farm, Pitlochry PH16 5JA
✆ (0796) 472318 Mrs P. Howman
Fax (0796) 473657

An attractive 18th-century farmhouse completely surrounded by its own land with lovely views of the hills, on the outskirts of Pitlochry. Sheep and pheasants are reared in the fields. Delicious food, candlelit dinners and picnic lunches are offered. Salmon Ladder 1 mile, 2 distilleries within walking distance, Blair Castle 6 miles.

Closed Xmas and New Year
3 bedrooms all ens. 🛁/🚻/WC (1 double; 2 twin).
🍴(12) ✚
Prices: B&B £27–29, EM £13.50–17.50.

Self-Catering

ABERFELDY Map 7 A1

Castle Menzies Home Farm, Aberfeldy, Perthshire PH15 2LY
✆ (0887) 820260 Mrs D. McDiarmid

There are 3 stone built comfortable cottages at separate locations on this arable farm. The Garden House sleeps 6, the West Lodge sleeps 4, and the White House sleeps 8. Cot and highchair provided. The farm is 2 miles west of Aberfeldy (B846), close to Castle Menzies. Golf, fishing and country walks all available nearby. Loch Tay 7 miles.

Open all year
✚ STB 👑 👑 👑 👑Classified
Prices: weekly £150–330.

Mains of Murthly Cottages, Aberfeldy, Perthshire PH15 2EA
✆ (0887) 820427 McDiarmid

This 400-acre mixed hill and arable farm is set in good walking country just outside Aberfeldy, near the whisky distillery. There are 2 cottages, each with 2 bedrooms, sleeping 3–6. Ground floor bedrooms, and cot supplied.

Open all year
✚ STB 👑 👑 👑
Prices: weekly £130–220.

BLAIRGOWRIE Map 7 A1

Easter Drimmie, Nr Blairgowrie, Perthshire PH10 7JD
✆ (0250) 886359 Mrs E.D. Church

Accommodation is available in 2 semi-detached stone cottages across an attractive courtyard from the farmhouse on this working upland stock farm in well-wooded countryside. The cottages have 2 and 3 bedrooms, sleeping 5–6. Tennis court on site, a duck pond, river fishing, and a variety of wildlife. The farm is just under 5 miles from Blairgowrie.

Open Easter-Xmas
✚ STB 👑 👑 👑Approved
Prices: weekly £110–170.

Easter Tullyweddie, Clunie, by Blairgowrie
✆ (0250) 884281
Contact: Mrs H. Wightman, Bankhead, Clunie, Blairgowrie PH10 6SG

For full farm description see p. 196. Accommodation also available in one self-catering unit, 1 bedroom, suit 2 adults, 2 children.

Open all year
ETB 👑Commended
Prices: weekly £85–90.

Fyal Farm, Alyth PH11 8LE
✆ (08283) 2997 Mrs M. Ferguson

Comfortable accommodation is offered in a peaceful situation on a working mixed farm with 100 cattle, 900 sheep and 350 pigs. The cottage sleeps 5–6, the bungalow sleeps 4–5. Situated east of Blairgowrie, just 2 miles from Alyth, this is a good centre for touring, walking, golf, shooting, fishing and skiing in winter.

Open all year
✚
Prices: weekly £120–170

Kerry Cottage, East Tullyfergus Farm, Alyth, Perthshire PH11 8JY
✆ (08283) 3251

Kerry Cottage stands in its own garden on a working farm. There are 2 ground floor bedrooms, sleeps 4–5. Located 2 miles from Alyth, 4 miles from Blairgowrie, the farm is well placed for touring. Glamis, Pitlochry, Dundee, Angus Glens, all within 25 miles.

Open all year
Prices: weekly £100–180.

Mains of Cargill, Meikleour, by Perth PU2 6DU
✆ (0250) 883235

This semi-detached farm cottage is set on a mixed arable farm amidst rolling farmland. It has a pleasant garden front and back, overlooks the River Tay and sleeps 6 (2 bedrooms). Ground floor bedroom and cot available. Salmon fishing on Tay close by. The farm is 10 miles north of Perth (A93). Blairgowrie and Rosemount Golf Course 4 miles.

Open Apr-Oct.
✦STB ☙ ☙ ☙Approved
Prices: weekly £140–170.✦ £5.

Newmill of Kinloch, Clunie, Blairgowrie,
Perthshire PH10 6SG
✆ (0250) 884263

For full farm description, see p. 196. A
2-bedroomed self-catering unit is also available,
sleeps 4–6. Wide doorways suitable for
wheelchairs.

Open all year
♿ ✦
Prices: weekly £125–250.

CALLANDER   Map 6 B1

Leny Estate, Callander, Perthshire FK17
8HA
✆ (0877) 31078
Leny House

For full description see p. 197. The estate has accommodation in 6 solid spruce log cabins, each
has 2 bedrooms plus sofabed, sleeps 4–6.

Open all year
STB ☙ ☙ ☙ ☙ ☙De Luxe
Prices: weekly £285–545.

CRIEFF   Map 7 A1

Kintocher, Crieff, Perthshire PH7 3NQ
✆ (076483) 258   Mrs C. Strang

This cottage stands on a working farm with lovely
views south across fields to the hills. The cottage
has 2 bedrooms, sleeps 4. Kintocher is 5 miles
from Crieff, south off A85 Perth road. Sma' Glen 5
miles. Perth 12 miles. Loch Earn 16 miles.

Open Apr-Sept.
STB ☙ ☙ ☙Commended
Prices: weekly £80–195.

KINROSS   Map 7 A1

Colliston, Glenfarg, Perth PH2 9PE
✆ (0577) 830434   Mrs J.D.S. Baillie

This pretty 2-bedroomed cottage, sleeps 4, is on
a beautifully situated working arable farm overlooking Loch Leven. The cottage has its own garden, cot can be supplied. This is a golfer's
paradise, many courses nearby including Gleneagles and St Andrews. The farm is on Glen-
farg-Milnathort road, 5 miles north of Kinross.
Riding School 1 mile. Gliding airfield 5 miles.

Open all year
✦ STB ☙ ☙ ☙Commended
Prices: weekly £90–250.✦ £15 per week.

LOCHEARNHEAD   Map 6 B1

Monachyle Mhor Farmhouse Hotel,
Balquhidder, Lochearnhead, Perthshire
FK19 8PQ
✆ (08774) 622
Fax (08774) 305

For full description see p. 199. Accommodation
is offered in 4 units with 1–3 bedrooms, sleeping
2–6.

Open all year
✦ STB ☙ ☙ ☙Commended
Prices: weekly £80–450.

PITLOCHRY   Map 7 A1

Auchnahyle Farm, Pitlochry PH16 5JA
✆ (0796) 472318   Mrs P. Howman
Fax (0796) 473657

For full farm description see p. 199. Accommodation is available in a 2-bedroomed cottage,
sleeps 5.

Closed Xmas and New Year
✦
Prices: weekly £160–310.

WALES

CLWYD

DENBIGH
Map 4 B2

Ty Coch Farm, Llangynhafal, Denbigh
LL16 4LN
℡ (0824) 790423   Mrs A. Lloyd Richards

Ty Coch dairy and sheep farm lies at the foot of the Clwydian Range, midway between Rhuthun and Denbigh. It has beautiful views over the Vale of Clwyd and pleasant walks, including Offa's Dyke part of which runs over the farm. The rooms are well-appointed and local produce is used in the excellent home cooking. Packed lunches on request, cot available. Nearby are riding stables, swimming pools, golf courses and a craft centre.

Closed Xmas
2 bedrooms (1 twin; 1 family), 1➡, 1WC.
⌂ ⅄ WTB 👑Merit
Prices: B&B £12–13, EM £6. ⌂ rates.

MOLD
Map 4 B3

Hill Farm, Llong, Mold CM7 4JP
℡ (0244) 550415   Mrs Ann M. Brown

This mixed dairy farm has 400 acres. The accommodation is in a large and spacious Georgian house with beams and open fires. The farm is 2 miles east of Mold on the Mold-Chester road. Golf, fishing and riding nearby. Convenient for Chester, Snowdonia and the coast.

Open all year
3 bedrooms (1 twin; 1 double; 1 family),
1➡,2WCs.
⌂ WTB 👑 👑
Prices: B&B £13–16, ⌂ rates.

Plas Penucha, Caerwys, Mold CH7 5BH
℡ (0352) 720210

This 16th-century farmhouse set on a working beef farm has been modernised to provide every comfort, Large lounge and library to relax in, tea/coffee facilities, packed lunches and afternoon teas available. Cot and highchair if required. The

garden overlooks the Clwydian Hills. The farm is 6 miles east of St Asaph (A55/B5722 to Caerwys). Denbigh and Bodelwyddan Castles 8 miles.

Open all year
5 bedrooms (2 twin inc. 1 ens. ⅃/WC; 2 double inc. 1 ens. ⅃/WC; 1 single), 2➡, 2WCs.
⌂ ⅄ WTB 👑 👑Commended
Prices: B&B £15.50, weekly £90. EM £7–8, weekly B&B plus EM £132. ⌂ rates.

RUTHIN
Map 4 B2

LLanbenwch Farm, LLanfair Dc, Ruthin
℡ (0824) 2340

This 13th-century farmhouse has all modern comforts as well as its period charm. Tea/coffee facilities and TV. The 40-acre mixed farm is set in superb scenery and convenient to all beauty spots, on A525 3 miles south of medieval Ruthin.

Open Mar-Oct.
3 bedrooms (1 twin; 1 double; 1 family), 1➡,
2WCs.

KEY TO SYMBOLS

Bath	🛁
Shower	⅃
Bathroom	➡
Disabled Guest Facilities	♿
No Smoking	⅄
Children Welcome	⌂
Dogs by Arrangement	🐕

⚘(5) WTB 🦢 🦢Commended
Prices: B&B £11, weekly £75. EM £5, weekly
B&B plus EM £105.

ST ASAPH   Map 4 B2

Bach-y-Graig, Tremeirchion, St Asaph LL17 0UH
✆ (0745) 730627

Bach-y-Graig is a 200-acre farm with a variety of
animals. The large 16th-century listed farmhouse
nestles at the foot of the Clwydian Range with
wonderful views over the surrounding countryside. The traditional furnishings and decor are in
keeping with the period features of the house, but
are combined with a modern emphasis on comfort and warmth. The farm is off the A541 from
Trefnant (A525). Packed lunches available on
request. There is a woodland trail on the farm and
craft centres nearby. Offa's Dyke and gliding
club 2 miles. 3 castles to visit within 5 miles. Bre-
nig Reservoir (windsurfing, fishing, sailing) and
golf 4 miles.

Open all year
3 bedrooms (1 twin ens.🛁/WC; 1 double
ens.🚿/WC; 1 family ens.🛁/WC), 1🛁, 1WC.
⚘ ⚑ WTB Farmhouse Award 🦢 🦢 🦢Highly
Commended
Prices: B&B from £16.⚘ rates.

Self-Catering

RUTHIN   Map 4 B2

Tyddyn Isaf, Rhewl, Ruthin
✆ (0824) 703367   Mrs Elsie Jones

Tyddyn Isaf is an 80-acre farm, 3 miles from
Ruthin on the A525 to Denbigh, growing cereals
and grazing sheep, beef cattle and pigs. Part of
the farmhouse is let to provide self-contained accommodation for 6 people. There is also the
newly converted granary – Y Granar – which
sleeps 2–4. Cot and highchair available. Horse
riding, Rhewl village with pub and shop 1 mile.
Golfing 5 miles.

Open all year
Prices: weekly from £90.

DYFED

CARMARTHEN   Map 1 B1

Glôg, Llangain, Carmarthen SA33 5AY
✆ (026783) 271   Mrs Maureen Gribble

Glôg is a 40-acre working farm with a beef suckler herd and horses, situated off the B4312, south
of Carmarthen and stands 5 miles equidistant between this busy market town and the quiet beach
and historic castle at Llanstephan. Comfortable
accommodation and fine food make this a pleasant place to stay. Cot and highchair available.

Open all year.
5 bedrooms (1 twin; 1 double; 2 family inc. 1
ens.🛁/WC; 1 single), 1🛁, 2🛁, 3WCs.
⚘ ⚑ WTB 🦢 🦢Merit Farmhouse Award
Prices: B&B £14.50–17.50, 3 nights £42–50, 7
nights £90–110. EM £6–8.⚘ rates.

Pantgwyn Farm, Whitemill, Carmarthen SA32 7ES
✆ (0267) 290247

This 300-year-old farmhouse is set on a small
working farm 4 miles from Carmarthen off the
A40, above the Towy Valley. Original features

retained such as oak beams, iron and slate fire-places. Farmhouse rooms detailed below, but 2 self-contained flats, sleeping 4 each, also available as self-catering or with meals taken at the farmhouse. One flat specifically designed for disabled guests. The food is highly acclaimed, Wales' winners of the Best Breakfast in Britain competition. The farm has sheep, lambs and a goat; donkeys give rides for children. Barn owls are being reared for release into the wild. Packed lunches by request. Cot available. An ideal centre for touring the West Lakes. Fishing in the Towy, Cothi and Gwili rivers.

Closed Xmas
3 bedrooms (1 twin priv.⏴/WC; 2 family 1 ens.⏴/WC, 1 ens. ⏴/WC).
⏶ WTB ⏶ ⏶ ⏶Highly Commended
Prices: B&B £16–23, weekly £101–165. EM £12.
Weekly B&B plus EM £176.50–235.00.

DEVIL'S BRIDGE   Map 4 A3
Erwbarfe Farmhouse, Devil's Bridge,
Aberystwyth SY23 3JR
☎ (097085) 251   Mrs Elaine Lewis

This comfortable stone farmhouse is situated on a 400-acre working farm with sheep and cattle. Good fresh farmhouse food is served and packed lunches on request. The farm lies off the A4120 Ponterwyd-Devil's Bridge road. The scenery is breathtaking and the farm is central to many attractions. Devil's Bridge Falls and Steam Railway 1 mile. Craft shops and silver lead mine 2 miles. Cardigan Bay and Aberystwyth town 12 miles

Open April-Oct.
2 bedrooms (1 double; 1 family), 1⏴, 1WC.
⏶ WTB ⏶ ⏶Merit
Prices: B&B £15–18, weekly £7–9. EM £100–120, weekly B&B plus EM £150–160.⏶ rates.

FISHGUARD   Map 1 A1
Tregynon Country Farmhouse Hotel,
Gwaun Valley, Nr Fishguard,
Pembrokeshire
☎ (0239) 820531
FAX (0239) 820808

Wales' 16th-century award-winning Country Farmhouse nestles in the foothills of the Preseli Mountains overlooking the Gwaun Valley, and 5 miles from the mile-long sweep of Newport Sands. Imaginative cuisine with wholefood and vegetarian dishes a speciality, as featured in 'Here's Health' and 'The Vegetarian'. Own smokehouse produces traditional oak-smoked

gammon and bacon. Licensed. Grounds include iron-age fort, 200ft waterfall, trout ponds and ancient forest. Two-Day Great Little Breaks, Nov-Mar. Winner of 8 awards including Pembrokeshire Coast National Park Award. All bedrooms ground floor. At the intersection of the B4313 and B4329, southeast of Fishguard, take the B4313 towards Fishguard, then first right and follow signs.

Open all year   **RAC**
8 bedrooms (4 double inc. 1 ens. ⏴/WC, 3 ens.⏴/WC; 4 family inc. 2 ens. ⏴/WC, 2 ens.⏴/WC).
⏶ WTB ⏶ ⏶ ⏶Highly Commended
Prices: B&B £22.50–29.75, EM £14–19. Weekly B&B plus EM £240–290. ⏶ rates.

HAVERFORDWEST   Map 1 A1
Bank House, Croesgoch, Haverfordwest,
Pembrokeshire SA62 6X2
☎ (0348) 831305

Bank House is a 60-acre dairy farm situated off the A487 Fishguard-St Davids road. The 100-year-old farmhouse has been fully modernised to provide comfortable accommodation. Good home produced food is served, packed lunches supplied on request. Coastal path and beach 1 mile. Pony riding and trekking 3 miles. St Davids, cathedral and city 6 miles. Fishguard harbour 10 miles.

Open Feb-Oct.
2 bedrooms (1 twin; 1 double), 1⏴, 1WC. ⏶
Prices: B&B £12–14, weekly £80–90. EM £7.
Weekly £120–130. ⏶ rates.

Crossways, Spittal Cross Farm, Spittal, Haverfordwest SA62 5DB

℗ (043787) 253   Mrs M. Evans

Every comfort is catered for in this new house on a dairy farm. Full Welsh breakfast is served in the dining room, the guests lounge overlooks the terrace, garden and beautiful Treffgarne Valley. Tea/coffee facilities. Situated centrally in Pembrokeshire, turn east 4 miles from Haverfordwest off A40 Fishguard road to Spittal. Nant-y-coy Mill 1 mile. Wolfscastle Pottery 3 miles. Llysyfran 7 miles.

Open Apr–Oct.
2 bedrooms (1 twin ens.⌂/WC; 1 double ens.⌐/WC), 1➡, 1WC.
⌂(10) ⊩ WTB ♛ ♛Highly Commended
Prices: B&B £16–17.50, weekly £105–115.⊩ £1 per day.

North Headborough, Dale Road, Walwyn's Castle, Haverfordwest SA62 3AE

℗ (0437) 781585

This attractive modernised farmhouse stands in a quiet south-facing position well away from the road. 5 miles southwest of Haverfordwest, off the B4327, the 23-acre smallholding supports sheep in winter and hay in summer, and some farm animals roam around the farm. Packed lunches provided on request. Beaches and coastal path under 3 miles. Bird sanctuaries and boats 5 miles. 2 ground floor bedrooms available.

Open April–Oct.
3 bedrooms (1 twin ens.⌐/WC; 1 double ens.⌂/WC;1 family ens.⌂/WC).
⌂(7) ⌇ WTB ♛ ♛
Prices: B&B £15–16, EM £7. Weekly B&B plus EM £140–147. ⌂ rates.

KILGEYTY   Map 1 A1

Carne Mountain Farm, Reynaltin, Begelly, Kilgeyty SA68 0PD

℗ (0834) 860546

The 200-year-old farmhouse is set on a 40-acre working farm amidst beautiful peaceful country-

side. Local produce used where possible for delicious home cooked meals served in our interesting dining room. Maps and books available to help plan your day. The farm is just under 4 miles south of Narberth. Riding, fishing and sailing (sea or river) 2 miles. Saundersfoot beach and harbour 4 miles. Tenby 6 miles.

Open all year
2 double bedrooms, 1➡, 1WC.
⌂(10) ⊩ WTB Listed
Prices: B&B £12.50–14.50, weekly £85–99. EM £8.50.

LAMPETER   Map 1 B1

Bryncastell, Llanfair Road, Lampeter SA48 8JY

℗ (0570) 422447

Bryncastell is a 140-acre riverside farm run by a traditional bilingual Welsh farming family. The luxury purpose-built farmhouse commands panoramic views across the beautiful Teifi Valley. Ground floor bedrooms available. Enjoy authentic Welsh recipes using home grown produce expertly prepared. Welsh breakfasts a speciality. Packed lunches and afternoon teas offered. The farm lies by the B4343 northeast of Lampeter. Trout and salmon fishing on river on farmland. Pony riding 4 miles. Golf course 5 miles. Gold mines 10 miles. Coast 13 miles.

Open all year
2 double bedrooms inc. 1 ens.⌂/WC, 1 ens.⌐/WC.
⌧ ⌂ WTB ♛ ♛Farmhouse Award
Prices: B&B £14.50–16, weekly £100–120. EM £8.50–9.50. Weekly £156–160. ⌂ rates.

MYNACHLOGDDU
Map 1 A/B1

Yethen Isaf, Mynachlogddu, Clywderwen, Pembrokeshire SA66 7SN

℡ (0437) 532256
Brian & Ann Barney

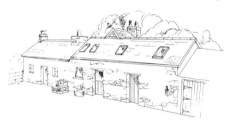

Yethen Isaf is a working sheep and beef farm set in the tranquil Preseli hills between the A478 and B4313. The farm breeds pedigree Welsh black cattle and Beaulah speckle faced sheep. The rooms are well-equipped and comfortable, with logfires and inglenook fireplace in the lounge. Packed lunches and afternoon teas provided on request. Cot and highchair available. Hill walking, Gors Fawr Stone Circle and Preseli Blue Stones site under 2 miles. Trout fishing 6 miles.

Open all year
3 bedrooms (2 twin; 1 double ens.☞/WC), 1🛏,
2WCs.
🕭 WTB ♛ ♛
Prices: B&B £13.50–18.50, weekly £94.50. EM £8.50, weekly £154. 🕭 rates.

NEW QUAY
Map 1 B1

Broniwan, Rhydlewis, Llandysul SA44 5PF

℡ (0239) 851261
Carole Jacobs

Broniwan is a 45-acre organic farm off the A487/486 at Rhydlewis. The Victorian stone farmhouse has lovely views of the Preseli Hills, and is full of books, paintings and friendly animals. Cooking is natural and wholesome using home grown produce. Vegetarian dishes a speciality. Packed lunches and afternoon teas on request. Ideally placed for exploring the area, Cardigan's sandy coast is 10 mins drive, fishing on River Teifi 15 mins and pony trekking 20 mins.

Open all year
3 bedrooms (2 twin inc. 1 ens.🕭/WC; 1 double),
1🛏, 2WCs.
🕭 ✖ WTB ♛ ♛Highly Commended Farmhouse Award
Prices: B&B £15–17, EM £8. Weekly B&B plus EM £150.

Nanternis Farm, Nanternis, New Quay SA45 9RP
℡ (0545) 560181

Nanternis is an 8-acre farm with sheep, goats, chickens and ducks, set in a quiet hamlet with attractive views. It lies off the A486 south of New Quay. The comfortable Edwardian farmhouse is spacious and well-run. Locally there are coastal walks, pony trekking and a good character pub. New Quay, with sandy beaches and watersports is less than 3 miles away. Cardigan (golf) 15 miles. Cot and highchair available.

Open Easter-Sept.
3 bedrooms (1 double; 1 family; 1 single), 1🛏,
2WCs. 🕭
Prices: B&B £13–14, weekly £91.

NOLTON HAVEN
Map 1 A1

Nolton Haven Farm, Nolton Haven, Haverfordwest, Pembrokeshire SA62 8NH
℡ (0437) 710263

The farmhouse is 50 yds from the sandy beach at Nolton Haven, off the A487 Haverfordwest-St Davids road. The house is open to guests all day and there is a separate dining room for their use. The 180-acre farm has a herd of suckler cows and calves, 10 horses and ponies which compete in local shows. Guests are welcome to assist around the farm and at shows. Cot and highchair available.

Open all year
6 bedrooms (1 twin; 2 double; 3 family inc. 2 ens.🕭/WC), 4🛏, 4WCs.
🕭 ✖ WTB Verified
Prices: B&B £14–16, weekly £98–112. EM £6. Weekly B&B plus EM £128–142. 🕭 rates.

PEMBROKE
Map 1 A1

Chapel Farm, Castlemartin, Pembroke SA71 5HW
℡ (0646) 661312
Mrs Ruth Smith

Chapel Farm has a 17th-century farmhouse offering comfortable accommodation for a relaxing holiday. The 260-acre dairy farm is a mile from the coast in the Pembrokeshire Coast National Park and has splendid views out to sea. Coastal footpath passes the farm, within 5 miles are wild surfing beaches, quiet coves, riding and fishing in sea in Bosherton Lilyponds. Good farmhouse food is served, packed lunches on request. The farm is 6 miles west of Pembroke off the B4320.

Open Apr-Oct.
2 bedrooms (1 twin; 1 family), 1🐾.
🐕 🐓
Prices: B&B £12–15, weekly £84–95. EM £7, weekly B&B plus EM £125–135. 🐕 rates.

SOLVA
Map 1 A1

Llanddinog Old Farmhouse, Solva, Haverfordwest, Pembrokeshire SA62 6NA
✆ (0348) 831224   Mrs Sarah C. Griffiths

The 16th-century stone farmhouse is set in secluded spacious grounds surrounded by sheep, calves, ponies and domestic pets. The farm is located off the A487 Haverfordwest-St Davids road. Packed lunches on request. Cot, highchair and babysitting available. Solva village and natural harbour and lots of beaches 5 mins drive. St Davids 12 mins.

Open all year
2 family bedrooms inc. 1 priv.🖭/WC, 1 ens.🖟/WC.
🐕 🐓 WTB 👑 👑 👑
Prices: B&B £15–16, EM £8. 🐕 rates.

Lochmeyler Farm, Pen-y-Cwm, Nr Solva, Haverfordwest, Pembrokeshire SA62 6LL
✆ (0348) 837724   Mrs Morfydd Jones

Lochmeyler is a 220-acre dairy farm set 3 miles inland in the centre of St Davids Peninsula off the A487 Haverfordwest-St Davids road. The 16th-century farmhouse has been renovated without losing its character. The rooms are comfortable and well-equipped, some have four poster beds. Ground floor bedroom available. Traditional and

vegetarian meals are offered, packed lunches on request and afternoon teas. Licensed. Smoking and non-smoking lounges for you to relax in, or saunter around the farm trails, walks and ponds where there is an abundance of wildlife and plants.

Open all year   RAC
6 bedrooms (2 twin ens.🖭/WC; 3 double ens.🖭/WC; 1 family ens.🖭/WC), 1🐾.
♿ 🐕(10) 🐓 WTB 👑 👑 👑 👑Deluxe
Prices: B&B £20, weekly £140. EM £9. Weekly B&B plus EM £185. 🐕 rates,🐓 £3 per day.

TENBY
Map 1 A1

Red House Farm, New Hedges, Tenby SA69 9DE
✆ (0834) 813918   Mrs Sally Oxley

Red House Farm is a small family run farm specialising in growing a variety of vegetables. Situated by the A478, the 18th-century farmhouse is homely and friendly and provides good country cooking. Children are welcomed with all sorts of toys and play equipment, plus cot and highchair. One ground floor bedroom. Good beaches 1–2 miles. Tenby 2 miles.

Open all year
5 bedrooms (1 twin; 2 double ens.🖟/🖭/WC; 2 family ens.🖟/🖭/WC), 1🐾, 3WCs.
🐕 🐓 WTB Listed
Prices: B&B £10–13, EM £4–6. 🐕 rates.

TREGARON
Map 1 B1

Neuaddlas Guest House, Tregaron SY25 6JL
✆ (0974) 298905   Margaret Cutter

Neuaddlas Country Guest House is set in 22 acres and is well established. This extremely peaceful spot overlooks the Cambrian Mountains and the Cors Caron Nature Reserve, with its rich variety of flora and fauna. There are no steps in the guest house, access to dining and sitting rooms is easy. Packed lunches on request. Neuaddlas is situated less than 2 miles northwest of Tregaron on the A485. Craft Centre 1 mile. But-

terfly and Nature Centre 6 miles. Pony trekking 10 miles. Seaside 12 miles.
Open all year
4 bedrooms (2 twin ens.♿/WC; 1 double ens.♿/WC; 1 family), 1🛏, 2WCs.
♿ 🏠 ✝ WTB ♛ ♛ ♛Commended
Prices: B&B £15–18, weekly £105–125. EM £8. Weekly B&B plus EM £161–182. 🏠 rates.

WHITLAND   Map 1 A/B1

Castell Pigyn, Llanboidy, Whitland
✆ (0994) 448391
Fax (0994) 448755

This cattle and sheep farm is situated on a peaceful hill top, 4 miles north of Whitland, with fabulous views of undulating farmland in all directions. Enjoy good home cooking, packed lunches and afternoon teas on request. Separate lounge and dining room for guests. Tea/coffee facilities. Pottery 1 mile, chocolate farm and fishing 3 miles, Llysyfran Dam 8 miles.

Open all year
3 bedrooms (1 twin ens.♿/WC; 1 family ens.♿/WC; 1 double ens. ♿/WC).
🏠 WTB ♛ ♛ ♛
Prices: B&B £16, EM £8, weekly B&B plus EM £161.🏠 rates.

Maencochyrwyn Farm, Login, Whitland SA34 0TN
✆ (0994) 419283

An ideal place for a peaceful holiday. The farm, an 80-acre working dairy farm, is situated just over 2 miles from the village of Llanboidy, 5 miles north of Whitland. The farmhouse has every modern amenity and offers good home cooking. Cot and highchair provided. A good base for touring Dylan Thomas country (12 miles) and the Preseli Mountains (10 miles). Tenby, Pendine Sands, Saundersfoot and Llysyfran Reservoir (renowned for brown trout) all within easy reach.

Open April-Oct.
3 bedrooms (1 twin; 1 family; 1 single), 1🛏, 1♿, 1WC.
🏠 ✝
Prices: B&B £12–14, weekly £80–90. 🏠 rates.

Self-Catering

CARDIGAN   Map 1 A1

Croft Farm Cottages, Llantood, Cardigan SA43 3NT
✆ (0239) 615179   Mr & Mrs Gow

Croft Farm is a working smallholding with lambs and calves in spring for the children to feed. Woo-

den play area and swings on site. The six cottages are converted slate farm buildings with 1–3 bedrooms, sleeping 2–7. Ground floor bedrooms available. The farm is 3 miles from Cardigan northwest off Cardigan-Fishguard road (A487/B4582). Riding 3 miles, beaches and coastal path 5 miles. Nevern Church with bleeding yew trees and 13th-century cross 5 miles.

Open all year
✝ WTB ♛ ♛ ♛ ♛
Prices: weekly £95–350.✝ £15.

CARMARTHEN   Map 1 B1

Cwmdwyfran Farm Cottages, Cwmdwyfran, Bronwydd Arms, Carmarthen SA33 6JF
✆ (026787) 419   Mrs J.S. Brandrick

These two superb holiday cottages have been converted from a stone farm building and are equipped to a high standard. Bordering the farmyard, each has a south facing verandah with beautiful views, sleeps 4/5 people, and has extra wide doorways to accommodate wheelchairs. Cot and highchair available. Cwmdwyfran Farm is off the A484, 3 miles north of Carmarthen. Gwili steam railway and fishing 1 mile. Golf course 3 miles. Beaches and pony trekking 9 miles.

Open all year
♿ 🏠 ✝ WTB Approved
Prices: daily £20–25, weekly £89–190. ✝ £5 per week.

Pantgwyn Farm, Whitemill, Carmarthen SA32 7ES
✆ (0267) 290247

For full description, see p. 203. Two self-contained flats, sleeping 4 each, are available as self-catering or with meals taken at the farmhouse. One flat specifically designed for disabled guests.

Closed Xmas.
2 bedrooms (1 twin; 1 double), ♿, 1WC.
♿ 🏠 WTB Grade 4
Prices: B&B weekly £100–250. ✝ £10 per week.

WHITLAND   Map 1 A/B1

Castell Pigyn, Llanboidy, Whitland
✆ (0994) 448391
Fax (0994) 448755

For full farm description, see above. Accommodation is available in a 2-bedroomed cottage, sleeps 4.

Open all year
WTB Grade 3
Prices: weekly £100–220.

Gwarmacwydd Farm, LLanfalteg, Whitland
✆ (0437) 563260   Mrs Angela Colledge

Five self-catering units of 1–3 bedrooms, sleeping 2–6, are available on this mixed working farm of 450 acres with milking cows and sheep. Also 2 miles of river with trout and salmon. The farm is north off A40, 3 miles west of Whitland. Oakwood Adventure Park 5 miles. Cerew Castle 8 miles. Tenby Beach 12 miles.

Open all year
⊁ WTB Grade 4
Prices: weekly £95–358.

GWENT

ABERGAVENNY   Map 2 A2

Chapel Farm, Nr Coalbrookvale, Blaina NP3 3DJ
✆ (0495) 290888   Mrs Betty Hancocks

Chapel Farm is a fine example of a 15th-century cruck farmhouse with steeply pitched roof and thick stone walls. Inside the charm of many oak beams is combined with all modern conveniences as the farm has been carefully renovated in recent years. The farm lies a mile off the A467 Brynmawr-Blaina road. Packed lunches on request. Cot available. Close by are the ruins of the Roundhouse Tower and Ty Mawr House, the Big Pit Mining Museum and Clydach Gorge.

Open all year
2 bedrooms (1 double ens.🛁; 1 family ens.🛁), 1🚿, 2WCs.
♨ WTB ➶ ➶Merit
Prices: B&B £15–20. EM £8. ♨ rates.

The Wenallt, Gilwern, Nr Abergavenny NP7 0HP
✆ (0873) 830694   Mr B.L. Harris

The Wenallt is a 16th-century Welsh longhouse set in 50 acres of farmland in the Brecon Beacons National Park, and commanding magnificent views over the Usk Valley. Retaining all its old charm with oak beams and inglenook fireplace, yet offering a high standard of comfort and good food, this makes an ideal base for touring the area. Packed lunches on request. Ground floor bedrooms, cot and highchair provided. Brecon-Monmouth Canal 1 mile. Big Pit Mining Museum 3 miles.

Open all year
8 bedrooms (2 twin inc. 1 ens.🛁/WC; 4 double inc. 2 ens.🛁/WC,1 ens. ➹/WC; 1 family ens.➹/WC; 1 single), 1🚿, 1WC.
♿ ♨ ⊁ WTB ➶ ➶ ➶
Prices ex. VAT: B&B £12.50–18, weekly £80.50–119. EM £8.50. Weekly B&B plus EM £133–171.50. ♨ rates.

PONTYPOOL   Map 2 A2

Pentwyn Farm, Little Mill, Pontypool NP4 0HQ
✆ (049528) 249

Pentwyn is a traditional Welsh longhouse set in a large garden with a swimming pool where good food and hospitality are of prime importance. Licensed. It is surrounded by 120 acres of grazing land and woods with rough shooting available. Games room for children. The farm lies off the A472 Usk-Pontypool road, on the edge of the Brecon Beacons National Park, with a choice of museums, castles and watersports within 10 miles.

Open Feb-Nov.
4 bedrooms (2 twin inc. 1 ens.🛁/WC; 2 double inc. 1 ens.🛁/WC), 1🚿, 2WCs.

&(4)
Prices: B&B £13–16.50, EM £10. Weekly B&B plus EM £144–165.

Ty'Ry-Ywen Farm, Lasgarn Lane, Trevethin, Pontypool NP4 8TT
✆ (049528) 200   Mrs S.D. Armitage

This 25-acre hill farm is set in Brecon Beacons National Park with marvellous 30 mile views down the Usk Valley. It can be found up a steep mountain track by the Trevethin Golf Club, just north of Pontypool on the A4043. The 16th-century house is spacious and well-appointed, four-poster bed and jacuzzi in two rooms. Note: access road not for the timid. Monmouth and Brecon Canal 2 miles. Llandegfedd Reservoir 4 miles. Caerphilly Castle 15 miles.

Open all year
3 bedrooms (1 twin ens.⌂/⇥/WC;2 double ens.⌂/⇥/WC).
⚡🕊 WTB 👑 👑 👑
Prices:B&B £16–35.

DINGESTOW   Map 2 A2
Lower Pen-y-Clawdd Farm, Dingestow, Monmouth NP5 4BG
✆ (060083) 223/677

Accommodation is offered on this working beef and sheep unit, which lies 6 miles west of Monmouth (A40). Raglan Castle 2 miles. Wye Valley 6 miles. Abergavenny and Brecon Beacons 10 miles.

Open Mar-Dec.
3 bedrooms (1 twin; 1 double; 1 family), 2🛁, 2WCs.
& 🕊 WTB 👑
Prices: B&B £14–16, weekly £90–105. &
rates,🕊 £3.

RAGLAN   Map 2 B2
Brooklands Farm, Chepstow Road, Raglan NP5 2EN
✆ (0291) 690782   Mrs Gwyneth Morgan

Brooklands Farm is a family run dairy farm with many small animals to feed. The house dates from the 1600s and is well modernised. The farm is 200 yds from Raglan village centre, off the A40 Abergavenny-Monmouth road. Cot and highchair available. Raglan Castle within walking distance.

Open all year
3 bedrooms (1 twin; 1 double; 1 family ens.⌂/WC), 2🛁, 2WCs.
& WTB 👑 👑
Prices: B&B £14–18, weekly £84–112. EM £8. Weekly B&B plus EM £140–154. & rates.

High House Farm, Bryngwyn, Raglan, Gwent NP5 2BS
✆ (0291) 690529   Mrs Jane S. Smith

High House, a traditional Welsh farmhouse dating back to 1640, offers comfortable accommodation on a working dairy farm. Set in a beautiful area between the Wye Valley and the Brecon Beacons National Park, 6 miles southeast of Abergavenny off the B4598 Usk road. Many superb golf courses within easy reach. Trekking and fishing available locally. Packed lunches and evening meals available. Cot and highchair provided. Monmouth and Raglan nearby.

Open all year
3 bedrooms (1 twin; double; 1 family ens.⌂/WC), 2🛁, 2WCs.
& 🕊 WTB Listed
Prices: B&B £14–18, weekly £98–126. EM £7.50–8, weekly £150–180. & rates.

Self-Catering

RAGLAN   Map 2 A2

Worcester House, Castle Farm, Raglan
NP5 2BT
✆ (0291) 690492

Worcester House is part of the Old Manor House
on Castle Farm, and is the oldest brick building in
Gwent. The farm is a working arable/dairy farm,
put down to corn, sheep and beef cattle. It is next
door to Raglan Castle in the village just off the
A40 Abergavenny-Monmouth road. The house
sleeps 6/7 and is well equipped. Cot, highchair,
baby bath provided. Brecon Beacons, Forest of
Dean 9 miles.

Open all year
⚘ ⛅ WTB Grade 4
Prices: weekly £100–250.

GWYNEDD

ANGLESEY   Map 4 A2

Bryntirion Open Farm, Dwyran, Anglesey
LL61 6BQ
✆ (0248) 430232   Patricia Naylor

Bryntirion is a working farm in an area of outstanding natural beauty. Guest dining room,
lounge and children's play area. The farm is situated on the A4080 southwest of the island. New-
borough Forest and beach 3 miles.

Open April-Sept.
3 bedrooms (1 twin; 2 double), 1🛁, 2WCs.
⚘ WTB ⚜
Prices: B&B £12, weekly £70. ⚘ rates.

Bwlchyfen Bentir, Bodffordd, Llangefni,
Anglesey LL65 3XL
✆ (0407) 720300   Jane Williams

Situated right in the centre of Anglesey (A5/
B5109), Bwlchyfen Bentir offers comfortable accommodation and home cooking in a peaceful
atmosphere. Cot and highchair available. The
nearest town, Llangefni, is 3 miles away.

Open Jan-Nov.
2 bedrooms (1 double; 1 family), 1🛁, 1WC.
⚘ ⛅
Prices: B&B £10, EM £4.

Drws y Coed, Llannerch-y-Medd,
Anglesey
✆ (0248) 470473   Mrs Jane Bown

This beautifully appointed award-winning farmhouse is set on a 550-acre working farm of beef,
sheep and arable surrounded by peaceful
wooded countryside, with panoramic views of
Snowdonia. The farm lies between the B5111
and B5108, east of Llannerch-y-Medd, in the
middle of the island. Games room and free pony
rides for children. Packed lunches on request,
plus delicious breakfasts and evening meals.
Fishing 3 miles. Riding, golf and sports centres 6
miles.

Open Jan-Nov.
3 bedrooms (1 twin ens.🛁/🚾/WC; 1 double
ens.🛁/🚾/WC; 1 family ens.🛁/🚾/WC).
⚘ WTB ⚜ ⚜ ⚜Highly Commended
Prices: B&B £16–18, weekly £112. EM £10.
Weekly £170. ⚘ rates.

Llwydiarth Fawr, Llanerchymedd,
Anglesey LLY1 8DF
✆ (0248) 470321/470540 Mrs Margaret Hughes

Excellent home cooking is provided in this attractive Georgian mansion. It stands on a 850-
acre beef, sheep and arable farm. Ground floor
bedrooms available. The farm is off the B5111, 6
miles north of Llangefni. Trout fishing 4 miles.

Open all year
4 bedrooms (1 twin ens. 🚾/WC; 1 double ens.
🛁/🚾/WC; 1 family ens. 🛁/🚾/WC; 1 single ens.
🛁/WC), 1🛁, 1WC.
⚘ WTB ⚜ ⚜ ⚜Highly Commended
Prices: B&B £20, weekly £140. EM £10–12.50,
weekly B&B plus EM £200. ⚘ rates.

Plas Cichle, Beaumaris, Anglesey LL58 8PS

℡ (0248) 810488   Mrs E.M. Roberts

This large period farmhouse with an extensive garden is set on a beef and sheep farm enjoying panoramic views over to Snowdonia. The rooms are spacious and well-appointed. Good home cooking is offered and packed lunches on request. The farm is just over a mile north of Beaumaris off the A545. Beaumaris attractions: Edwardian castle, childhood museum, jail and yachting facilities. Also golf, riding, boat trips on the Straits and fishing. 16th-century priory, wishing well and dovecot 1 mile.

Open Mar-Nov.
3 bedrooms (1 twin ens.⋔/WC; 2 double inc. 1 ens.⊟/⋔/WC, 1 ens.⋔/WC).
๑๑(6) WTB ☞ ☞ ☞Highly Commended, Farmhouse Award
Prices: B&B £17–18, weekly £105–112. EM £12. Weekly £165–175. ๑๑ rates.

Plas Trefarthen, Brynsiencyn, Isle of Anglesey LL616SZ

℡ (0248) 430379   JM Roberts

This Georgian country house is surrounded by a 200-acre arable farm with cattle and sheep. Cot, highchair and games provided. Ground floor bedroom available. Standing at the edge of the Menai Straits, 6 miles from the Menai Bridge just off A4080, opposite Snowdonia, it make an ideal base for touring the area. Plas Newydd (NT) House 3 miles. Sandy beach 6 miles.

Open all year
6 bedrooms (1 double ens. ⋔/⊟/WC; 5 family inc 1 ens. ⋔/WC, 4 ens. ⋔/⊟/WC), 2➡, 1WC.
๑๑ WTB ☞ ☞ ☞Highly Commended
Prices: B&B £16–18, EM £10.

Tre'r Ddol Farm, Llannerch-y-Medd, Anglesey LL71 7AR

℡ (0248) 470278   Ann Astley

Tre'r Ddol is a 200-acre working farm by the B5109 Llangefni-Bodedern road. The farmhouse is an interesting 17th-century building, once a manor house, with spacious accommodation and many period details. Ground floor bedrooms available. Mrs Astley believes passionately in good farmhouse fare, homely comfort, cleanliness and maintaining a Welsh atmosphere. Children enjoy free pony rides and help on the farm. Cot, highchair and games provided. Working windmill 3 miles. Beaches 5 miles. Beaumaris Castle, Old Jail and Menai Suspension Bridge within 10 miles.

Open Jan-Nov.
4 bedrooms (1 twin ens.⋔/WC; 1 double ens.⋔/WC; 2 family ens.⊟/WC), 1WC.
๑๑ ๑ ↾ WTB ☞ ☞ ☞Highly Commended
Prices:B&B £17, weekly £115. EM £9. Weekly B&B plus EM £170. ๑๑ rates,↾ £2 per day.

BALA   Map 4 B3

Erw Feurig Farm Guest House, Cefnddwysarn, Bala LL23 7LL

℡ (06783) 262   Mrs G.M. Jones

Erw Feurig is a 160-acre hill farm with sheep and beef cattle. The old farm cottage, magnificently situated facing the Berwyn Mountains, has been extended to accommodate guests in spacious, comfortable rooms. Ground floor bedroom available. Coarse fishing on the farm which lies on the A494, just over 3 miles northeast of Bala and the largest natural lake in Wales, Llyn Tegid. Packed lunches on request, cot and highchair provided.

Open Feb-Nov.
5 bedrooms (1 twin; 1 double; 2 family inc. 1 ens.⋔/WC; 1 single), 1⋔, 1➡, 2WCs.
๑๑ WTB ☞ ☞Highly Commended
Prices: B&B £13–16, weekly £90–110. EM £7. Weekly £130–160. ๑๑ rates.

Talybont Isa, Rhyduchaf, Bala LL23 7SD

℡ (0678) 520234   Mrs Ann Skinner

The comfortable modern house stands a little away from the farm buildings on this 120-acre dairy farm. Sheep, hens and ducks also feature in the farmyard. Evening meals, cot and highchair can be provided, all rooms have tea/coffee facilities. Ground floor bedrooms available. The farm

---

KEY TO SYMBOLS

Bath	⊟
Shower	⋔
Bathroom	➡
Disabled Guest Facilities	๑
No Smoking	✄
Children Welcome	๑๑
Dogs by Arrangement	↾

stands 2 miles from Bala off the A4212 Traws-fynydd road.

Open Jan-Nov.
3 bedrooms (1 twin;1 double; 1 family), 2🛏,
2WCs.
⚜ ⛄ WTB ⛄Commended
Prices: B&B £13–15, weekly £90–98. EM £5–6, weekly B&B plus EM £112–126.

BANGOR   Map 4 A2

Goetre Isaf Farmhouse, Caernarfon Road, Bangor LL57 4DB
℗ (0248) 364541

Superb country situation with magnificent views. Although isolated Goetre Isaf is only 2 miles from Bangor mainline station. Ideal touring centre for the mountains of Snowdonia, Isle of Anglesey, and the beaches of the Lleyn Peninsula. Imaginative farmhouse cooking. Special diets accommodated and vegetarians welcome. The farmhouse is adjacent to the Caernarfon road, southwest of Bangor. Packed lunches on request. Stabling by arrangement. Pony trekking, riding, golf and fishing nearby.

Open all year.
3 bedrooms (2 twin inc. 1 ens.🍽/WC; 1 double), 2🛏, 3WCs.
⚜ ⛄
Prices: B&B £13–18, EM £5.50–8.

DYFFRYN ARDUDWY   Map 4 A3

Byrdir, Dyffryn Ardudwy LL44 2EA
℗ (0341) 247200

This traditional stone farmhouse has exposed beams and large fireplaces. The farm is a mixed working unit. Guests are well looked after with packed lunches and delicious evening meals. The area has lakes, mountains, beaches and wonderful walks in every direction. Byrdir is midway between Harlech and Barmouth off A496 at Dyffryn Ardudwy on road to Cwm Nantcol.

Open Mar-Oct.
5 bedrooms (1 twin/double ens.🛁; 2 family ens. 🛁/WC; 1 double ens.🍽/WC; 1 single), 1WC.
⚜ ⛄ WTB ⛄ ⛄ ⛄Highly Commended
Prices: B&B £15.50–18, weekly £105–115. EM £8, weekly £155–165. ⚜ rates.

Ystumgwern Hall Farm, Dyffryn Ardudwy LL44 2DD
℗ (03417) 249

This 1000-acre working farm lies a mile from golden beaches, mountains and shops, on the A496 Harlech-Barmouth road. The 16th-century farmhouse is full of character, with oak beams and open fires, and is well-known for excellent cooking, with an emphasis on fresh produce. There is a separate lounge and two dining rooms for guests, plus a ground floor bedroom. Some bedrooms have private lounge and kitchen area. Cot and highchair available.

Open all year
6 bedrooms (2 twin ens.🍽/WC; 2 double ens.🍽/WC; 2 family ens.🛁/WC).
⚜ ⛄ WTB Highly Commended
Prices: B&B £18, weekly £125. ⚜ rates.

BETWS-Y-COED   Map 4 A3

Maesgwyn, Pentre Foelas, Betws-y-Coed LL24 0LR
℗ (06905) 668

Maesgwyn is a mixed farm situated a mile from Pentre Foelas on the B5113. This 17th-century farmhouse offers the opportunity to explore one of the most famed beauty spots of North Wales. Close by are Snowdonia, slate miles, forestry walks, mountain lakes, pony trekking, hill walking and climbing. Betws-y-Coed 6 miles. Tea/coffee facilities in rooms.

Open April-Nov.
2 bedrooms (1 double; 1 family), 1🛏, 1WC.
⚜ ⛄ WTB Listed Commended
Prices: B&B £12–14, weekly £80. ⚜ rates.

CAERNARFON   Map 4 A3

Pengwern Farm, Saron, Llanwnda, Caernarfon LL54 5UH
℗ (0286) 830717

This charming, spacious farmhouse is beautifully situated between mountains and sea, with unobstructed views of Snowdonia, The farm covers 130 acres which run down to Foryd Bay, noted for its birdlife. Meals are cooked to a professional standard using fresh produce including home produced beef and lamb. Packed lunches on request. Cot and highchair available. Golf 2 miles.

Open Feb-Nov.
3 bedrooms (1 twin ens.⋔/⊟/WC; 2 double ens.⋔/⊟/WC).
🐾 ⚄ WTB ⚘ ⚘ ⚘Highly Commended Farmhouse Award
Prices: B&B £15–18, weekly £105–126. EM £9. Weekly B&B plus EM £149–182. 🐾 rates.

CONWY
Map 4 A2

Henllys Farm, Llechwedd, Conwy LL32 8DJ
✆ (0492) 593269

Henllys is a 150-acre mixed farm set on the roadside amidst quiet beautiful scenery just south of Conwy. Good home cooking from fresh local produce is emphasised, with own farm lamb a speciality. Conwy Castle, quay, the smallest house, Plas Mawr, Aberlonwy House and Bodnant Gardens all close by.

Open Mar-Nov.
3 bedrooms (1 double; 1 family; 1 single) 2🚬, 2WCs. 🐾
Prices: B&B £13–16, weekly £80–100. EM £7. Weekly B&B plus Em £125–160. 🐾 rates.

DOLGELLAU
Map 4 A3

Glyn Farm, Dolgellau LL40 17A
✆ (0341) 422286   Mrs E. Wyn Price

This 300-year-old farmhouse sits on a hill with all windows facing the picturesque Mawddach estuary. The farm lies close to the A493, just west of Dolgellau. The warm and well-equipped accommodation assures a pleasant stay. Cot and highchair available. Precipice walk 1 mile. Pony trekking, Cader Idris 2 miles. Sea 6 miles.

Open Mar-Nov.
5 bedrooms (1 twin; 2 double; 1 family; 1 single), 1🚬, 2WCs.
🐾 ⚓ WTB ⚘
Prices: B&B £12–14.

PORTHMADOG
Map 4 A3

Tyddyn Du Farm, Gellilydan, Ffestiniog LL41 4RB
✆ (0766) 85281   Mrs Paula Williams

This working farm is an excellent location for exploring North Wales' numerous attractions, beaches and spectacular walks. The beautiful 17th-century farmhouse has charm and character with inglenook fireplace, antiques, exposed beams and stonework. TV and tea/coffee facilities in bedrooms, one superb private cottage suite. Candlelit dinners with home-made soups, buns and fresh wholesome food. Vegetarians welcome. Packed lunches on request. Ducks, bottle-fed lambs, ponies on farm. The farm is just off the A470 near the A487 junction at Gellilydan. Send stamp for brochure.

Open all year
4 bedrooms (1 twin; 2 double ens.⋔/WC; 1 family ens.⋔/WC), 1🚬, 1WC.
🐾 WTB ⚘ ⚘ ⚘Highly Commended
Prices: B&B £14–16.50, EM £7.50. Weekly B&B plus EM £133–150. 🐾 rates.

PWLLHELI
Map 4 A3

Mathan Uchaf Farm, Boduan, Pwllheli LL53 8TU
✆ (0758) 720487   Mrs J. Coker

This is a dairy farm with 80–100 milking cows, calves, dogs that play with children and a friendly Shetland pony. The farm lies off the A497 Pwllheli-Nefyn road. Swing, games, cot and highchair available. Adventure Farm and riding stables 2 miles. Sea 4 miles.

Open May-Oct.
3 bedrooms (1 twin; 1 double; 1 family), 1🚬, 2WCs.
🐾 ⚓ WTB ⚘ ⚘
Prices: B&B £15–17, weekly £100–120. EM £7–8. Weekly £150–180. 🐾 rates.

TRAWSFYNYDD
Map 4 A3

Bryn Celynog Farm, Trawsfynydd, Blaenau Ffestiniog LL41 4TR
✆ (076687) 378

In the centre of Snowdonia National Park this farmhouse has a reputation for excellent food and friendliness. Separate lounge and dining room for guests. Tea/coffee facilities. Packed lunches on request. On the farm are 2 lakes, a Roman castle ruin and an old railway. The farm is 3 miles east of Trawsfynydd (A4212).

Open all year
3 bedrooms alll ens. 🚿/WC (1 twin; 1 double; 1 family), 1🛁, 1WC.
🧒 🐕 WTB ♛♛ ♛Commended
Prices: B&B £14–16.50, weekly £98–115. EM £7, weekly £147–164. 🧒 rates.

TYWYN
Map 4 A3

Dolffanog Fach, Talyllyn, Tywyn LL36 9AJ
✆ (0654) 761235 Mrs Meirwen Pughe

The farmhouse is stone built and set at the foot of Cader Idris in the Snowdonia National Park, with fantastic views of Talyllyn Lake from the garden. The farm has 1000 acres on the mountain with sheep and suckler cows. It is located on the B4405 (off the A487) northeast of Tywyn. Good farmhouse cooking offered and packed lunches on request.

Open Mar-Nov.
3 bedrooms (1 twin; 1 family; 1 double ens. 🚿/🛁/WC), 1🛁, 1WC.
🧒 WTB ♛♛ ♛
Prices: B&B £14–17, weekly £95–112. EM £7.50. Weekly B&B plus EM £145–155. 🧒 rates.

Hendy Farm, Tywyn, Meirionnydd
✆ (0654) 710457 Anne Lloyd-Jones

Hendy is a working mixed farm of 220 acres to be found just off the A493 Tywyn-Bryncrug road. The large stone built farmhouse offers well-equipped accommodation with separate sitting and dining room for guests. Packed lunches available on request. Hendy has its own halt for the Talyllyn Railway on the farm. Beach 2 miles. Golf course 4 miles.

Open Easter-Oct.
3 bedrooms with priv. facilities (1 twin; 2 double), 1🛁, 1WC.
🧒 🐕 WTB ♛♛ ♛Highly Commended
Prices: B&B £13.50–15, weekly £94.50–105. EM £7.50. Weekly B&B plus EM £133–154. 🧒 rates.

Tan y Coed Ucha, Abergynolwyn, Tywyn LL36 9UP
✆ (0654) 782228 Gweniona S. Pugh

This is a mixed farm with cattle and sheep. The farmhouse is over 100 years old, but has been modernised for comfort and convenience. The atmosphere is welcoming and homely. The farm lies off the B4405 between Abergynolwyn and Dolgoch Falls. Packed lunches on request and cot and highchair available. Talyllyn Railway runs through the farmland. At the back of the farmhouse begins the climb up Bird Rock. Dolgoch Falls 1 mile. Talyllyn Lake 3 miles, fishing available. Twywn beach 6 miles.

Open Mar-Nov.
4 bedrooms (1 twin ens. 🚿/🛁/WC; 1 double; 2 single), 1🛁, 1WC.
🧒 🐕 WTB Listed
Prices: B&B £11–14, weekly £77–98. EM £7.50. Weekly B&B plus EM £129.50–150. 🧒 rates.

Self-Catering

ANGELSEY
Map 4 A2

Llwydiarth Fawr, Llanerchymedd, Anglesey LLY1 8DF
✆ (0248) 470321/470540 Mrs Margaret Hughes

For full farm descrption, see p. 211.There are 6 self-catering units on the farm, sleeping 4–6 people.

Open all year
🐕 WTB Grade 5
Prices: weekly £100–500.

Plas Trefarthen, Brynsiencyn, Isle of Anglesey LL616SZ
✆ (0248) 430379 JM Roberts

For full farm description see p. 212. One wing of the large house is let as self-catering accommodation, 3 bedrooms, sleeps 6.

Open all year
Prices: weekly £120–260.

BEAUMARIS
Map 4 A2

Yr Orsedd, Llanddona, Beaumaris, Anglesey
✆ (0248) 810443   Hilary Bebb-Parry

Yr Orsedd is a working dairy farm situated 3 miles northwest of the historic town of Beaumaris (B5109). The self-catering farmhouse sleeps 5 in comfort. Cot available. It is a traditional farm cottage with exposed beams, overlooking the village of Llanddona. Llanddona beach 3 miles. Red Wharf Bay 7 miles.

Open all year
♿ ☪ WTB Grade 5
Prices: £70–400.

CRICCIETH
Map 4 A3

Chwilog Fawr, Chwilog, Pwllheli LL53 6SW
✆ (0766) 810506   Mrs Catherine Jones

This is a traditional Welsh farmhouse situated on a working beef and sheep farm, 4 miles west of Criccieth (A497/B4354). Panoramic views can be enjoyed from the 6 chalets, 2 and 3 bedroomed, sleeping 4 and 6. Ground floor bedrooms available. Chwilog Fawr is surrounded by lovely country walks, beaches 2 miles, golf, fishing and sailing within easy distance.

Open Mar-Oct.
WTB Grade 4 and 5
Prices: weekly £100–350.

DYFFRYN ARDUDWY
Map 4 A3

LLys Bennar, Dyffryn Ardudwy LL44 2RX
✆ (0341) 247316   Catrin Rutherford

These cottages are attractively converted old farm buildings. Although not on a working farm, they are surrounded by grazing sheep and cattle. There are 3 cottages, with 2–3 bedrooms, sleeping 4–7. Ground floor bedrooms available. Llys Bennar is 5 miles from Barmouth (north on coast road via Tal-y-bont). Beach nearby, fishing 2 miles, Harlech Castle and golf 5 miles.

Open all year
☪ WTB Grade 4
Prices: weekly £150–366, ☪ £15.

Planning a day out?
See RURAL ATTRACTIONS

Ynys Ystumgwern Hall Farm, Dyffryn Ardudwy LL44 2DD
✆ (03417) 249

For full description see p. 213. The 16th-century farm cottages have been renovated to a high standard. Well equipped and warm, ideal for winter lets, they sleep 2–8 people. There is a picnic and barbecue area, plus a children's playroom. Cot and highchair available. The farmhouse will happily provide breakfast if required.

Open all year
☪ ☪ WTB Grade 5
Prices: weekly £125–420. ☪ rates.

PORTHMADOC
Map 4 A3

Tyddyn Madyn, Golan, Garn Dolbenmaen LLS1 9YY
✆ (0766) 75605

The stone built farmhouse is set on a 35-acre working farm with panoramic views of the beautiful Pennant Valley. With 3 bedrooms, it is fully equipped for 6 people. Fishing rights on the farm and well-stocked lakes within 30 mins drive. The farm lies 5 miles northwest of Porthmadoc, on the main Porthmadoc-Caernafon road.

Open Apr-Oct.
Prices: weekly £160–200.

PWLLHELI
Map 4 A3

Blaenau Uchaf, Llithfaen, Nr Pwllheli LL53 6PD
✆ (075885) 472   Mr D. Clifford

This farm dates back to 1541 as the thick stone walls and exposed beams show. There are magnificent views across Cardigan Bay and St Tudwals Island. The farm is on the outskirts of the small village of Llithfaen, 10 miles northwest of Pwllheli (A499/B4417). The 4-acre smallholding has sheep, donkeys, cats and dogs. The stable conversion has one bedroom plus sofa bed in lounge, sleeps 4, and is equipped to the highest standards. Easy access to all the Lleyn Peninsula's lovely beaches.

Closed Xmas and New Year
Prices: weekly £100–180.

Gwynfryn Farm, Penrallt, Pwllheli LL53 5UF
✆ (0758) 612536   Mrs R.A. Ellis

Gwynfryn is an organic dairy farm situated northwest of Pwllheli on the Llannor road. Accommodation is offered in 8 cottages, sleeping 2–8, converted from farm buildings. There is a games room, play area and launderette. Bed and breakfast also available. Two cottages have ground floor bedrooms. The sea, marina and leisure centre 2 miles. Snowdonia 20 miles. Slate mines 30 miles. Dogs are welcome, but not in July and August.

Open all year
🕭 🐾 🛏 WTB 😤 😤 😤 😤/ 😤
Prices: weekly £94–450, short break £70.50. 🛏 £10 per night.

Ty'n Don, Llanengan, Abersoch, Pwllheli LL53 7LG
Contact: Mrs Elizabeth Evans, Peulan, Rhos Isaf, Caernafon LL547NG

Eight self-catering cottages, sleeping 5–8, are set on this 120-acre sheep farm, a mile from the village of Llanengan (leave the A499 at Abersoch). Two cottages are all on the ground floor. From this uniquely attractive position, the sea almost surrounds the peninsula, the holidaymaker has over a dozen coves and beaches to choose from. The closest is 300 yds from the farm. Cot and highchair provided.

Open all year
🐾 🛏 WTB Grades 3 & 4
Prices: weekly £89–£390.

Reduced rates are sometimes available.
Ask your host about weekend breaks.

POWYS

BRECON   Map 1 B1

Brynfedwen Farm, Trallong Common, Sennybridge, Brecon LD3 8HW
✆ (0874) 636505   Mrs Mary Adams

Brynfedwen, meaning Hill of the Birch Trees, is a family run farm high above the valley of the River Usk, with splendid views of the Brecon Beacons. The modernised stone farmhouse is warm and welcoming. Rooms include a ground floor twin bedded granny flat specially designed for disabled guests, to let either as self catering or as B&B. Cot and highchair provided. Packed lunches on request. The farm is off the A40, 7 miles west of Brecon, within the Brecon Beacons National Park.

Open all year
3 bedrooms (1 twin ens.🛁/WC; 2 family inc. 1 ens.🚿/WC;1 ens.🛁/WC).
🕭 Non-smokers preferred WTB 😤 😤 😤
Highly Commended
Prices: B&B £16, EM £9. 🐾 rates.

Lower Rhydness, Llyswen, Brecon LD3 0AZ
✆ (0874) 754264   Mrs M.E. Williams

This 150-acre working farm with sheep, beef cattle and one Shetland pony lies 10 miles northeast of Brecon, off the A470. The farmhouse is very old and full of character with oak panelling, exposed beams and an open fire on cold days. There is also a large garden for guests to enjoy. Cot and highchair available. The surrounding area has much to offer: Brecon canal and Beacons, Dan-yr-Ogof caves, Llangorse Lake, Elan Valley and Welsh wool factory.

Open Mar.–Dec.
3 bedrooms (1 twin; 1 double; 1 family), 1🛁, 2WCs.
🐾 🛏 WTB Listed
Prices: B&B £12, weekly £80. EM £6.50. Weekly B&B plus EM £119.

Tre-graig Farm, Bwlch, Brecon LD3 7SJ
✆ (0874) 730973

An impressive new farmhouse on a 45-acre working farm enjoying panoramic views of the Usk Valley and surrounding mountain ranges within the Brecon Beacons National Park. Easy access to a network of footpaths gives full enjoyment of the breathtaking scenery. Tea/coffee facilities, open fire and TV in guest lounge. The farm is off A40 a mile from Bwlch.

Open Apr-Oct.
3 bedrooms (1 twin; 1 double; 1 family), 1🛏,
2WCs.
🙌 WTB 👑 👑Commended
Prices: B&B £14–18, weekly £95. EM £7.50,
weekly B&B plus EM £147.

Trehenry Farm, Felinfach, Brecon LD3 0UW
✆ (0874) 754312　　　　Mrs Theresa Jones

Enjoy the beauty of the Welsh countryside at our spacious 18th-century farmhouse on a 200-acre farm with sheep, cattle and cereals. Our aim is to make your stay enjoyable with good home cooking, a friendly welcome and a large garden to relax in. Cot available. Trehenry Farm is off the A470 Brecon-Bronllys road. The Brecon Beacons and Black Mountains make this a paradise for walkers. Also locally fishing, riding, boating, swimming and golf.

Open Mar-Dec.
3 bedrooms (1 twin ens.🛁/WC; 1 double
ens.🛁/WC; 1 family ens.🛁/🖤/WC), 1🛏, 1WC.
🙌 WTB 👑 👑 👑 Highly Commended
Farmhouse Award
Prices: B&B £16, weekly £110. EM £9–10.
Weekly B&B plus EM £170. 🙌 rates

BUILTH WELLS　　　　　　　　Map 1 B1

Disserth Mill, Builth Wells, LD2 3TN
✆ (0982) 553217

Disserth Mill is on a mixed farm. Packed lunches on request and good home cooking in the evenings. The Mill is 3 miles north of Builth Wells (A483). Llandrindod and Spa waters 4 miles.

Elan Valley Reservoir 13 miles. Hay-on-Wye 18 miles.

Open Mar-Oct.
3 bedrooms (1 twin; 2 double), 1🛏, 1WC.
🙌 🐓 WTB Classified
Prices: B&B £14, weekly £98. EM £8, weekly
B&B plus EM £150. 🙌 rates.

New Hall, Llandewircwm, Builth Wells LD2 3RX
✆ (0982) 552483

New Hall is a smallholding with fields and a wood extending down to a stream. The 17th-century farmhouse nestles in magnificent unspoilt scenery overlooking the Wye Valley. It is to be found under 2 miles from Builth Wells on the B4520. Packed lunches on request, ground floor bedrooms, cot and highchair available. Golf, sports centre and scenic park by the River Wye at Builth Wells. Royal Welsh Showground 2 miles.

Open all year
5 bedrooms (1 twin; 2 doubles inc 1 ens.🛁;1
family ens.🖤/WC; 1 single ens.🛁), 1🛏, 2WCs.
🙌 WTB 👑 👑Commended Guest House Award
Prices: B&B £14–18, weekly £98–114. EM
£4.50–7. Weekly £147–157.50. 🙌 rates.

Ty-isaf Farm, Erwood, Builth Wells LD2 3S2
✆ (0982) 560607

This mixed working farm of 340 acres lies just off the A470, south of Builth Wells. The farmhouse is comfortably furnished throughout. Good home cooking served and packed lunches provided on request. Cot and high chair available. Locally – pony trekking, golf, swimming, fishing, birdwatching and beautiful walks by the River Wye.

Open all year
3 bedrooms (1 twin; 1 double; 1 family), 1🛏,
2WCs.
🙌 🐓 WTB 👑 👑Merit Farmhouse Award
Prices: B&B £11–12.50, weekly £77. EM £5–6.
Weekly B&B plus EM £112–126. 🙌 rates.

KNIGHTON Map 2 A1
Cefnsuran, Llangunllo, Knighton LD7 1SL
✆ (054781) 219

Relax in this 16th-century farmhouse on a working farm amidst beautiful countryside. A play area, games room with snooker table and table tennis, plus good walks, nature trails with abundant wildlife, riding, boating and coarse fishing are all offered. Packed lunches and afternoon teas provided. The farm is under 7 miles west of Knighton, (A488 then B4356 north).

Open all year
4 bedrooms (2 twin inc. 1 ens. ⋔/WC, 1 ens. ♱/WC; 1 double ens. ⋔/WC; 1 family ens. ⋔/WC), 2♒, 2WCs.
⚿ WTB ♛ ♛Commended
Prices: B&B £14–16, weekly £91–105. EM £8.50–11, weekly £140–210. ⚿ rates.

Monaughty Poeth, Llanfair-Waterdine, Knighton LD7 1TT
✆ (0547) 528348   Jim & Jocelyn Williams

The Victorian farmhouse stands on an ancient site amid sheep covered hills. Guests are beauti-

KEY TO SYMBOLS	
Bath	♒
Shower	⋔
Bathroom	♱
Disabled Guest Facilities	♿
No Smoking	⚤
Children Welcome	⚿
Dogs by Arrangement	🐕

fully looked after with delicious home baked pies and fresh flowers in the pretty rooms. The farm is 3 miles northwest of Knighton off B4355 Newtown road. Within easy reach of the Elan valley and Dam, and medieval Ludlow. Offa's Dyke passes through the farm.

Open end Apr-Nov.
2 bedrooms (1 twin/family; 1 double), 1♒, 2WCs.
⚿(10) 🐕
Prices: B&B £15.50–16.50, weekly £105.

LLANDRINDOD WELLS Map 1 B1
Brynhir Farm, Chapel Road, Howey, Llandrindod Wells LD1 5PB
✆ (0597) 822425   Mrs C. Nixon

On a 150-acre hill farm in a beautiful mountain setting, this charming 17th-century farmhouse offers a relaxing holiday. The surrounding countryside is renowned for its interesting birdlife and lovely views. Conducted badger tours offered. The farm is situated a mile from Howey off the A483. There is trout fishing nearby and farmhouse cooking a speciality. Packed lunches on request, ground floor bedrooms available. Spa town of Llandrindod Wells 2 miles. Elan Valley 11 miles.

Open Mar-Nov.
10 bedrooms (4 twin inc. 1 ens. ⋔/WC; 4 double inc. 1 ens. ⋔/WC;1 family ens. ⋔/WC; 1 single), 2♒, 3WCs.
⚿ 🐕 WTB ♛ ♛ ♛Commended
Prices: B&B £14.50–15, weekly £92–102. EM £6.50–7. Weekly £140–150. ⚿ rates.

Holly Farm, Howey, Llandrindod Wells LD1 5PP
✆ (0597) 822402

Holly Farm set in beautiful countryside offers guests a friendly welcome under 2 miles south of Llandrindod Wells. Excellent base for exploring lakes, mountains and birdwatching. Beverage trays, log fire and TV lounge. Superb meals using home produce.

Open April-Nov.
3 bedrooms (2 double; 1 family), 1🛏, 1WC. 🐕
Prices: B&B £14–17, EM £7–8. Weekly
£140–150. 🐕 rates.

Three Wells Farm, Chapel Road, Howey, Llandrindod Wells LD1 5PB
✆ (0597) 822484 Ron, Margaret & Sarah Bufton
✆ (0597) 824427

Voted the Best Small Hotel In Wales in 1990, Three Wells Farm is a licensed farm guest house and working farm overlooking a fishing lake in beautiful countryside. The farm lies a mile south of Llandrindod Wells off the A483 at Howey. All rooms have tea/coffee facilities, TV and telephones. Some bedrooms have four poster beds and private lounges. Good home cooking is served from a varied menu with a good selection of wines in the attractive dining room. There is also a lounge with adjoining sun lounge, TV room, snug bar and lounge bar. Three Wells Farm is well placed for rambling and birdwatching. FHG Diploma, Rural Tourism Award for Accommodation and Catering.

Open Feb-Nov.
14 bedrooms (6 twin inc. 2 ens.🛁/WC, 4 ens.🚽/WC;6 double inc. 2 ens.🛁/WC, 4 ens.🚽/WC; 1 single ens.🛁/WC; 1 family ens.🚽/WC), 2WCs. 🐕(10)
Prices: B&B £16–21.50, EM £8. Weekly B&B plus EM £150–185.

LLANFYLLIN   Map 4 B3
Cyfie Farm, Llanfihangel-yng-Ngwynfa, Llanfyllin, Montgomeryshire
✆ (0691) 648451   George & Lynn Jenkins

The 17th-century farmhouse stands on a working farm of 180 acres, high above a delightful valley, with views from the patio and colourful garden. Bedrooms are furnished to a very high standard, and the private stable suite offers every comfort. Superb traditional meals are served in the attractive dining room with conservatory feature. Packed lunches and afternoon teas available on

request. Highchair provided. The farm lies 4 miles north of the A495. Lake Vyrnwy and Llanfair/Welshpool Light Railway 6 miles. Pistyll Rhaedr, Llanrhaeadr Waterfall (the highest in Wales) 9 miles. Powys Castle 11 miles.

Open all year
3 bedrooms (1 twin priv.🚽/WC; 1 double ens.🚽/WC; 1 family ens.🛁/WC).
🐕 WTB 🏆 🏆 🏆Highly Commended
Prices: B&B £16.50–22.50, EM £9. Weekly B&B plus EM £150–178. 🐕 rates.

LLANGORSE   Map 1 B3
The Old Stables, Trefeinon Farm, Llangorse, Brecon LD3 0PS
✆ (087484) 607   Mrs L. Sheppard

Trefeinon is a working farm with deer and horses, wild flower meadows and fresh spring water. In this idyllic spot, a barn has been converted into self-contained units let as self-catering or B&B. Ground floor accommodation available, cot, highchair and playroom provided. From the A40, Trefeinon is off the B4560 Bwlch-Talgarth road after Llangorse. Just over a mile from the farm lie the Black Mountains and Llangorse Lake. Brecon 6 miles. Hay-on-Wye 10 miles.

Open all year.
11 bedrooms (6 twin inc. 2 ens.🛁/WC, 4 ens.🚽/WC; 4 double inc. 2 ens.🛁/WC, 2 ens.🚽/WC; 1 family ens.🛁/WC).
🐕 🍴
Prices: B&B £20. 🐕 rates,🐕 £10 per week.

LLANIDLOES   Map 4 B3
Dol-llys Farm, Llanidloes
✆ (05512) 2694   O.S. Evans

Dol-llys is a 17th-century farmhouse situated on the banks of the River Severn within walking distance of the market town of Llanidloes, off the A470. The house often intrigues our guests because it has so many levels and small staircases, but all agree on the high standard of the accommodation. This is a working farm of 150 acres. You can fish in the Severn on our farmland. Golf, tennis and bowls available locally.

Open all year
2 bedrooms (1 twin ens.⬜/WC; 1 double ens.⬜/WC), 1⬥,2WCs.
WTB ♛ ♛Highly Commended
Prices: B&B £12–15.

MACHYNLLETH   Map 4 A3

Br_yncelyn Farm, Dinas Mawddwy, Machynlleth
✆ (0650) 531289   Mrs E.M. Edwards

The Edwards family offer a comfortable holiday in a peaceful valley of Cywarch at the foot of Aran Fawddwy. Spacious bedrooms, packed lunches and evening meals provided. The farm is 2 miles from the village of Dinas Mawddwy, 10 miles northeast of Machynlleth on A470/489.

Open all year
2 twin bedrooms priv.⬜/WC.
⬥ (9) ✚ WTB ♛ ♛ ♛
Prices: B&B £15–17, EM £6–7.

Bryn Sion Farm, Cwm Cywarch, Dinas Mawddwy, Machynlleth
✆ (0650) 531251

This old stone farmhouse is set in the picturesque valley of Cywarch, 10 miles north east of Machynlleth off A489/470. The farm is mostly sheep, 700 ewes, but some Welsh Black cattle are also kept. Packed lunches on request. Fishing, shooting and hill walking available on the farm. Pony trekking, golf, swimming within easy reach. Beaches 40 mins.

Open all year
2 double bedrooms, 1⬥, 1WC.
⬥ ✚ WTB Listed
Prices: B&B £12–14, weekly £84–98. EM £5–7, weekly B&B plus EM £119–147. ⬥ rates.

MONTGOMERY   Map 4 B3

The Drewin Farm, Church Stoke, Montgomery
✆ (0588) 620325

Offa's Dyke footpath runs through this mixed working farm of sheep, cattle and corn which is located off the B4385 west of Church Stoke (A489). There are panoramic views from the 17th-century farmhouse where you can enjoy good home cooking served in the oak beamed dining room with a large inglenook log fireplace. The games room has a snooker table. Drewin Farm is well placed for exploring the area. Montgomery 5 miles. Powys Castle, Stokesay Castle, Welshpool-Llanfair Light Railway and Acton Scott Farm Museum 12 miles. Ludlow 18 miles.

Open April-Nov.
2 family bedrooms inc. 1 ens.⬜/WC, 1⬥, 2WCs.
⬥ ✂ ✚ WTB ♛ ♛ ♛Highly Commended
Prices: B&B £14–16, weekly £98–112. EM £7–8. Weekly B&B plus EM £149–160. ⬥ rates.

Little Brompton Farm, Montgomery SY15 6HY
✆ (0686) 668371   Mrs G. Bright

Two miles south of the Georgian town of Montgomery on the B4385 (A489) stands this working mixed farm and attractive 17th-century farmhouse. The house is traditionally furnished, offering comfortable accommodation and excellent home cooking. Packed lunches provided on request. Cot, highchair and children's games available. Little Brompton Farm makes a good base for touring Mid Wales and the Border country. Offa's Dyke passes through the farm. Powys Castle and the Welshpool-Llanfair Light Railway 10 miles.

Open all year
3 bedrooms (1 twin ens. ⬜/WC; 1 double ens.⬜/WC; 1 family ens.⬜/WC), 2⬥, 2WCs.
⬥ ✚ WTB ♛ ♛ ♛Highly Commended
Prices: B&B £14–16, weekly £98–112. EM £7–8.50. Weekly B&B plus EM £147–170. ⬥ rates.

NEWTOWN
Map 4 A3

Cefn-Gwyn Farm, Trefeglwys, Nr Caersws, Newtown SY17 5RF
✆ (05516) 648

This picturesque house stands on a mixed family run farm in a superb location for walking and bird-watching. High standards are kept throughout and the superb traditional cooking is of special note. Packed lunches and afternoon teas on request. Situated on B4569 between Trefeglwys and Caersws, 6 miles north of Llanidloes. Golf 2 miles. Lakes 4 miles. Newtown 8 miles.

Open all year
3 bedrooms (2 double; 1 family ens. ☞/WC), 1🡒, 2WCs.
🏵 🡒 WTB ♛ ♛Commended
Prices: B&B £12.50–14.50, weekly £87.50–101.50. EM £8.50–9.50, weekly B&B plus EM £147–168. 🏵 rates.

TALGARTH
Map 2 A2

Lodge Farm, Talgarth, Brecon
✆ (0874) 711244

Lodge Farm is a small family run mixed hill farm nestling on the Black Mountains in peace and tranquility, yet under 2 miles from Talgarth off the A479. The 18th-century house offers spacious, traditionally furnished accommodation with interesting and wholesome food, including vegetarian. Cot, highchair and children's play area provided. The farm is ideal for walking and exploring the National Park. Bronllys Castle 2 miles. Hay-on-Wye 8 miles.

Open Feb-Dec.
3 bedrooms (1 twin ens. ☞/WC; 1 double ens.🛁/WC; 1 family ens.🛁/WC), 1🡒, 2WCs.
🏵 🡒 WTB ♛ ♛
Prices: B&B £16–18, EM £9–10. Weekly B&B plus EM from £150. 🏵 rates.

TALYBONT-ON-USK
Map 1 B1

Llanddetty Hall Farm, Talybont-on-Usk, Brecon LD3 7RY
✆ (087487) 267

The 17th-century oak beamed farmhouse of Llanddetty Hall stands on a 175-acre hill sheep and beef farm that ranges from the foot of the mountain down to the banks of the River Usk within Brecon Beacons National Park. The Brecon-Monmouth canal flows through the farmland. Good home cooking is offered and packed lunches on request. Cot available. The farm is situated on the B4558 (A40) Talybont-on-Usk-Llangynidr road. Talybont Reservoir 3 miles. Tretower Court 5 miles.

Open April-Oct.
3 bedrooms (1 twin; 1 double; 1 family), 1🡒, 2WCs.
🏵 WTB ♛ ♛Commended Farmhouse Award
Prices: B&B £14–17, weekly £95–119. EM £7–7.50. Weekly B&B plus EM £147–168. 🏵 rates.

WELSHPOOL
Map 4 B3

Lower Trelydan, Guilsfield, Welshpool SY21 9PH
✆ (0938) 553105   Graham & Sue Jones

This beautiful old black and white house is set on a mixed sheep, beef and arable farm. Every comfort welcomes guests, lovely accommodation, beverage trays and delicious cuisine bar. Licensed, residential and restaurant. Cot and highchair available. The farm is 2 miles north of Welshpool (A490/B4392).

Open all year
3 bedrooms (1 twin; 1 family; 1 double ens. ⋔/WC), 3🛁, 3WC.
⚿ WTB 🍵 🍵 🍵
Prices: B&B £14.50–16, weekly £101.50–112. EM £9, weekly B&B plus EM £164.50–175.

Moat Farm, Welshpool SY21 8SE
✆ (0938) 553179   Mrs Gwyneth Jones

Moat Farm is a 250-acre dairy farm off the A483, 3 miles south of Welshpool. Good home cooking is served in the fine timbered dining room. Cot and highchair provided, and older guests will appreciate the pool table and tennis lawn. Riding school 2 miles. Swimming bath, Welshpool-Llanfair Light Railway and canal trips 3 miles. Golf course 4 miles.

Open April–Oct.
3 bedrooms (2 double ens.⋔/WC; 1 family ens.🛁/WC), 1⋔, 1WC.
⚿ WTB 🍵 🍵 🍵Highly Commended
Prices: B&B £16–18, weekly £112–126. EM £8–9. Weekly B&B plus EM £168–175. ⚿ rates.

Tynllwyn Farm, Welshpool SY21 9BW
✆ (0938) 553175   Mrs Freda Emberton

A warm welcome awaits you in the large brick farmhouse at Tynllwyn Farm. From its hillside position, this working beef and sheep farm has splendid views over the surrounding countryside. Mrs Emberton offers excellent country cooking and packed lunches on request. Licensed. The farm lies a mile north of Welshpool on the A490. Nearby you can take boat trips on the canal or ride the Welshpool-Llanfair Light Railway. Powys Castle 2 miles. Moors Farm (Rare Breeds Collection) 3 miles.

Open all year   **RAC**
6 bedrooms (2 twin; 2 double; 2 family), 2🛁, 3WCs.
⚿ ᴛ
Prices: B&B £12–12.50, weekly £84–86. EM £7–7.50. Weekly B&B plus EM £117–120. ⚿ rates.

Self-Catering

KNIGHTON   Map 2 A1
Cefnsuran, Llangunllo, Knighton LD7 1SL
✆ (054781) 219

For full farm description see p. 219. A wing of the farmhouse has been made into a self-contained flat with 3 bedrooms, sleeps 7.

Open all year
WTB Grade 5
Prices: weekly £164–286.

LLANGORSE   Map 1 B3
The Old Stables, Trefeinon Farm, Llangorse, Brecon LD3 0PS
✆ (087484) 607   Mrs L. Sheppard

For full farm description see p. 220. A barn has been converted into 6 self-contained units, sleeping 2–5.

Open all year
⚿ ᴛ WTB Grade 3
Prices: weekly from £120. ᴛ £10 per week.

WELSHPOOL   Map 4 B3
Tanyffridd, Brooks, Welshpool
✆ (0686) 640296   Mrs M. Williams
Contact: Llwyn-onn, Brooks, Welshpool

This is an 18th-century cottage set on a 20-acre smallholding which keeps a wide variety of animals. A large enclosed lawned garden looks over a delightful rural scene. The cottage has 3 bedrooms, sleeps 6. The smallholding is 8 miles from Welshpool, A483 southwest via Berriew. Ideal for touring Wales and the Border counties, Powys Castle 8 miles.

Open all year
ᴛ WTB Grade 3
Prices: weekly £65–190.

KEY TO SYMBOLS	
Bath	⊽
Shower	⋔
Bathroom	🛁
Disabled Guest Facilities	⚷
No Smoking	🚭
Children Welcome	⚿
Dogs by Arrangement	ᴛ

WEST GLAMORGAN

SWANSEA Map 1 B1

Coynant Farm, Felindre, Swansea SA5 7PU
✆ (0269) 595640/592064

Just 6 miles from Swansea the peaceful 18th-century farmhouse of Coynant Farm stands in 200 acres of land amid lakes, woods and hills with magnificent views in all directions. The house provides good food, a licensed bar and log fires. Situated under 3 miles from Felindre village north of the A48 (between M4, Jcts 46 & 47), the farm is convenient for the Gower peninsula and beaches. Riding and fishing on the farm. Black Mountains and National Park 6 miles. Carreg Cenen Castle 7 miles.

Open all year
5 bedrooms (2 double ens.🛁/WC; 2 family ens.🛁/WC; 1 single ens.🚿/WC).
🐕
Prices: B&B £17.30–18.50, EM £3.🐕 rates.

CHANNEL ISLANDS

JERSEY
Self-Catering
ST HELIER

Woodlands Farm, Mont-a-L'Abbe, St Helier JE2 3MG
℗ (0534) 864663   Nicola Le Boutillier

This 17th-century granite farmhouse is set in beautiful countryside on a dairy farm with 95 milking cows and 40 followers. Jersey Royal new potatoes are also grown. There are large gardens and barbecues for guests to use. Four self-catering apartments sleep 3–5 adults, all fully equipped. Cots and highchairs available. The farm is 200 yds from the A9 St Helier-St Johns main road. Five clean beaches within 2 miles of the farm. The many Jersey tourist attractions, castles, museums etc. and watersports are all within easy reach of the farm.

Open all year 𝄞
Prices: weekly £250–545.

GUERNSEY
Self-Catering
LE BIGARD

Les Merriennes, Le Bigard, Forest
℗ (0481) 63262   Mr & Mrs D.A.J. Erskine

At Les Merriennes 2 luxury self-contained flats have been converted from an old barn, each with its own sheltered sunny garden. Each sleeps 2. The farm is in a very quiet rural position, lovely cliff walks within 3 mins, Occupation Museum 8 mins. Small hamlet with shops 10 mins.

Open Mar-Nov.
𝄞 (9) ↟
Prices: weekly £200–330. ↟ £10 per week.

NORTHERN IRELAND

CO. ANTRIM

BUSHMILLS Map 10 C1

Carnside Farm Guest House, 23 Causeway, Bushmills
✆ (02657) 31337

This large old-style farmhouse, on a 150-acre working dairy farm stands on a hill overlooking beaches and the Causeway coastline. Packed lunches, cot, highchair and games provided. Ground floor bedrooms available. Carnside Farm is 2 miles from Bushmills, just off A2. Bushmills Distillery, Bush River and fishing 2 miles. Carrickarede Rope Bridge 4 miles.

Open Feb-Nov.
8 bedrooms inc. 1 double ens. 🛁/WC, 1 family ens. 🛁/WC, 1🛏, 3🛁, 3WCs.
⚜ NITB Grade B
Prices: B&B £13-17, weekly £86-114. EM £8-9. ⚜ rates.

BOARDMILLS Map 10 C1

Bresagh Farm, 55 Bresagh Road, Boardmills, Lisburn BT27 6TU
✆ (0846) 638316

This warm comfortable farmhouse is situated on an 80-acre mixed farm, 4 miles north of Ballynahinch (A24). Water skiing on Lough Henney close by. Rowallane Gardens (NT) Saintfield 4 miles.

Open all year
2 bedrooms (1 double; 1 family), 1🛏, 1WC.
⚜ ⚘
Prices: B&B £13.50-15. ⚜ rates.

CARRICKFERGUS Map 10 C2

Beech Grove, 412 Upper Road, Troopers Lane, Carrickfergus
✆ (09603) 63304

Beech Grove is a rural farmhouse standing on a 16-acre mixed farm near the coast. Good country cooking is offered, and packed lunches on request. Located a mile south of Carrickfergus off

the A2, within 3 miles of the farmhouse there are opportunities for golf, fishing and riding, as well as Belfast Zoo and Carrickfergus Castle. Convenient for Larne and Belfast harbours.

Open all year
7 bedrooms (1 twin ens.WC; 1 double ens.🛁/WC; 2 family ens.🛁/WC; 3 single), 1🛏, 2WCs.
⚜ 🐓
Prices: B&B £12-12.50, weekly £80. EM £5. Weekly B&B plus EM £108. ⚜ rates.

Craig's Farm, 90 Hillhead Road, Ballycarry, Larne
✆ (09603) 53769

This comfortably renovated farmhouse is on a beef rearing farm. Separate lounge for guests, cot and packed lunches provided. The farm is midway between Carrickfergus and Larne, 2 miles off the coast road (A2). Carrickfergus Castle 6 miles. Gobbins, Island Magee 4 miles.

Open all year
3 bedrooms (1 twin; 1 double; 1 family), 2🛁/WC, 1🛏, 1WC. ⚜
Prices: B&B £12-15, weekly £80-100. ⚜ rates.

GLENARIFFE Map 10 C1

Dieskirt Farm, 104 Glen Road, Glenariffe, Cushendall
✆ (02667) 71308/71796

Dieskirt is a 2000-acre sheep farm with scenic walks throughout the farm giving breathtaking views of the glen and across to Scotland. The paths also lead to Glenariffe Forest, adjacent to the farm, with many more walks and waterfalls. The modern farmhouse offers all facilities for the tourist, and situated near Waterfoot (A2 from Larne) it is convenient for visiting all the attractions of the region. Close by: sea angling trips and an outdoor activity centre. 20 mins drive: Watertop Open Farm and Rathlin Island. 1 hour drive: Giants Causeway, Bushmill's Distillery and Cultra Museum.

Open May-Nov.
3 bedrooms (2 double; 1 family ens.🛁), 1🛏,
1WC.
🅿 🐾 NITB Farmhouse
Prices: B&B £11–14, weekly £77–90. EM
£6–9.50. 🅿 rates.

PORTRUSH
Map 10 C1

Islay View, 36 Leeke Road, Portrush BT56 8NH
🕾 (0265) 823220   Mrs Eileen M. Smith

Islay View is a warm comfortable bungalow on a 60-acre mixed farm with a superb view of Giants Causeway. Every attention is paid to guests' requirements. For disabled visitors there is a wheelchair ramp and specially equipped bathroom. The farm lies off the B62, a mile south of the A2 Portrush-Bushmills road. White Rocks, beach and Dunluce Castle 1 mile. Royal Portrush golf course 2 miles. Bushmills Distillery 4 miles. Giants Causeway 6 miles.

Open Easter-Sept.
3 bedrooms (1 double; 2 family), 1🛏, 2WCs.
♿ 🅿
Prices: B&B £12.50–14, weekly £87. 🅿 rates.

CO. ARMAGH
PORTADOWN
Map 10 C2

Green Acres, 57 Red Lion Road, Portadown
🕾 (0762) 352610

The redbrick farmhouse of Green Acres stands in 50 acres of orchard and mixed farming, 3 miles southwest of Portadown on the B77 Loughgall

road. Cot, highchair and babysitting available, under 5s free lodging. Ideally placed for sailing and waterskiing on Craigavon Lakes, fishing, and golf at Tandragee. Armagh 5 miles.

Open all year
3 bedrooms (2 twin; 1 double), 1🛏, 1WC.
🅿
Prices: B&B £12. 🅿 rates.

CO. DOWN
BALLYMARTIN
Map 10 C2

Sharon Farm Guest House, 6, Ballykeel Road, Ballymartin, Newry, Kilkeel BT34 4PL
🕾 (06937) 62521   Mrs Marley Bingham

Just a mile from the coast lies this working farm, mainly sheep with working sheepdogs, chickens, bantams and pheasants. In the warm farm bungalow you will find a friendly atmosphere and the opportunity to enjoy Mrs Bingham's afternoon teas. The guest house is off the A2, 2 miles northeast of Kilkeel, by Ballymartin village. Kilkeel has the largest fishing fleet in Ireland. This is a good spot for mountain walks, golfing, fishing and birdwatching. Mountains of Mourne 4 miles.

Open all year
3 bedrooms (1 twin; 1 double; 1 family), 1🛏, 2🛁, 2WCs.
🅿 NITB Approved
Prices: B&B £13, weekly £87. 🅿 rates.

Ashcroft, 12, Ballykeel Road, Ballymartin, Kilkeel BT34 4PL
🕾 (06937) 62736   Esther Orr

This mixed farm is situated off the A2, 2 miles northeast of Kilkeel, by Ballymartin village. Based in the comfortable farmhouse you can enjoy the beauty of both the Mountains of Mourne and the coast. Cot available. Annalong corn mill 3 miles. Silent Valley 4 miles.

Open Mar-Oct.
4 bedrooms (1 twin; 2 double; 1 family ens.🛁/ WC), 1🛏, 1🛁, 2WCs.
🅿 🍴 NITB Registered
Prices: B&B £12–14, weekly £80. 🅿 rates.

BANBRIDGE
Map 10 C2

The Moor Lodge Farm Guest House, 20 Ballynafern Road, Annaclone, Banbridge BT32 5AE
🕾 (08206) 71516   Brigid and Jim McClory

A comfortable chalet bungalow on a mixed beef and sheep farm situated off the B10 Banbridge-Rathfriland road in Bronte countryside. Children are welcomed with swings, slide, playroom and games. Packed lunches and afternoon teas available on request. The Bronte Glen and original homestead are within walking distance. Close by there is golf, fishing and a Leisure Centre. Corbet and Loughbrickland Lakes 3 miles. Banbridge 5 mles. Mourne Mountains 11 miles. Forest Parks of Castlewellan and Tollymore 14 miles.

Open all year
4 bedrooms (1 twin; 2 double; 1 family), 1⇒, 2WCs.
☐ ☐
Prices: B&B £12, weekly £80. EM £7. Weekly B&B plus EM £129. ☐ rates.

NEWTOWNARDS   Map 10 C2

Ballycastle House, 20 Mountstewart Road, Newtownards BT22 2AL
✆ (024774) 357   Margaret Deering

This 200-year-old stone built farmhouse has been extensively and tastefully modernised to provide every modern comfort whilst preserving the house's undoubted character. Cot available. The small working farm has cattle and pigs, and maintains a display of antique farming equipment. Ballycastle House lies off the A20, 5 miles southeast of Newtownards. Mountstewart Estate (NT) 1 mile. Ballycopeland Windmill 5 miles. Bangor 9 miles. Belfast, Ulster Folk and Transport Museum and Rowallane Gardens 14 miles. Castleward House 16 miles.

Open all year
4 bedrooms (3 double inc. 1 ens.☐/WC, 1 ens.☐/WC; 1 single), 1⇒, 1WC.
☐ ☐
Prices: B&B £14–15. ☐ rates.

Reduced rates are sometimes available.
Ask your host about weekend breaks.

Beechhill Farm, 10 Loughries Road, Newtownards BT23 3RN
✆ (0247) 818404

This mixed farm has beef and cattle, horticulture, cereals, potatoes and a variety of vegetables. Packed lunches and evening meals on request. There are separate guests TV lounge and dining room. Situated 4 miles east of Newtownards off A20. Horseriding available locally, sailing, and flying 4 miles, golf 5 miles.

Open all year
5 bedrooms (3 twin inc. 1 ens.☐/WC, 1 ens. ☐/WC, 1 ens. ☐; 1 double; 1 family), 1⇒, 2WCs.
☐
Prices: B&B £13.50, weekly £94.50. Dinner £10, high tea £8.50. ☐ rates.

Gordonall, 93 Newtownards Road, Grey Abbey, Newtownards
✆ (024774) 325   Mrs A. Martin

Gordonall is a 160-acre mixed farm of mainly beef and sheep in a superb position overlooking Strangford Lough and the Mountains of Mourne. Mrs Martin is happy to provide a light supper on request. Cot and highchair available. The farm is situated on the A20 southeast of Newtownards, within walking distance of Grey Abbey village, with its several antique and craft shops, and Mountstewart House (NT).

Open April–Sept.
2 bedrooms (1 twin; 1 family), 1⇒, 1WC.
☐ ☐NITB Farmhouse
Prices: B&B £13–15. ☐ rates.

Greenlea Farm, 48 Dunover Road, Ballywalter, Newtownards BT22 2LE
✆ (02477) 58218   Evelyn McIvor

This mixed farm of 73 acres looks out across the sea towards the Scottish coast. The spacious farmhouse offers every comfort and good home cooking, beginning with a traditional Ulster Fry, and including lunch and afternoon tea. Small parties are catered for. Cots and highchair available. Greenlea lies half a mile off the A2 by Ballywalter village. Bowls, tennis and fishing 1 mile. Riding school, antique and craft shops, and Mount-stewart (NT) 4 miles. Kirkliston Racing 7 miles.

Open all year
5 bedrooms (2 twin; 1 double; 1 family; 1 single), 1🛏, 1♨, 2WCs.
🐾 ⚓
Prices: B&B £12–13, weekly £75–80. EM £6–8. Weekly B&B plus EM £119–126. 🐾 rates.

CO. FERMANAGH

ENNISKILLEN   Map 10 B2

Bayview Guest House, Tully, Churchill, Enniskillen
© (0365) 64250

From the bay windows of this modern farmhouse you can look out over Lough Erne. The house is surrounded by gardens and attached to a work-ing dairy farm where guests are welcome to view the animals. You can enjoy good home cooking, with lunch, afternoon tea and packed lunches on request. Ground floor bedroom, cot, highchair and children's games available. The guest house is situated on the A46 11 miles northwest of Enniskillen. Within walking distance stands Tully Castle with its 17th-century gardens and shore walks. World famous Belleek Pottery 10 miles. Lough Navar, via beautiful forest drive, 3 miles.

Open Mar-Oct.
4 bedrooms (1 twin ens.♨/WC; 2 double inc. 1 ens.♨/WC; 1 family), 1🛏, 2WCs.
🐾
Prices: B&B £13–15, weekly £84–98. EM £7, weekly £130–144. 🐾 rates.

Lakeview Farm Guesthouse, Drumcrow, Blaney, Enniskillen
© (0365) 64263   Mrs Jason Hassard

The modernised farmhouse of Lakeview over-looks and adjoins one of the most beautiful parts of Lower Lough Erne. The house is surrounded by shrubs and gardens, approached on a tarmac drive approx. 200 yds from the A46 Enniskillen-Belleek road. Mrs Hassard offers good country hospitality with quantities of excellent home cooking. Lunch, packed lunches and afternoon teas provided. Ground floor bedroom, cot and highchair available. Tully Castle 2 miles. Lough Navar and forest drive 7 miles.

Open Jan-Nov.
4 bedrooms (1 twin; 1 double; 2 family inc. 1 ens.♨/WC), 1🛏, 2WCs.
🐾 ✂ NITB Grade A
Prices: B&B £12–13, weekly £84–91. EM £7–7.50. Weekly B&B plus EM £125–130.

Mulagh Kippin Farm, Carrybridge, Lisbellaw, Enniskillen
© (0365) 87419   Mrs Hazel Johnston

The farmhouse on this 120-acre dairy farm offers warm and comfortable accommodation and good home cooking. Full board, packed lunches and afternoon teas all provided as required. Ground floor bedrooms available. Situated 4 miles south of Enniskillen, off the A34 a mile from Carrybridge, the farm is convenient for Florence-court and Marble Arch Caves (7 miles). Locally this is an excellent spot for birdwatching and fishing.

Open May-Sept.
2 double bedrooms ens.♨/WC, 1🛏, 2WCs. 🐾
Prices: B&B £12, weekly £77. EM £7. 🐾 rates.

Riverside Farm Guesthouse, Gortadrehid, Culkey P.O., Enniskillen
© (0365) 322725   Mary Isobel Fawcett

This modern farmhouse is situated on a working beef farm in a peaceful rural setting, 2 miles west of Enniskillen (A4/A509). Afternoon tea, packed lunches and evening meals provided. Cot, high-chair, playroom and children's games available. Facilities for disabled guests. Centrally placed for the Erne Loughs, Marble Arch Caves, Flo-rencecourt House and Castlecoole.

Open all year
6 bedrooms (3 twin; 1 double; 2 family ens. ♨/WC), 3🛏, 4WCs.
♿ 🐾 NITB Farm Guesthouse
Prices: B&B £13–13.50, weekly £91–94. EM £6–8, weekly &B plus EM £125–130.

Tullyhona Farm Guest House, Marble Arch Caves Road, Florencecourt
© (036582) 452   Mrs Rosemary Armstrong

Your comfort and enjoyment are assured with the award-winning hospitality of Tullyhona Farm. Mrs Armstrong's home cooking offers a choice of menus with flexible meal times and snacks where preferred. Special diets catered for. This is a beef and sheep farm, calving tours are offered in sea-son and pony trekking. Children are welcomed with games, playhouse, trampoline and climbing frame. Cot and highchair provided. The guest house is 400 yds from Florencecourt (NT), off the A32 southwest of Enniskillen, and just over a mile from the Marble Arch Show Caves. Central for fishing, golf, boating, watersports and hill climbing.

Open all year
7 bedrooms (2 twin; 2 double inc. 1 ens. ⋔/WC; 3 family ens. ⋔/WC), 2🐎, 2WCs.
♿ 🏠 NITB Grade A
Prices: B&B £14–16, weekly £98–105. EM a la carte. 🏠 rates.

CO. LONDONDERRY

COLERAINE   Map 10 C1

Ballylagan House, 31, Ballylagan Road, Coleraine BT52 2PQ
✆ (0265) 822487

Ballylagan House is a comfortably furnished traditional farmhouse on a working dairy farm. You can enjoy true country hospitality in a homely atmosphere, with delicious home baking. A bedtime supper is provided at no extra cost. Packed lunches available on request. Children's needs are well met with outdoor swing, slide, tractor and trailor, bicycles and a large play yard, plus cot and highchair. The farm is located 2 miles from Portrush, a mile off the B17 Coleraine-Bushmills road. Central for touring, within an easy distance are Giants Causeway, Bushmills Distillery and the attractive Antrim coast.

Closed Xmas and New Year
3 bedrooms (1 double; 2 family), 1🐎, 1WC.
🏠 ✄
Prices: B&B £10–12.50. 🏠 rates.

Heathfield, 31, Drumcroon Road, Garvagh
✆ (02665) 58245   Mrs Heather Torrens

You will receive a warm welcome at this charming old 17th-century farmhouse on a working mixed farm. Located on the A29 Garvagh-Coleraine road, Heathfield is an ideal base for touring the area. Giants Causeway, Bushmills Distillery and the Antrim coast road 20 miles. Championship golf course 12 miles. Pony trekking 4 miles.

Open all year
4 bedrooms (1 twin; 1 double; 1 single; 1 family), 1🐎, 2WCs.
Prices: B&B £13.50–15.

See STOP PRESS
for more farms

Killeague Farm House, 156 Drumcroon Road, Blackhill, Coleraine
✆ (0265) 868229   Mrs Margaret Moore

Our motto is good food, fun and fellowship. Our 3-storey Georgian farmhouse, built in 1783, stands on the A29 midway between Coleraine and Garvagh, surrounded by a 130-acre dairy farm. Stabling if required, with an outdoor arena and riding instruction by arrangement. Forest parks all around provide delightful country walks, and you can fish in the river on the farm. Cot, highchair and children's games available. Golf nearby. Jet adventure area 4 miles. Giants Causeway, beaches and waterskiing 10 miles.

Open all year
4 bedrooms (2 double; 1 family ens. ⋔/WC; 1 single), 2🐎, 3WCs.
🏠
Prices: B&B £14–15, weekly £95. EM £8. Weekly B&B plus EM £150. 🏠 rates.

Tullans Farm, 46 Newmills Road, Coleraine BT52 2JB
✆ (0265) 42309

A comfortable and cosy farmhouse on a working sheep and cattle farm. Visitors are welcome to explore the farm. Prize-winning baking a speciality. Supper, packed lunches and afternoon teas provided. Cot, highchair and games available. The farm is a mile east of Coleraine. Fishing, swimming, skating, bowling, horseriding, tennis, birdwatching all within 2 miles.

Open all year
3 bedrooms (2 double ens. ⋔/WC; 1 family), 1🐎, 1WC.
🏠NITB Approved Farmhouse
Prices: B&B £12, weekly £79. 🏠 rates.

LONDONDERRY   Map 10 C1

Tully Farm, 109 Victoria Road, Newbuildings, Londonderry BT47 2RN
✆ (0504) 42832

This warm and comfortable farmhouse lies on a sheep and cattle farm, 4 miles from the historic walled city of Londonderry, off A5 Strabane road. Golf course 2 miles. Fishing 5 miles.

Open all year
5 bedrooms (2 twin; 1 double; 1 family ens.⋒/WC; 1 single), 1🛏, 1WC.
⚶ NITB Approved Farmhouse
Prices: B&B £11.50, ⚶ rates.

CO. TYRONE

DUNGANNON Map 10 C2

Cohannon, 225 Ballynakelly Road, Dungannon BT71 6HJ
✆ (08687) 23156 M.J. Currie

A warm welcome awaits you at this comfortable farm bungalow with open fires, a friendly atmosphere and good quality home produced food. This is a small arable farm, grazing and horticulture, and a splendid sight in May amid the apple blossom. The farm is situated off the A45 by M1, Jct 14. Argory (NT) 2 miles. Peatlands Park, open bog area rich in wildlife, 3 miles. Ardress House (NT) and Tyrone Crystal Factory 4 miles.

Open all year
2 bedrooms (1 twin; 1 double), 1🛏, 1WC.

⚶ ✄
Prices: B&B £11.50, EM £5–6. ⚶ rates.

OMAGH Map 10 B/C2

Greenmount Lodge, 58, Greenmount Road, Omagh BT79 0YE
✆ (0662) 841325

Greenmount Lodge, a modern country house on an early 18th-century estate, is approached by a tree-lined avenue in mature and peaceful woodland. The 1780 courtyard remains intact and the new house offers luxurious accommodation. One twin room has full facilities for wheelchair users. is The Lodge has a reputation for superb food. Game shooting available on the estate. Situated 6 miles south of Omagh (A5/B84), there is a choice of local golf courses. Ideal base for touring the Sperrins, Ulster-American Folk Park (8 miles), Clogher Valley (7 miles) and Fermanagh Lakeland.

Open all year
8 bedrooms (4 twin ens.⋒/WC; 2 double ens.⋒/WC; 2 family ens.⋒/WC), 1🛏, 3WCs.
⚿ ⚶ NITB Grade A
Prices: B&B £14.50–15.50. EM £8–12.50. ⚶ rates.

REPUBLIC OF IRELAND

CO. CARLOW

BALLON   Map 10 C3

Sherwood Park House, Kilbride, Ballon
✆ (0503) 59117   M.& P. Owens

Enjoy timeless elegance and a warm welcome from your hosts and their young family. This early Georgian house is on a 100-acre mixed farm set in rolling parklands and tranquil countryside. Open fires, romantic bedrooms, all meals provided from local and home-grown produce. Guests may bring their own wine for dinner. Games room with pool table, sega, swings plus cot and highchair supplied. The farm is 8 km south of Tullow, signed from Jct N80/N81.

Open all year
4 bedrooms (2 double; 2 family inc. 1 ens.🛁/🚿/WC), 2🛏, 2WCs.
🐾 Bord Failte Farmhouse
Prices: B&B £16–20, weekly £100–125. EM £15, weekly B&B plus EM £200–225. 🐾 rates.

KEY TO SYMBOLS	
Bath	🚿
Shower	🛁
Bathroom	🛁
Disabled Guest Facilities	♿
No Smoking	🚭
Children Welcome	🐾
Dogs by Arrangement	🐕

CAVAN

BELTURBET   Map 10 B2

Hilltop Farm, Belturbet
✆ (049) 22114   Elizabeth B. Dunne

This farmhouse is set on a working dairy farm 5 km from Belturbet. In the local area you can go fishing, boating, cruising and play golf. Packed lunches and afternoon teas provided on request. Ground floor bedrooms, cot and highchair available.

Open all year
10 bedrooms (1 twin; 1 double; 8 family inc. 6 ens. 🛁/WC, 1 ens. 🚿/WC), 3🛏, 5WCs.
🐾 🐕 Bord Failte Farmhouse
Prices: B&B £12–14, weekly £77–112. EM £10–12, weekly B&B plus EM £150–185.

COOTEHILL   Map 10 B2

Riverside Farm Guesthouse, Cootehill
✆ /Fax (049) 52150   Joe & Una Smith

This large farm guesthouse provides packed lunches and evening meals on request. Cot, highchair. games and playroom available for children. The guesthouse is 2 km southwest of Cootehill off the Cavan road. Cavan 24 km.

Open all year
6 bedrooms (2 twin; 2 double inc. 1 ens.🛁/WC; 2 family inc. 1 ens.🚿/EC), 5🛏.
🐾 Bord Failte Farmhouse
Prices: B&B £13–15, weekly £84. EM £12, weekly B&B plus EM £165. 🐾 rates.

Self-Catering

BELTURBET
Map 10 B2

Hilltop Farm, Belturbet
✆ (049) 22114   Elizabeth B. Dunne

Detailed farm description, p. 232. Accommodation is also offered for self-catering in a 2-bedroomed unit, sleeps 2.

Open all year
Prices: weekly £180.

CO. CLARE

BALLYVAUGHAN
Map 10 B3

Rocky View Farmhouse, Coast Road, Fanore, Ballyvaughan
✆ (065) 76103

A comfortable modern bungalow style house on the coast overlooking Aran Islands where guests are welcomed with tea or coffee on arrival. The farm rears a suckling herd and is an ideal spot for a quiet relaxing holiday. Packed lunches and evening meals on request. Rocky View is on the coast road by Blackhead on Galway Bay, 13 km from Ballyvaughan. Rock-climbing, water-skiing, sea angling, rock fishing, horse riding, all within 12 km.

Open 21 April-Oct.
5 bedrooms all ens. ⌂/WC (2 twin; 2 double; 1 family), 1WC.
⌂(10) ✂
Prices: B&B £13, weekly £89. ⌂ rates.

DOOLIN
Map 10 A3

Horseshoe Farmhouse, Fisher Street, Doolin
✆ (065) 74006   Moloney Family
Fax (O65) 74421

This spacious bungalow is set on a dairy farm overlooking Doolin, a village famous for traditional Irish music. Well equipped rooms, cot available. Licensed. Tennis court. The farm lies west of N67 Ennistymon-Ballyvaughan road.

Good base for touring the Burren and Cliffs of Moher. Pony trekking and cycle hire locally.

Open all year
5 bedrooms all ens.⌂/WC (3 twin; 2 double), 2WCs. ⌂
Prices: B&B £14–16.

KILRUSH
Map 10 A3

Fortfield Farm, Donail, Killimer, Kilrush
✆ (065) 51457   S.& B. Cunningham

In an agricultural area overlooking the River Shannon, this spacious modern residence is off the N67 ferry road south of Kilrush. Fortfield is a working farm with dairy and beef cattle, and an agricultural zoo. Cot and children's games available. High tea as well as evening meals offered. Golf, fishing, seaside and music locally. Killimer car ferry 2 km. Kilrush Creek marina 6 km.

Open April-Nov.
5 bedrooms (1 twin; 2 double; 2 family ens.⌂/WC), 2➡.
⌂ ⛏
Prices: B&B £12.75, EM 10.50, high tea £7.50. ⌂ rates.

MOUNTSHANNON
Map 10 B3

Derg Lodge, Mountshannon
✆ (0619) 27180   Colette Waterstone

With beautiful scenic views on all sides this 27-acre farm with dry stock is situated near Lough Derg. The modern bungalow of Derg Lodge is just outside Mountshannon village on the R352 Ennis-Portunna road. Ideally located for anglers with stocks of pike, trout, perch, bream, rudd and tench. Afternoon tea and packed lunches provided. Cot available. On Holy Island, a short distance from the harbour, stands a 7th-century monastic settlement and round tower.

Open all year
4 bedrooms (1 twin; 2 double; 1 family), 1➡, 1⌂/WC.
⌂ ⛏
Prices: B&B £12–15.⌂ rates.

CO. CORK

BANTRY   Map 10 A4

O'Mahony's Farmhouse Accommodation, Lisheens, Kealkill, Bantry
✆ (027) 66041   Mrs Chrissie O'Mahony

A warm welcome is assured at O'Mahony's large and comfortable two-storey farmhouse, on the T65 Ballylickey-Kealkill road, north of Bantry. Ground floor accommodation, cot, highchair and children's games provided. Full board is available including packed lunches and afternoon teas. You can relax in the garden or watch the workings of the dairy farm. The lakes and rivers in this scenic area provide good fishing and boating nearby. Golf and horse riding also available locally.

Open May-Sept.
3 family bedrooms, 2➥, 2WCs.
&. ♨
Prices: B&B £12, weekly £80. EM £6–10. Weekly B&B plus EM £120–150. ♨ rates.

BLARNEY   Map 10 B4

Birch Hill House, Grenagh, Blarney
✆ (021) 886106   Dawson Family

A Victorian family home on a dairy and cattle farm. The house overlooks mature trees and a river. Inside log fires and home baking add to your comfort. Evening meals available. Cot and highchair can be supplied. The farm is 6 km north of Blarney, via Waterloo. Fishing, horse riding and golf nearby. Convenient for car ferry and airport. Blarney Woodland Farm 5 km.

Open Apr-Oct.
6 bedrooms (2 twin; 2 double; 2 family), 2➥, 2WCs.
♨ 🜓
Prices: B&B £13, dinner £11, high tea £8. Weekly B&B plus dinner £165. ♨ rates.

Garrycloyne Lodge, Garrycloyne, Blarney
✆ (021) 886214   Mrs Catherine Hallissey

A comfortable and attractive farmhouse situated 5 km from Blarney (R617), this dairy farm has sheep and cattle on 160 acres. Spacious mature gardens include a play area for children. The farmhouse is suitable for the disabled, all bedrooms ground floor, and children's equipment available. There are log fires and good

home baking, including a packed lunch if required. Blarney Castle and Woollen Mills to visit locally. Cork 10 km. Fota Wildlife Park 12 km.

Open April-Nov.
4 bedrooms (1 double ens.🜓/WC; 3 family ens.🜓/WC), 1➥, 1WC.
&. ♨ ⤨ 🜓 Board Failte Approved
Prices: B&B £13, weekly £88. EM £12. Weekly B&B plus EM £165. ♨ rates.

CLONAKILTY   Map 10 A4

An Garran Coir, Castlefreke, Clonakilty
✆ (023) 48236

Set in a peaceful picturesque valley this split level farmhouse is found off the N71 at Clonakilty. Located on the scenic west Cork coastline the working dairy farm offers landscaped gardens, animals, pony rides and mapped walks of local forest, cliffs and bird sanctuary. Renowned cuisine with seafood, cream teas and packed lunch available. Full children's facilities provided. Irish music evenings for groups by arrangement. Sandy beaches, golf, pitch and putt, surfing, yachting and other watersports all within a short distance from the farmhouse. Stone Circle 8 km.

Open all year
10 bedrooms (3 twin inc. 1 ens.🜓/WC; 5 double inc. 2 ens.🜓/WC; 2 family inc. 1 ens.🜓/WC), 2➥, 2WCs.
&. ♨ 🜓
Prices: B&B £11–12.50, weekly £75–88. EM £8–11. Weekly £120–145. ♨ rates.

Ard Na Greine, Ballinascarty, Clonakilty
© (023) 39104   Norma Walsh

At this warm modern farmhouse near Ballinascarty village (N71 north of Clonakilty) the emphasis is strongly on Norma Walsh's delicious home cooking and baking with wholesome fresh food. A 5-course dinner or a la carte menu is offered, also packed lunches and afternoon teas. Winner of the Galtee Breakfast Award, Agri-Tourism Award and the BHS Area Award, this farmhouse comes highly recommended. It is an excellent base for touring the area's many attractions: Blarney Castle, Bantry, Glengarriff, Glandore, Gougane Barra and a choice of sandy beaches.

Open all year
6 bedrooms (3 twin inc. 2 ens.🛁/WC; 1 double; 2 family ens.🛁/WC), 2🐂.
🐴 🐕
Prices: B&B £13–15, weekly £91–105. EM £13. Weekly B&B plus EM £182–189. 🐴 rates.

Liscubba House, Rossmore, Clonakilty
© (023) 38679   Mrs Phyl Beechinor

This old style farmhouse is on a 130-acre beef and silage farm, situated 14 km from Bandon (signposted on the N71 and R588). Mrs Beechinor provides good country cooking using fresh farm produce, with packed lunches and afternoon teas on request. For relaxation you can stroll in the landscaped garden or curl up with a book before a roaring log fire. Cot, highchair and well equipped playground available. Convenient for beaches, Rossmore Castle 2 km, Ballynacarriga Castle 6 km.

Open all year
6 bedrooms (1 twin; 2 double; 2 family; 1 single), 2🐂, 4WCs.
🐴 🐕
Prices: B&B £12.75, weekly £87.50. EM £11, high tea £7.50. Weekly B&B plus EM £165. 🐴 rates.

GLANDORE   Map 10 A4
Kilfinnan Farm, Glandore
© (028) 33233   Mehigan Family

The large modernised farmhouse overlooks Glandore Harbour. Glandore is on the R597, off the N71 Skinnereen-Clonakilty road. An ideal location for fishing, country walks and water sports, with sandy beaches and Drombeg Stone Circle close by. This mainly dairy farm also produces its own meat, eggs, fruit and vegetables to provide guests with partial board including optional packed lunches, afternoon teas and high teas. Cot, highchair and playroom available.

Open all year
4 bedrooms (1 twin; 2 double inc. 1 ens.🛁/WC; 1 family ens.🛁/WC), 2🐂, 2WCs.
🐴 Board Failte Approved
Prices: B&B £12.75–15, EM £12, high tea £6. 🐴 rates.

INNISHANNON   Map 10 B4
Ballymountain House, Innishannon
© (021) 775366   Tim & Sheila Cummins

The 200-year-old country house is on a cattle and sheep farm, off the N71 midway between Cork and Clonakilty, 3 km from Bandon. Home cooking is a speciality, with full breakfasts and a 5-course dinner served. Cot available. Ballymountain House is ideally placed for touring Co. Cork and the south coast. Kinsale and south coast beaches 16 km. Cork 25 km.

Open March-mid Nov.
8 bedrooms (4 twin; 2 double; 2 family), 3🐂, 3WCs.
🐴 🐕
Prices: B&B £13, weekly £85. EM £11.50. Weekly B&B plus EM £165. 🐴 rates.

YOUGHAL   Map 10 B4
Ballymakeigh House, Killeagh, Youghal
© (024) 95184   Browne Family

A delightful 250-year-old farmhouse set in tranquil surroundings, Ballymakeigh House is found off the N25 Youghal-Midleton road. Here you will discover excellent cuisine imaginatively served using home grown produce by the winner of the Housewife of the Year Award 1990, and the Agritourism Award 1992. The dairy farm has a full size tennis court and a games room, three golf courses are within 20 km. Cot, highchair and playroom available. Fota Wildlife Park 20 km.

Open Feb-Oct.
6 family bedrooms ens.☞/WC).
꿈 ♙
Prices: B&B £17.50, weekly £119. EM £15. Weekly £217. ꙮ rates.

Cuilin Farm, Shanacoole, Kinsalebeg, Youghal
© (024) 92537   Mrs M. Collender

This 200-year-old farmhouse has all modern conveniences and stands in beautiful countryside overlooking Youghal Bay. Cuilin Farm is on N25, under 6 km north of Youghal. The mixed farm has some cows, a donkey and poultry. Packed lunches and afternoon teas on request.

Open Apr-Oct.
6 bedrooms (1 twin; 2 double; 1 family ens. ꙮ/☞/WC; 1 triple), 2♙, 2WCs.
ꙮ Bord Failte Farmhouse
Prices: B&B £13, EM £11.

CO. DONEGAL
DOWNINGS   Map 10 B1
An Crosseg, Downings, Letterkenny
© (074) 55498   Marrietta Herraghty

Relax and enjoy your stay in this quiet farmhouse, set on a mixed farm overlooking Sheephaven Bay, against a backdrop of rugged hills and woods. Evening meals include locally caught fish. Situated just off the Atlantic Drive Scenic Route, the farm is 1 km from Downings on the

Rosguill Peninsula, 30 km north of Letterkenny (R245). Blue flag beach, golf, sea angling and horse riding 1 km.

Open May-Oct.
4 bedrooms (2 family; 2 double inc. 1 ens. ꙮ/WC), 2♙, 2WC.
ꙮ Bord Failte Approved
Prices: B&B £13–14, weekly £80. EM £11, weekly B&B plus EM £155. ꙮ rates.

GLENTIES   Map 10 B1
Oakdale, Derries, Glenties
© (075) 51262   Mrs Teresa O'Donnell

This modernised farmhouse is situated in a scenic area 3km from Glenties village, 26 km northwest of Donegal on the N56. Good home baking, with fresh farm eggs, is provided and a warm turf fire in the TV lounge. The farmhouse is suitable for disabled guests, with ramp entrance for wheelchairs. There is local fishing and attractive country walks. Ardara Caves 6 km. Portnoo beach 12km.

Open Mar-Oct.
4 bedrooms (2 twin ens.ꙮ/WC. 2 double inc. 1 ens.ꙮ), 1♙, 2WCs.
♿ ♙ Board Failte Approved
Prices: B&B £13, EM £11.50. Weekly B&B plus EM £165–170.

LIFFORD   Map 10 B1
The Hall Greene, Porthall, Lifford
© (074) 41318   Mervyn & Jean McKean

The 16th-century farmhouse, complete with antique furnishings, overlooks the River Foyle and the Sperrin Mountains with an uninterrupted

view for miles. Hall Greene is signposted 3 km from Lifford (N14). This working farm has beef, sheep, pigs and tillage. Guests are welcome to participate. Children will enjoy the donkey, pet goats, lambs and antique tractor rides. Cot and highchair available. Full board is offered including afternoon teas and packed lunches. Beltony Stone Circle 11 km. Greenan ancient stone fort and Derry Railway Museum 19 km. Fishing, golf, driving range and pitch and putt nearby.

Open all year
4 bedrooms (1 double; 3 family inc. 1 ens.🛁/WC), 1🛏, 2WCs.
🛇 Board Failte Approved
Prices: B&B £13, weekly £85. EM £11. Weekly B&B plus EM £165. 🛇 rates.

The Haw Lodge, The Haw, Lifford
☎ (074) 41397   Eileen Patterson

A very pretty traditional farmhouse set on a 50-acre beef farm, 2 km southwest of Lifford on N15 Lifford-Sligo road. Good salmon and trout fishing in River Finn that flows through farm. Some bedrooms ground floor. Packed lunches, cot and highchair on request. Within 3 km, golf (2 and 18 hole, pitch and putt, driving range), swimming pool, greyhound racing.

Closed Xmas
4 bedrooms (1 twin ens. 🛁; 1 double; 2 family ens. 🛁/WC), 1🛏, 2WCs.
🛇 🐦 Bord Failte Approved
Prices: B&B £12–13.50, weekly £75–85. High Tea £7, Dinner £10. Weekly B&B plus dinner £140–150. 🛇 rates.

PORTSALON   Map 10 B1
Avalon, Tamney, Fanad Peninsula via Letterkenny
☎ (074) 59031   Mrs Maureen Borland

This very comfortable, traditional style 2-storey farmhouse is a Home Baking winner. Packed lunches, afternoon teas and evening meals are all available. Cot, highchair and games provided. The farm with grazing land is 30 km north of Letterkenny on the Fanad Peninsula west of Portsalon. Beach and golf 5 km.

Open Apr-Nov.
4 bedrooms (1 twin; 1 double; 1 single; 1 family ens. 🛁/WC), 1🛏, 2WCs.
🛇 ✂
Prices: B&B £11.50–13.50, weekly £75. High Tea £7.50, dinner £10. Weekly B&B plus dinner £145.🛇 rates.

Swilly View Farmhouse, Portsalon, Kerrykeel PO
☎ (074) 59119

The farmhouse is situated 5 km south of Portsalon (32 km north of Letterkenny) by Lough Swilly. Ideally placed for touring the peninsula. Sandy beaches, golf, fishing and pitch and putt are all nearby. Primarily this is a dairy and sheep farm, but there are also ponies. Afternoon teas are provided if required. Cot available.

Open Feb-Oct.
4 twin bedrooms, 1🛏,1🛁, 2WCs. 🛇
Prices: B&B £12.75, EM £10. 🛇 rates.

RAMELTON   Map 10 B1
Gleann Oir Farmhouse, Ards, Ramelton
☎ (074) 51187   Rosemary Crawford

This modern bungalow is on an elevated site overlooking the River Lennon, 3 km west of Ramelton, north of Letterkenny (R245/249). The mixed farm has cattle, sheep and tillage. Visitors are welcome to join in with the milking, and feeding calves and lambs. Excellent salmon and trout river borders the farm. Good home cooking includes lunch and afternoon tea. Ground floor bedrooms, cot and highchair available.

Open Mar-Oct.
4 bedrooms (1 twin ens.🛁/WC; 1 double ens.🛇/WC; 2 family ens.🛁/WC), 1🛏, 2WCs.
♿ 🛇 🐦
Prices: B&B £13, weekly £90. EM £11. Weekly B&B plus EM £165. 🛇 rates.

CO. DUBLIN
SKERRIES   Map 10 C2
Woodview Farmhouse, Margaretston, Skerries
☎ (01) 491528   Mary Clinton

Enjoy warm hospitality and good home cooking at this comfortable farmhouse situated just 4 km from the seaside town of Skerries (N1). Packed lunches provided on request. Ground floor bedrooms, cot and highchair available. Ardgillan Park is within walking distance. Newgrange, ancient burial grounds 20 km. Convenient for Dublin airport and ferry points.

Open all year
6 bedrooms (2 twin inc. 1 ens. ⋔/WC; 2 double inc. 1 ens. ⋔/WC; 2 family ens. ⋔/WC), 3🛏,
3WCs.
🚱 ⚘ ✝
Prices: B&B £12–14, weekly £80. EM £9–11. Weekly B&B plus EM £140. ⚘ rates.

CO. GALWAY

CONG
Map 10 A2

Leckavrea View House, Maam Valley
℗ (092) 48040   Mrs B. Gavin

This large farmhouse stands on the northern shores of Lough Corrie on a mixed farm. The farm is 4 km east of Maam on the Maam-Cong road L101, and overlooks Castle Kirk (Grace O'Malley's Castle). Boats and gillies for hire, cruises to castle, hill walking, painting, pitch and putt all available locally. The farmhouse offers all meals; cot, highchair, playroom and games available for children.

Open all year
6 bedrooms all ens. ⋔/WC (1 double; 4 family; 1 single), 1🛏, 3WCs.
⚘ ✝ Bord Failte Farmhouse
Prices: B&B £14, EM £14. Weekly B&B plus EM £165. ⚘ rates

HEADFORD
Map 10 A2

Balrickard Farm, Galway Road, Headford
℗ (093) 35421   James & Margaret McDonagh

This Gothic style farm residence, part of which is 300 years old, now operates as a guest house. It is surrounded by a mixed farm of 60 acres with beef, suckling cow, sheep and two beehives. The honey is for family and guest use only. Balrickard Farm is on the N84 Headford-Galway road, 1 km from Headford. Local attractions include a par 3 golf course opposite the house, riding school, river fishing and Ross Abbey, 15th-century monastic ruins.

Open Mar-Nov.
3 bedrooms (1 twin; 1 double; 1 family), 2🛏, 1⋔,
2WCs.
⚘ ✝
Prices: B&B £12–13, EM £12. ⚘ rates.

Corrib View Farm, Annaghdown
℗ (091) 91114   The Scott Family

This charming 100-year-old farmhouse is set on a beef and sheep farm near Lough Corrib, 3 km off N84 Galway-Headford road south of Headford. Agri-Tourism Award winners 1992, this is an ideal base for touring Connemara and Clifden. Galway

City 15 km. Annaghdown Pier and St Brendan's Monastery ruins 3 km. Nature walks near farm.

Open Easter-mid Sept.
5 bedrooms (2 double; 2 family inc. 1 ens. ⋔/WC; 1 single), 1🛏, 1⋔, 2WCs.
⚘ Bord Failte Farmhouse
Prices: B&B £14.50–16.50, EM £15. ⚘ rates.

LEENANE
Map 10 A2

Glen Valley House and Stables, Glencroff, Leenane
℗ (095) 42269   Josephine O'Neill

This comfortable farmhouse is set in a peaceful valley, surrounded by mountains with sea nearby. The farm rears sheep, cattle and Conemara ponies. Pony trekking from farm daily. Dinner available, cot and highchair provided. The farm is off the N59 Clifden-Westport road. Ashleigh Waterfall 10 km.

Open Easter-Sept.
4 bedrooms (2 twin; 1 double ens. ⋔/WC; 1 family ens.🖉/WC), 2🛏, 2WCs.
⚘ Bord Failte Listed
Prices: B&B £12, weekly £80. EM £13, weekly B&B plus EM £150. ⚘ rates.

ORANMORE
Map 10 B3

Hazelwood House, Creganna, Oranmore
℗ (091) 94275   Patricia Kavanagh
FAX (091) 94608

Hazelwood House is a charming old style residence in a secluded wooded area 1 km off the N18 Limerick-Galway road, signposted midway between Oranmore and Clarenbridge. Centrally heated and log fires in the entrance hall and

drawing room. International reputation for good food. Dinner bookings by noon. Wine licence. Some horses are kept on the farm which is small and mainly woodland. 18 hole golf links, sailing and horse riding all 5 mins. Galway city 15 mins. Winter breaks a speciality, golfing, foxhunting or just a quiet holiday. Groups by arrangement.

Jan-Nov
6 bedrooms (1 twin; 3 double inc. 2 ens. ⌂/WC; 2 family inc. 1 ens.⌂/WC), 1➡, 1WC.
Prices: B&B IR£13–15, weekly IR£90–100. EM IR£15.

OUGHTERARD   Map 10 A2

Cashel Rock Farmhouse, Raha, Oughterard
✆ (091) 80213   Mrs Sheila Walsh

This comfortable farmhouse is set on a beef and sheep farm overlooking Lough Corrib and an 18-hole golf course. Situated 2 km off N59, 6 km from Oughterard village. There are mountain walks on the farm. Corrib cruises, fishing, riding, tennis and swimming pool, 15th-century castles 2 km. Packed lunches and 4 course evening meals available. Cot provided.

Open Easter-Oct.
7 bedrooms (2 double inc. 1 ens. ⌂/WC; 2 twin inc. 1 ens. ⌂/WC; 2 family ens.⌂/WC;1 single ens. WC).
☙ Bord Failte Approved
Prices: B&B £13–15, weekly £105. EM £12–15, weekly B&B plus EM £210. ☙ rates.

CO. KERRY

KILLARNEY   Map 10 A4

Glebe Farmhouse, (off) Tralee Road, Killarney
✆ (064) 32179   Mrs Betty O'Connor

You will find a friendly homely atmosphere in this modern two-storey farmhouse with views of the mountains, situated off the N22 Killarney-Tralee road, just over 5 km from Killarney. The farm has sheep and beef cattle, and a large collection of vintage farm machinery. Ground floor bedroom,

cot and babysitting available. Glebe makes a good base for touring: the Ring of Kerry route begins 5 km, and the Dingle Peninsula route 9 km, from the farmhouse.

Open April-mid Dec.
5 bedrooms (1 twin; 2 double inc.1 ens. ⌂/WC; 2 family inc. 1 ens.⌂/WC), 2➡, 3WC. ☙
Prices: B&B £10.75–11.75, weekly £74–84. EM £9.50. Weekly B&B plus EM £140. ☙ rates.

Islandmore House, Clonkeen, Killarney
✆ (064) 53009   Kathleen Spillane

This 60-acre dairy farm is located 15 km south of Killarney on the N22. The modern two-storey farmhouse offers comfortable accommodation, with fishing in the River Flesk and mountain climbing opportunities locally. Golf and boating in Killarney.

Open May-Oct.
4 bedrooms (1 twin ens.⌂/WC; 2 double inc. 1 ens.⌂/WC; 1 single), 1⌂, 2WCs.
☙ Board Failte Farmhouse
Prices: B&B £13, weekly £77. ☙ rates.

Lios Na Manach Farmhouse, off Mill road, Killarney

This quiet and secluded farm offers guests lunch, tea and an evening meal. Accessible from both N22 and N71,the farmhouse is 5 km southeast of Killarney. Muckross House and Gardens nearby.

Open 15 Jan-15 Dec.
6 bedrooms (1 double; 4 family inc. 1 ens.☞/ ⌂/WC, 1 ens. ⌂/WC; 1 single).
Prices: B&B £12.50–14, weekly £80. EM £11, weekly B&B plus EM £160. ☙ rates.

See STOP PRESS
for more farms

Lynch's Farm, Tralee Road, Kilcummin, Killarney
© (064) 31637   Kathleen Lynch

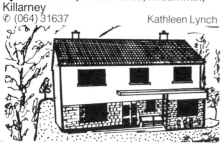

There are fine views of Killarney Lakes and mountains from the bedrooms of this modern farmhouse. You will receive a warm welcome at Lynch's dairy farm, and you are invited to watch the cows being milked. Evening meals are served at Xmas and in the quiet season. Highchair and children's games available.

Open all year
5 bedrooms all ens. ⋔/WC (2 twin; 2 double; 1 single), 3➤, 3WCs.
⚘ ☈
Prices: B&B £12.75–13.50. EM £10. ⚘ rates.

KILLORGLIN   Map 10 A3

Hillview Farm, Killorglin, Tralee Road, Milltown
© (066) 67117

This modern farm bungalow is on the main N70 between Killorglin and Milltown, overlooking the Slieve Mish Mountains and the hills of Kilderry. Hillview is a family run dairy and sheep farm with ducks, hens, pony, donkey, pet rabbits, fish, dogs and cats. Relax in a home from home atmosphere. Complimentary refreshments on arrival, packed lunches provided on request. Cot available. A central touring base for all the beauty spots of Kerry, west Cork and (via ferry) Clare. Fishing, scenic walks, mountain climbing and sandy beaches nearby. New golf course, designed by Eddie Hackett, within walking distance of the house. Kerry Airport 12 km.

Open 17 Mar-Oct.
6 bedrooms (1 twin ens. ⋔/WC; 2 double; 3 family inc. 2 ens. ⋔/WC), 2➤, 2WCs.
⚘ ☈
Prices: B&B £13–14, EM £12 (5 courses).
Weekly B&B plus EM £165. ⚘ rates.

VENTRY   Map 10 A3

Garvey's Farmhouse, Kilvicadownig, Ventry, Dingle
© (066) 59914

This traditional style house is set on a dairy and sheep farm less than 2 km from the beach. Dunkery Fort, Beehive Hut and many attractive walks by the farm, which is 11 km west of Dingle on the main Slea Head road after Ventry. Packed lunches, cot and highchair available on request.

Open Mar-Oct.
4 bedrooms (2 twin; 1 double ens. ⋔/WC; 1 family), 2➤, 2WCs.
⚘ Bord Failte Approved
Prices on application.

Moriarty's Farmhouse, Tigh-Iosagain, Rahinnane, Ventry, Dingle
© (066) 59037   Mrs Brid Moriarty

On the Dingle Peninsula, this spacious and comfortable farmhouse lies in peaceful surroundings with panoramic views of mountains and sea from every window. The farm covers 113 acres of grassland and mountain with mainly sheep and cattle. Full board with home produce is offered plus packed lunch and afternoon tea. Ground floor bedrooms, cot and playground available. Ventry is on the R559 5 km west of Dingle. Numerous local attractions and amenities include Norman Castle, Ventry beach (blue flag status), horse riding, bicycle hire from the farm, boat and sailboard hire, boat trips to Blasket Islands and, of course, Fungie the dolphin in Dingle harbour.

Mar-Oct.
6 bedrooms (3 double ens.🛁/WC; 3 family ens.🛁/WC).
🐕
Prices: B&B £13, EM £12.50. Weekly B&B plus EM £170. 🐕 rates.

CO. KILDARE

ATHY   Map 10 C3

Ballindrum Farm, Athy
☎ (0507) 26294   Mary & Vincent Gorman

A comfortable modern farmhouse on the rich grasslands of south County Kildare, 9 km north-east of Athy, turning off the N78 at the Norman Moat of Ardscull. The farm is mainly dairy and farm tours can be arranged. Lunch, tea and evening meals available, with home baking a speciality. Toys, cot and highchair for children. Kilkea Castle, Moone High Cross and golf course 6 km.

Open Apr-Oct.
4 bedrooms (1 twin; 1 double; 1 family; 1 single), 2🚿, 2WCs.
🐕 Bord Failte Approved
Prices: B&B IR£13, weekly IR£88. EM IR£11, weekly B&B plus EM IR£165.

CASTLEDERMOT   Map 10 C3

Kilkea Lodge Farm, Castledermot
☎ (0503) 45112

This 250-acre working tillage farm and riding centre lies in open rolling countryside. Full board is offered and the food is of a high calibre. Kilkea is situated on the R418 Athy road, less than 6 km from Castledermot. The forest provides attractive walks and there is a selection of excellent golf courses nearby. Irish National Stud 25 km.

Open Mar-mid Dec.
5 bedrooms (1 twin ens.🛁/WC; 2 double; 1

family ens.🛁/WC; 1 single), 1🚿, 3WCs.
🐕(12)
Prices: B&B £23-25, EM £12-18. 🐕 rates.

CO. KILKENNY

KILKENNY   Map 10 B3

Blanchville House, Dunbell, Maddoxtown
☎ (056) 27197   Tim & Monica Phelan

Blanchville is an elegant Georgian house in the centre of a working farm situated 8 km from the medieval city of Kilkenny, off the N10 Carlow-Kilkenny road. This is a family home where guests are offered home cooking with own produce and country hospitality in pleasant surroundings. Packed lunches provided on request. Cot and highchair available. Local amenities include golf, hunting, racing (Gowran Park), fishing (trout and salmon in River Nore), sandy beaches at Tranmore and Dunmore East. Riding schools locally, also children's pony on farm (tuition by arrangement).

Open Mar-Oct.
6 bedrooms (2 twin ens.🛁/WC; 2 double ens.🛁/WC; 2 family), 6🚿, 3WCs.
🐕 🐕
Prices: B&B £20-23, EM £16. 🐕 rates.

The Bungalow Farmhouse, Clomantagh, Woodsgift
☎ (056) 35215   Sean & Gretta Power

Set on a mixed sheep and cattle farm, this farmhouse offers lunch, tea and evening meals. Cot and highchair available. The farm is 5 km east of Urlingford (N8), on the Urlingford-Kilkenny road

KEY TO SYMBOLS	
Bath	🛁
Shower	🚿
Bathroom	
Disabled Guest Facilities	♿
No Smoking	🚭
Children Welcome	🐕
Dogs by Arrangement	🐕

(R693). Golf, swimming, hill walking and horse riding all locally. Nilcooly Abbey 6 km. Kilkenny City 19 km.

Closed Xmas
4 bedrooms (3 double inc. 1 ens. 🚿/WC; 1 single), 1🛁, WC. 👪
Prices: B&B £11.50–12.50, EM £8–10. 👪 rates.

NEW ROSS Map 10 C3

Garranavabby House, The Rower, Inistioge
✆ (051) 23613 Johanna Prendergast

This lovely old farm residence is part 17th-century, and lies in scenic surroundings between the Rivers Nore and Barrow, on the outskirts of The Rower, N79/T20/L18A north of New Ross. Home cooking and produce a speciality. Packed lunches available and evening meals if booked in advance. Fishing on both rivers, golf 9-hole at New Ross 7 km, 18-hole at Borris 15 km.

Open Apr-Sept.
3 bedrooms (1 twin; 1 double; 1 family), 2🛁, 3WCs.
👪 🐕 Bord Failte Farmhouse
Prices: B&B £15, weekly £100. Dinner £15, High Tea £11. 👪 rates.

THOMASTOWN Map 10 B3

Grove Farmhouse, Ballycocksuist, Inistioge, Thomastown
✆ (056) 58467 Nellie Cassin

Grove Farmhouse is a quiet and peaceful 200-year-old Georgian style house situated in the scenic countryside of the Arrigle Valley, to be found off the R700 Inistioge-Thomastown road. The house, with antique furnishings and log fires, has its own mature gardens and woodland areas, beyond which is the working beef, sheep and tillage farm. Packed lunches and afternoon teas served on request. Cot, games and children's playground available. Fishing locally. Golf 8 km. Jerpoint Abbey 10 km. Kilkenny city 25 km.

Open May-Sept.
4 bedrooms (1 twin; 2 double inc. 1 ens. 🚿/WC; 1 family), 1🛁, 3WC. 👪
Prices:B&B £12–14. EM £10. 👪 rates.

CO. LAOIS

DONAGHMORE Map 10 B3

Castletown House, Donaghmore
✆ (0505) 46415 Moira Phelan

Castletown House is an 1990 Award winning farm guesthouse, northeast of Roscrea (N7/L27). The early 19th-century residence is set in peaceful surroundings on a 200-acre beef and sheep farm. Fresh farm produce and home baking is offered. Tea served at night, packed lunches on request. One ground floor bedroom, cot, high-chair and children's games available. The house has a lovely view of the Slieve Bloom mountains. River Erkina and remains of a Norman castle on the farm. Golf, tennis, fishing and Irish music locally.

Open Mar-Nov or by arrangement
5 bedrooms (2 twin ens. 🚿/WC; 2 double ens. 🚿/WC; 1 family ens. 🚿/WC).
♿ 👪 🐕
Prices: B&B £12.75, weekly £88. EM £10.50, high tea £8. Weekly B&B plus EM £165. 👪 rates.

PORTLAOISE Map 10 B3

Park House, Stradbally, Portlaoise
✆ (0502) 25147 Mrs Bridget Cushen

Located a short way from Stradbally on the N80 Portlaoise road, this 250-year-old farmhouse stands on a tillage and dry stock farm. All fruit and vegetables are grown on the farm, and guests are welcome to assist in harvesting. Park House has a large mature garden for visitors use, a playroom for children with pool table, basketball and swingball. Free babysitting. Home cooked meals and pastries are provided, packed lunch if requested. Rock of Dunamaise within walking distance. Round tower in Timahoe and fishing 5 km. Emo Court Gardens 9 km. Ballyfin House and Slieve Bloom Mountains 11 km.

Open May-mid Oct.
3 bedrooms (2 double; 1 family), 1🛏, 2WCs. 🐾 ☈
Prices: B&B £12, weekly £80. EM £10. Weekly B&B plus 6EM £140. 🐾 rates.

CO. LEITRIM

BALLINAMORE   Map 10 B2

Riversdale Farmhouse, Ballinamore
© (078) 44122   Thomas Family

At Riversdale you can enjoy every luxury in a peaceful rural setting. The spacious residence includes an indoor heated swimming pool, sauna, squash court and games room. The cuisine is excellent, and packed lunches are provided if required. Ballinamore is south of Enniskillen (A32/R202) amid beautiful scenery of lakes and mountains. Golf (9 hole) 5 km. Horse riding 12 km. Lough Rynn House and Gardens 15 km. Forest Parks 20 and 30 km. Marble Arch Caves 32 km.

Open all year
6 bedrooms (1 twin; 4 family inc. 2 ens.🛁/WC; 1 single), 1🛏, 1🛁, 4WCs.
🐾(8) Board Failte Approved
Prices: B&B £15–19, weekly £90–105. EM £10. Weekly £148–160. 🐾 rates.

MANORHAMILTON   Map 10 B2

Drummonds Farmhouse, Glencar, Manorhamilton
© (072) 55197   Eileen McGowan

This comfortably modernised farmhouse is surrounded by 35 acres of farmland with beef cattle. Waterfalls and forest walks nearby. Packed lunches, 5 course dinners, cot and highchair available. The farm is 6 km east of Manorhamilton (N16), golf course 17 km.

Open Apr-Oct.
4 bedrooms (1 twin; 2 double; 1 family), 2🛏, 2WCs.
🐾 ☈ Bord Failte Listed
Prices: B&B £12, EM £11. 🐾 rates.

CO. LIMERICK

ADARE   Map 10 B3

Hollywood House, Adare, Croagh
© (061) 396237 Peter & Miriam O'Shaughnessy

This 300-year-old farmhouse is set in peaceful rural parkland surrounded by a natural game sanctuary. The rooms are spacious and beautifully furnished, log fires in the drawing room. Afternoon tea is served. Cot available. The house is 5 km from Adare (N20 south of Limerick) and signposted from the village hall. Clonshire Equestrian Centre 3 km, golf, fishing and archaeological sites 5 km.

Open Apr-Oct.
4 bedrooms (2 double priv.🛁/WC; 2 family priv.🚾/🛁/WC).
🐾 Bord Failte Approved
Prices: B&B £15. 🐾 rates.

CROOM   Map 10 B3

Bridge House Farm, Grange, Bruff
© (061) 390195   Mrs Patricia Barry

This 200-year-old farmhouse on a cattle and sheep farm offers guests good home cooking with organically grown vegetables. Packed lunches and afternoon teas available. The farm is by the Camogue River 14 km south of Limerick

City on the Limerick-Bruff road (R152), 6 km north of Bruff. Lough Gur nearby. Equestrian Centre 6 km, greyhound racing, golf and fishing 10 km.

Open Apr-Sept.
5 bedrooms (1 twin; 1 double ens.⌂; 1 family ens.⌂/WC; 2 single inc. 1 ens.⌂), 1🛏, 3WCs.
⚘ Bord Failte Approved
Prices: B&B £13, weekly £85. EM £11, weekly B&B plus EM £155. ⚘ rates.

Cronin Farmhouse, Ballymacamore, Croom
✆ (061) 397497　　　　Mrs Mary B. Cronin

Cronin Farmhouse is a modern bungalow on a beef and sheep farm in the heart of the Golden Vale, an unpolluted and unspoilt area with delightful scenery. The picturesque village of Adare is only 8 km from the farm. Situated off the L118 Croom-Ballingarry road, west of the N20, Cronin's is ideally placed for touring Cork, Kerry, Clare and Tipperary. Fishing and golf nearby. Lough Gur, Knockfierna and Bunratty Folk Park within easy reach. Mrs Cronin offers good home cooking, with packed lunches and afternoon teas on request. Ground floor bedrooms available, also cot and highchair.

Closed Xmas
3 bedrooms (1 treble; 2 family inc. 1 ens. ⌂/WC), 1🛏, 3WCs.
♿ ⚘ 🛏
Prices: B&B £13, weekly £85. EM £7. ⚘ rates.

KILMALLOCK　　　　Map 10 B3
Flemingstown House, Blackpool, Kilmallock
✆ (063) 98093

View cows being milked morning and evening at this 250-year-old farmhouse placed at the intersection of 3 counties. Wonderful views over green fields to the Galtee Mountains. Visitor lounge with tea/coffee facilities. Packed lunches available. The house is 3 km southeast of Kilmallock on R512 Limerick-Mitchelstown road. Ballyhoura Way 6 km.

Open all year
6 bedrooms (3 twin inc. 2 ens.⌂/WC;1 double ens.⌂/WC; 1 family ens.⌂/WC;1 single).
⚘ 🛏
Prices: B&B IR£15, weekly IR£100. Dinner IR£15, High Tea IR£10. ⚘ rates.

LIMERICK　　　　Map 10 B3
Millbank House, Murroe, Limerick
✆ (061) 386115

Millbank House is a 250-year-old Georgian farmhouse in a quiet and peaceful setting, 3 km off the N24 Limerick-Tipperary road. Children enjoy meeting the farm animals, goats and donkey. Cot and highchair available. Packed lunches supplied on request. The Mulcaire River flows through the farm providing trout and salmon fishing. An excellent choice for a truly relaxing break, within 10 mins drive are forest walks, pitch and putt, equestrian centre and greyhound racing. Limerick 18 km.

Open May-Sept.
5 bedrooms (1 twin; 1 double; 1 single; 2 family ens.⊟/WC), 3🛏, 2WCs.
🐕 🐓
Prices: B&B £13–15, EM £12.50. 🐑 rates.

TARBERT   Map 10 A3
Dillane's Farmhouse, Doonard, Listowel Road, Tarbert
✆ (068) 36242

This modern farmhouse is set on a 50-acre mixed farm which is all cattle and no tillage. The farm is just outside Tarbert on the N69 Limerick-Tralee road via Listowel. Tarbert House, Shannon car ferry 3 km. Glin Castle 6 km. Carrigfoyle Castle 8 km.

Open May-Oct.
5 bedrooms (1 twin ens.🛁/WC; 1 double; 3 family inc. 2 ens.🛁/WC), 1🛏.
🐑 Bord Failte Approved
Prices: B&B £12–15. 🐑 rates.

Self-Catering

CROOM   Map 10 B3
Cronin Farmhouse, Ballymacamore, Croom
✆ (061) 397497   Mrs Mary B. Cronin

For full farm description, see p. 244. Accommodation is also offered in the former farmhouse which stands in its own grounds in a scenic wooded area at the centre of the farm. The 5-bedroomed house sleeps 8–10. Ground floor bedrooms and bathroom suitable for wheelchair users.

Open all year
♿ 🐑 🐓
Prices: weekly £120–140.

See STOP PRESS
for more farms

CO. LONGFORD

GRANARD   Map 10 B2
Toberphelim House, Granard
✆ (043) 86568   Dan & Mary Smyth

This Georgian farmhouse with period furniture is set on a 200 acre family run cattle and sheep farm. For childen there are swings, climbing frame, highchair and playroom. The house is on the Castlepollard road 2 km from Granard, and makes a good base for exploring Longford and surrounds. Tullynally Castle, Lough Rynn Estate, Carraglass Manor all within 25 km. Coarse fishing 5 km.

Open May-Sept.
3 bedrooms (1 twin; 2 family ens.🛁/WC), 1🛏, 2WCs.
🐑 Bord Failte Approved
Prices: B&B £14–16, weekly £85–100. EM £8.🐑 rates.

CO. LOUTH

DROGHEDA   Map 10 C2
Tubbertoby, Termonfeckin, Drogheda
✆ (041) 22124   Mary Flanagan

This is a modern farmhouse furnished with antiques and possessing fascinating records of life on the site dating back to 1773. The farm has a pedigree herd of Holstein cows producing milk for the liquid milk and manufacturing market. Packed lunches and afternoon teas provided on request. The farm lies on the Clogherhead coast road northeast of Drogheda, just 10 mins walk from a safe sandy beach. Within 15 km are the Newgrange Burial Chambers (circa. 3000 BC), also Knowth, Monasterboice, Slane and the Hill of Tara.

Open June-Sept.
4 bedrooms (2 twin; 1 double; 1 family), 2🛏, 2WCs.
🐑 Board Failte Approved
Prices: B&B £13. 🐑 rates.

CO. MAYO

BALLINA
Map 10 A2

Garder Hill Farmhouse, Killala
℃ (096) 32331

This modern farmhouse is on a beef and sheep farm, with hens in enclosure. Packed lunches and afternoon teas available. Ground floor bedroom, ramp available, cot and highchair provided. The farm is just outside Killala, north of Ballina on R134. Sandy beaches 2 km. Ogham Stones 5 km, Moyne and Rossock Abbeys 3–6 km, River Moy (salmon) 11 km.

Open all year
5 bedrooms (1 twin; 2 double; 2 family), 4 ﬁ/WC, 1➥, 1WC.
⚘ Bord Failte Farmhouse
Prices: B&B £12.50–13.50, weekly £85–93. EM £10–12, weekly B&B plus EM £155–177. ⚘ rates.

Kilmurray House, Castlehill, Crossmolina
℃ (096) 31227
Joe & Madge Moffat

A large attractive house set on a 955-acre mixed farm. There is a tennis court, cot and highchair plus babysitting available. Packed lunches, afternoon teas and evening meals provided. Guests may bring their own wine. The farm is 5 km south of Crossmolina (N59 west of Ballina). Fishing, scenic tours and heritage centre nearby.

Open Apr-Oct.
6 bedrooms (1 twin; 1 double ens. ﬁ/WC; 3 family inc. 2 ens. ♨/WC, 1 ens ﬁ/WC; 1 single), 2➥, 2WCs.
⚘ Bord Failte Approved

Prices: B&B £12.50–13.50, weekly £90. EM £12, weekly B&B plus EM £150. ⚘ rates.

CLAREMORRIS
Map 10 B2

Valley Lodge, Facefield, Claremorris
℃ (094) 65180
Mrs Mary Barrett

This comfortable farmhouse is on a mixed farm with goats, donkey and poultry in a peaceful valley, signposted off N60 Claremorris-Balla road, 10 km from Claremorris, 7 km from Balla. Ideal touring centre for Westport, Achill Island, and Knock Shrine (10km). Ground floor bedrooms and cot available, packed lunches on request. Horse riding and golf 10 km.

Open April-Sept.
5 bedrooms (1 twin ens. ﬁ/WC; 3 double; 1 single ens. ﬁ/WC), 1➥, 2WCs.
⚘ Bord Failte Approved
Prices: B&B £11.75–12.75, EM £6–10.

LOUISBURGH
Map 10 A2

Cuaneen House, Carramore, Louisburgh
℃ (098) 66460
Mrs Teresa Sammon

This friendly family run farm is right by the sea with magnificent views across Clew Bay to the islands from all windows. There are a pony and donkey on the farm, and delicious home cooking to be enjoyed. Playroom with toys, cot and babysitting service available. The farm is off the T39 west of Westport, by a safe sandy beach. Ideal for touring Mayo and Connemara.

Open April-Oct.
5 bedrooms (2 twin; 2 double inc. 1 ens. ﬁ/WC; 1 single), 3➥, 4WCs. ⚘
Prices: B&B £13, EM £11. Weekly B&B plus EM £165. ⚘ rates.

WESTPORT
Map 10 A2

Seavilla Farmhouse, Lecanvey, Westport
℃ (098) 64803

This modern farmhouse under Croagh Patrick Mountain overlooks Clew Bay, many of the rooms have views of the sea and islands. This is a sheep farm, pure border collies are bred here and demonstrations given. Packed lunches and evening meals provided, and full Irish breakfasts. All rooms are ground floor, orthopaedic beds. A choice of beaches and mountain walks. Seavilla is 10 km west of Westport on Westport-Louisburgh coast road.

Open Apr-Nov.
6 bedrooms (4 twin inc. 3 ens. 🚿/WC; 2 double inc. 1 ens. 🚿), 1 🛁, 1WC.
👪 Bord Failte Approved
Prices: B&B £13–14, EM £11. 👪 rates.

Self-Catering

BALLINA — Map 10 A2

Kilmurray House, Castlehill, Crossmolina
✆ (096) 31227 — Joe & Madge Moffat

For full farm description, see p. 246. A self-catering bungalow is available, 4 bedrooms, sleeps 7.

Open Apr-Oct.
Bord Failte Approved
Prices: weekly £175–200.

WESTPORT — Map 10 A2

Seavilla Farmhouse, Lecanvey, Westport
✆ (098) 64803

For full farm description see B&B entry above. Self-catering is available in a well-equipped 2-bedroomed unit, sleeps 5–6.

Open Apr-Nov.
Prices: weekly £150.

CO. MEATH

DUNSHAUGHLIN — Map 10 C2

Gaulstown House, Dunshaughlin
✆ (01) 8259147

Regional winner of 1992 AIB Agri-Tourism awards, this early 19th-century farmhouse stands on a drystock farm overlooking a 27-hole golf course. Packed lunches on request. The farm is 3 km east of Dunshaughlin, off Ratoath road. Tara 9 km, Trim 22 km. Dublin 27 km.

Open Apr-Oct.
3 bedrooms (1 twin ens. 🚿; 1 double; 1 family ens. 🚿/WC), 1 🛁, 2WCs.
👪(10) 🚭 Bord Failte Farmhouse
Prices: B&B £15–17, weekly £100. EM £11, weekly B&B plus EM £175. 👪 rates.

KELLS — Map 10 C2

Deer Park Farm, Crossakiel, Kells
✆ (046) 43609 — Mrs Mary Rountree

This is an ideal spot for relaxing or using as a base for touring. The modern bungalow, set on a beef farm, is in an area rich in archaeological treasure on the rolling plains of Meath. The farm lies 11 km west of Kells on the Kells-Oldcastle road. Mrs Rountree provides good home cooking and a cot and games are available for children. Golf course 6 km. Newgrange 16 km. Hill of Tara 12 km. Trim 10 km.

Open May-Sept.
3 double bedrooms ens. 🚿/WC), 1 🛁, 1WC. 👪
Prices: B&B £18, EM £10. 👪 rates.

NAVAN — Map 10 C2

Balreask House, Navan
✆ (046) 21155 — Mrs Ellie McCormack

This modern farmhouse is set back from the road and is surrounded by a mixed drystock (cattle and sheep) farm. Balreask House is 4 km south of Navan off N3 at Old Bridge Inn. 13 km from Newgrange, the largest passage grave site in Europe, and ideal for exploring the Boyne Valley. Mellifont Abbey, Knowth, Tara, Bective Abbey, Slane and Dunsaney all within easy distance.

Open Apr-Oct.
4 bedrooms (1 twin; 1 double; 2 family), 2 🛁, 2WCs.
👪 Bord Failte Farmhouse
Prices: B&B £13, weekly £85.

CO. OFFALY

BIRR — Map 10 B3

Minnocks Farmhouse, Roscrea Road, Birr
✆ (0509) 20591

On this dairy farm visitors are welcome to take part in milking the cows and feeding the calves. Packed lunches and afternoon teas available. TV in all bedrooms. The farmhouse is suitable for the disabled with ground floor bedrooms and ramps.

KEY TO SYMBOLS

Bath	🛀
Shower	🚿
Bathroom	🛁
Disabled Guest Facilities	♿
No Smoking	🚭
Children Welcome	👪
Dogs by Arrangement	🐕

The farm is 3 km south of Birr (N62). Local attractions include Georgian town of Birr and Birr Castle and Gardens, Heritage Centre, nature trails. Slieve Bloom Mountains 10 km.

Open all year
7 bedrooms all ens.⋔/WC (1 twin; 1 double; 5 family).
& ⅏ ⊁ Bord Failte Farmhouse
Prices: B&B £14, weekly £98. Dinner £12, High Tea £11. Weekly B&B plus dinner £165. ⅏ rates.

CO. SLIGO

BALLYMOTE   Map 10 B2
Temple House, Ballymote
✆ (071) 83329   Mrs D. Perceval

Temple House is an elegant mansion situated in 1000 acres of farm and woodland overlooking a lake and Templar Castle. The present house was redesigned and refurnished in 1864. It retains its old atmosphere with turf and log fires and some canopied beds. Meals are thoughtfully prepared using produce from the walled garden. Wine license. Recommended in the Irish Food Guide. The farm, 2 km off the N7 Sligo-Charlestown road, has sheep, pigs and Kerry cattle. Coarse fishing is provided on the lake and boats for hire. Cot and highchair available.

Open April-Nov.
5 bedrooms (2 twin inc. 1 ens.⇗/WC, 1 priv.⋔/WC; 2 double inc. 1 ens.⇗/WC, 1 ens.⋔/WC; 1 single ens.⋔/WC). ⅏
Prices: B&B £30. EM £16. ⅏ rates.

CO. TIPPERARY

CASHEL   Map 10 B3
Ardmayle House, Cashel
✆ (0504) 42399   Annette V. Hunt
Fax (0504) 42420

This 200-acre dairy farm has been owned by the family since 1840, the farmhouse is 250 years old. Guests are welcome to explore the farm which has sheep and horses, and to fish for brown trout on a mile private stretch of River Suir. Packed lunches available, cot, highchair, swings

and games provided. Ardmayle House is 7 km north of Cashel, L185 via Ardmayle village. Rock of Cashel 6 km. Holy Cross and Athassel Abbeys 11 km.

Open Mar-Oct.
5 bedrooms (1 twin; 4 family inc. 2 ens. ⋔/WC), 2🛁, 2WCs.
⅏ ⊁ Bord Failte Farmhouse
Prices: B&B £13.50-14.50, weekly £90. EM £12, weekly B&B plus EM £165. ⅏ rates.

CLONMEL   Map 10 B3
Clover Hill Farm, Knocklofty, Clonmel
✆ (052) 38226   Mrs Patricia Conway

This modern bungalow farmhouse is set in a panoramic scenic location on a working beef and sheep farm. Home cooking is a speciality, packed lunches available on request. Salmon and trout fishing, mountain and forest walks locally. Pony trekking 5 km. Golf and historic castles 6 km. The farm is 5 km west of Clonmel via Knocklofty Bridge.

Open Apr-Oct.
4 bedrooms (1 twin; 1 single; 2 family inc. 1 ens. ⋔/WC), 1🛁, 2WCs.
⅏ Bord Failte Approved
Prices: B&B £13-15, EM £10.75. ⅏ rates.

TIPPERARY   Map 10 B3
Homeleigh Farmhouse, Ballinacourty, Glen of Aherlow
✆ (062) 56228

Homeleigh is a 50-acre dairy farm with some sheep in a beautiful position between the Galtee Mountains and Slievenamuck, off the N24 south of Tipperary. The modern bungalow is very comfortable with all bedrooms on the ground floor. Good country cooking with packed lunches and afternoon teas on request. The Galtee Mountains are ideal for walks. Putting green and tennis court on the farm. Trout fishing nearby, horse riding 5 km. Moore Abbey ruins 5 km. Rock of Cashel 25 km.

Open all year
5 bedrooms (2 twin ens.⋔/WC; 2 double; 1 single ens.⋔/WC), 2🛁, 2WCs.
& ⅏ ⊁
Prices: B&B £13.50-15.50, weekly £84. EM £12. Weekly B&B plus EM £147-161. ⅏ rates.

Planning a day out?
See RURAL ATTRACTIONS

CO. WATERFORD
CLONMEL   Map 10 B3
Nire Valley Farmhouse, Ballymacarbry
℗ (052) 36149   Mrs Mary Doocey

This award winning farmhouse lies 9 km south of Clonmel on the R671. It is set on a beef and sheep farm overlooking the scenic Nire Valley, an ideal location for touring the South. The dining room overlooks the patio and large mature gardens. Mrs Doocey provides excellent home cooking with 5-course dinners. Packed lunches provided on request. Trout fishing on the farm. Heritage Centre 6 km.

Open April-Sept.
5 bedrooms (2 twin; 1 double ens.⌂/WC;1 family ens.⌂/WC; 1 single), 2🛁, 3WCs. ♿ ⚲
Prices: B&B £12–14, weekly £84. EM £10. Weekly B&B plus EM £150. ⚲ rates.

DUNGARVAN   Map 10 B4
Ballyguiry Farm, Dungarvan
℗ (058) 41194   Mrs Kathleen Kiely

The farmhouse was built in 1833 and is part of a mixed farm situated south of Dungarvan off the N25. Children are particularly welcome with a pony to ride, playground and hard tennis court. Cot and highchair also provided. There are many scenic drives in this attractive region. 18 hole golf course adjacent to farm. A choice of uncrowded beaches, pitch-and-putt, 2 heated swimming pools and pony trekking nearby. Touraneena Heritage Centre 13 km.

Open April-Oct.
3 bedrooms (1 double ens.⌂/WC; 2 family ens.⌂/WC), 1🛁, 2WCs. ⚲ ⚲
Prices: B&B £13–15, weekly £91. EM £10. Weekly B&B plus EM £155. ⚲ rates.

The Castle Farm, Millstreet, Cappagh
℗ (058) 68049

An exciting place to stay, this farmhouse is in the restored wing of a 15th-century castle. It stands in a beautiful valley on a 120-acre dairy farm, signposted off the N72 Dungarvin-Cappoquin road. There is a wine licence. Packed lunches supplied on request. For children, a playroom, playground, swings, slide, pony rides and hard tennis court are available. Cot and highchair provided. Lismore Castle 12 km. Vee Drive 14 km. Cahir Castle 25 km.

Open Mar-Oct.
5 bedrooms (1 twin ens.⌂/WC; 2 double ens.⌂/WC;2 family ens.⌂/WC), 1🛁, 1WC. ⚲ ⚲
Prices: B&B £16, weekly £110. EM £11.50. Weekly B&B plus EM £170. ⚲ rates.

DUNMORE EAST   Map 10 B4
Elton Lodge, Rossduff, Dunmore East
℗ (051) 82117   E. Richardson

This 18th-century farmhouse is set in pleasant mature gardens on a dairy farm. Cot provided. The farm is 6 km from Dunmore East.

Open June-Sept.
5 bedrooms (2 twin ens.⌂/WC; 1 family ens.⌂/WC; 2 double inc. 1 ens.⌂/WC, 1 ens.⌂/WC).
⚲ ⚲ Bord Failte Farmhouse
Prices: B&B IR£14–15, weekly IR£155. ⚲ rates.

CO. WESTMEATH
CASTLEPOLLARD   Map 10 B2
Whitehall Farmhouse, Castlepollard
℗ (044) 61140   Abigail Smyth

An old style farmhouse set among the lakes of the Midlands makes an ideal base for touring, fishing, horse riding and golfing holidays. Packed lunches, afternoon teas, and evening meals available. Cot and games supplied. The farmhouse is 15 km north of Mullingar on R394, 5 km from Castlepollard.

Open Mar-Oct.
3 bedrooms (2 twin; 1 double), 2♨, 2WCs.
⌂ Bord Failte Approved
Prices: B&B £13, weekly £84–91. Dinner £10, EM £7.50. Weekly B&B plus dinner £154–161. ⌂ rates.

MOATE   Map 10 B2

Temple, Horseleap, Moate
✆ (0506) 35118   Declan & Bernadette Fagan

This is an award-winning Victorian farmhouse with a lovely garden amid the park-like setting of a beef cattle and sheep farm. Afternoon tea on arrival begins a relaxing, well looked after stay. The cooking is imaginative using fresh farm and garden produce. Licensed. There is a library and games room for guests use, and cycling can be arranged. The farm is to be found 1 km off the N6 Moate-Kilbeggan road, 6 km from Moate. Packed lunches supplied on request. Ground floor bedroom, cot and highchair available.

Open Mar-Oct.
4 bedrooms (2 double ens.⌂/WC: 2 family inc. 1 ens.⌂/WC,1 ens.⌂/WC). ⌂
Prices: B&B £18, weekly £105. EM £12. ⌂ rates.

MULLINGAR   Map 10 B2

Annascanan House, Killucan, Kinnegad
✆ (044) 74130   Mrs Pamela Cooney

The Royal Canal flows through the grounds of this lovely old house. The farm, 350 acres of cows, cattle, sheep and tillage, is to be found 3.3 km off the N4 at Kinnegad, southwest of Mullingar. Packed lunches and afternoon teas are available, a cot can be provided. Kinnegad has 5 restaurants. Fishing in the canal on the farm. Mullingar with golf and lakes 16 km.

Open April-Oct.
3 bedrooms (1 twin; 1 double 1 family), 3♨,3WCs.
⌂ 🐎
Prices: B&B £14, weekly £88.50.

Mearescourt House, Rathconrath, Mullingar
✆ (044) 55112   Eithne Pendred

This is a gracious Georgian mansion set amidst ancient trees and sweeping parkland offering seclusion, elegance and comfort. The farm has 336 acres of rolling pasture with cattle and sheep. Delicious country cooking and wine licence. Packed lunches also provided. Situated 15 km west of Mullingar, signposted off Ballymahon road (R392), in a central location for touring. Golf, riding and fishing close by.

Closed Xmas
5 bedrooms (3 twin ens.⌂/WC; 1 double; 1 family ens.⌂/WC), 7♨, 7WCs. ⌂
Prices: B&B £16–20, EM £16. ⌂ rates.

Mornington, Multyfarnham, Mullingar
✆ (044) 72191   Warwick & Anne O'Hara
Fax (044) 72338

Mornington has been the home of the O'Hara Family for 5 generations. It is tucked away on a slope above Lough Derravaragh surrounded by mature trees and pastureland, ringed by the hills of north Westmeath. Dinner is provided, wine licence. An ideal location for exploring the

Midlands. Tullymally Castle 15 km. For the farm turn off the R394 Mullingar-Castlepollard road at Crookedwood and follow signs. Mullingar 14 km.

Open 9 April-8 Nov.
3 bedrooms (1 twin ens. 🛁/WC; 1 family ens. 🛁/WC;1 double ens. 🚿/WC), 3🛏, 2WC. 🐾
Prices: B&B £22.50, weekly £157.50. EM £16, weekly £200. 🐾 rates.

Self-Catering

MULLINGAR   Map 10 B2

Mearescourt House, Rathconrath, Mullingar
℡ (044) 55112   Eithne Pendred

For full farm description, see p. 250. Two self-catering units are available, each has 2 bedrooms, sleeps 4.

Closed Xmas
Prices: weekly £160.

Mornington, Multyfarnham, Mullingar
℡ (044) 72191   Warwick & Anne O'Hara
Fax (044) 72338

For full farm description see B&B entry above. Self-catering also available in one 3-bedroomed unit, sleeps 5.

Open 9 April-8 Nov.
Prices: weekly £175. 🐾 rates.

CO. WEXFORD

FERNS   Map 10 C3

Ballyorley House, Boolavogue, Ferns
℡ (054) 66287

An ideal place for a restful rural holiday. The Georgian residence is set on a mixed farm surrounded by a wealth of wildlife, good woodland walking, and for those who like to hunt rabbits and pigeons are plentiful. The farm lies just over 6 km from the N11 Enniscorthy-Gorey road. Afternoon teas are available and there is a playground for the children. Golf nearby. Beaches and dog racing 14 km. Herit-

age Park 25 km. Kennedy Memorial Park 30 km. Rosslare Harbour 40 km.

Open all year
4 bedrooms (2 double inc. 1 ens. 🛁/WC; 2 family), 2🛏, 2WC.
🐾 🐴 Board Failte Approved
Prices: B&B £16-17.50, EM £14. Weekly B&B plus EM £170. 🐾 rates.

WEXFORD   Map 10 C3

Killiane Castle Farmhouse, Drinagh
Mrs Kathleen Mernagh

This family home stands on a mixed farm adjacent to a 13th-century Norman Castle in an appealing setting of 230 acres of pastureland. The farm has pleasant gardens, a hard tennis court, farm walks and a lounge with games and books. Evening meals served, wine licence. Cot and highchair available. Killiane Castle is 7 km south of Wexford, signposted off N25, 10 mins from Rosslare ferry. Close by are beaches and golf courses. National Heritage Centre, Johnstown Castle, swimming pools and riding all within easy reach.

Open Mar-Nov.
8 bedrooms inc. 3 ens. 🛁/WC (3 twin; 2 double; 2 family; 1 single), 4🛏, 5WCs.
🐾 Bord Failte Farmhouse
Prices: B&B £13-15, EM £12. 🐾 rates.

Self-Catering

WEXFORD   Map 10 C3

Killiane Castle Farmhouse, Drinagh

For full farm description see previous entry. Accommodation is also available in four 2-bedroomed units, sleeping 4–6.

Open Mar-Nov.
Prices: weekly £180.

CO. WICKLOW

BALTINGLASS   Map 10 C3

Beechlawn, The Old Rectory, Kiltegan
✆ (0508) 73171   Mrs Evelyn Jackson

This Georgian farmhouse, whose hospitality has won a national award, is surrounded by a 50-acre beef farm. Situated north of Shillelagh on the R747 8 km off the N81 at Baltinglass, the house has large secluded gardens with picnic area and swing. Cot and highchair, packed lunches and afternoon teas available on request. Tennis and pitch and putt are both in the village. Golf 8 km. Riding stables 14 km.

Open Mar-Oct.
5 bedrooms (2 twin; 1 family; 2 single), 2🛏,

KEY TO SYMBOLS

Bath	⛉
Shower	🚿
Bathroom	🛁
Disabled Guest Facilities	♿
No Smoking	🚭
Children Welcome	♧
Dogs by Arrangement	🐕

2WCs. ♧
Prices: B&B £13.50. Dinner £12.50. High Tea £9. ♧ rates.

SHILLELAGH   Map 10 C3

Park Lodge Farmhouse, Clonegal
✆ (055) 29140

Park Lodge is a charming Georgian 18th-century farmhouse set in the peaceful surroundings of a 200-acre family run farm. Fishing, golf, sandy beaches and the famous Wicklow Way for good walks, are all within 30 mins drive. The farm lies in scenic countryside off the R725 Gorey-Carlow road, between the N11 and N81. Packed lunches and afternoon teas supplied on request. Cot and highchair available. Clonegal Castle, the oldest inhabited in Ireland, 5 km.

Open all year
4 bedrooms (2 twin; 1 double ens.🚿/WC; 1 family), 2🛏, 2WC. ♧
Prices: B&B £13.50–15, weekly £90. EM £9.50–12.50. Weekly £160. ♧ rates.

WICKLOW   Map 10 C3

Moordale, Ballinaclough, Wicklow
✆ (0404) 67539

Guests are welcome to roam the fields and hills of this dairy farm and enjoy the beautiful scenery. Historic mass rock is on the hill. Situated on the main Wicklow-Wexford road (N11) 4 km from Wicklow, there is golf and sea angling within 5 km. Brittas Bay beach 8 km. Mount Usher Gardens 6 km. Avoca Handweavers 20 km.

Open Apr-Sept.
3 bedrooms ens.🚿 (1 double; 2 family triples), 1🛏, 2WCs.
♧ 🐕 Bord Failte Farmhouse
Prices: B&B £12.50. ♧ rates.

Motor Insurance

The quickest route to better insurance value

CALL NOW FOR YOUR FREE QUOTATION

0800 678000

or contact your local RAC Insurance branch below during normal working hours

Belfast: (0232) 232640
Birmingham: 021-475 8811
Bournemouth: (0202) 752950
Bristol: (0272) 238499
Cardiff: (0222) 495333
Croydon: 081-681 1546
Darlington: (0325) 369 269
Edinburgh: 031-657 3444
Exeter: (0392) 58335
Glasgow: 041-221 5665
Gloucester: (0452) 300715
Leeds: (0532) 460404

Liverpool: 051-258 1441
Manchester: 061-832 2536
Newcastle: 091-230 0066
Norwich: (0603) 632056
Nottingham: (0602) 691933
Oxford: (0865) 514077
Plymouth: (0752) 228591
Sheffield: (0742) 788044
Southampton: (0703) 335361
Stockport: 061-429 0100
Watford: (0923) 817839

Insurance Services

All the cover you'll ever need

Stop Press

ENGLAND

BUCKINGHAMSHIRE

AYLESBURY
Map 2 B2

New Farm, Oxford Road, Oakley, Aylesbury HP18 9UR
✆ (0844) 237360   Mrs B. Pickford

Situated on the Oxfordshire/Buckinghamshire boundary, New Farm lies just outside Oakley off the B4011 north from Thame. This working farm of 163 acres comprises arable, sheep and beef cattle. Staying in a fully modernised farmhouse, with the luxury of log fires and central heating in winter, you can enjoy good food using free range eggs and home grown vegetables. Adjacent to Bernwood Forest Nature Reserve. Waterperry Gardens 6 miles. Oxford 7 miles.

Closed Xmas and New Year
3 bedrooms (1 twin; 2 double), 1🛁, 1WC.
🐾(6) ETB Listed and Commended
Prices from: B&B £16, weekly £112. EM £10, weekly B&B plus EM £182. 🐾 rates.

CHESHIRE

CONGLETON
Map 5 A2

Sandhole Farm, Hulme Walfield, Congleton
✆ (0260) 224419   Mrs Veronica Worth

Sandhole Farm is on the A34, 2 miles north of Congleton. The old Cheshire farmhouse is surrounded by fields affording beautiful views. Accommodation is available within the farmhouse and also in the original stable block which has re-

cently been converted into luxurious bedrooms. Two rooms are on the ground floor. Cot and high-chair provided. Ideally located for touring the Peak district (30 mins), The Potteries (30 mins) and visiting local stately homes, Gawsworth Hall, Little Moreton Hall, Capesthorne.

Open all year.
stable: 10 ens. bedrooms (8 twin; 2 double); house: 3 bedrooms (1 single; 1 twin; 1 family), 2🛁.
🔥 🐾 ⚹ 🛒 ETB 👑 👑Commended
Prices: B&B from £17.50. 🐾 rates.

MARTON
Map 5 A2

Sandpit Farm, Messuage Lane, Marton, Nr Macclesfield SK11 9HS.
✆ (0260) 224254   Mrs Kennerley

Sandpit Farm stands on the outskirts of the village of Marton, off the A34 southwest of Macclesfield. This 100-acre arable farm in a tranquil rural setting has a comfortable farmhouse with period features, oak beams and staircase, log fires. Capesthorne Hall 3 miles. Little Moreton Hall 5 miles.Bidulph Grange Gardens 6 miles. Quarry Bank Mill and Museum 10 miles.

Open all year.
3 bedrooms (1 twin ens. 🚿/WC; 1 double ens. 🚿/WC; 1 single), 1🛁, 1WC.
🐾(3) ⚹ 🛒 ETB 👑 👑
Prices: B&B £13–17.50. 🐾 rates.

CORNWALL

LAUNCESTON
Map 1 B3

Tredidon Barton, St Thomas, Launceston
PL15 8SJ
✆ (0566) 86288

Spacious accommodation is offered in this beautiful period listed homestead with country garden surrounded by a sheep and arable farm. Flowers, antiques, log fires, imaginative cuisine and home comforts pamper guests. Gym, games room, coarse fishing all inclusive. The farm is off the A395 4 miles west of Launceston. Leisure Farm, pay and play golf 2 miles. Norman Castle, steam railway 4 miles. Otter Farm and moors 5 miles.

Open Mar-Oct.
3 bedrooms (1 twin; 2 double), 2🛁, 2WCs. 👶
Prices: B&B £15, EM £9. 👶 rates.

PENZANCE
Map 1 A3

Mulfra Farm, Newmill, Nr Penzance TR20 8XP
✆ (0736) 63940
Mrs Monica Olds

High on the edge of the Penwith Moors stands this 50-acre smallholding with 200-acre hill. Tea/coffee facilities and TV in attractive bedrooms. There are cows, calves and horses. The 17th-century farmhouse has a comfortable lounge with a Cornish Stone oven and inglenook fireplace, separate dining room and sun porch. Plenty of good food. Situated west of the B3311, Penzance-St Ives road. Superb walking country, open moorland, ancient monuments and good

beaches all within easy reach. Car essential. Penzance 3 miles. St Ives 10 miles. Land's End 14 miles.

Open April-Oct.
2 double bedrooms ens. 🛁/WC).
👶(12)
Prices: B&B £15. EM £5.50. Weekly B&B plus EM £125.

Self-Catering

CAMELFORD
Map 1 A3

Aldermoor Farm, Advent, Camelford
PL32 9QQ
✆ (0840) 213366
Hanne & Jimmy Golding

Just over a mile outside Camelford, close to both moors and beaches, stands this small cattle and sheep farm. Self-catering accommodation is available in three attractive old buildings: Sarah's Cottage sleeps 6, Primrose Cottage sleeps 4, and the Old Barn sleeps 2. All have retained their period charm, with a wealth of exposed beams, thick walls and even a couple of four-poster beds. Away from any main roads, Aldermoor Farm is ideal for children and those searching for peace and tranquility. Gardens and barbecue areas. Tintagel 7 miles. Boscastle and Port Isaac beach within easy reach.

Open all year.
Prices: weekly £100–310.

Old Newham Farm, Otterham, Camelford
PL32 9SR
✆ (08403) 470
C.A.& M. Purdue

This is a small farm with many animals including friendly sheep and a pig called Beryl. There are 3 self-catering cottages with 1–3 bedrooms, sleeping 2–6. Ground floor bedroom available. Otterham is 8 miles north of Camelford (A39). Coast and moors 3 miles. Boscastle 5 miles.

Open all year
ETB♪♪♪♪
Prices on application.

KEY TO SYMBOLS

Bath	☐
Shower	🛁
Bathroom	🛁
Disabled Guest Facilities	♿
No Smoking	✂
Children Welcome	👶
Dogs by Arrangement	🐕

LAUNCESTON   Map 1 B3

Tredidon Barton, St Thomas, Launceston
PL15 8SJ
✆ (0566) 86288

For farm description, see farm entry p. 255. Self-catering accommodation is available in a converted granary, sleeps 4.

ETB *ʃʃʃʃ*
Prices on application.

DERBYSHIRE

Self-Catering

BUXTON   Map 5 A2

The Hayloft, Stanley House Farm, Great
Hucklow SK17 8RL
✆ (0298) 871044   Margot Darley

Situated northeast of Buxton (A6/B6049), the Hayloft is an attractive conversion from the original barn on Stanley House Farm. All the principal rooms face south with uninterrupted views. The Hayloft is fully fitted out for 4 people to a high degree of comfort and convenience. Stanley House is a working farm, and as stock is kept on the farm and in the surrounding fields please keep dogs on leads. An ideal centre for exploring the Peak District. Cressbrook Dale is within walking distance, Chatsworth House 3 miles, Bakewell 2 miles.

Open all year.
2 twin bedrooms inc. 1 ens. 🛁/WC; 1 ens.
🚿/WC.
🐕(12) ✝ ETB*ʃʃʃʃ*Commended
Prices: £135–205.

DEVON

NEWTON ABBOT   Map 1 B3

Bulleigh Park, Ipplepen, Newton Abbot
TQ12 5UA
✆ (0803) 872254   Angela Dallyn

From the windows of our small family farm you can admire the extensive views of the surrounding Devon countryside or watch our sheep, cows, calves and horses grazing close by. In our comfortable home enjoy large English breakfasts with homemade marmalade and jams. Special diets catered for. Cot, highchair, games and secure garden with sandpit and climbing frame provided. Bulleigh Park lies south of Newton Abbot off the A381, ideally suiting guests who want to explore the region. Compton Castle (NT) and a good Devon country pub within walking distance. Paignton Zoo and Steam Train 3 miles. Golf 1 mile. Dartmoor and Dartmouth 11 miles.

Open all year.
2 bedrooms (1 double; 1 family ens. 🛁/WC), 1🛏,
1WC.
🐕 ETB 👑 👑
Prices: B&B £12–16.50, weekly £84–105. 🐕 rates.

Self-Catering

SIDMOUTH   Map 1 B3

Hawkerland Valley Cottages, Stoneyford
Cottage, Stoneyford, Colaton Raleigh,
Sidmouth EX10 0HY
✆ (0395) 68843   Mrs J.M. Jackson

Our holiday cottage in the country is surrounded by farmland (but with one or two pretty cottages nearby). Our farm is a couple of miles away. A stream runs through the garden. The fully equipped 3-bedroomed cottage sleeps 5. Wheelchair ramps, cot and highchair available. Situated midway between Sidmouth and Budleigh Salterton off the A376, this is a good area for quiet country walks. Sidmouth, Budleigh Salterton and Exmouth 5–7 miles. Exeter 10 miles.

Open Easter-New Year
&c. & ⚘ ✹
Prices: weekly £120–280.✹ £10 per week, one dog only.

DORSET

BLANDFORD FORUM   Map 2 A3

Rivermead Farm, Childe Okeford, Blandford Forum DT11 8HB
✆ (0258) 860293   Mr & Mrs D.N. Cross

A delightful homely farmhouse set in beautiful countryside. The comfortable rooms have tea/coffee facilities, and there is a large sitting room and garden for guests. The farm grows organic vegetables and has working Shire horses and rare breed cattle. Rivermead Farm is north of the A357 Blandford Forum-Sturminster Newton road, 7 miles from Blandford Forum. Iron Age hill forts of Hambledon and Hod close by. Bulbarrow 4 miles.

Open all year
2 bedrooms (1 twin ens.⌑/WC; 1 family ens.⌑/WC).
&(5) ✂ ETB 👑 👑
Prices: B&B £15–16.50, weekly £100. & rates.

CORFE CASTLE   Map 2 B3

Bradle Farmhouse, Nr Corfe Castle, Wareham
✆ (0929) 480712   Mrs Gillian Hole

Bradle Farmhouse was built in 1862. It lies in a peaceful valley between Church Knowle and Kimmeridge, less than 3 miles southeast of Wareham off the A351. This is a working farm of 550 acres with cows, sheep and corn. There is direct access from the farm to the Purbeck Hills, with a wide choice of scenic walks. Packed lunch on request. Cot and highchair provided. Evening meals available locally. Corfe Castle ruins 2 miles. Sandy beaches of Studland 8 miles. Kimmeridge Bay, rock pools and shale, 2 miles.

Open all year
3 bedrooms (1 twin; 1 double; 1 family), 2🛏,2WCs.
&ETB 👑 Commended
Prices: B&B £15–18, weekly £90–110. & rates.

GILLINGHAM   Map 2 A3

Cole Street Farm, Cole Street Lane, Gillingham SP8 5JQ
✆ (0747) 822691

This 300-year-old farmhouse retains many traditional features, like oak beams and flagstone floors, but has been renovated to a high standard. The grounds have free range chickens, ducks and geese, with a stream and duck pond. Cot and highchair available. The farm is south of Gillingham off B3081 Gillingham-Shaftesbury road, and is surrounded by fields and footpaths. Shaftesbury 4 miles.

Open all year
4 bedrooms (1 twin; 1 single; 2 family inc. 1 ens.⌑/WC, 1 ens.⌑/WC),1🛏, 1WC.
& ✂
Prices: B&B £15, & rates.

Self-Catering

BLANDFORD FORUM   Map 2 A3

Rivermead Farm, Childe Okeford, Blandford Forum DT11 8HB
✆ (0258) 860293   Mr & Mrs D.N. Cross

For full farm description see B&B entry above. Accommodation is also offered in a 1-bedroomed unit, sleeps 2.

Open all year
Prices: weekly £80–200.

GILLINGHAM   Map 2 A3

Cole Street Farm, Cole Street Lane, Gillingham SP8 5JQ
✆ (0747) 822691

See B&B entry above for full farm description. Self-catering in 5 cottages, all highly individual, converted from farm buildings. Each has a patio and garden, 1–3 bedrooms, sleeping 3–6. Also children's beds and cots provided.

Open all year
Prices on application.

GLOUCESTERSHIRE

GLOUCESTER Map 2 A2
Kilmorie, Gloucester Road, Corse,
Staunton, Nr Gloucester GL19 3RQ
℗ (0452) 840224 Sheila Barnfield

Kilmorie is a Grade 2 listed smallholding keeping
sheep, goats, ponies, poultry and fruit. Children
may join in looking after the animals and ride the
ponies. All rooms are well equipped including tea
trays and radio alarms. Separate lounge and dining room and a large garden for guests to enjoy.
This is a warm and friendly place to stay. The farm
is on the A417 Gloucester-Ledbury road, 7 miles
from Gloucester. Malvern Hills 5 miles. Falconry
Centre 6 miles. Cotswolds 10 miles. Within 40
mins drive: four castles, farm and wildlife parks.

Open all year
7 bedrooms (1 twin ens.; 3 double; 2 family
ens.; 1 single), 2, 3WCs.
(5) ETB
Prices: B&B £10, EM £5.50. rates.

HAMPSHIRE

PETERSFIELD Map 2 B3
Brocklands Farm, West Meon, Petersfield
GU32 1JN
℗ (0730) 829228 Mrs S. Wilson

Brocklands Farm is a 300-acre arable farm in the
Meon Valley. The farm entrance is on A32 south
of West Meon, which is west of Petersfield. The
farmhouse is modern but furnished traditionally,
with very good views and well off the road.
Packed lunches and afternoon teas on request. A
disused railway line and grass headlands around
the farm make attractive walks. We also have a
small caravan site, very quiet with no building in
sight. Old Winchester Hill 1 mile. Hinton Ampner
House and Garden 3 miles. Winchester, Petersfield and Alton approx. 10 miles.

Closed Xmas.
3 bedrooms (1 twin; 2 double), 1, 1, 2WCs.
ETB Listed
Prices: B&B £15–16.

HEREFORD & WORCESTER

HEREFORD Map 2 A2
Little Green Farm, Newton St Margarets,
Vowchurch, Hereford HR2 0QJ
℗ (098123) 205 Mrs Joan Powell

This warm modernised farmhouse faces south,
peacefully situated between Golden Valley and
the Black Mountains 14 miles west of Hereford
via A465 (B4349/B4348). Little Green is a working farm with cattle and sheep. We offer good
farmhouse fare with mainly home grown produce
and every comfort. Packed lunches on request,
cot and playroom available. Many places of historic interest and natural beauty lie within easy
reach in unspoilt countryside. Wye Valley, picturesque Tudor villages and castles, golf courses,
Hay-on-Wye 15 miles. Malvern Hills 30 miles.

Closed Xmas.
3 bedrooms (2 double; 1 family), 1, 2WCs.
ETB Registered
Prices: B&B £10–12.50, weekly £70–87. EM
£16–18. Weekly B&B plus EM £112–126.
rates.

LEOMINSTER Map 2 A1
Woonton Court Farm, Leysters,
Leominster HR6 0HL
℗ (0568) 87232 Mrs Elizabeth Thomas

This beamed farmhouse stands on a working
farm where visitors are welcome to walk and
observe the animals. Farm produce available,
afternoon teas offered. Cot, highchair and swing
supplied for children. The farm is off A4112 Leo-
minster-Tenbury Wells road, before Leysters vil-

lage. A good base for touring, Ludlow Castle, Hereford Cathedral, Leominster Priory all within easy reach.

Open all year
2 bedrooms (1 twin; 1 double ens. 🛇/WC).
🐾🛏
Prices: B&B £12.50–15.

Self-Catering

LEOMINSTER   Map 2 A1

Woonton Court Farm, Leysters, Leominster HR6 0HL
✆ (0568) 87232   Mrs Elizabeth Thomas

For full farm description, see above. A half-timbered detached millhouse situated 50 yds from the farmhouse with its own patio garden offers self-catering accommodation for 3–4 in 2 bedrooms.

Open all year
🛏 ETB♪♪♪♪Commended
Prices: weekly £130–250, short breaks £95.

HUMBERSIDE

BARTON-UPON-HUMBER   Map 5 B2

West Wold Farm, Deepdale, Barton-upon-Humber DN18 6ED
✆ (0652) 33293   Mrs P.C. Atkin

An attractive 19th-century farmhouse with large gardens and paddock surrounded by farmland. There is a small private yard of horses, guests' horses and ponies stabled. Tea making facilities. Packed lunches and evening meals on request. The farm is 2 miles south of Barton-upon-Humber. Nature reserve, Barton Claypits, historic churches 2 miles. Viking Way 2 miles

Open all year
2 bedrooms (1 twin; 1 double), 2🐄.
🐾 🛏
Prices: B&B £14–16, EM £7–15.

KENT

ASHFORD   Map 3 B3

Arketts Farm, Charing, Ashford TN27 0HN
✆ (023371) 2893   M.M. Okell

The farmhouse is a Grade 2 listed building with beams and fireplaces set amidst 60 acres of pasture and woodland. Here we offer good home cooking and packed lunches on request. Designated an Area of Outstanding Natural Beauty, the quiet rural area is ideal for walking and riding, with extensive broadleaf woodlands and abundant wildlife. Situated 8 miles northwest of Ashford, innumerable castles, gardens, villages and historic sites lie within an hour's drive. Leeds Castle 8 miles. Faversham 9 miles. Canterbury and Maidstone 14 miles.

Open all year.
2 bedrooms (1 twin; 1 double), 1🐄, 2WCs.
🐾(4)✄ 🛏 ETB Listed
Prices: B&B £12.50–13.50, weekly £85–92. EM £5. 🐾 rates,🛏 £1 per night.

LANCASHIRE

SCARISBRICK   Map 4 B2

Sandy Brook Farm, Wyke Cop Road, Scarisbrick, Southport PR8 5LR
✆ (0704) 880337   Mrs W. Core

This small comfortable arable farm is situated in the rural area of Scarisbrick, midway between the seaside town of Southport and the ancient town of Ormskirk, just off the A570. The converted farm buildings are attractively furnished and also cater to the needs of disabled guests. Cot and highchair provided. Martin Mere Wildfowl Trust 6 miles. Rufford Old Hall 7 miles. Tarlton Leisure Lakes 8 miles.

Open all year
6 bedrooms (3 twin ens. 🛁/WC; 1 double ens. 🛁/WC;2 family ens. 🛁/WC).
♿ 🐾 ETB 🏆 🏆
Prices: B&B £14, weekly £88.20. 🐾 rates.

NORFOLK

BECCLES   Map 3 B1

Shrublands Farm, Burgh St Peter, Nr
Beccles NR34 0BB
✆ (050277) 241

This homely farmhouse is situated on the Waveney Valley on the Suffolk border, west of Low-
estoft. In fact the River Waveney itself flows
through the 480 acres of mixed working farmland. An ideal spot for birdwatching as well as
touring Norfolk, and Suffolk as Beccles, Low-
estoft, Great Yarmouth and Norwich are all within
easy reach. River Centre, swimming, sauna,
jacuzzi, gymnasium and restaurant 1 mile from
farmhouse.

Closed Xmas
3 bedrooms (1 twin; 1 double; 1 family), 3🛏,
2WCs.
🏠(5) ETB 👑 👑
Prices: B&B £14–15, weekly £98–105. 🐾 rates.

HARLESTON   Map 3 B1

Weston House Farm, Mendham,
Harleston IP20 0PB
✆ (098682) 206   Mrs June E. Holden

A warm welcome and good country cooking
await you at this 17th-century Grade 2 listed
farmhouse, set in an acre of garden overlooking
pastureland. Weston House Farm is a stock and
arable farm covering 300 acres, just east of the
A143 Diss road. Ground floor bedroom, cot,
highchair and children's games available. Tea/
coffee facilities in rooms. Otter Sanctuary 6 miles.
Bressingham Steam Museum 15 miles. Suffolk
Heritage coast 18 miles. Norwich, Minsmere Bird
Sanctuary and Stowmarket 20 miles.

Open Mar-Nov.
3 bedrooms (2 twin inc. 1 ens. WC; 1 family ens.
🚿/WC), 1🛏, 2WCs.
🏠 🐾 ETB 👑 👑
Prices from: B&B £14.50, weekly £87.50. EM
£8.50. 🐾 rates.

NORTHUMBERLAND

HEXHAM   Map 7 B3

Low Barns, Wall, Hexham
✆ (0434) 606680   Mrs L.L. Newall

This is a mixed farm with sheep, cattle, horses
and grain. There are wild flower meadows and
river walks, all set in the National Park. All meals
are offered. Tea/coffee facilities and heated
swimming pool add to the enjoyment. Wall is on
A6079, 3 miles north of Hexham. The area has
much to offer, Hadrian's Wall, Hexham Abbey,
Derwent Reservoir and many country house gardens in the vicinity.

Open all year
4 bedrooms (1 twin priv. 🚿/WC; 2 double inc. 1
priv. 🚿/WC, 1 ens. 🛁; 1 single priv. 🚿/WC).
🏠🐴🐾
Prices: B&B £17.50. 🐾 rates.

Self-Catering

BERWICK-ON-TWEED   Map 7 B2

The Old Smithy, Brackenside, Bowsden,
Berwick-on-Tweed TD15 2TQ
✆ (0289) 88293   John & Mary Barber

Our mixed farm lies south of Berwick-on-Tweed
west of the A1, near the B6525/B6353. The farm
comprises a suckler herd, sheep, wheat, barley,
oats, mixed woodland and conservation area.
Accommodation is offered in the beautifully renovated Old Smithy, sleeps 6. It is fully equipped
including cot, highchair and attractive wood
burning stove. Within easy reach of Brackenside
are the border and coastal castles, and a number
of NT properties. Steam train 4 miles. Lindisfarne
7 miles. Farne Islands 20 miles.

Open all year
🛁 🏠 🐾
Prices: weekly £160–320.

HEXHAM   Map 7 B3

Low Barns, Wall, Hexham
✆ (0434) 606680   Mrs L.L. Newall

For full farm description, see above. Self-catering
accommodation available in 2 houses converted
from farm buildings. One looks across the valley,
the other over sunny gardens. Each has 2
bedrooms, sleeping 5–6.

Open all year
🛁
Prices on application.

NORTH YORKSHIRE

PATELEY BRIDGE — Map 5 A1

Bewerley Hall Farm, Bewerley, Pateley Bridge, Nr Harrogate HG3 5JA
✆ (0423) 711636 Eileen & Neville Bulmer

Bewerley Hall Farm is a Grade 2 listed farmstead built in 1870 as the home farm of the Yorke Estate. It stands in a secluded position near the River Nidd 12 miles northwest of Harrogate (B6265). On this family run working beef and sheep farm you can enjoy every comfort. The food is of the highest quality, packed lunches on request. Licensed. A private stretch of trout and grayling fishing is exclusively for guests' use. Horse riding arranged locally. The area is noted for bird-watching and walking. Tennis, golf and dry skiing available near Harrogate, horse race meetings at Ripon and Thirsk.

Open Jan-Nov.
5 bedrooms (1 twin; 1 double; 2 ensuite; 1 family), 1🛁, 2WCs.
👪 🐕
Prices from: B&B £13.50, weekly £91. EM £9.25. Weekly B&B plus EM £155.75. 🐕 £2 per night.

SCARBOROUGH — Map 5 B1

Island Farm, Staintondale, Scarborough
✆ (0723) 870249 Mary Clarke

Nine miles north of Scarborough off the A171, this farm is in the North York Moors National Park, close to both the coast and the sea. The spacious accommodation includes a large games room with a full size snooker table. Comfort and good breakfasts provide a welcoming atmosphere. Cot available. Whitby 12 miles.

Open April-Nov.
3 bedrooms (2 twin ens.🚿/WC; 1 family ens.🚿/WC), 1WC.
👪 🚭 🐕 ETB ♛ ♛
Prices: B&B £14–16, weekly £100. 👪 rates.

Self-Catering

WHITBY — Map 5 B1

Blackmires Farm, Danby Head, Danby, Whitby YO21 2NN
✆ (0287) 660352 Mrs G.M. Rhys

Blackmires Farm lies by the moors, south of the A171 Whitby-Guisborough road. This small family farm has cattle, goats, sheep and poultry. The 17th-century farmhouse has a modern 3-bedroomed bungalow attached and a well-equipped modern static caravan, both sleep 6. Cot, swing and sandpit provided. Moors and walks adjacent to the farm. National Park Danby Moors Centre 4 miles. Whitby beach 15 miles. Hutton le Hole folk museum 10 miles.

Open Mar-Oct.
ETB⚷⚷⚷Approved
Prices: weekly from £150.

OXFORDSHIRE

WALLINGFORD — Map 2 B2

North Farm, Shillingford Hill, Wallingford OX10 8NB
✆ (086732) 8406 Mrs Hilary Warburton

This spacious comfortable farmhouse is set on a 500-acre working farm with sheep, pygmy goats and chickens. Walks by the River Thames and fishing available. The farm is 2 miles north of Wallingford. Take A324 north to Shillingford Bridge Hotel, farm track leads from the car park.

Open all year
2 bedrooms (1 twin; 1 double ens.🛁/WC), 1🛁.
👪(5) 🚭 ETB ♛ ♛Commended
Prices: B&B £17.50–30.

SHROPSHIRE

CLUN — Map 2 A1

Lower Duffryn Farm, Newcastle-on-Clun, Clun, Craven Arms SY7 8PQ
✆ (0588) 640239 Mrs Thelma Davies

A warm welcome awaits you with good home cooking at this working mixed farm of cattle and sheep. It is set amid rolling hills in unspoilt countryside with lovely views. Packed lunches and evening meals available. Tea/coffee facilities. Lower Duffryn is situated on B4368 15 miles west of Craven Arms. Offa's Dyke 1 mile.

Open Easter-Oct.
3 bedrooms (1 twin; 2 double), 1🚽, 1WC.
🐕(10) ⊬ ETB Listed Commended
Prices: B&B £13–15, weekly £84. EM £6–7, weekly B&B plus EM £126. 🐕 rates.

SOMERSET
YEOVIL   Map 2 A3
Vicarage Farm, Northover, Ilchester, Nr Yeovil
✆ (0935) 840631   Mrs Irene King

This former vicarage is set amongst beautiful lawns and gardens on an 800-acre corn, sheep, dairy and beef farm. Packed lunches and afternoon teas available. The farm is on A37, 5 miles north of Yeovil. Ideal for a touring centre. Golf courses 5 miles, coarse fishing on the farm. Close to Yeovilton with museum, pubs and restaurants.

Open all year
3 bedrooms (1 twin; 1 double; 1 single), 1🚽, 2WCs. 🐕
Prices: B&B £12.50–15. 🐕 rates.

WARWICKSHIRE
WARWICK   Map 2 B1
Shrewley Pools Farm, Haseley, Warwick
✆ (0926) 484315   Mrs Cathy Dodd

This beautiful 17th-century farmhouse retains many of its original features and is set in an acre of fabulous garden. The farm has barley, oats, oilseed rape, turkeys, pasture and geese. Afternoon teas and evening meals available. The farm is 4 miles from Warwick. Packwood House 3 miles. Kenilworth Castle 6 miles. NAC 7 miles. NEC 10 miles.

Open all year
2 bedrooms (1 twin; 1 family ens.🖘/WC), 1🚽, 2WCs.
🐕 ETB Commended
Prices: B&B £18–23, EM £5–6.50. 🐕 rates.

SCOTLAND
CULLODEN MOOR   Map 9 A2
Balaggan Farm, Culloden Moor, by Inverness, Highlands IV1 2EL
✆ (0463) 790213   Mrs P. Alexander

A warm welcome is found at this comfortable farmhouse with good food, home baking and open fire in the sitting room. Packed lunches on request. The 90-acre farm rears stock and crops for winter feed. Fishing in the River Nairn, Clava Cairns, Culloden Battlefield and Cawdor Castle close by. The farm is off B9006 from Inverness (7 miles).

Open Apr-Oct.
2 bedrooms (1 twin; 1 family), 1🚽, 1WC.
🐕 🦃 STB Listed Commended
Prices: B&B £13–14, weekly £91. EM £8, weekly B&B plus EM £145. 🐕 rates.

ELGIN   Map 9 A2
Gladhill Farm, Fochabers, Elgin, Moray, Grampian
✆ (034387) 331   Mrs Lorna Smith

The farmhouse is situated o a 500-acre arable and livestock farm by the sea, 6 miles from Elgin. We specialise in seed potatoes, cereals, sheep and beef cattle. A warm welcome, good food and home baking are provided for all our guests. Beaches close by and golf 1 mile. Brodie Castle and Whisky Trail 10 miles.

Open all year
3 bedrooms (1 twin; 1 family/double; 1 single), 1🚽.
🐕🦃
Prices: B&B £13, weekly £78. EM £20. 🐕 rates.

PEEBLES   Map 7 A2
Winkston Farm, Edinburgh Road, Peebles, Borders
✆ (0721) 21264

The Georgian listed farmhouse provides comfortable and friendly accommodation. The surrounding smallholding of 45 acres farms sheep and horses. Packed lunches on request. Cot and highchair available. Winkston Farm has a good central location for touring, 2 miles from Peebles on A703 Peebles-Edinburgh road. Walking, fishing and golf 2 miles.

Open Easter-Oct.
3 bedrooms (1 twin; 2 double), 1🚽, 1WC.
🐕 STB 🏵 🏵Highly Commended
Prices: B&B £13–14. 🐕 rates.

REPUBLIC OF IRELAND

KILLARNEY
Map 10 A4

Kylie Farmhouse, Pallas, Beaufort, Co Kerry
✆ (064) 44197   John & Mary Anne O'Sullivan

This comfortable family bungalow on a 50-acre dairy farm enjoys an enviable position overlooking Killarney Lakes, MacGillycuddy Reeks, Dunloe and River Laune. The farm is off the R562, 10 km west of Killarney. Cot and highchair available. Golf 5 km.

Open Jun-Oct.
3 bedrooms (1 double ens.⌂/WC; 2 family inc. 1 ens.⌂/WC), 1🛪, 2WCs.
⚘ 🛏 Board Failte Approved
Prices: B&B £12–14, EM £12.

FERNS
Map 10 C3

Clone House, Ferns, Enniscorthy, Co Wexford
✆ (054) 66113   Tom & Betty Breen

This award-winning farmhouse is 3 km southwest of Ferns off the N11 Enniscorthy-Gorey road. The farmhouse dates back to 1600 and is set in lovely gardens with the ruins of a 12th-century church and the River Bann flowing through the farm. Fishing, shooting, hunting and golf can all be found locally. The Breens have won the Galtee Irish Breakfast Award, Best Farmhouse Garden Award and the National Agri-Tourism Award. The farmhouse is licensed. Children are welcomed and well provided for. In Ferns stands a 12th-century castle.

Open Mar-Oct.
5 bedrooms (1 twin; 1 double ens.⌂/♒/WC; 3 family inc. 1 ens.⌂/♒/WC, 1 ens.⌂, 1 priv.⌂/WC), 1WC.
⚘ Board Failte Approved
Prices: B&B £14.50–16.50, weekly £108–115. High Tea £10. EM £13.50. Weekly B&B plus EM £180.⚘ rates.

Rural Attractions

ENGLAND

AVON

Priston Mill
Priston, Nr Bath
✆ (0225) 423894

King Athelstan gave this watermill to the Abbot of Bath in 931. It is still working, driven by a spectacular waterwheel. Friendly staff describe its history and workings. Scenic wagon rides and play areas. On sale: gifts. Location: 6 miles southwest of Bath, signposted from A39 at Marksbury Church

Open: April-Sept daily, 1415–1700
Entrance charges: Adults £2.20, children £1.50, OAP/concessions £1.50
WC ★ ✗ SHOP

Radford Farm and Shire Horse Stables
Radford Farm, Radford, Timsbury, Bath BA3 1QF
✆ (0761) 470106

Radford Farm is worked as it would have been between 1940 and 1955. Horses do most of the work. There are Shire Horses, older breeds of sheep, goats, pigs and poultry. A hands on experience – bottle feeding lambs, hand milking goats, ride in a horse and cart. Play area, pets corner and nature trails. Fun for all the family, many attractions under cover if wet. Location: Signposted from A367 Bath-Exeter road.

Open: Apr-Oct daily, 1030–1700
Entrance charges: Adults £2.50, children £2, OAP/concessions £2.
WC ★ & partial access ☞

BUCKINGHAMSHIRE

Bekonscot Model Village
Warwick Road, Beaconsfield HP9 2PL
✆ (0494) 672919

The oldest model village in the world, it covers one and half acres with landscaped gardens, miniature houses, castles, shops, churches and railway stations (160 buildings) with fine Gauge One model railway 400 metres long. Play area and picnic facilities. On sale: souvenirs. Location: Signposted from M40, Jct 2.

Open: Mar-Oct daily, 1000–1700.
Entrance charges: Adults £2.50, children £1.25, OAP/concessions £2.
WC & ☞ SHOP

Bucks Goat Centre
Layby Farm, Old Risborough Road, Stoke Mandeville HP22 5XJ
✆ (0296) 612983

Most comprehensive collection of goats in Britain, 12 breeds, plus pony, donkeys, sheep, pigs, poultry and pets. Guided tours by appointment. Educational programmes for groups – schools, playgroups, senior citizens, etc. Pony rides. Visitor centre, farm, plant nursery. Cheese and cider tastings by arrangement. On sale: Farm produced goat cheese, milk, fudge and ice cream, plus non-goat farm produce and gifts. Location: off A4010 outside Stoke Manderville travelling towards Princes Risborough.

Open: Tues-Sun & bank hols, summer 1000–1730, winter 1000–1700.
Entrance charges: Adults £1.50, children £0.75.
WC ★ & ☞ SHOP

CAMBRIDGESHIRE

Sacrewell Farm & Country Centre
Sacrewell, Thornhaugh, Peterborough PE8 6HJ
✆ (0780) 782222

530-acre mainly arable farm but with sheep, pigs, goats, rabbits, poultry, peacocks, etc. Working watermill, huge collection of farm, domestic and craft bygones. Farm, nature and general interest trails. Maze, trampolines, toys and games. Schools, birthdays, adult groups, all welcome. On sale: souvenirs, gifts. Location: off A47 8 miles west of Peterborough.

Open: daily, 0900–2100
Entrance charges: Adults £1.50, children £0.50,
OAP/concessions £1
WC 🅃 ♿ ⌸ SHOP

Welney Wildfowl and Wetlands Centre
The Wildfowl and Wetlands Trust, Pintail
House, Hundred Foot Bank, Welney Nr
Wisbech PE14 9TN
✆ (0353) 860711

A relaxing day out. Enjoy exploring a remnant of
original fenland. In winter thousands of wintering
birds can be viewed from a comfortable hide.
Also picnic facilities, exhibition area. On sale:
books, gifts. Location: 12 miles north of Ely signposted from A10.

Open: all year, daily, 1000–1700.
Entrance charges: Adults £2.70, children £1.35,
OAP/concessions £2.20, family £7.50.
WC ♿ ⌸ SHOP

The Windmill
Swaffham Prior, Cambridge CB5 0JZ
✆ (0638) 741009

Foster's Mill, a 4-storied tower windmill built
c.1860, is back in working order and once more
produces stoneground organic wholemeal flour
by windpower only. On sale: flour. Location:
northwest side of B1102 in Swaffham Prior
village.

Open: April-Oct, 1st & 3rd Suns, Bank hols Sun
& Mon, 1400–1700, or by appointment.
Donation suggestions: Adults £1, children
£0.50, OAP £0.50.
SHOP

CHESHIRE
Cheshire Ice Cream Farm
Drumlan Hall, Newton Lane, Tattenhall, Nr
Chester CH3 9NE
✆ (0829) 70995

A real working dairy farm. Watch the ice cream
being made (weekdays in summer) and see the
cows milked (1330–1530). Sample the products
then take some home. On sale: ice cream and
other dairy produce from farm, preserves, gifts.
Location: south of Chester, follow signs from A41
Chester-Whitchurch road.

Open: all year except except Xmas, New Year
and last 2 weeks in January, daily, 1000–1730.
Entrance free
WC 🅃restricted, ♿ ⌸ SHOP

CLEVELAND
The Botanic Centre
Ladgate Lane, Acklam, Middlesbrough
TS5 7HF
✆ (0642) 594895

A unique centre developed by trained horticulture and construction personnel. Example of
industry and public sector initiative. Enviro-world
incorporating exhibition hall, gallery, demonstration gardens, theme gardens, gold medal-win-
ning white garden, visitor centre. On sale: Green
shop with organic produce, gifts and peat free
compost. Location: 4 miles from Middlesbrough
town centre, A19/A174.

Open: all year, Wed-Sun, 1100–1800
Entrance charges: Adults £2, children £0.50,
OAP/concessions £1.30.
WC 🅃 ♿ ⌸ SHOP

CORNWALL

Callestock Cider Farm
Penhallow, Truro TR4 9LW
℃ (0872) 573356

Working farm making cider, country wines, jams and preserves. Museum of cidermaking, tractor and trailer rides through orchards, friendly farm animals and free samples of all products in farm shop. On sale: Farm produce, incl. Cornish scrumpy, country wines, jams, preserves and honey. Location: Signposted at Penhallow on A3075 Newquay-Redruth road.

Open: Feb-Mar, Nov-Dec Mon-Fri 0900–1700, Apr-Oct Mon-Sat 0900–1800.
Entrance free.
WC ♪ &restricted, ☞ peak season only, SHOP

Museum of Historic Cycling
The Old Station, Camelford PL32 9TZ
℃ (0840) 212811

The nation's foremost museum of cycling history, covering 1818 to modern times. On sale: Books, mementos. Location: a mile north of Camelford on Boscastle road.

Open: Easter-Oct, Sun-Thur 1000–1700
Entrance charges: Adults £2, children £1.50, OAP/concessions £1.50.
WC & SHOP

Tamar Otter Park & Wild Wood
North Petherwin, Nr Launceston PL15 8LW
℃ (0566) 85646

A branch of the famous Otter Trust where British otters are bred for reintroduction to the wild. 20 acres of woodland with 3 species of deer roaming free, 2 waterfowl lakes, wallabies, pheasants and peacocks. Visitor centre, free parking. On sale: unusual gifts mainly connected with conservation. Location: signposted from B3254 Launceston-Bude road at Langdon Cross, Launceston 5 miles.

Open: Apr-Oct & Good Fri, daily 1030–1800.
Entrance charges: Adults £3, children £1.50, OAP/concessions £2.50.
WC & ☞ SHOP

CUMBRIA

The Watermill
Little Salkeld, Penrith CA10 1NN
℃ (0768) 881523

A fine example of an 18th-century country corn mill, milling organic stoneground flours the tra-

ditional way by waterpower. Close to Long Meg Stone Circle for visitors touring the area. On sale: large range organic flours, cereal products and groceries. Location: under 2 miles northeast of Langwathby, off A686 Penrith-Alston road.

Open: Jan-Dec, Mon-Fri 1030–1700
Entrance charges: Adults £1.50, children £1, OAP/concessions £1.
WC & partial access, ☞ SHOP

DERBYSHIRE

Poole's Cavern & Buxton Country Park
Green Lane, Buxton SK17 9SA
℃ (0298) 26978

Beautiful showcave with a rich variety of cave formations, a thousand stalactites, stalagmites and an archeological dig. Guided tour lasts 40 mins. Visitor centre with exhibition and video, 100 acres of woodland with nature trail. On sale: books, minerals, souvenirs and children's gifts. Location: off A54 Leek road just outside Buxton.

Open: Good Fri-Oct. daily 1000–1700, closed Weds Apr/May/Oct.
Entrance charges: Adults £2.70, children £1.50, OAP/concessions £2.20.
WC & ♪ woodland only, ☞ SHOP

Speedwell Cavern
Winnats Pass, Castleton, Hope Valley S30 2WA
℃ (0433) 620512

An amazing underground boat journey through an 18th-century Derbyshire lead mine, to the famous Bottomless Pit. Fully guided tours leave every 15 mins, duration 45 mins. On sale: Locally made blue john stone jewellery, gifts. Location: Off main A625 west of Castleton village.

Open: daily Oct-Mar 0930–1700, April-Sept 0930–1730
Entrance charges: Adults £4, children £2.50, OAP/concessions £3.25
WC ♪ ☞ SHOP

Treak Cliff Cavern
Castleton S30 2WP
℃ (0433) 620571

A range of underground caverns with stalactites, stalagmites, and all kinds of beautiful formations. Views of blue john stone, 330 million-year-old fossils. A working blue john mine and now designated a site of special scientific interest. Covered and outdoor picnic areas. On sale: cavern mined blue john ornaments and jewellery. Location: on A625 west of Castleton.

Open: daily, summer 0930–1730, winter
0930–1600
Entrance charges: Adults £3.50, children £1.70,
under-5s free, OAP/concessions £2.80.
WC ♥ ☐ SHOP

DEVON

Canonteign Falls & Country Park
Canonteign, Chudleigh
✆ (0647) 52434

A memorable and dramatic day out for all the
family at England's highest waterfall. On sale:
gifts. Location: 3 miles off A38 at Chudleigh.

Open: Mar-Oct, daily 1000–1730
Entrance charges: Adults £3, children £2, OAP/
concessions £2.50
WC ♥ &partial access, ☐ ✕ SHOP

Exemoor Rare Breeds Farm
Week-St-Mary, Holsworthy EX22 6UX
✆ (056681) 366

A trail over modern and traditional farmland with
rare and commercial breeds of cattle, pigs,
sheep, goats and ponies in natural surroundings.
With 38 different breeds this is one of the largest
collections in North Cornwall. Conservation area
has 2 ponds with waterfowl, ducks and geese.
Picnic area, pets corner, antique farming arti-
facts on display. On sale: souvenirs. Location:
east of A39 Camelford-Bude road at Wainhouse
Corner.

Open: Easter-Oct.
Entrance charges: Adults £1.75, children £1,
OAP/concessions £1
WC & SHOP

The Milky Way & North Devon Bird of Prey Centre
Downland Farm, Clovelly, Bideford, EX39
5RY
✆ (0237) 431255

Top open farm, nominated for ETB Best Tourist
Attraction 1992. Pet and feed baby animals,
hand milk a cow, watch a falconry display, even
throw your own pot. Adventure playground.
Pidler Countryside Collection. Face painting.
Laser clay pigeon shooting. On sale: dairy products, local crafts, books. Location: A39 Bideford-Bude road, 2 miles south of Clovelly.

Open: April-Oct, daily 1030–1800
Entrance charges: Adults £3.50, children £2,
OAP/concessions £3
WC ♥ & ☐ SHOP

Museum of Dartmoor Life
West Street, Okehampton EX20 1HQ
✆ (0837) 52295

New display tells the story of the people who
have lived and worked on Dartmoor from prehis-
toric times to the present day. Displays also
examine issues such as the environment and the
effects of social change. On sale: crafts, books,
gifts. Location: Signposted from A30 into
Okehampton.

Open: April-Oct, Mon-Sat 1000–1700 Jun-Sept,
Sun 1000–1700.
Entrance charges: Adults £1, children £0.60,
OAP/concessions £0.80.
WC ♥ &partial access ☐ SHOP

Otterton Mill Centre & Working Museum
nr Budleigh Salterton EX9 7HG
✆ (0395) 68521

You can watch every stage of turning wheat into
bread at this waterpowered working cornmill with
bakery attached. Mill restored in 1977 and powered by River Otter. Audio-visual slide sequence
shows history and operation of this Domesday
mill. On sale: Home baked goods from our own
flour, crafts: pottery, glass, paintings, wood-
turning. Location: off A376 north of Budleigh
Salterton.

Open: daily, Mar-Jan 1030–1730, Jan-Mar
1130–1630
Entrance charges: Adults £1.50, children £0.70,
Groups – adults £0.80, children £0.60
WC ♥ & ☐ ✕ SHOP

Tuckers Maltings
Osborne Park, Teign Road, Newton Abbott
✆ (0626) 334734

Guided tours of the only traditional working
malthouse open to the public in England, making
malt from barley for Real Ale. Working Victorian
machinery – turn the grain yourself. Audio
effects, video programme, picnic area. Excellent
educational fun for all the family in a truly unique
building. On sale: special bottled beers & wines,
local preserves & chutneys, traditional toys, malt,
gifts. Location: signposted from railway station.

Open: Easter-Oct. Sun-Fri 1000–1700
Entrance charges: Adults £3, children £1.90,
OAP/concessions £2.65.
WC ♥ &partial access, ☐ ✕ SHOP

DORSET

Dorset Heavy Horse Centre
Edmonsham Road, Verwood
© (0202) 824040

In a quiet corner of Dorset come and enjoy seeing six breeds of Gentle Giant plus Miniature Shetland ponies, in their own miniature stable yard. Wagon rides weather permitting. Don't miss the commentaries (1130, 1430 & 1615 hrs). Picnic and play area, video. On sale: gifts. Location: signposted from Verwood (A31/B3081 4 miles from Ringwood).

Open: Easter-Oct, daily 1000–1730
Entrance charges: Adults £2.95, children £1.95, OAP/concessions £2.50.
WC ⊷ & ⌨ SHOP

Park Farm Museum
Milton Abbas, Blandford DT11 0AX
© (0258) 880704

Farm animals to touch and feed, picnic site with panoramic views (picnic barn if wet). Farming, local history and Bygone museum. Chimney pot collection. Pony and tractor trailer rides, Sundays in summer, daily in school holidays. On sale: local farm produce, eggs, butter, cheese, ice cream. Location: signposted from Milton Abbas (off A354 Blandford-Puddletown road).

Open: Mar-Nov, 1000–1800
Entrance charges: Adults £2, children £0.75, family £5.
WC ⊷ restricted, & ⌨ SHOP

Putlake Adventure Farm
Langton Matravers, Swanage BH19 3EU
© (0929) 423751/422917

See how a real farm works. You can bottle feed lambs and goats and hand milk cows. There are pigs, horses, goats, ducks, geese, chickens, rabbits and guinea pigs. Farmland trail, pets corner and picnic area. On sale: gifts. Location: on B3069, off A351 Swanage-Wareham road.

Open: Easter-Oct, Sun-Fri 1100–1800
Entrance charges: Adults £2.75, children £1.75, OAP/concessions £2.25
WC ⊷ & ⌨ SHOP

DURHAM

Beamish Open Air Museum
Beamish DH9 0RG
© (0207) 231811

The living museum showing life around 1913 in the North country. Costumed staff welcome visitors to a working farm with animals, exhibitions and cheese making, a town, a colliery village and a railway station. Walk into the houses and see how people really lived. And suffered – look at the equipment in the dentist's surgery. Allow at least 5 hours for a visit. Special events in summer. Picnic areas. On sale: Beamish cheese, souvenirs. Location: on A693, 4 miles west of A1(M) Chester-le-Street exit.

Open: Apr-Oct, daily 1000–1800, Nov-Mar, Tues-Sun 1000–1700
Entrance charges (1992): winter-summer adults £4–7, children £2.50–4, OAP/concessions £2.50–4.
WC ⊷ & partial access, ⌨ SHOP

EAST SUSSEX

Barkham Manor Vineyard
Piltdown, Uckfield TN22 3XE
© (0825) 722103

Tour of vineyard and winery with tutored tastings. Large 18th-century thatched barn venue for banquets, weddings, etc. All surrounded by beautiful gardens. This is a genuine working vineyard, no special facilities for children. On sale: wine related gifts. Location: off A272 between Haywards Heath and Uckfield.

Open: Easter-Xmas Eve, Tues-Sun 1000–1700
Entrance charges: Adults £2.30 with tour, £1.50 without guide.
WC ⊷ & ⌨ by arrangement, SHOP

Bartley Mill
Bells Yew Green, Nr Frant, TN3 8BH
© (0892) 890372

13th-century working watermill milling organic grain. Trout hatchery, trout fishing, coarse fishing, rare pigs, and walks. Trout fishing for children (rod hire £1), trout hatchery tours, educational school trips catered for. On sale: Flour, muesli, preserves, biscuits, cakes, eggs. Location: 3 miles southeast of Tunbridge Wells off B2169 towards Lamberhurst.

Open: daily Mar-Sep 1000–1800, Oct-Mar 1000–1700
Entrance charges: Adults £1.50, children £1, OAP/concessions £1, family £3.50
WC ⊷ ⌨ ✕ SHOP

Drusilla's Park
Alfriston BN26 5QS
© (0323) 870656

Famous zoo with breeding groups of animals in natural habitats. Major new addition – Down on the Farm – life size model cow to be milked.

Lambing most times of the year. Railway and adventure playground. All in beautiful rural setting, winner of England's Family Welcome of the Year. Gardens planned to suit needs of disabled and partially sighted visitors. On sale: books, pottery, toys, plants, fudge, gifts. Location: off A27 Lewes-Polegate road.

Open: daily 1000–1700.
Entrance charges: Adults £4.75, children £4.25, OAP/concessions £3.50.
WC ♈ restricted, ♿ ☞ ✗ SHOPS

Michelham Priory
Upper Dicker, Hailsham BN27 3QS
✆ (0323) 844224

Visit the 13th-14th century buildings and Tudor house furnished in period. Exhibitions in Picture Gallery and Tudor Barn, Sussex crafts, coachsmiths and rope museum, working water mill, physic garden. The house and restaurant are in 6 acres of gardens surrounded by one of the largest moats in England. On sale: souvenirs, books. Location: near Hailsham, off A22 & A27.

Open: 25 Mar-Oct, daily 1100–1730. Mar & Nov, Sun 1100–1600.
Entrance charges: Adults £3.30, children £1.90, OAP/concessions £2.90.
WC ♿ ☞ ✗ SHOP

Seven Sisters Sheep Centre
East Dean, Nr Eastbourne BN20 0DG
✆ (0323) 423302

Everything sheepish – on this family run farm. Over 40 breeds of British sheep, seasonal demonstrations, lambing, shearing, sheep milking, cheese making. Other young farm animals – pigs, goats, calves, rabbits and chicks – to feed and cuddle both outside and under cover. 17th-century flint barn. On sale: sheeps milk, cheese, yoghurt and ice cream. Coloured fleeces, knitwear and sheep gifts. Location: a mile from Beachy Head, off A259.

Open: Mar-Sept, daily 1400–1700 (restricted opening in May)
Entrance charges: Adults £2, children £1.25, OAP/concessions £1.60
WC ♿ ☞ SHOP

ESSEX

Epping Bury Farm Centre
Upland Road, Epping CM16 5SA
✆ (0992) 578400

Rare breeds farm centre. Pets corner rabbits, guinea pigs, etc. Chickens, ducks and turkeys roam the farmyard. Adventure barn with safe but exciting ropes, slides, nets, ballpond, hanging slide, obstacles. Nature trail. On sale: eggs and souvenirs. Location: off the B1393 north of Epping, signed Epping Green

Open: daily 0930–2000
Entrance charges: Adults £2, children £1.25, under-5s free, OAP/concessions £1.25.
Adventure Barn £2
WC ♈ ♿ ☞ ✗ SHOP

Marsh Farm Country Park
Marsh Farm Road, South Woodham Ferrers, Chelmsford CM3 5LD
✆ (0245) 321552

A working farm with beef cattle, sheep, free range chickens and pigs. Hand milking demonstrations, pets corner, adventure play area, country walks and nature reserve. On sale: free range eggs. Location: signposted from A130 Rettendon Turnpike roundabout.

Open: mid-Feb-Nov, Mon-Fri 1000–1630, weekends & bank hols 1000–1730
Entrance charges: Adults £1.95, children £1.45, OAP/concessions £1.45
WC ♈ restricted, ♿ ☞ SHOP

GLOUCESTERSHIRE

Cotswold Farm Park
Guiting Power, Cheltenham GL54 5UG
✆ (0451) 850307

The most comprehensive collection of rare breeds of farm livestock in the country in a beautiful farm setting high in the Cotswolds. Pet corner, adventure playground, farm trail, lambing, shearing and other seasonal attractions. On sale: gifts. Location: off the B4077 Stow-on-the-Wold to Tewkwsbury road.

Open: April-Sept, daily 1030–1800
Entrance charges: Adults £3 children £1.50, OAP/concessions £2.
WC ♿ ☞ SHOP

Cotswold Falconry Centre
Batsford Park, Moreton-in-Marsh GL56 9QB
✆ (0386) 701043

Daily demonstrations in the art of falconry. Flying eagles, hawks, owls and falcons. Many different types of birds of prey to be seen, the emphasis is on their breeding and conservation. On sale: gifts. Location: west of Moreton-in-Marsh on A44 west.

Open: Mar-Oct, daily 1030–1730, Nov-Dec Sat-Sun only
Entrance charges: Adults £2.50, children £1, OAP/concessions £1.50
WC 🐕 ♿ ☕ SHOP

Slimbridge Wildfowl and Wetlands Trust
Slimbridge, Gloucester GL2 7BT
✆ (0453) 890065

A fun day out for the family to enjoy walks, secluded hides, beautiful scenery and a world famous collection of exotic waterfowl in their natural setting. Exhibitions, tropical house and spectacular views of wintering wildfowl. On sale: books, gifts. Location: signposted from M5, Jcts 13 & 14

Open: all year except Xmas, 0930–1700 (summer), 0930–1600 (winter)
Entrance charges: Adults £4.50, children £2.25, OAP/concessions £3.40
WC ♿ ☕ SHOP

Westonbirt Arboretum
Tetbury GL8 8QS
✆ (0666) 880220

One of the largest and most imposing collections of trees and shrubs in the world, covering 600 acres of beautifully landscaped Cotswold countryside. Visitor centre, exhibitions and 17 miles of footpaths. Best in spring with colourful displays of rhododendrons, azaleas, camelias, magnolias and bluebells. Autumn colours magnificent, especialy the maples. On sale: country gifts. Location: 3 miles south of Tetbury.

Open: all year daily, 1000–2000/dusk
Entrance charges: Adults £2, children £1, OAP £1.20.
WC 🐕 restricted to 480 acres, ♿ ☕ SHOP

HAMPSHIRE

The Watercress Line
The Railway Station, Alresford S024 9JG
✆ (0962) 734200/733810

Hampshire's Rural Railway, once used to carry watercress to London's markets, climbs through rolling countryside between Alton and Alresford. The 4 stations are authentically restored, period advertising, agricultural goods. Ropley has a rustic ramble, superb views, locomotive yard and picnic areas. On sale: souvenir and bookshops at terminus stations. Ropley Station also has collectors' items, videos, sometimes plants. Location: Alton and Alresford signposted off A31.

Open: varies with seasons, call talking timetable (0962) 734886.
WC 🐕 ♿ ☕ ✕ SHOP

Whitchurch Silk Mill
28, Winchester Street, Whitchurch RG28 7AL
✆ (0256) 893882

Working silk mill situated on River Test. Historic looms weaving silk, waterwheel powered machinery. Video and audio on silk production. On sale: silk on roll, ties, scarves, handkerchiefs. Location: A34 Winchester to Newbury.

Open: all year except Xmas-New Year, Tues-Sun 1030–1700
Entrance charges: Adults £2.50, children £0.60, OAP/concessions £1.90, family £5.50.
WC ♿ ☕ SHOP

HEREFORDSHIRE

Bewdley Museum
Load Street, Bewdley DY12 2AE
✆ (0299) 403573

Housed in the town's old Butcher's Shambles, the museum's emphasises the crafts and industries of Bewdley and the Wyre Forest area. Displays cover tanners, charcoal burners, basketmakers, bee keepers and brass founders. Daily rope and clay pipe making. On sale: craftware, souvenirs, books. Location: Bewdley is on A456, 4 miles west of Kidderminster.

Open: Mar-Nov, Mon-Sat 1000–1730, Sun 1400–1730
Entrance charges: Adults £0.60, unaccompanied children £0.30, otherwise free, OAP/concessions £0.30
🐕 ♿ SHOP

Bromyard Heritage Centre
Rowberry Street, Bromyard
✆ (0885) 582314

The Year of the Hop exhibition traces the growing and picking cycle and changes in cultivation. Three dimensional display. Displays relating to the railway, education and local history. Tourist information centre. On sale: souvenirs.

Open:Easter-Sep.
Entrance free
WC SHOP

Cider Museum & King Offa Distillery
Pomona Place, off Whitecross Road, Hereford
© (0432) 354207

Displays in a former cider works include 17th-century French Beam Press, a cooper's shop, 1920s factory bottling line, champagne cider cellars and cider brandy distillery. On sale: local cider, perry & King Offa Distillery products, china, pottery. Location: off A438, near city centre.

Open: April-Oct, daily 1000–1730; Nov-Mar, Mon-Sat 1300–1700. Last admissions 45 mins earlier
Entrance charges: Adults £1.80 children £1.25, OAP/concessions £1.25
WC ⚓ &restricted & no WC, SHOP

Domestic Fowl Trust
Honeybourne Pastures, Honeybourne, Nr Evesham WR11 5QJ
© (0386) 833083

The only Conservation Centre specialising in the display and breeding of all pedigree domestic ducks, hens, bantams and turkeys. All breeds are in labelled paddocks. Also children's farm and adventure playground. On sale: poultry related gifts, equipment, books, feedstuffs, housing and young stock. Location: signposted off A46 Broadway-Stratford-on-Avon road.

Open: all year, Sat-Thur 1030–1700
Entrance charges: Adults £3, children £1.75, OAP/concessions £2.50
WC & ⚓ SHOP

Dunkertons Cider Company
Luntley, Pembridge, Leominster HR6 9ED
© (05447) 653

Ciders and perry made from traditional varieties of cider apples and perry pears. Tastings from oak casks. Mill usually open with information on process. On sale: cider and perry, much is organic. Location: a mile from A44 at Pembridge.

Open: all year, Mon-Sat 1000–1800
Free entrance
& partial access, SHOP

L'Escargot Anglais
Credenhill Snail Farm, Credenhill, Hereford
© (0432) 760218

All aspects of snail farming both indoors and out. Guided tours of farm, display of British methods and equipment. Display of wild British snails and tastings of snail dishes. On sale: frozen recipe snail dishes, snail preparation dishes, snail farm-

ing books and souvenirs. Location: On A480 near Credenhill village.

Open: May-Sept, daily 1030–1800, Oct-Apr, Mon-Fri 1100–1700
Entrance charges: Adults £1.50, children £1, under-8 free, OAP/concessions £1.20.
WC ⚓ SHOP

Jinney Ring Craft Centre
Hanbury Road, Hanbury, Bromsgrove B60 4BU
© (0527) 821272

Twelve craft shops where crafts people can be seen at work. Craft and art gallery, needlework department. Something for all the family, set in beautiful old farm buildings in the midst of the wonderful Worcestershire countryside. On sale: craft goods. Location: on B4091, just north of B4090 Droitwich-Alcester road.

Open: all year, Tues-Sun, 1030–1700
Free entrance
WC ⚓ & partial access, ⚓ SHOPS

Wye Valley Heritage Centre
Doward, Symonds Yat, Ross-on-Wye
© (0600) 890474

A private collection of antique tractors, farming bygones and hundreds of tools used by country craftsmen. Also many antique domestic items. This is probably the largest collection of rural bygones open to the public in the country. Picnic area and play area. Location: signposted west of Symonds Yat.

Open: Easter-Oct, daily 1030–1730
Entrance charges: Adults £2, children £1, OAP/concessions £1.50
WC ⚓ &partial access, ⚓ SHOP

HERTFORDSHIRE

Mill Green Museum
Mill Green, Hatfield AL9 5PD
© (0707) 271362

Local history museum and fully restored water powered corn mill. Visitors can see the grinding of the corn in the traditional way. Small local history museum with changing programme of temporary exhibitions in the former miller's house adjoining the mill. Craft demonstrations on Summer weekends. On sale: flour, souvenirs, books. Location: signposted from A1000 and A414.

Open: Jan-Dec, Tues-Fri 1000–1700, Sat-Sun & Bank hols 1400–1700
Entrance charges on application
WC & partial access, SHOP

KENT

Brattle Farm Museum
Brattle Farm, Staplehurst TN12 0HE
✆ (0580) 891222

A personal collection of agricultural bygones including tractors, vintage cars, motor cycles, bicycles, blacksmith's and wheelwright's equipment and a pair of working oxen. Many items of local manufacture. On sale: souvenirs and pottery. Location: off the A229 in Staplehurst.

Open: Easter-Oct, Sun & bank hols 0930–1830
Entrance charges: Adults £1.50, children £1, OAP/concessions £1
WC ✝ & ☕ SHOP

Iden Croft Herbs
Frittenden Road, Staplehurst TN12 0DH
✆ (0580) 891432

A peaceful tranquil herb centre with a walled garden and 4 acres of gardens showing beauty and use of herbs. National Origanum Collection, representative collections of Mint and Thyme. Herb courses throughout the year. Garden especially for blind/disabled visitors. Many seats in shade and sun. On sale: enormous range of herbs, aromatic and herbaceous plants, herbal medicines, books, terracotta. Location: signposted from A229 south of Staplehurst.

Open: all year, Mar-Sept, Mon-Sat 0900–1700, Suns & Bank hols 1100–1700; Oct-Feb Mon-Sat 0900–1700.
Donation suggestion £1
WC ✝ & ☕ SHOP

Parsonage Farm Rural Heritage Centre
North Elham, Nr Canterbury CT4 6UY
✆ (0303) 840766/840356

Since 1270 Parsonage Farm has been in the Elham Valley, now designated an Area of Outstanding Natural Beauty. The same family has owned the farm since medieval times. This family run working farm has displays illustrating past and present, and traditional and rare breeds of farm animals. Farm and nature trail, picnic area. On sale: eggs, honey, jam, local crafts and souvenirs. Location: signposted from B2065 (off A2 from Canterbury).

Open: Easter-Sept, Tues-Sun & Bank hols 1030–1700
Entrance charges: Adults £2.30, children £1.40, OAP/concessions £1.60
WC & ☕ SHOP

Rare Farm Animals of Hollanden
Great Hollanden Farm, Mill Lane, Hildenborough, Nr Sevenoaks TN15 0SG
✆ (0732) 832276

Over 60 rare breeds, pets corner, adventure playground, tractor-trailer rides, recreation of an Iron Age settlement, PYO fruit. School visits catered for. Picnic area. On sale: fresh fruit and vegetables, meat and dairy produce, gifts. Location: 7 miles south of M25, off A21 on B245.

Open: 26 Mar-30 Sept, daily 1030–1700
Entrance charges: Adults £3.40, children £2.20, OAP/concessions £2.75.
WC & ☕ SHOP

South of England Rare Breeds Centre
Highlands Farm, Woodchurch, Ashford TN26 3RJ
✆ (0233) 861493

Kent's newest and greenest attraction opened April 1992. Ninety acres of rolling Kent countryside, 65 breeds of British farm animals – pigs, poultry, cattle, sheep, goats, ducks, and geese. Childrens corner. Most animals can be seen under cover, especially in winter months. On sale: delicatessen, farm produce. Location: on B2067 west of Ham Street (M20, Jct 10/A2070).

Open: all year, daily, summer 1030–1730, winter 1030–1630.
Entrance charges: Adults £2, children £0.50, OAP/concessions £1.75.
WC & ☕ ✕ SHOP

Toy & Model Museum
Forstal Farm, Goudhurst Road, Lamberhurst TN3 8AG
✆ (0892) 890711

Situated in a converted Oast on a working hop farm, this collection is guaranteed to bring back childhood memories: Rupert bear books and memorabilia, dolls and teddy bears, model railway, working model 1920s fairground and Chequered History – toy and model Grand Prix racing cars through the century. Mock village street with crafts and collectables in individual shops. Also, duck pond, picnic area, woodland and riverside walks. On sale: crafts, toys, collectables. Location: on A262 east of A21.

Open: all year, daily 1000–1800.
Entrance charges: Adults £2, children £1.25, OAP/concessions £1.25.
WC ✝ & ☕ SHOP

Whitbread Hop Farm
Beltring, Paddock Wood TN12 6PY
© (0622) 872068
FAX (0622) 872630

This leading Kent Tourist attraction, featuring the largest collection of Victorian oast houses in the world, is the home of the famous Whitbread Shire horses. Also: hop story exhibition, animal village, pottery workshop, nature trail, play area. On sale: gifts, souvenirs. Location: M20 Jct 4, then via Tonbridge to Paddock Wood.

Open: all year, daily 1000–1700
Entrance charges on application.
WC ⊨ ও ☐ ✕ SHOP

LANCASHIRE
Martin Mere Wildfowl & Wetlands Centre
Burscough, Ormskirk L40 0TA
© (0704) 895181

A fun day out for the family to enjoy walks, secluded hides, beautiful scenery and seeing the many species of waterfowl. On sale: books, gifts. Location: 6 miles from Ormskirk, signposted from M6, M61 & M58.

Open: all year, daily, summer 0930–1730, winter 0930–1600
Entrance charges: Adults £3.50, children £2.50, OAP £2.50, family £8.75.
WC ও ☐ SHOP

LEICESTERSHIRE
Melton Mowbray Cattle Market
Market Place, Melton Mowbray
© (0664) 67771

Cattle market established in 1324. Visitors can watch sales both inside and outside the auction rings. Sheep, cattle, pigs, goats, poultry, and much more. On sale: from livestock to budgies, hay and outdoor wear. Location: near town centre, A606 Nottingham-Melton Mowbray road.

Open: Tues 0900–1600
Free entrance
WC ⊨ ও ☐ ✕ SHOP

Rutland County Museum
Catmos Street, Oakham, Rutland LE15 6HW
© (0572) 723654

Museum of Rutland Life includes farm equipment, machinery and wagons, rural tradesmen's tools, domestic collections, local archaeology. Accommodated in a splendid late 18th century indoor riding school. Special gallery on Volunteer Soldier in Leicestershire and Rutland. Location: on A6003 near Oakham town centre.

Open: daily, Mon-Sat 1000–1700, Apr-Oct Sun 1400–1700, Nov-Mar Sun 1400–1600
Entrance Free
WC ও SHOP

LINCOLNSHIRE
Springfields
Camelgate, Spalding PE12 6ET
© (0775) 724843

In spring this 25 acre show garden provides a spectacle of tulips, daffodils, hyacinths etc. In summer dazzling display of bedding plants. Spalding Flower Festival 1st May. On sale: gifts. Location: a mile outside Spalding (A151).

Open: Apr-Sept, daily 1000–1800.
Entrance charges: Adults £2.50, accompanied children free, OAP/concessions £2.30.
WC ও ☐ SHOP

NORFOLK
Letheringsett Water Mill
Riverside Road, Letheringsett, Holt NR25 7YD
© (0263) 713153

See the ancient craft of flour making with stones powered by water. This watermill was built in 1802 and is now restored and fully functional. Working afternoons, with full guided tours 1400–1630. Demonstrations Tues, Thurs & Sun. Also hungry ducks outside. On sale: 100% wholewheat flour, bread, eggs, vegetables, pet food and gifts. Location: a mile west of Holt off A148.

Open: all year, Tues-Fri 0900–1300 & 1400–1700, Sat 1000–1300, Sun (Whit-Sept) 1400–1700.
Entrance charges: viewing/demonstration Adults £1/2, children £0.75/1.25, OAP/concessions £1/1.50.
WC SHOP

NORTHAMPTONSHIRE
The Old Dairy Farm Centre
Upper Stowe, Nr Weedon NN7 4SH
© (0327) 40525

Working farm with converted listed farm buildings containing craft workshops, antique and clothes shop. Animals including rare breeds on view. Location: off A5, 5 miles north of Towcester.

Open: daily, Jan-Feb 1000–1630, Mar-Dec 1000–1730

Entrance free, animal viewing £0.50
WC & ♿ ✕ SHOP

NORTH HUMBERSIDE

Sewerby Hall
Church Lane, Sewerby, Bridlington
✆ (0262) 673769(Grounds)/677874(Hall)

Set in 50 acres of grounds the 18- and 19th-century Hall has an art gallery, museum, archaeology display, vintage motor cycle collection and Amy Johnson Trophy Room. Grounds have Formal Garden, Old English Garden, Rose Garden, mini-zoo, aviary, golf, putting, bowls, herds of deer, llamas and wallabies. Ring for calendar of special events. Location: 2 miles north of Bridlington.

Open: Easter-Sept Sun-Fri 1000–1800, Sat 1330–1800; Oct/Nov/Xmas/Feb-Easter daily 1100–1600.
Entrance charges: Adults £1.60, children £0.80, OAP/concessions £1.20.
WC ↟ & partial access, ♿ ✕ SHOP

NORTHUMBERLAND

Chipchase Castle
Wark-on-Tyne NE48 3NT
✆ (0434) 230685

The castle is set in an idyllic position overlooking rolling parkland with sheep and cattle down to the North Tyne River. Guided tours of the interior of this Jacobean house, unattended viewing of 18th-century chapel and 14th-century Pele Tower. Also a walled vegetable garden, herbaceous borders, wild garden with lake and wildfowl. On sale: books and plants. Location: east of Wark (B6320) north of Hadrian's Wall.

Open: 1–28 Jun daily, house 1400–1700, gardens 1000–1800, April-14 July & Sept, gardens only
Entrance charges: All/Gardens only Adults £3/1, children £1.50/0.50
WC & gardens only, SHOP

NORTH YORKSHIRE

The Hawes Ropemakers
Hawes DL8 3NT
✆ (0969) 667487

See how the twist is put in - watch traditional rope-making in which many fine yarns are twisted to make a strong rope. Cattle halters, horse leading reins, bannister, church bell ropes, dog leads. Note: disabled access limited on Sats. Location: on A684 opposite children's playground.

Open: all year Mon-Fri 0900–1730, July-Oct Sats 1000–1730
Free entrance
WC & ✕ SHOP

Lightwater Valley Theme Park
North Stainley, Ripon HG4 3HT
✆ (0765) 635321

125 acres of country park and lakeland with unique rides, skill testing activities and the world's biggest rollercoaster. Shopping mall. On sale: toys and fancy goods, preserves. Location: 3 miles north of Ripon on A6108.

Open: Jun-Aug, daily 1030–1700/1800. April-May & Sept-Oct selected days.
Entrance charges: ✆ (0765) 635368 for 1993 prices
WC & ♿ ✕ SHOPS

Yorkshire Dales Falconry and Conservation Centre
Crows Nest, Nr Giggleswick, Settle N. Yorks LA2 8AS
✆ (0729) 822832/825164

A day out for all the family and the chance to see the largest bird of prey in the world free flying – the Andean Condor. An all weather attraction. Free flying displays daily, inside if raining. A chance to hold a bird on your fist. Henry Hedgehog Park (playground). Falconry school and courses available. On sale: falconry equipment, pottery, prints, gifts, educational toys. Location: signposted off A65 out of Settle.

Open: all year, daily 1000–1800.
Entrance charges: Adults £3.95, children £2.25, OAP/concessions £2.95, family £10.50
WC & ♿ SHOP

NOTTINGHAMSHIRE

The White Post Modern Farm Centre
Farnsfield, Nr Newark NG22 8HL
✆ (0623) 882977

Modern working farm with indoor and outdoor exhibitions showing over 4000 animals including: chicks, piglets, cattle, deer, rabbits, owls, amphibians, reptiles, bees, snails, spiders, rheas, quails and butterflies. New night-time walk. Winner of 1991 Family Welcome of the Year Award. On sale: home produce. Location: 12 miles north of Nottingham on A614.

Open: daily, Mon-Fri 1000–1700, weekends 1000–1800
Entrance charges: Adults £2.50, children £1.50, under-4s free, OAP/concessions £1.50.
WC & ♿ SHOP

OXFORDSHIRE

Ardington Pottery
15 Home Farm, School Road, Ardington, Nr Wantage OX12 8PN
✆ (0235) 833302

Working studio pottery with displays of handmade stoneware and porcelain ceramics made on the premises since the 19th century. Picture tiled dairy. On sale: pottery. Location: 2 miles east of Wantage, off A417.

Open: daily, Mon-Sat 1000–1700, Sun 1130–1700.
Free entrance
WC ♟ & ♿ SHOP

Cogges Manor Farm Museum
Church Lane, Cogges, Witney OX8 6LA
✆ (0993) 772602

Living museum of farming and rural Oxfordshire life set in a manor house with walled garden. Daily craft and farming demonstrations, a variety of animals, nature and history trails and picnic areas. On sale: souvenirs, books, garden produce. Location: signs from A40, footpath from town centre.

Open: Apr-Oct, Tues-Fri 1030–1730, weekends 1200–1730
Entrance charges: Adults £2.50, children £1.25, OAP/concessions £1.25
WC & ♟ ♿ SHOP

The Herb Farm and Saxon Maze
Peppard Road, Sonning Common, Reading RG4 9NJ
✆ (0734) 724220

Demonstration gardens and a collection of horticultural and agricultural hand tools. The maze, created 1991, is a symbolic hedge maze covering an acre, an intriguing puzzle for all the family. On sale: herb related products – toothpaste, potpourri – and garden sundries, scented plants, herbs, wild flowers, 200 varieties. Location: 4 miles north of Reading on B481.

Open: Tues-Sun, 1000–1700
Entrance charges (maze): Adults £0.50, children £0.25
WC ♟ & ♿ SHOP

Waterfowl Sanctuary and Rescue Centre
Wiggington Heath, Nr Hook Norton, Banbury OX15 4LB
✆ (0608) 730252

Set in 22 acres of unspoiled Oxfordshire countryside, a unique collection of rare breeds of domestic fowl, poultry and farm animals. Children

Food on sale for larger animals. Incubation and hatching eggs on view periodically. Picnic areas. On sale: education packs, fact sheets for teachers, souvenirs. Location: signposted from A361 & B4035.

Open: all year, daily 1030–1930.
Entrance charges: Adults £2, children £1
WC & SHOP

SHROPSHIRE

Hoo Farm Animal Kingdom
Hoo Farm, Preston-on-the-Weald Moors, Telford TF6 6DJ
✆ (0952) 677917

Hoo Farm offers all those things normal farms can't: sheep racing, steeplechasing ostriches, wooden cows, tame llamas, plus cattle, sheep, deer, and goats. Demonstrations of country crafts and skills beekeeping, weaving, spinning, shoeing, pheasant-rearing. On sale: home produce eg, trout, venison, eggs, plus game, preserves, farm ice cream, woolcrafts. Location: off A442 on Preston/Horton road north of Telford.

Open: Easter-Sept, Wed-Sun & Bank hols 1100–1800
Entrance charges: Adults £2, children £1.50, OAP/concessions £1.50
WC ✠ restricted, & ☐ SHOP

Pimhill Mill Farm Shop
Lea Hall, Harmer Hill, Shrewsbury SY4 3DY
✆ (0939) 290342

The farm mill grinds organic wheat to be bought in this shop along with other organic and specialist foods: organic meats, cheeses, preserves, fruit, vegetables, bread, cakes. Picnic/barbecue site with friendly farm animals for all to see. Location: A528 Shrewsbury-Ellesmere road, 6 miles from Shrewsbury.

Open: all year, Wed-Sat 1000–1700
Entrance free
WC ☐ Tues-Sat, SHOP

SOMERSET

Chewton Cheese Dairy
Priory Farm, Chewton Mendip, Nr Bath BA3 4NT
✆ (0761) 241666

Watch traditional farmhouse cheddar cheesemaking and sample the produce. Note: no cheesemaking Thurs or Sun. Best viewing time 1130–1430. Guided tours, video available. Unusual animals, and gardens for picnics. On sale:

cheese, butter, cream and other local produce. Location: 5 miles north of Wells on A39

Open: all year, 0930–1630.
Entrance charges (guided tour): Adults £1.50, children £1
WC & ☐ ✗ SHOP

Hornsbury Mill
Elieghwater, Chard TA20 3AQ
✆ (0460) 63317

A restored and working 200-year-old waterwheel and cornmill, in 5 acres of landscaped gardens with trout and duck lake and bygones museum. Evening restaurant and bar meals, functions and conference facilities. On sale: local crafts, toys and produce. Location: on A358 between Chard and Ilminster.

Open: all year, Mon-Sat 1000–2330, Sun 1000–1800.
Entrance charges (museum only): Adults £1.50, children £1, OAP/concessions £1.
WC ✠ & ☐ ✗ SHOP

John Wood (Exmoor) Ltd
Old Cleeve Tannery, Minehead TA24 6HT
✆ (0984) 40291

Visit the Tannery, located amid beautiful rural scenery, and see skilled craftsmen at work. Guided tours around the factory at 1045, 1130, 1415 and 1500 hrs. See sheepskins going through all the various stages to become rugs, slippers, gloves, paint roller skins, etc. On sale: factory seconds plus coats, rugs, wool jumpers, leather goods and toys. Location: signposted on A39 Williton-Minehead road.

Open: all year, Mon-Fri 0900–1700, Sat 1000–1600
Entrance charges: Adults £0.50, children £0.25, OAP/concessions £0.25.
WC & ☐ SHOP

Willow & Wetlands Visitor Centre
Meare Green, Stoke St Gregory, Taunton TA3 6HY
✆ (0823) 490249

Willow growing and basket making is a traditional Somerset craft, here all aspects of the industry can be seen from willow preparation to finished basket and other withy products. Guided tours last one hour. Historic items displayed plus RSPB exhibition of flora and fauna of surrounding wetlands. On sale: basketware and books. Location: signposted at West Lyng on A361 Taunton-Glastonbury road.

Open: all year, Mon-Sat 0900–1700.
Willow tour charges: Adults £1.75, children
£0.75, OAP/concessions £1.50.
WC ⋔ ⌂ SHOP

SOUTH YORKSHIRE

Wigfield Farm, Worsbrough Mill Museum
Worsbrough Country Park, Worsbrough
Bridge, Barnsley S70 5LJ
✆ (0226) 774527

Historic working waterpowered cornmill and
open farm with rare and commercial breeds set
in 200-acre country park with fishing reservoir.
On sale: stoneground flour, other mill products.
Location: off A61, 2 miles north of M1, Jct 36

Open: Wed-Sun 1000–1700/dusk
Entrance – optional small donations
WC ⋔restricted, & ⌂ SHOP

STAFFORDSHIRE

Blackbrook World of Birds
Wink Hill, Nr Leek
✆ (0565)873282/(0538) 308293

On this rapidly expanding site in the Staffordshire
moorlands there are many species of unusual
birds on view – kookaburras, sacred ibis, rheas.
Also pets area, farm animals and domestic
waterfowl. Waterfowl range from massive Tou-
louse geese to miniature Call ducks. Picnic area.
On sale: bird-orientated gifts. Location: on Alton
Towers turning, off A523 Leek-Ashbourne road.

Open: April-Oct, daily 1130–1730.
Entrance charges: Adults £2, children £1, OAP/
concessions £1.
WC & ⌂ SHOP

Moorlands Farm Park
Ipstones, Stoke-on-Trent ST10 2LP
✆ (0538) 266479

Open farm and rare breeds with farm walks, picnic areas with panoramic views, children's play
areas. Free bag of feed provided to feed the
friendly animals. Location: signposted off A523
Leek-Ashbourne road.

Open: Apr-Nov, daily 1030-dusk
Entrance charges: Adults £1.50, children £0.75,
OAP/concessions £0.75
WC ⋔ & ⌂ SHOP

SUFFOLK

Boyton Vineyard
Stoke-by-Clare, Sudbury CO10 4AN
✆ (0440) 61893

Tour of vineyard and tastings in wine lodge. Gardens, listed 15th-century farmhouse and picnic
area. On sale: estate produced wine. Location:
signposted from A1092, south of Bury St
Edmunds

Open: April-Oct, daily 1030–1830
Entrance charges: Adults £1.50, children/OAP/
concessions free
WC ⋔ & ✕ by appointment, SHOP

Craft at the Suffolk Barn
Fornham Road Farm, Great Barton, Bury
St Edmunds IP31 2SD
✆ (028487) 317

Display and sale of East Anglian crafts and plants
centred on an old Suffolk barn, herb and wild
flower garden, wide selection of home cooking
made on the premises to traditional recipes. Location: signposted from A143 at Great Barton.

Open: Mid-Mar-Xmas, Wed-Sat 1000–1730,
Sun 1200–1730.
Free entrance
WC ⋔ & ⌂ SHOP

Easton Park Farm
Easton, Nr Wickham Market
✆ (0728) 746475

A Victorian farm, setting for many species of farm
animals including rare breeds. Modern dairy with
viewing gallery, unique Victorian dairy, green
trail, Suffolk horses and early farm machinery.
Adventure playground. Location: signposted
from Easton (A12/B1116).

Open: 21 Mar-30 Sept, daily 1030–1800
Entrance charges: Adults £3.70, children £2,
OAP/concessions £3.
WC ⋔ & ⌂ SHOP

Tangham Trail
Tangham, Woodbridge IP12 3NF
✆ (0394) 450164

Phoenix Trail is over 3 miles partially suited to
wheelchairs, and with shortcuts. 3 Forest Cycle
Trail is 25 miles on forest tracks and public roads,
suits mountain bikes. Follow footprint or cycle
signs from B1084 Woodbridge-Oxford road. Picnic areas. Phoenix Trail leaflet £0.50, Cycle Trail
leaflet & map £0.80.

Open: daily, dawn-dusk.
WC ⋔ &

SURREY

Rural Life Museum
Reeds Road, Tilford, Farnham GU10 2DL
✆ (025125) 2300/5571

Displays on all aspects of past village life, forge, wheelwright's shop, wagons, forestry, etc. Arboretum, woodland walks, picnic area. On sale: crafts. Location: off A287 Farnham-Haslemere road.

Open: Apr-Sept. Wed-Sun, 1100–1800
Entrance charges: Adults £2.50, children £1.25, OAP/concessions £2
WC ⊁ ᕷ ⨅ SHOP

TYNE AND WEAR

Washington Wildfowl & Wetlands Centre
District 15, Washington NE38 8LE
✆ (091) 4165454

A fun day out for the family to enjoy with walks, secluded hides, beautiful scenery and seeing the many species of wildfowl. On sale: books and gifts. Location: east of Washington, signposted on A195 & A1231.

Open: daily, summer 0930–1700, winter 0930–1600.
Entrance charges: Adults £2.95, children £1.50, OAP/concessions £7.50, family £7.50.
WC ᕷ ⨅ SHOP

WEST MIDLANDS

Dudley Canal Trust
Black Country Museum, Tipton Road, Dudley
✆ (021) 5205321

Narrowboat trips into Dudley Canal Tunnel and Singing Cavern limestone mine. Audo-visual dis-play. Refreshments only on prebooked evening trips. On sale: souvenirs at towpath shop. Location: signposted off A4123 Birmingham-Wolverhampton road.

Open: Mar-Nov, daily 1000–1700.
Entrance charges: Adults £1.70, children £1.30, OAP/concessions £1.30
⊁ ᕷ SHOP

WEST SUSSEX

Arundel Wildfowl & Wetlands Centre
Mill Road, Arundel BN18 9PB
✆ (0903) 883355

A fun day out for the family to enjoy with walks, secluded hides, beautiful scenery and seeing the many species of wildfowl. On sale: books and gifts. Location: a mile north of Arundel town centre.

Open: daily, summer 0930–1830, winter 0930–1700
Entrance charges: Adults £3.50, children £1.75, OAP/concessions £2.50, family £8.75.
WC ᕷ ⨅ ✖ SHOP

Weald and Downland Open Air Museum
Singleton, Chichester
✆ (024363) 348

Unusual collection of rescued historic buildings from southeast England, including medieval farmstead, farmhouses and agricultural buildings reconstructed in this country park setting with livestock. Ideal for anyone interested in farming and rural life. On sale: books, souvenirs. Location: on A286 Chichester-Midhurst road.

Open: Mar-Oct, daily 1100–1700, Nov-Feb, Wed & Sun 1100–1600
Entrance charges: Adults £3.60, children £1.75, OAP/concessions £3
WC ⊁ ᕷ partial access, ⨅ SHOP

SCOTLAND

DUMFRIES AND GALLOWAY

Caerlaverock Wildfowl & Wetlands Centre
Eastpark Farm, Caerlaverock, Dumfriesshire
© (38777) 200

Thousands of different species of waterfowl can be viewed from screened approaches, an observatory with three towers and 20 hides. Location: signposted from A75 in Dumfries.

Open: daily 1000–1700
Entrance charges: Adults £2.70, children £1.35, OAP/concessions £2, family £6.75.
WC ₺ ⌨

GRAMPIAN

Aden Country Park
Mintlaw, Peterhead, Aberdeenshire AB42 8FQ
© (0771) 22857

Award-winning agricultural museum and working farm set within beautiful woodlands of Aden Country Park. On site are also tourist information centre, picnic and play area, Best Caravan Park

In Scotland 1992. On sale: crafts. Location: a mile west of Mintlaw on A950.

Open: May-Sept, daily 1100–1700, Apr & Oct Sat-Sun 1200–1700
Entrance charges: Adults £1, children free
WC ⱦ ₺ ⌨ SHOP

STRATHCLYDE

Ayrshire Museum of Country Life & Costume
Dalgarven Mill, Dalry Road, Kilwinning KA13 6PL
© (0294) 52448

Step back in time at this working water mill, country life museum and costume collection all in an idyllic setting with riverside walks. The listed vernacular mill and farm buildings give this attraction a distinctive ambience. Hideaway/camp site. On sale: home baked bread, cakes, milled flour and oatmeal, pewter. Location: on the A737 Kilwinning-Dalry road.

Open: all year, Mon-Sat 1000–1700, Sun 1230–1730
Entrance charges: Adults £2.50, children £1, OAP/concessions £1.50
WC ⱦrestricted, ₺ ⌨ SHOP

CHANNEL ISLANDS

JERSEY

Jersey Shire Horse Farm Museum
Champ Donne, Route de Trodez, St Ouen
© (0534) 482372

One of the most popular tourist attractions on the Channel Islands. Come and see Shire horses and foals, Shetland ponies, donkeys, coach house, driving vehicles, bygones collection, sheep, goats, poultry, pigs, aviaries. Take a carriage ride or watch the parade, twice daily. On sale: gifts.

Open: Mar-Nov, Sun-Fri 1000–1730
Entrance charges: Adults £3, children £1, under-3s free, OAP/concessions £2.50.
WC ₺ ⌨ SHOP

WALES

DYFED

Llanelli Wildfowl & Wetlands Centre
Penclacwydd, Llwynhendy, Llanelli SA14 9SH
✆ (0554) 741087

A fun day out for the family to enjoy walks, secluded hides, beautiful scenery and seeing the many species of wildfowl. On sale: books, gifts. Location: off A484 Swansea road, 3 miles east of Llanelli.

Open: daily, summer 0930–1700, winter 0930–1600
Entrance charges: Adults £2.95, children £1.50, OAP/concessions £2.20. family £7.50.
WC & ☛ SHOP

Llangloffan Farmhouse Cheese Centre
Castle Morris, Haverfordwest
✆ (03485) 241

Watch the cheesemaking process from milk to classic Llangloffan hard cheese. Visitors should arrive by 1000. Milk is from our Jersey cows, the farm is run on organic principles. On sale: Welsh cheeses. Location: off A487 Fishguard-St David's road.

Open: Cheesemaking session 1000–1230, May-Sept Mon-Sat, April& Oct Mon Wed Thur Sat.(Farm shop daily except Sun)
Entrance charges: Adults £1.50, children £1, OAP/concessions £1.25
WC ☛ & ☛ SHOP

Museum of the Welsh Woollen Industry
Drefach Felindre, Llandysul SA44 5UP
✆ (0559) 370929

Working museum shows the history of the woollen industry and its people, with regular demonstrations of the skilled process of turning fleece into fabric. Located alongside a working woollen mill and craft shops. On sale: crafts, souvenirs. Location: on A484 Carmarthen-Lampeter road, 4 miles east of Newcastle Emlyn.

Open: April-Sept Mon-Sat, Oct-Mar Mon-Fri, 1000–1700
Entrance charges: Adults £1, children £0.50, OAP/concessions £0.75
WC & partial, ☛ SHOP

POWYS

Centre for Alternative Technology
Machynlleth SY20 9AZ
✆ (0654) 702400

Discover the world of green living. Seven acres of working displays include wind turbines, water power, solar energy, recycling, smallholding and energy conservation. Waterpowered cliff railway, organic gardens and adventure playground. On sale: gifts, books. Location: on A487 north of Machynlleth.

Open: Mar-Oct, daily, 1000–1700, Nov-Feb bookings only
Entrance charges (1992): Adults £2.95, children £1.90, OAP/concessions £2.70
WC & ☛ ✕ SHOP

SOUTH GLAMORGAN

Llanerch Vineyard
Hensol, Pendoylan CF7 8JU
✆ (0443) 225877

Visit the only vineyard in Wales producing estate bottled wine. There is a 6-acre vineyard with winery, and 10 acres of woodland and lakes. On sale: wine, souvenirs and cider. Location: a mile south of M4, Jct 34.

Open: Easter-Xmas, daily 1000–1700
Entrance charges: Adults £2, children £1, under-10s free
WC & ☛ SHOP

NORTHERN IRELAND

CO ANTRIM

Leslie Hill
Ballymoney BT53 6QL
✆ (02656) 66803

Idyllic setting with old farm buildings, large collection of horse drawn machines, farm animals, poultry, pets, carriages, museums, lakes, walks, trap rides, adventure playground and walled garden. On sale: home produce – eggs, jams, plants plus crafts. Location: signposted from the A26 (Ballymoney bypass) roundabout.

Open: Easter-Jun & Sept Sat, Sun & Bank hols 1400–1800, Jul-Aug Mon-Sat 1100–1800, Sun 1400–1800
Entrance charges: Adults £1.90, children £1.30, OAP/Concessions £1.30
WC & partial, ⊡ SHOP

CO DOWN

Castle Espie Wildfowl & Wetlands Centre
Ballydrain Road, Comber BT23 6EA
✆ (0247) 874146

A fun day out for the family to enjoy walks, secluded hides, beautiful scenery and seeing the many species of wildfowl. On sale: books, gifts. Location: signposted from the A22 Comber-Killyleagh road.

Open: Mon-Sat 1030-dusk, Sun 1400-dusk
Entrance charges: Adults £2.20, children £1.10, OAP/concessions £1.50
WC ⊡ ✕ SHOP

REPUBLIC OF IRELAND

CO KILDARE

Ardkill Farm,
Carbury
✆ (0405) 53009

Children feed pet lambs and see the farm animals: ducks, geese, bronze turkeys, chickens and peacocks. A sheep shearing demonstration takes place at 1600 hrs, children help to roll up the fleece. Peatland tours. Ardkill Farm won a conservation award in 1992 for the Preservation of A Raised Peat Bog, with its unique habitat. 97% of boglands have been destroyed, a tour with our guide is both educational and stimulating. On sale: homemade bread, jams, honey, peatland conservation souvenirs. Location: turn off N4 Dublin road at Enfield, farm 6 miles

Open: Apr-July, daily 1400–1800, Sep-Oct peatland only
Entrance charges: Adults IR£2, children IR£1.50, OAP/concessions IR£1.50.
WC & ⊡ SHOP

Key to Map Pages

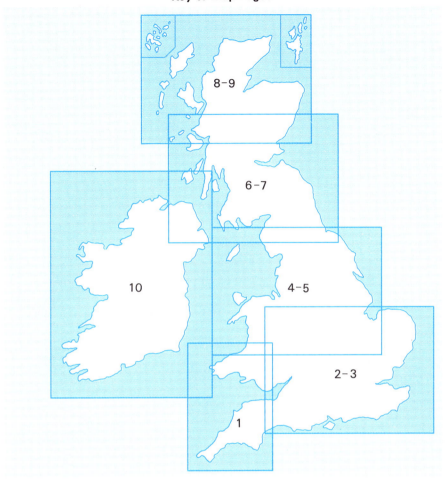

8-9

6-7

10

4-5

2-3

1

LEGEND

● Cheddar	Farm Locations
━②━	Motorways
A3	Primary Routes
A385	Other Routes

Scale 20 miles to 1 inch approx.

0   20   40   60   80 Kilometres

0   10   20   30   40   50 Statute Miles

Ireland produced at 27 miles to 1 inch approx.

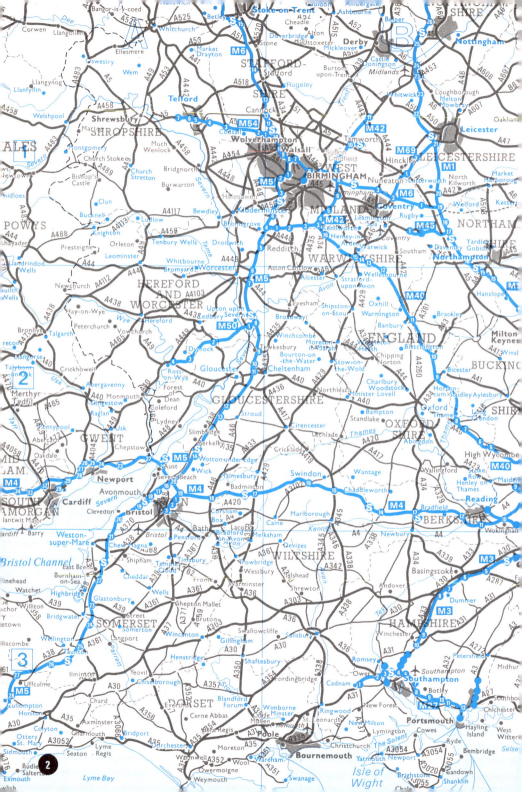

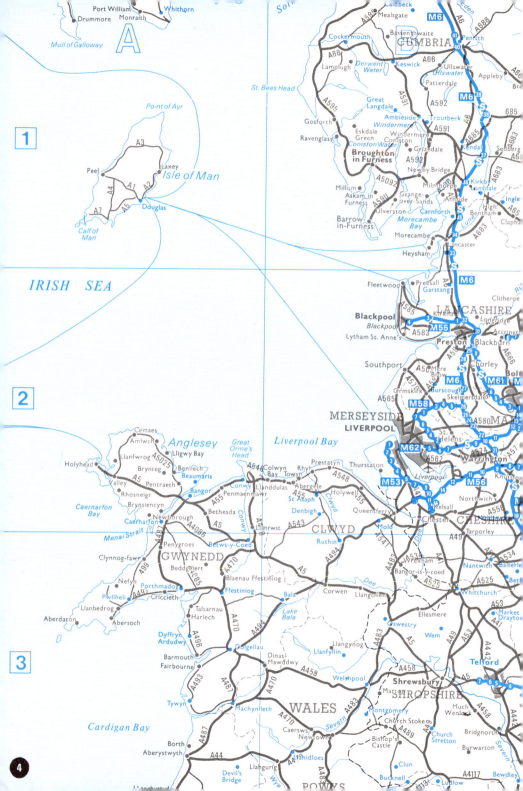

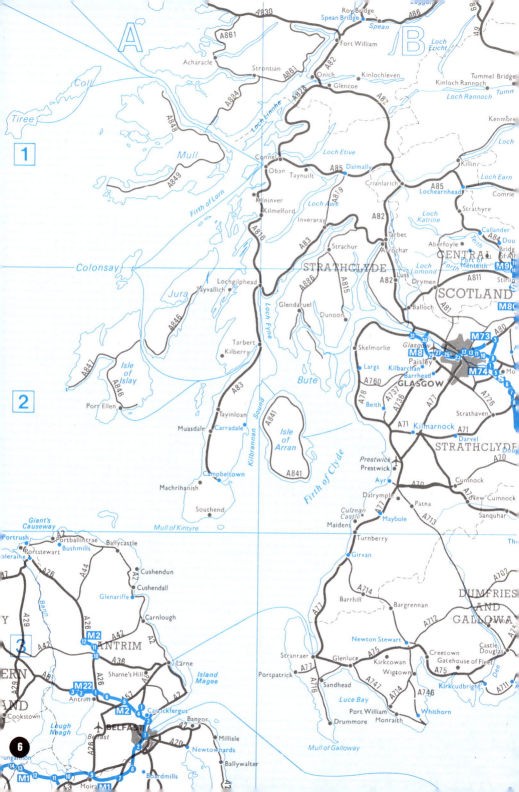

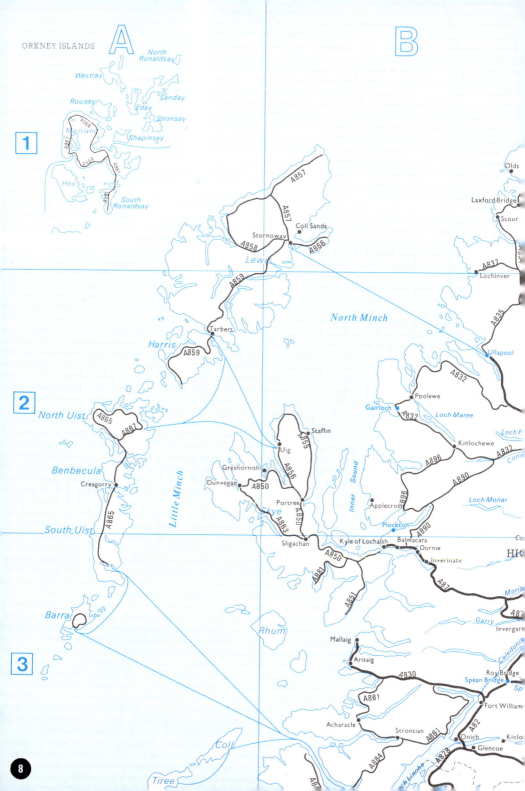

ORKNEY ISLANDS

A **B**

1

North Ronaldsay
Westray
Rousay
Sanday
Eday
Mainland
Stronsay
A966
A965
Shapinsay
A967
A964
A961
Hoy
A967
South Ronaldsay

A857

A857

A858 Stornoway Coll Sands
Lewis A866

A859

Tarbert

Harris

A859

Olds

Laxford Bridge

Scour

A837

Lochinver

North Minch

Ullapool

A832

2

North Uist A865
A867

Benbecula

Creagorry

South Uist

A865

Little Minch

Staffin
A855
Uig
A856
Greshornish
Dunvegan
A850
Portree
Skye
A863 A850
Sligachan
A851
A881

Gairloch
A832
Poolewe
Loch Maree
Loch F
Kinlochewe
A832
A896
Con
A896
A890
Loch Monar
Applecross
A896
Plockton
A890
Kyle of Lochalsh
A850
Balmacara
Dornie
Inverinate
HIG
A87
Moris
A87
Garry
Invergar

Inner Sound

3

Barra

Rhum

Mallaig
Arisaig
A830
Roy Bridge
Spean Bridge
Sp
Fort William
A82
A861
Acharacle
Strontian A861
Onich
Kinlo
Glencoe
A884
A828

Coll

Tiree

8

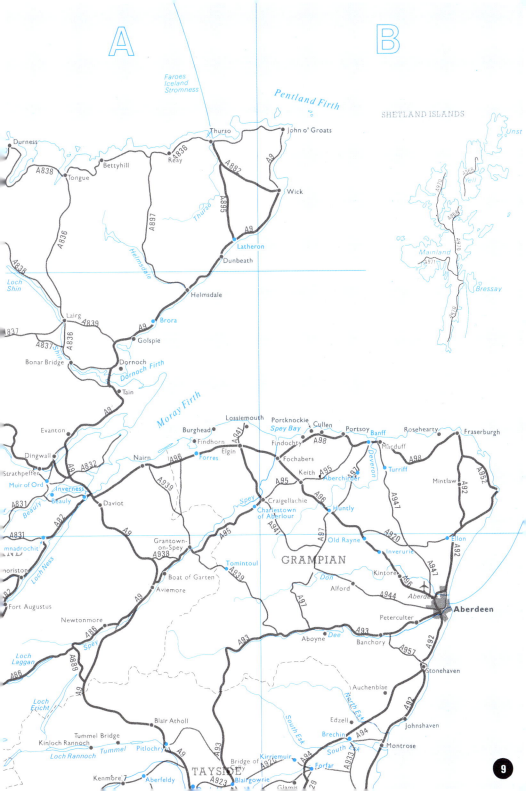